During the nineteenth century, the shrine cities of Najaf and Karbala᾿ in Ottoman Iraq emerged as the most important Shiʻi centers of learning. In a major contribution to the study of pre-modern Middle Eastern religious institutions, Meir Litvak provides the first in-depth discussion of the internal social and political dynamics of these communities. Tracing the historical evolution of Shiʻi leadership throughout the century, he explores the determinants of social status among the ʻulama᾿, the concept of patronage in the relationship between master and disciple, the structures of learning, questions of ethnicity, and financial matters. He also assesses the role of the ʻulama᾿ as communal leaders who, in the face of an unfriendly Sunni government in Baghdad, often needed Iranian support and were, therefore, obliged to adopt a more quietist political stance than their counterparts in Iran.

This is an important book which in its historical and political interpretations sheds light on the formation of contemporary Shiʻism and on the surrounding debates.

MEIR LITVAK is lecturer in the Department of Middle Eastern Studies and African History at Tel Aviv University.

Cambridge Middle East Studies

Shi'i scholars of nineteenth-century Iraq

The 'ulama' of Najaf and Karbala'

Cambridge Middle East Studies 10

Editorial Board
Charles Tripp (general editor)
Shaul Bakhash   Michael C. Hudson   Noah Lucas
Deniz Kandiyoti   Rashid Khalidi   Basim Musallam
Roger Owen

Cambridge Middle East Studies has been established to publish books on the nineteenth- and twentieth-century Middle East and North Africa. The aim of the series is to provide new and original interpretations of aspects of Middle Eastern societies and their histories. To achieve disciplinary diversity, books will be solicited from authors writing in a wide range of fields including history, sociology, anthropology, political science and political economy. The emphasis will be on producing books offering an original approach along theoretical and empirical lines. The series is intended for students and academics, but the more accessible and wide-ranging studies will also appeal to the interested general reader.

Shi'i scholars of
nineteenth-century Iraq

The 'ulama' of Najaf and Karbala'

Meir Litvak

CAMBRIDGE
UNIVERSITY PRESS

PUBLISHED BY THE PRESS SYNDICATE OF THE UNIVERSITY OF CAMBRIDGE
The Pitt Building, Trumpington Street, Cambridge, United Kingdom

CAMBRIDGE UNIVERSITY PRESS
The Edinburgh Building, Cambridge CB2 2RU, UK
40 West 20th Street, New York NY 10011–4211, USA
477 Williamstown Road, Port Melbourne, VIC 3207, Australia
Ruiz de Alarcón 13, 28014 Madrid, Spain
Dock House, The Waterfront, Cape Town 8001, South Africa

http://www.cambridge.org

First published 1998
First paperback edition 2002

Typeface Plantin 10/12 pt.

A catalogue record for this book is available from the British Library

Library of Congress Cataloguing in Publication data
Litvak, Meir.
Shi'i scholars of nineteenth-century Iraq: the ulama of Najaf
and Karbala / Meir Litvak.
        p.   cm. – (Cambridge Middle East studies)
Includes bibliographical references (p.   ) and index.
ISBN 0 521 62356 1 (hb)
1. Shī' ah – Iraq – Najaf – History.   2. Shī' ah – Iraq – Karbala – History.
3. Shiite shrines – Iraq – Najaf.   4. Shiite shrines – Iraq – Karbala.
5. Iraq – History – 1534–1921.   6. Iraq – Politics and government.
I. Title.   II. Series.
BP192.7.I7L58   1998   297.8′2′095675–dc21   97-35821   CIP

ISBN 0 521 62356 1   hardback
ISBN 0 521 89296 1   paperback

Dedicated to my mother and father
to Nava, Omri, and Adi

Contents

Acknowledgments

I wish to thank Professor Roy P. Mottahedeh of Harvard University and Professor Abbas Amanat of Yale University for their encouragement, thoughtful guidance, and, in particular, warm and generous attitude, which enabled me to pursue the task of researching and writing this book.

The Center for Middle Eastern Studies at Harvard University, where I did much of my research, provided a most congenial environment and much financial assistance during my studies. I am grateful to its academic and administrative staff for the years I have spent there, particularly Professors Nadav Safran, Roy P. Mottahedeh, and William Graham.

I wish to thank my present academic home, the Dayan Center for Middle Eastern Studies at Tel Aviv University, for providing me with the financial help and moral support necessary for the completion of the book. I am particularly grateful to its director, Professor Itamar Rabinovich, whose far-sighted advice brought me to the fascinating world of the Shi'i 'ulama', as well as to Professor Asher Susser and Dr. Martin Kramer.

Thanks are also due to the Avi Fellowship Foundation in Zurich and the German Foreign Academic Council (DAAD), whose financial support enabled me to carry out research in Europe. I am also grateful to the Seminar for European History at Tel Aviv University and to the Parviz and Pouran Nazarian Chair for Modern Iranian Studies at Tel Aviv University for their financial support in making the revision to a book possible.

I thank the staffs of the Middle Eastern Department at the Widener Library, Harvard University; the Public Record Office (Kew Gardens, London); the India Office Library (London); the British Library (London); the Archives de Ministère des Affaires Etrangères (Paris); and the Schiabibliothek at the Orientalischeseminar at the University of Cologne. In addition I wish to thank Professor Juan Cole for providing me with his personal copy of a most valuable manuscript necessary for this work.

The writing of this book has been enriched by the advice of friends and colleagues, who kindly read parts or all of this work and made numerous suggestions for improvements. I am particularly beholden to the sound advice of Ofra Bengio, Gad Gilbar, Yosef Kostiner, David Menashri, Yitzhak Nakash, Joshua Teitelbaum, Ehud Toledano, David Wasserstein, Michael Winter, and the two anonymous readers. I also wish to thank Mira Reich for editing my non-native English, and my brother Nathaniel for his help, which cannot be properly described in words.

It was a pleasure working with the Cambridge University Press staff: Marigold Acland, the Middle East editor, who guided me through the process of revision; the series general editor Charles Tripp; my copy-editor Mary Starkey, for her patience, expertise, and dedication; Philippa Youngman, Jayne Matthews, and all the other people engaged in producing this book.

Last but not least, I should like to thank my wife Nava, who has endured many years of my research and writing for the book, for providing me with the invaluable support necessary for the completion of the task.

A note on transliteration

The transliteration system used in this book is based on the standard
Encyclopaedia of Islam transliteration from Arabic. The exceptions are
the omission of diacritical marks over long vowels and the use of the
letter J for the Arabic letter *jim*.

Both Persian and Turkish names have been transliterated from the
original Arabic, e.g. Muhammad and not Mohammad or Fadil and not
Fazel. The prefix al- has been added whenever necessary to names of
Arab persons, in order to distinguish them from members of other
ethnic groups.

For geographical names which often appear in English such as Tehran
and Isfahan the common English usage has been employed.

Abbreviations

BSOAS	*Bulletin of the School of Oriental and African Studies*
CCC	Correspondance Consulaire et Commerciale
CPC	Correspondance Politique des Consuls
EI²	*Encyclopaedia of Islam (Second Edition)*
EIr	*Encylopaedia Iranica*
FO	Foreign Office
IGFD	India Government Foreign Department
IJMES	*International Journal of Middle Eastern Studies*
IOL	India Office Library
IS	*Iranian Studies*
ISE	*Islamic Shiʿite Encyclopedia*
JAOS	*Journal of the American Oriental Society*
JESHO	*Journal of the Economic and Social History of the Orient*
JNES	*Journal of Near Eastern Studies*
JSSR	*Journal of the Scientific Study of Religion*
L/P&S/	Letters, Political & Secret
MES	*Middle Eastern Studies*
PRO	Public Record Office
SI	*Studia Islamica*
WI	*Die Welt des Islams*
ZDMG	*Zeitschrift der Deutchen Morgenlandischen Gesselschaft*

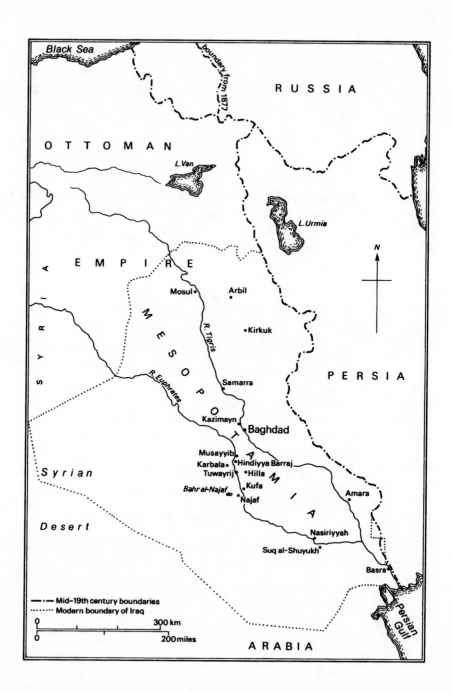

Black Sea

boundary from 1877

RUSSIA

OTTOMAN

L.Van

L.Urmia

N

EMPIRE

S Y R I A

Mosul •

• Arbil

M E S O P O

R. Tigris

• Kirkuk

PERSIA

Samarra

R. Euphrates

Kazimayn

Baghdad

Musayyib

Karbala •   • Hindiyya Barraj

Tuwayrij   • Hilla

Bahr al-Najaf   • Kufa

• Najaf   • Amara

Nasiriyyah

Suq al-Shuyukh •

Basra

Persian Gulf

Syrian

Desert

M
I
A

---·— Mid-19th century boundaries
············ Modern boundary of Iraq

|___|___|___|___|___| 300 km
0
|___|___|___|___| 200 miles

A R A B I A

Introduction

Knowledge (*'ilm*) lifts the lowly person to heights. Ignorance keeps the youth of noble birth immobile.[1]

The 'ulama', or men of learning in the Muslim world, have often been described as the one group that makes the Islamic community "Islamic" rather than something else.[2] Such a broad statement of course needs to be historicized with reference to specific periods and places, yet, it is particularly appropriate for the Shi'i 'ulama' in the two shrine cities (*'atabat-i 'aliyat,* lit. sublime thresholds) – the holiest pilgrimage sites in Shi'ism – Najaf and Karbala' in Iraq during the years 1791–1904.

During this time Najaf and Karbala', where the first and third Shi'i Imams, 'Ali and Husayn, are buried, emerged as the most important centers of learning and religious leadership in the Shi'i world, a status they would gradually lose during the twentieth century.[3] Equally important, it was in these places and years that the structure and content of higher Shi'i learning and of the institution of religious leadership achieved their final shape, which has remained largely in effect to this day. Likewise, it is during this period that the 'ulama' finally secured their role as almost exclusive custodians of Shi'i tradition and religious life by defeating all rival religious trends, and by appropriating the various manifestations of popular religion. Concurrently, the Shi'i 'ulama' did not face the encroachment of secular education either in Iran and Iraq to the extent that eroded the power base of their Sunni counterparts in the Middle East.

The uniqueness of the community of learning in the shrine cities was largely due to the fact that it was founded by the 'ulama' themselves to serve as a center of erudition and scholarship, rather than by rulers or lay notables to serve political, administrative, and social purposes. Consequently, in contrast to contemporary Sunni religious establishments, the community of learning in the shrine cities was independent of the rulers, and was much more oriented toward the lay Shi'i constituency than toward the state. As Shi'i towns in the Sunni

1

Ottoman Empire, it was the community rather than the state that constituted the primary socio-religious frame of reference discussed in this book, with the 'ulama' playing a central role as religious, communal, and political leaders.

Few if any other centers of learning in the Middle East assumed the character of a "university town" like Najaf, where the civic economy and social organization revolved around pilgrimage and learning. Thanks to this combination of pilgrimage, learning, and trade, Najaf emerged as the heart of a "Shi'i International," attracting students and visitors from all parts of the Shi'i world.[4] The presence of a large foreign, mostly Iranian, population of teachers, students, and pilgrims inside Ottoman Iraq placed the shrine cities in the unique situation of being simultaneously an integral part of two very different societies, polities, and cultures, those of Qajar Iran and Ottoman Iraq.

The peculiar nature of the two communities as centers of learning independent of the state is best described by the Shi'i term *hawza 'ilmiyya* (lit. territory of learning) or community of learning, denoting a communal whole which encompasses scholarship, inter-personal and social bonds, as well as the organizational and financial spheres. The 'ulama' of the two shrine cities constituted a distinct social stratum whose members possessed a strong self-consciousness and group identity formed by shared values, interests, and lifestyle, as well as by the continuous interaction between members.[5]

A major factor in the 'ulama''s self-esteem lay in their being a small literate minority in an otherwise mostly illiterate society both in Iran and Ottoman Iraq. Although women could study and attain high ranks of learning in Shi'ism, the community of 'ulama' in the shrine cities was predominantly a society of men, particularly as many of the students could not afford to marry.[6]

Pre-modern Iranian society was characterized by vertical social divisions determined by religion, ethnicity, and ecological factors. Whereas the focus of identity for many of these social groupings was primarily defense against outsiders, the focus of identity of the 'ulama' community was basically different.[7] Entry to the ranks of the 'ulama' was often voluntary, whether out of genuine piety or as a means of social betterment. The ethos of the 'ulama' as heirs to the Prophet and Imams was another major factor in forging this identity. Consequently, while economic factors tended to increase the importance of class divisions in Iran, partially supplanting many of the former vertical divisions, the 'ulama' community retained its nature as a status group.

The study of the social organization of Muslim learning and of the 'ulama' as a social stratum has made important gains in recent years, but for obvious reasons has been focused on the majority Sunni community.[8] The study of Shi'ism and of the Shi'i 'ulama' has also progressed considerably, largely under the impact of the 1978–79 revolution in Iran. The majority of the latter studies have concentrated on doctrinal developments, particularly Shi'i political theory, and on the role of the 'ulama' in politics, thus dealing primarily with the 'ulama' elite. Likewise, most of these studies have focused on Iran itself as the largest and most important Shi'i society,[9] rarely delving into the internal organization of the Shi'i religious stratum, or giving the shrine cities their due share, as this study aims to do.

The Shi'i 'ulama' have been mainly associated with Iran, and the communities of 'ulama' in the shrine cities have mostly been seen as part of the larger Iranian context, without looking deeply at their uniqueness as centers of learning and as consisting predominantly of migrants. Recent studies on Shi'ism in Iraq, primarily by Batatu, Luizard, Mallat, Nakash, and Wiley have focused mainly on the Shi'i tribal population or on the twentieth century.[10]

This study, therefore, seeks to fill this gap by examining the internal dynamics of a community of 'ulama' in the two most important centers of Shi'i learning and to place them in three different, but partly related, historical contexts: first, the institutions of higher learning in Islam and the evolution of the 'ulama' as a social stratum; second, socio-political developments in Iraq, particularly through the prism of Sunni–Shi'i relations; and finally, the relations between religion and state in Iran. Likewise, it seeks to encompass both the upper and lower level of the 'ulama' and provide, as much as is made possible by the available sources, a history of the 'ulama' from below.

The nineteenth century was a period of profound change in the Middle East produced by the interaction between internal developments and western influences and pressures. Yet, large segments of local society in Iraq and Iran remained deeply traditional and highly religious as far as their worldview and modes of social organization were concerned. Within this context the 'ulama' acted as a bastion of religious tradition and social continuity. An additional aspect is suggested by the provincial small-town nature of Najaf and Karbala', which sets the community apart from the Sunni 'ulama' in metropolitan centers such as Istanbul, Cairo, or Damascus. A major purpose of this study, therefore, is to examine the relative impact of external and internal forces on the social makeup and organization of the community of 'ulama' and on its relations with other historical players.

What holds together a community of scholars and students in a situation where the state is unfriendly, and does not play the simultaneous role of benefactor and overseer? The key is the preponderance of informal interpersonal ties, which serve as the basis for social interaction in the society of the 'ulama', and is manifested by patron–client relationships. These ties have often been associated in a cause-and-effect relationship with the absence of formal organizations and overall administrative mechanisms in Muslim communities of learning. As this study will show, both these elements encompassed most aspects of life in the shrine cities, ranging from the mode of teaching to finances and the institution of leadership. Equally important, they remained largely intact during the entire period under study and well into the twentieth century.

The 'ulama' are examined here in three expanding circles. Part 1 analyzes the internal aspects of Shi'i learning and of the community of 'ulama' in the shrine cities. Most important, it seeks to analyze the interaction and role of the two key factors underlying the social organization of the 'ulama' community, that is, scholarship and patronage. Consequently, we see how links of patronage cut across and superseded class and ethnic divisions in the shrine cities, even though they did not annul them.

The mode of teaching in the shrine cities is also closely linked to the system of patronage. Students were affiliated with individual teachers and not with institutions. Likewise, the diploma was awarded by the teacher as a personal matter between him and the student, giving a formal stamp to the patronage ties that linked them.

The importance of patronage is highlighted by the nature of finances in the shrine cities which was based on donations and religious dues – alms and the fifth – provided by believers, rather than on landed endowments (*awqaf*) as was the case in the Ottoman Empire and even Qajar Iran. The dependence on donations required the teachers to construct networks of patronage composed of former students and followers, mainly merchants, who channeled funds to them. The centrality of these ties to the sustenance of the community of learning, and the religious obligation of emulation (*taqlid*) of the leading scholars by their lay followers rendered these networks more significant for the 'ulama' of the shrine cities than their links of patronage with state officials. Since patronage relationships were exclusive to the teacher and did not pass to his sons, the latter could not succeed to their father's status and position, as was the case in the Ottoman Empire and Iran, and had to justify their status on their own merits. Consequently, the community of learning in the shrine cities has remained open to talented newcomers throughout the last two centuries. While networks of patronage were being formed and dissolved throughout the period the practice itself showed remarkable durability.

Chapters 2 to 5 deal with the institutionalization and evolving nature of leadership in the scholarly community in both towns as well as in the wider Shi'i world, using the leadership issue as a focus to analyze the various other aspects of the community of learning.

In contrast to Catholicism, the Islamic *shari'a* rejected the need for a clerical institution to mediate between man and God in order to attain spiritual salvation. Rather, in view of the judicial, social, and administrative duties of the 'ulama', and the close links between religion and state in Islamic history, official religious hierarchies were established on the initiative of the state to serve its own purposes. Such was the case with the Ottoman *Ilmiyeh*, which was headed by the Shaykh al-Islam of Istanbul, the office of Shaykh al-Azhar in Egypt, or even the Imam Jum'a of Lucknow in the Shi'i kingdom of Awadh. All these religious leaders could, therefore, be termed "officials," since they derived their authority from organizational and bureaucratic positions.

By contrast, the Shi'i mujtahids, those scholars eligible to issue religious rulings, fit the definition of informal leaders who, in the often-quoted words of the nineteenth-century British historian John Malcolm, "fill no office, receive no appointment, [and] have no specific duties but who are called, from their superior learning, piety and virtue, by the silent but unanimous suffrage of the inhabitants ... to be their guides in religion, and their protectors against the violence and oppression of their rulers."[11]

Malcolm's description, which alludes to certain charismatic qualities, captures the dual role of the Shi'i mujtahids as both spiritual and social leaders. This was particularly true of the religious leadership in the shrine cities in view of its independent and informal character and the centrality of personal loyalties.

Shi'i religious leadership and particularly the institution of Supreme Exemplar (*marja'iyyat-i taqlid*) resulted from the development of the concept of general deputyship (*niyaba 'amma*), which enabled the 'ulama' to claim charismatic authority inherited from and wielded on behalf of the Hidden Imam, and through socio-political processes which culminated with the reinstatement of Usulism – the rationalist school and methodology for deducing legal norms – in the eighteenth century. However, whereas the concept of emulation (*taqlid*) and the prerequisites for *ijtihad* (the process of inferring legal norms using reason) were instrumental in designating a religious elite of mujtahids, they were insufficient to create a clear hierarchy within it.[12]

There is a theory in contemporary Shi'ism that at any given time in Shi'i history there was one 'alim who was recognized as the supreme religious authority. Consequently, there are historiographic attempts to draw a continuous line of exemplars back to the days of the Twelfth Imam.[13] This theory, however, is relatively new and ungrounded. The institution of a supreme religious authority under one mujtahid first appeared under the Safavids when Shah Tahmasp bestowed the title "Mujtahid of the Age" (*mujtahid-i zaman*) upon 'Ali al-Karaki al-'Amili in 1533. The title, however, entailed neither systematic doctrinal authority nor formal leadership over the administration of religious institutions. Only the office of Mullabashi established in the late seventeenth century formally recognized a mujtahid as the highest religious authority in Safavid Iran.[14] The destruction of the Safavid state in 1722 marked the demise of that institution.

The integration of the clerical community into an independent establishment during the early years of the Qajar dynasty prompted both the 'ulama' and their constituent groups to search for a more systematic line of authority. The recognition of a "head" or a leader was intended to answer the need for a superior model who, by embodying both rational capacity and moral piety, could sanctify the righteousness of the entire 'ulama' establishment.[15]

Theoretically, the designation of the spiritual leader or the Supreme Exemplar was determined by his superiority in the three major qualifications for *ijtihad*, i.e. '*ilm* (knowledge of the law), '*adl* (justice in the practice of law) and *wara*' (piety). Of the three, *a'lamiyat* (superiority in learning) was held as the most important. The idea of emulating the most learned mujtahid was implicit in Muhammad Baqir Bihbihani's (d. 1791) writing. Mirza Abu al-Qasim Qummi (d. 1815–16) advanced it by reestablishing the concept of *mutaba'a*, i.e. the conscious following of the opinion of a superior mujtahid both in doctrine and in practice, thereby facilitating the emergence of an informal hierarchy among the mujtahids.[16]

The coherent concept and institution of *marja'iyya* appeared only during the second half of the nineteenth century. It was Murtada Ansari who formulated the concept, which nullified all religious acts not performed in emulation of the exemplar. Ansari's excessive caution in exercising his authority, however, raises some questions as to the actual application of the theory during his period. Likewise, none of the leading nineteenth-century mujtahids claimed doctrinal or spiritual authority.[17]

The rationalism propounded in Usuli theory largely contradicted the spiritual standing attributed to the exemplars in order to enhance their prestige among their followers. In order to obscure this paradox, unworldly qualities such as asceticism and extreme devotion were often assigned to them.[18] Miracles (*karamat*) which happened to or were performed by the mujtahid, and dreams in which the Imams appeared to him, endowed him with the necessary charismatic aura.

There was of course a large gap between the theory and the actual practice of selecting an exemplar. The requirements for *marja'iyya* were too vague and subjective, paving the way for conflicting claims and arbitrary denials of qualifications, problems to which the more formal western academic system is also not immune. Likewise, the procedure for pronouncing the choice, i.e. the attestation of these qualifications by two just men, contained the same vagueness and could have led to an uncontrolled proliferation of exemplars. Even the simple question of whether the evaluation of knowledge is a prerogative of the 'ulama' or of every believer is left ambiguous. Consequently, the criteria could hardly be applied in a systematic and practical way to determine scholastic superiority among the mujtahids. In practice, these criteria enabled the believer to choose or shift from one exemplar to another as he pleased and whenever it suited his interests.[19]

Equally important, doctrinal obstacles inhibited the full institutionalization of a religious hierarchy and particularly the position of Supreme Exemplar. The presence (or actually the material absence) of the Hidden Imam made any attempt toward the theoretical elaboration of a supreme authority a matter of controversy and conflict. The absence of a centrally organized structure in the learning complex in the shrine cities or in Iran and the fact that any mujtahid could bestow *ijazat ijtihad* – the diploma permitting the practice of ijtihad – on his students made the ranking of mujtahids difficult. A certain incompatibility also existed between the stress of otherworldliness attributed to the *marja'iyya* and the requirements necessary for carrying out his role of social and communal leadership.[20]

Consequently, in the Shi'i context it is more instructive to focus on the institution of *ri'asa*, i.e. the combination of religious and communal leadership. The difference between *ri'asa* and *marja'iyya* parallels in a way the implicit tensions over seniority between pure scholarship and academic administration in western hospitals or universities, as each role requires different qualifications.[21] Whereas *marja'iyya* implied the intellectual and spiritual superiority of one mujtahid, *ri'asa* reflected the amorphous structure of the Shi'i establishment, where numerous religious leaders coexisted with each other. Even so, the Shi'i *ri'asa* had greater spiritual authority than the more administratively constituted Ottoman religious leadership.

The Usuli concept of religious leadership and hierarchy also differed from the model espoused by Sufi Islam which stipulated a hierarchical order in which man is defined in terms of his spiritual perfection. By contrast the Usuli notion of hierarchy refers more to rational knowledge of the law. The Shi'i Perfect Man is clearly a charismatic figure who is described as the heart of the *umma*, yet he has no worldly power and lives with his wishes unfulfilled.[22] The mujtahid on the other hand, is only partially a charismatic figure, and his authority extends to every aspect of religious life.

While I do not seek to provide an exhaustive account of every struggle for leadership in the shrine cities, these chapters trace the continuous pendulum between centralization and diffusion of leadership and the development of the concept and actual practices of leadership in the shrine cities and the Shi'a as a whole.

In Sunni communities the 'ulama' competed among themselves for the favor of the rulers or for positions in madrasas in their struggle for leadership. The focus of the leadership struggles in the shrine cities was different, since endowed chairs were fewer due to the scarcity of substantial *awqaf*. Consequently, in order to attain the status of exemplar, mujtahids needed both symbolic and material resources. Symbolic resources, that is a reputation for scholarship and a certain charismatic quality expressed as piety and justice, were necessary, but by no means sufficient, preconditions for attaining leadership status since they did not represent by themselves the necessary link with the mujtahid's constituents.

The complementary material capital was the close link with the Bazaar community in Iran which provided the financial mainstay of the 'ulama'. However, those who have discussed the importance of the mujtahids' relations with the merchant community have failed to point out to the importance of networks of patronage composed of former students. These students, who were stationed in the various communities, provided the crucial link between the leader and his followers by collecting the religious dues for their teacher, by referring students, pilgrims, and legal questions to him, and by disseminating his rulings among the followers.

The various ascriptive factors, such as clerical or sayyid origins, were helpful, but again were neither necessary nor sufficient conditions for the attainment of leadership. Consequently, this study will show how the leadership ranks in the shrine cities were more open to talented newcomers than was the case in either the Ottoman religious hierarchy or Qajar Iran. The major reason for this openness was the central role of teaching in the shrine cities and the relatively minor role of endowments as a source of funds and status, in contrast to the holding of official positions as was the case in Sunni countries. Further, a distinction is made between the various levels and meanings of status, such as scholarly vs. socio-political eminence; recognition by peers, by students, or by the wider masses; and the acknowledgment of the seniority of a fellow mujtahid as compared with the acceptance of subordination to him.

During the nineteenth century the Shi'i religious leadership underwent centralization from the multiple places of learning to the shrine cities, particularly Najaf. However, as this study shows, no mujtahid was ever able fully to concentrate the religious leadership in his own person and achieve the universal recognition and subordination of his peers. More important, neither a theory nor a mechanism for the selection or appointment of leaders was ever formulated. Despite the centralization, therefore, no formal religious hierarchy was ever established in the shrine cities or among the Shi'a as a whole. Again the patronage system was both a cause and effect of this pattern.

Part 2 examines the political and social activity of the 'ulama' within a political triangle formed together with the Ottoman rulers of Iraq and the Qajar dynasty in Iran. The 'ulama' of the shrine cities found themselves in the peculiar situation of being a part of an oppressed minority in Iraq but also members of the powerful religious establishment of Iran. Since most of their constituents and financial support came from Iran, the shrine cities were directly affected by all the important socio-economic developments in that state. Concurrently, the 'ulama' played a prominent role in the complex relations between Sunnis and Shi'is as well as between center and periphery in Iraq.

This dual and opposing position in two adjacent countries had a profound impact on the 'ulama''s political conduct and activity in both arenas, which was markedly different from that of their counterparts in Iran. Thus in the context of the historiographical debate on the political role of the 'ulama' in nineteenth-century Iran, this study supports the view describing the relations between the 'ulama' and the Qajars as multi-faceted. In addition to periods of tension and rivalry between certain segments of the 'ulama' and the Qajars, there was also a commonality of interests, implicit and also some explicit recognition of Qajar legitimacy during some parts of the nineteenth century, and even cooperation against heretic revolutionary movements such as Babism.

Moreover, whereas various studies have concluded that the shrine cities were centers of opposition to the Qajars, I argue that the dependence of the 'ulama' in these cities on the Qajar government to offset various discriminatory Ottoman policies and pressures, as well as the nature of the shrine cities as centers of learning, rendered the 'ulama' there much more politically quietist than their colleagues in Iran.[23]

The evolving relationship between the 'ulama' and the British in Iraq adds another though somewhat less important factor and dimension to the 'ulama'–Ottoman–Qajar triangle. Research on British penetration in Iraq has focused mainly on the strategic and economic issues. This study examines how the British forged relations with the Shi'i community, initially as part of their interests in India, but subsequently, as their involvement in Iran grew, so did their interest in the community of 'ulama' *per se*. British involvement in the shrine cities adds another facet to the role of the external factors of change affecting the community of learning.

The local and urban history of Iraq has been a fairly neglected area of research, mostly due to the paucity of sources. While this study does not focus principally on this topic, it attempts to shed light on various aspects of local Iraqi history. Whereas most studies of nineteenth-century Ottoman reforms examine the peasants or the major urban centers in the Middle East, this study will discuss their impact on local society in smaller peripheral towns. Thus part 2 treats both the common and the divergent interests of the 'ulama' and those of the local sayyid elite. It shows how the 'ulama' elite assumed the role of urban notables, as formulated in Albert Hourani's paradigm, as mediators between the population and the Sunni government in Baghdad.[24]

Various historians have often pointed out the close links between the 'ulama' and the urban mafia-type gangs in Middle Eastern towns. In the shrine cities these relationships were much more tenuous than in other places. The 'ulama', who were often harassed by the gangs, occasionally even preferred Sunni Ottoman rule to gang lawlessness. Overall, however, the study shows that while various 'ulama' were integrated into the larger Middle Eastern Ottoman pattern of notables, their Shi'i identity, the fact that most of them did not become landowners, and none joined the Ottoman bureaucracy, set them as a distinct group within the larger phenomenon.

The basic methodology used in this book is prosopographical, defined as collective biography of a group of actors in history. The technique employed makes detailed investigations into the genealogy, interests, and political activities of the group, combined with detailed case studies.[25]

The peculiar situation of the 'ulama' of the shrine cities in being simultaneously members of the dominant religious establishment in Iran and part of an oppressed minority in Iraq raises the interesting question of locating them on the church–sect social continuum. The term "church" refers to a religious group that accepts the culture of the social environment in which it exists, and tends to be large, conservative, and universalist. A church tends to acquire a certain amount of social and political power, which it often retains by association with the government or the ruling classes. A sect is a religious group that does not accept the social environment in which it exists. Sects are often small, exclusive, and uncompromising. Members are mostly voluntary converts, and their lives are pretty much controlled by and revolve around the sect. In this sharp and schematic dichotomy most religious groups fall somewhere between the two extremes.

The church–sect continuum was originally devised for western protestant societies.[26] However, while recognizing the differences between Muslim and western societies, these concepts may serve as a useful device to analyze the conduct of the 'ulama' in a variety of spheres: the structure of the learning community; the leadership question; and particularly their attitude toward external challenges to their authority coming from the Akhbari, Sufi, Shaykhi, and Babi movements; and finally the conduct of the 'ulama' as part of the 'ulama'–Ottoman–Qajar triangle.

The Shi'i 'ulama' in history

During the first three centuries of Islam the Imami Shi'i community followed the leadership of the infallible Imams, with the scholars remaining much in their shadow. The geographical expansion of Shi'ism in the third/ninth century and growing 'Abbasid persecution obliged the last three active Imams to delegate much of their authority to their disciples, the 'ulama'.[27]

The Imami community overcame the crisis caused by the occultation (ghayba) of the Twelfth Shi'i Imam in 260/874 largely thanks to the leadership provided by the 'ulama'. The 'ulama', however, lacked the essential qualification on which the authority of the Imams rested, their infallibility. Their own authority, which rested on their knowledge of the transmitted commands and statements of the Imams as well as on their role as jurisprudents was legal-traditional rather than charismatic.[28]

The dominant legal school in Imami–Twelver Shi'ism since the fifth/eleventh century has been the Usuliyya, named after its reliance on usul al-fiqh (principles of jurisprudence) as the methodology for deducing legal norms. The science of Usul was supposed to deal, on the basis of preponderant supposition (zann), with legal problems for which there were no clear answers in the Qur'an or Traditions (akhbar). The process of inferring legal norms using reason and relying on the other sources of law was called ijtihad.[29]

Ijtihad developed in response to the changing needs of the Shi'i community, while also reflecting the need to assert and justify the 'ulama''s general deputyship (niyaba 'amma) of the Imam in his absence. No question requiring ijtihad could be settled conclusively through the consensus of the 'ulama' without confirmation from the Imam. Ijtihad, therefore, must remain an open process in an effort to reach the closest approximation to the objective truth until the return of the Imam.

In the course of this process, the 'ulama' appropriated many of the Imam's prerogatives. The most important of these were the collection and distribution of alms (zakat) and the fifth (the khums, which every Shi'i is obliged to give to the Imam from his annual income); the administration of justice; the conduct of the Friday prayer; and the declaration of Jihad.[30] The assumption of these prerogatives gave the 'ulama' the power to legitimize Shi'i rulers. In addition, it advanced the process of professionalization of the 'ulama' since it established the jurisdiction of the calling, i.e. the particular areas of work with which it deals, and their restriction to eligible persons.[31]

The exercise of ijtihad was confined to qualified persons, while the ordinary believer was required to follow and emulate (taqlid) the decisions of those learned in law. The Usuli school, therefore, divided society into two strata: a majority of followers and emulators (muqallidun) and a minority of mujtahids who are to be followed (muqalladun). Since Islam theoretically encompasses all aspects of life, the mujtahids could combine religious and social leadership, thus enjoying greater authority than their Sunni counterparts.[32]

Concurrently, the individual practicing of ijtihad perpetuated the diffused nature of authority within the ranks of the Shi'i 'ulama'. Norms were derived by individuals and gradually accepted by a consensus, rather than by formal ecclesiastical bodies as in Christian churches.

The proclamation in 1501 by the new ruler of Iran, Shah Isma'il Safavi, of Twelver Shi'ism as the state religion marked a turning point in the history of both Shi'ism and Iran. Twelver Shi'ism was transformed from mainly an Arab minority sect to a state religion dominated by Iranians. The endorsement of Shi'ism marked a turning point in Iranian history by making it a central element of Iranian identity and culture, and by transforming the 'ulama' into a powerful social stratum.

To diffuse Twelver Shi'ism in Iran, the Safavids invited large numbers of Twelver Shi'i 'ulama' from Lebanon, Arab Iraq, and Bahrayn. While the adoption of Twelver Shi'ism brought the Shi'i 'ulama' to unprecedented social and economic power, it simultaneously raised new problems, as the religious institutions in Iran were subordinated to the state, and the 'ulama' had to reconcile the charismatic bases of Safavid authority with Twelver Shi'i beliefs.[33]

However, the newly arrived Arab 'ulama' were too dependent on the Safavids' patronage to challenge them on this issue. Nor did they wish to undermine the Safavid state which was propagating Shi'ism. Gradually, however, the 'ulama' forged alliances with the merchant community and artisan guilds. They were also appointed as trustees of charitable endowments (*awqaf*) and were able to amass extensive wealth. In the decades after their accession to power, the Safavids suppressed the various Sufi orders whose messianism seemed to threaten the stability of the state, thereby eliminating a major rival to the 'ulama'.[34]

As Safavid rule weakened in the second half of the seventeenth century, the 'ulama' emerged as a hierocracy, that is, an establishment relatively independent of the state. As their power grew, the 'ulama' changed their attitude toward the legitimacy of the state, as some of them argued that the ruler should be both a sayyid and a senior jurisprudent.[35]

The fall of the Safavid dynasty in 1722 under the invasion of the Sunni Afghans began a prolonged period of wars and economic hardship in Iran. In addition to loss of life and property, the 'ulama' were deprived of government patronage. Concurrently, the fall of the Safavids advanced the 'ulama''s monopolistic control over Shi'ism, as it dealt a mortal blow to the extremist heritage (*ghuluw*) in Shi'ism. They were also relieved of the anomalous position of legitimizing charismatic Safavid authority, which contradicted their beliefs.[36]

With the accession of Nadir Shah (1736–47) to power, the 'ulama' faced another danger. Nadir expropriated the religious endowments in Iran in order to sustain his massive armies, and to undermine the economic and political position of the 'ulama'. Seeking to preserve the unity of his religiously mixed army, he sought to reconcile Shi'a and Sunna and to transform Shi'ism into the fifth legal school (*madhhab*) of Sunni Islam, instead of a separate sect.[37] A conference of Sunni and Shi'i 'ulama' which he convened in Najaf in 1743 produced an imposed agreement to that effect, but its impact was short lived as neither the Shi'i 'ulama' nor the Ottomans could reconcile themselves to it. Nadir Shah's policies collapsed with his assassination in 1747.[38]

Persecution by the Afghans and also by Nadir Shah as well as the worsening conditions in Iran resulted in a massive emigration of 'ulama' from Iran to the shrine cities and to India. This emigration together with the decline of learning in Iran transformed the shrine cities into the leading Shi'i centers of scholarship during the eighteenth century.

Concurrently, these factors were largely responsible for the reemergence of the *Akhbariyya* as a major school in Twelver Shi'ism.[39]

Akhbariyya had existed as the tradition opposed to the Usuli school since the Buyid era (945–1055), and was revitalized by Mulla Muhammad Amin Astarabadi (d. 1033/1624 or 1036/1627). The differences between Usulism and Akhbarism revolved around three issues: the sources of law, the means of attaining knowledge, and the authority of the 'ulama' as heirs to the Imams. In contrast to the Usulis, Astarabadi argued that the single most important source of law was the Imams' traditions. The central idea underlying the Akhbari view was that there was no essential difference between the legal state of the community before and after the Occultation. The Imams made certain that all major questions which might arise in the future would be addressed in the traditions. Consequently, Akhbarism rejected the exercise of ijtihad, and with it the extension of the Imam's authority to the 'ulama'.[40]

Akhbarism became the dominant school in the shrine cities since the 1730s. The fall of the Safavids dealt a serious blow to the Usuli school in Iran, which argued that the central institutions of the Islamic state can exist during the absence of the Imam. Henceforth, Usulism was taught only in a few provincial towns.[41] When the Iranian refugees came to the shrine cities, they adopted the Akhbarism of their local hosts. The most prominent eighteenth-century Akhbari scholar was Shaykh Yusuf Bahrani (1695–1772) of Karbala'. He pursued moderate Akhbarism, adopting a more selective approach toward the Traditions, and came close to adopting the Usuli position on the role of the jurist.[42]

The dominance of Akhbarism in the shrine cities was first openly challenged by Aqa Muhammad Baqir Isfahani Bihbihani, whose personal biography largely reflects the history of Shi'ism during the eighteenth century. Born in Isfahan to a respectable 'ulama' family, Muhammad Baqir emigrated to Najaf following his father's death and the Afghan invasion. In Najaf he studied the Traditions with Sayyid Sadr al-Din Qummi, under whose influence he became an Akhbari. Following Nadir Shah's invasion of Iraq, he moved to Bihbihan in southern Iran, where he established links with the local elite by marrying the daughters of the headman of Qanawat quarter and of a respectable merchant.[43] In Bihbihan he reverted to Usulism, possibly following theological and communal clashes with Akhbari 'ulama' from Bahrayn who lived there. In the early 1760s he decided to settle in Karbala' either due to the worsening economic situation in Bihbihan,[44] or more probably because he realized that the struggle between the two rival schools would be decided in the learning centers of the shrine cities.

In Karbala' Bihbihani (as he was now called) began teaching Usuli texts in secret due to the great Akhbari hostility toward the Usulis. Although few Usulis reportedly still lived in Karbala', they had to practice dissimulation.[45] In addition, Bihbihani set out to refute Akhbarism and prove the validity of ijtihad. When he felt sufficiently confident, he openly challenged Bahrani to a public debate on the tenets of the two schools and to allow the latter's disciples to study under him. Bahrani did not oppose Bihbihani's challenge and continued to maintain friendly personal relations with him, a plausible reaction considering his moderate Akhbari views.[46] This story suggests that Bahrani in fact prepared the ground for the shift from Akhbarism to Usulism, which was, therefore, smoother than the picture presented by the hagiographic accounts of Bihbihani.

Bihbihani apparently had strong merchant contacts through his in-laws in Bihbihan and his half-brothers in Isfahan and Shiraz supporting him with charitable funds and seeking his rulings on commercial disputes. Such funds were crucial for attracting a growing number of students and providing them with stipends to live on. Consequently, whereas the first generation of Iranian refugees in the shrine cities may have felt obliged to accept Akhbari superiority and patronage, the second generation were probably more confident in reverting to the traditional Usuli approach, which gradually became the dominant school in the shrine cities.[47]

Akhbarism failed first and foremost because of its rigidity. For Bihbihani and his disciples the first priority was to use deductive reasoning to draw conclusions applicable to practical needs. The political changes and the crisis of legitimacy of the post-Safavid period required such an approach in order to give the 'ulama' the necessary means to play their part in the affairs of the world.[48] While the Akhbari disregard for such needs may have suited the small and isolated scholarly community of the shrine cities up to the eighteenth century, Usulism was better suited to a state-wide community with divergent constituencies.

Akhbari denial of the 'ulama''s authority to conduct Friday prayers and to collect and disburse the *khums* and *zakat* taxes went against the previous historical development of Shi'i doctrine. In the long run, to paraphrase Robert Michels' "iron law of oligarchy," no religious establishment would reject a system or a doctrine that provides it with power.[49] The passing of a generation of leading Akhbaris during the 1770s without leaving successors suggests the weaknesses of Akhbarism in that respect. Henceforth, Usulism has dominated orthodox Shi'ism to the present day.

The shrine cities in history

The town of Karbala', which emerged around the grave of the slain Imam Husayn, is situated some 90 kilometers southwest of Baghdad. As early as 65/684–85 Husayn's grave became a pilgrimage site for Shi'is. The caliph al-Mutawakkil destroyed the tomb and its annexes in 236/850–51 and prohibited the visitations to the holy places in both towns, but the graves were subsequently rebuilt. In 369/979–80 the Buyid amir Adud al-Dawla built shrines over the graves of 'Ali in Najaf and Husayn in Karbala' which henceforth became the centers for Shi'i visitations.[50]

The town of Najaf lies about 160 kilometers south of Baghdad and 9 kilometers west of Kufa on a flat barren height from which the name Najaf is taken. It came into existence during the reign of Harun al-Rashid, after a dome was built over Imam 'Ali's grave in about 170/786–87. Outside Najaf stretches Wadi al-Salam, which serves as a huge graveyard for pious Shi'is who wish to be buried near 'Ali's tomb. Najaf's location on the old trade route from Basra to Baghdad and the pilgrimage route to the Hijaz compensated for its barren earth and the shortage of water.[51] Najaf emerged as a Shi'i center of learning when Shaykh al-Ta'ifa, Muhammad b. Hasan Tusi (d. 1067), moved there in 1056 after the pillaging of his house following the Seljuk takeover of Baghdad. During the Ilkhanid period (13th–15th centuries) it was overshadowed by Hilla and Aleppo.[52]

The rise of Safavid Iran in 1501 and the Ottoman turn to the east under Selim I and Suleiman transformed Iraq into a battle zone between the two rival empires. The struggle for political supremacy was expressed in terms of the Sunni–Shi'i strife, with the shrine cities perceived as a prize by the Safavids. Baghdad and the shrine cities changed hands several times between the Safavids and the Ottomans at a heavy cost to the population of Iraq and its economy.

Throughout most of the period of Ottoman rule (1533–1918) the territory of present-day Iraq was a frontier region in terms of distance and isolation from the Ottoman political center and by being a battle zone between the rival empires. During the years 1747–1831 the pashalik of Baghdad was ruled by Mamluk officers of Georgian origin, who enjoyed local autonomy but were an integral part of the Ottoman system.[53]

Economically, Iraq was one of the least developed areas of the Ottoman Empire. The weakness of the central government and the breakdown of the irrigation system confined agriculture to the vicinity of the cities. The country also suffered from major outbreaks of plague and cholera. Concurrently, Iraq served as a trade route from the Mediterranean to the Indian Ocean as well as being part of a regional market which encompassed Najd and the Gulf.[54]

The two brief periods of Safavid rule over the shrine cities (1508–1533 and 1622–1638) resulted in some construction, but the Safavids cultivated Isfahan and Mashhad as rival learning and pilgrimage centers for political and economic reasons.[55]

As the burial sites of the two most revered Imams, 'Ali and Husayn, Najaf and Karbala' rank after Mecca and Medina in holiness for Shi'is. Whereas Shi'is revered Mecca and Medina out of religious duty, their feelings toward Karbala' were deeper and more emotional, due to their profound empathy with the tragedy of Husayn and its centrality in their religious life. Traditions attributed to the various Imams exalted the virtues of the pilgrimage (*ziyara*) and residence (*mujawara*) in the shrine cities, absolving the believers from all their sins and rewarding them generously in heaven.[56]

Visitation to the shrines of the Imams in Iraq became a major feature of popular Iranian Shi'ism. It was intended to acknowledge the Imams' authority as leaders of the community, and to maintain the contract (*'ahd*) between the Shi'i believer and the Imam, who would intercede with God on his behalf on the day of resurrection. Equally important, the visitation, particularly at Karbala', aimed at preserving Shi'i collective memory and group identity as distinguished from that of the Sunnis. Since it could be made throughout the year, the visitation became a most popular pilgrimage destination.[57]

Karbala' was the larger of the two towns, with a population of about 50,000 persons in the early 1900s, most of whom were Iranian pilgrims and immigrants.[58] Najaf, with a population of about 30,000 by the early 1900s, remained a predominantly Arab town with a strong tribal imprint on its society and culture.[59]

To sum up, the eighteenth century was a turning point in the history of the shrine cities, brought about through the confluence of several parallel processes. The fall of the Safavids and the crisis in Iran drove 'ulama' to migrate from Iran and Bahrayn to Iraq. The failure of Nadir Shah and Karim Khan Zand to take over Iraq and the weakness of the Ottoman–Mamluk regime in Baghdad gave the 'ulama' of the shrine cities sufficient latitude to build important centers of study without government interference. Growing pilgrimage and improved supply of water provided the necessary financial and physical infrastructure for learning. Finally, the reemergence of Usulism supplied the 'ulama' with doctrinal tools to exercise a greater and more active religious and communal role. Thus on the eve of the nineteenth century, the shrine cities faced a new era during which they would emerge as the two most important centers of learning in Shi'ism.

This study begins with the death of Muhammad Baqir Bihbihani in 1205/1791, and the emergence of a new generation of religious leaders in Shi'ism. This period roughly coincided with the rise to power of the Qajar state in Iran.[60] The reinstatement of Shi'ism as the state religion and the restoration of stability to the country prompted the return of 'ulama' from the shrine cities to Iran, opening a new era in the relations between state and religion in Iran, and in the relations of the shrine cities with their Iranian constituents. At the close of our period, the 1905 Constitutional Revolution in Iran marked a new era in the history of the 'ulama' in Iran and the shrine cities. Overall, the study examines a community during a period of transition and change, primarily in its relations with the outside world and other social actors, while still retaining many traditional characteristics in its internal structure.

Part 1

The community: learning and leadership

1 The community of learning: concept and organization

The communities of learning that evolved in the shrine cities during the nineteenth century were the product of centuries of Muslim tradition, as far as the mode of teaching and the centrality of patronage as a social bond were concerned. At the same time, their emergence as Shi'i centers within a Sunni state played a major role in shaping their peculiar social, organizational, and financial features. Unlike other centers of learning in the Muslim world, they were not set up or sustained on a regular basis by political elites in order to provide themselves with legitimacy and juridical manpower. Nor did they act primarily as an arena for stipendiary posts (*mansab* pl. *manasib*), in which knowledge was exploited as a form of capital by notables in order to acquire social and political distinction.[1] Rather, they grew from below through the efforts of the 'ulama' themselves as centers for teaching and scholarship, forming the heart of social and religious networks linking mujtahids, low-ranking 'ulama', and ordinary believers throughout the Shi'i world.

The purpose of this chapter is to analyze the internal workings and mechanisms of the community of 'ulama', especially by demonstrating the key role of informal social networks based on interpersonal and patronage ties and their crucial impact on almost all other aspects of life in the shrine cities, such as ethnicity and class. I will also seek to review the main features of Shi'i higher learning, its strengths and weaknesses, in order to show the close links between the structure of learning and the wider social structure of the 'ulama' community and its influence on other questions such as leadership and finance.

By the nineteenth century the 'ulama' of the shrine cities had become a distinct social stratum as a result of a centuries-long process of professionalization which culminated in the reinstatement of Usulism, and because they consisted primarily of immigrants, most of them from ethnic groups foreign to the local Arab population. Sunni 'ulama' were often incorporated into government bureaucracies, while the Usuli 'ulama' functioned as hierocracy, i.e. as an establishment semi-independent of the state. They were clearly distinct from the Sunni Ottoman

21

elites in Iraq, and equally so from the bureaucratic and military elite in Qajar Iran in their social and educational backgrounds and career opportunities.

In view of these circumstances the proper unit for discussion regarding the 'ulama' should be the term preferred by the Shi'i sources themselves, i.e. the *hawza 'ilmiyya* or community (lit. territory) of learning. The *hawza* denotes a communal whole which encompasses scholarship, interpersonal and social bonds, as well as organizational and financial aspects.[2] It was characterized by an amorphous structure without an overall formal and hierarchical organization and by the absence of regulatory bodies regarding the curriculum of studies, finance, or administration like those in western and also in Ottoman institutions of education.[3]

We can speak, however, of a process of institutionalization in the shrine cities in the sense of patterns of behavior which crystallize and persist in the course of time, and to which people become attached as a result of their role in the formation of identity or through social interest. Thus, whatever regularization there was regarding the curriculum or the stages of study during the period under discussion, it was based on conventions and customs, rather than on formal decisions by elected or appointed bodies. This situation stood in contrast to the hierarchical Ottoman learned establishment, whose structure and mode of operation were largely determined by the state.

While the 'ulama' of the shrine cities vied among themselves for students, prestige, funds, and influence, this competition took a form other than that prevailing in Sunni centers of learning, because of the absence of an overall administration and government patronage. These rivalries were oriented toward the community and much less toward securing the favor of government officials.

Notwithstanding the amorphous structure of the community of learning a major element in its evolution was the creation of boundaries determining affiliation to or exclusion from mainstream Shi'ism, which also functioned to impose internal discipline. While the rules of conduct were unwritten, they were not necessarily flexible or lenient and their violation drew punishment. In the absence of governmental enforcement agencies, the most powerful instrument for imposing social discipline was excommunication (*takfir*). Its introduction by Muhammad Baqir Bihbihani as a weapon in internal disputes in the mid-eighteenth century endowed the efforts of the 'ulama' to eliminate any threats to their authority with greater effectiveness.[4]

A remarkable example of such internal disciplining designed to establish the boundaries of social legitimacy is that of Hadi Tehrani, one of the leading *usul* teachers in Najaf since the 1870s. Tehrani is mentioned as having enlightened views, which might have meant adherence to Babism. In addition, he did not hide his contempt for his contemporaries and for some of the greatest authorities of Shi'i *fiqh*. Personal insults alone have never been lacking in disputations between mujtahids, but Tehrani's views were also perceived as a threat to the foundations of the community. Consequently, he was declared unclean, i.e. an infidel, during a meeting of the leading 'ulama' and students in 1303/1885–86. The excommunication led to violent clashes between the disciples of the respective mujtahids in which Tehrani's disciples suffered a crushing defeat. Most of them abandoned his class out of fear for their lives. Yet, in the absence of a supreme regulatory authority, few mujtahids contested the excommunication as an extreme measure which should not have been used in such matters. Tehrani never regained his status, and reportedly left for Tehran.[5] However, the fact that *takfir* was not often used indicates its effectiveness as a deterrent. After the Constitutional Revolution the use of *takfir* against political rivals became a more common weapon in struggles within the community of learning.

Clientalism in the community of learning

The community of learning centered around individual mujtahids who gave their own classes, and sometimes supported lower-level teachers. As in the medieval period, the madrasas in the shrine cities, which served mainly as housing and for ensuring an endowed income to one teacher, were part of a larger community of learning and intellectual activity. Most classes were given at mosques, the shrine courtyards and the mujtahids' private homes. Students, therefore, were regarded as disciples of a specific mujtahid, and not of the madrasa as an institution. Berkey's observation on medieval Cairo that "education was judged not on *loci* but on *personae*"[6] applies to the shrine cities five centuries later as well.

The informal nature of higher Muslim learning has often been contrasted with the formal structure of the medieval European university. The difference is generally attributed to the nature of Islamic law which recognizes only the physical individual as the juristic person, since each individual stands in direct unmediated relation to God. In contrast, Roman law recognizes the corporation as a juristic entity with acknowledged and secured interests.[7] Such a view, however, seems to accord too much power to laws in shaping societies, and does not take into account the possibility that laws merely reflect or legitimize existing social situations. Alternatively, the predominance of informal relationships and institutions has been seen as typical of societies where boundaries between social groups are seldom distinct and fixed, and where associations are few in number. The reluctance of the Middle Eastern states to tolerate the development of independent and tightly structured bodies, thus hindering the rise of an independent indigenous bourgeoisie, is another likely factor.[8]

The informal character of the learning institutions has always been linked with the "personalistic nature" of Middle Eastern society, in which "the unifying point for the disparate elements of life resides in the single person" rather than in formal associations.[9] The complementary component of this concept, suggested both as its cause and effect, is the system of clientalism or patron–client relationships, which dominated almost all aspects of life in the community of learning.

Clientalism is common in societies which have been chiefly characterized by extensive and extractive economies, and by intensive exploitation of a fixed resource basis. In other words, such societies resemble the patrimonial model, in which the rulers attempted to control the ownership of land in their own hands. Most other social actors, therefore, have a relatively low degree of autonomous access to the major socioeconomic and political resources needed to implement their goals, or to control their own resources. Authority in such societies is often incompletely centralized and is shared between rulers and patrons who play the role of intermediaries between various social groups and the government. In these complex but not fully bureaucratized societies, kinship and other ascriptive ties often cannot regulate the allocation of power and resources, while the universal categories of class, party, and citizen typical of modern states are still underdeveloped.

Consequently, there is a strong tendency in these societies to create an institutional means of bridging the gap between elites and lower strata. These institutions often have the same symbolic and affective tone as kinship solidarity, and may even be expressed as (fictive) kinship, as was the case in the medieval Mamluk system. Like kinship, they entail mutual long-term obligations of personal exchange. The religious systems of such societies are mediated by professional clergy, or the 'ulama' in the Muslim case. Patrons who exert some sort of emotional or moral hold over their clients can expect more enduring relations with them, minimizing the possibility that other patrons may entice away their wards through simple material promises.[10]

The influence of the centuries during which Shi'i scholarship was developed by individual mujtahids independently of state intervention reinforced the informal nature of Shi'i learning. The principle of emulation (*taqlid*) of a living mujtahid, and the prohibition on emulating a dead one also enhanced the importance of patronage in creating distinct, unequal reciprocal relations between two individuals.

In a society largely shaped by a continuous influx of immigrant students and teachers vying for financial resources, status, and influence, the creation of networks of patronage was a necessity for both parties in securing their places. In the absence of a central administration to look after their needs, the only means of survival for young students coming to a foreign place in their teens was to attach themselves to a teacher-patron.[11] In addition, clientalism enabled the 'ulama' of the shrine cities, and Muslims in general, to overcome ethnic and regional divisions in a diverse and heterogeneous society. Moreover, it served the interests of the leading mujtahids to preserve their dominance over their students and junior colleagues by preventing them from forging a collective group consciousness. Consequently, the community of learning could serve as a micro-model of a clientalist system.

Clientalism in the shrine cities consisted of the classical type of dyadic relation between the mujtahid and the single student which permeated almost every aspect of life. These patronage relationships closely resembled the medieval companionship (*suhba*) between students and teachers, although that specific term was not in use. The Shiʻi sources use such medieval terms as *lazama* (adhered to) the teacher in describing master–disciple relationships reflecting the continuity of the medieval model in both concept and conduct.[12] Clientalism in the shrine cities, however, was less engrossing and demanding than in the Sufi parallels. The Sufi *murid* (disciple) was supposed to leave his soul's salvation entirely in his master's hands, and obey his teacher at all costs. In return, the Sufi master was seen as capable of interceding before God for his disciples. In Shiʻism both these elements were reserved to the Imams and were not assigned to the mujtahids.[13]

Students, even when residing at a madrasa, were affiliated and identified with the study circle of a specific mujtahid. In each study circle students were divided into two groups: an inner circle of senior and close students, the *khawass* (entourage), who served as teaching assistants and aides, and the larger student group. The medieval meaning of *khawass* referred to the ruler's entourage, and its use among the 'ulama' reflects the importance and status of its members. Affiliation to the *khawass* was not formal, but depended on personal relations with the mujtahid. Ansari is mentioned as having appointed his close disciple, Hasan Ashtiyani, as *imam al-talaba*, which probably meant his closest aide for student affairs.[14]

Patronage is based on an imbalance in resources and on reciprocity in services rendered, which most often favors the patron. The shrine cities diverged somewhat from the classical model, as the teacher-patron was the one who first provided services to his client during the early years of this relationship. In Sunni systems of learning students received stipends from the madrasa's endowment. By contrast, in the shrine cities, due to the scarcity of *awqaf*, most students were dependent for their livelihoods on their teacher through the donations he managed to elicit. Again, personal acquaintance with the teacher was the key element. Dawlata-badi, an unsympathetic observer, asserts that Mirza Hasan Shirazi (d. 1895) personally decided the stipend each student should receive. Students did not know how much their colleagues received, and an atmosphere of jealousy developed among them. In this way, presumably intended to promote healthy competition among the students, Shirazi held all of them "between hope and fear."[15] Quchani, who was often penniless during his student days, recounts that in order to receive a stipend from Akhund Khorasani he needed the personal intercession of fellow students from Khorasan.[16] It seems that due to the voluntary nature of study in the shrine cities, and the students' dependence on their teachers, there was no need for strict disciplinary measures apart from denial of the stipend. At least the available sources do not mention any.

Patronage relations extended to areas beyond pure academics. Muhsin al-Amin declared that in contrast to most centers of learning, teachers in Najaf used to inquire about the personal situation of the students, about their food, housing, debts, whether they had received letters from home, their dreams for the future, and the like. Hasan al-Sadr's statement that the students and 'ulama' who were supported by Shirazi "were all as family to him in all their affairs" portrays the mujtahid's network as a scholarly version of an extended household.[17] The more intimate type of patronage compared with the one prevailing in Iran was due to the centrality of teaching in the shrine cities compared with the focus on the administration of justice in Iranian centers, as well as the competition among teachers for students who would later serve them as agents.

Marriages between the masters' daughters and promising students, which were common to other religious establishments as well, both symbolized and cemented the relationships of patronage. They often cut across ethnic lines, and even superseded family obligations, as was the case with Ja'far Kashif al-Ghita' who gave his daughter to his disciple, disregarding his nephew's protest that tribal traditions gave precedence to the family. Since married students received larger stipends, they had to obtain their masters' permission if they wanted to marry. Students of Akhund Khorasani who defied their teacher's disapproval of such marriages lost their grants.[18] The mujtahid's attention and goodwill were essential even for obtaining a room in the madrasa.[19]

Unlike the more coercive type of relations between peasants and landlords, clientalism in the shrine cities was voluntary thanks to the centrality of teaching and the absence of overall administration. Students could join a teacher's class or leave it and join another's at will for a variety of reasons, not all of them academic. This freedom enhanced the students' bargaining position, which was an essential element of the system.

As shown above, the reciprocity of patronage often favored the patron. In the shrine cities, however, the mujtahids' dependence on their students was greater than in other centers of learning due to the absence of secured income from *awqaf*. The mujtahids needed the students to publicize their courses among their colleagues in order to attract a greater following. In some instances students wrote juridical works at their teacher's instruction as well as copying his own works and compiling his rulings (*fatwas*) into *risalat 'amal* (a religious manual, which supported his claim to religious leadership).[20] Some mujtahids, such as Ja'far Kashif al-Ghita', employed their students in enforcing their rulings or even intimidating their political rivals in Najaf. In cases where disputes between mujtahids were resolved by force, the students' role was especially important.[21]

A case in point is the story of Baqir al-Bata'ihi, a son of a local religious leader in Suq al-Shuyukh in southern Iraq. Baqir was a student in Najaf when his father, Shaykh 'Ali, died. The "leaders of the religious authority" (*hay'a diniyya*) in Najaf at the turn of the twentieth century, Husayn Khalili, Akhund Khorasani, and Muhammad Taha Najaf, agreed among themselves to persuade him to accept the role of religious leadership in the Muntafiq region, due to his fame and popularity there. The nomination followed a subtle negotiating process, which possibly also reflected some tensions between Iranian mujtahids and local Arab 'ulama', since Baqir was reluctant to leave Najaf. He finally agreed on the condition that he would be able to issue *fatwas* independently.[22] That the mujtahids could not force him to go to the Muntafiq region shows that there were certain limits of their power over lower-level 'ulama'. It is quite possible that in an age of many competing leaders, local 'ulama' could maneuver among them in order to obtain greater leeway for themselves. On the other hand, Shaykh Baqir's insistence on issuing his own *fatwas* points to the degree of centralization in religious affairs. Apparently, local Arab 'ulama' had not been able to issue *fatwas* by themselves, either because they were deemed unqualified or more likely in order to preserve the authority of the mujtahids in the shrine cities.

Durability of clientalist relationships was flexible since students could move from one teacher to another. However, most students adhered to their principal master even after returning home, until his death. Most aspiring mujtahids became independent teachers only after the death of their principal teacher. When a disciple decided to have his own independent study circle while his teacher was still alive, and without his permission, it usually meant a break in their relations.

Allegiance to the master was personal and exclusive to him. It did not necessarily extend to his entire family or his sons, who did not bestow knowledge upon the student. I was able to trace only a few recorded cases in which patronage relations continued along several generations. In this event the mujtahid's sons usually enjoyed scholarly reputations themselves.[23] These one-generational ties were unlike the Sufi master–disciple relationships, where the master's son often succeeded his father as a spiritual leader and patron. The mujtahid could not pass his legal expertise on to his son, but the Sufi master could bestow his charisma on his successor by an act of designation.[24]

When the teacher died, his study circle dissolved and the former disciples set up their own classes, often in competition with each other. The rivalries among Ansari's students after his death, and the disintegration of the community of learning in Samarra' following the death of Shirazi are but two prominent illustrations of the importance of the vertical rather than the horizontal allegiance of student peer groups.[25]

Patronage networks linking the teacher and his former disciples who resided as 'ulama' in various Shi'i localities came close to the ideal type of radially connected network. In this model each member is directly linked to the central figure, i.e. the teacher, and members communicate with one another only through him.[26] It is possible that in the mujtahid–disciple network, the latter did communicate with each other directly, although there are no data to show it. However, even if they did, these links were of secondary importance compared with the single link each member had with the mujtahid. Activating them politically, then, was dependent on the mujtahid's lead, rather than on other members.

The master–disciple networks were often organized in a pyramid-type patronage pattern in which links between the patron and his clients were introduced beyond the first layer, once the disciple had his own students and clients.[27] When the mujtahid died, his network dissolved. The various members most often attached themselves to the network of another mujtahid, since the top level of the mujtahid ranks would consist of only a limited number of mujtahids and consequently only a certain number of networks could coexist.[28] Shi'i traditions describe

Muhammad b. Makki al-'Amili the Shahid I (d. 1384) as the first mujtahid to establish a network when he appointed his agents throughout Syria. It is more likely, however, that such networks dated back to the days of the Imams and their agents.[29]

The diffused lines between social groups in medieval Muslim societies and the importance of vertical allegiances well into the nineteenth and twentieth centuries raises the question whether students had acquired collective consciousness and interests besides their common pursuit of stipends.[30] Unquestionably, attainment of stipends was the major criterion in distinguishing between students who were registered and recognized as disciples of specific mujtahids and newcomers. In addition, the distinction between students and local society was quite clear, since most of them were immigrants of different ethnic origins who came to the shrine cities with the explicit purpose of studying.

Typically of networks elsewhere in the Middle East, students often developed a sense of pride in their circle of study and shared a group identity (*asabiyat*) as disciples of a specific mujtahid, combined with rivalry against competing networks.[31] What is uncertain, however, is whether this collective consciousness survived the death of the teacher and the dispersal of the students. When politics began to occupy a more prominent place in the shrine cities during the 1905 Constitutional Revolution, the activity of students as a body became a more common and significant feature.[32]

An important institution which complemented the vertical teacher–student relationship, and which contributed to the sense of a community in the shrine cities, was the socio-academic and poetry session or salon (*majlis* or *diwan*) in which educational, literary, and socio-political activities were fused. Such sessions, which were called the "soul of Najaf," reputedly dated from the city's early history. They took place on Thursdays and Fridays and particularly during nights of Ramadan when classes were not held, serving as a respite from intensive intellectual activity. The establishment of such a *majlis* often signaled a claim of high status by a mujtahid acting as an important tool in expanding his social networking. The *majalis* also provided mechanisms for conflict resolution in Shi'i society, and produced a certain cultural syncretism between Arab, Persian, and Indian cultures, primarily in the field of poetry.[33]

The importance of interpersonal allegiances did not nullify the role of the family as a primary unit of loyalty and power. Families and clans determined a person's identity, affiliation, and allegiance in a traditional society. A family that managed to build a mosque or a madrasa could use these to perpetuate its high status for more than one generation. The Bahr al-'Ulum clan and their relatives the Tabataba'i family of

Karbala' used their control of the Oudh Bequest (see below) as an important instrument to consolidate their power base, with members of the two families receiving the bulk of the funds. The families maintained close ties with each other through marriages and study. The Kashif al-Ghita' clan acted as a unit to maintain its leadership status with one member recognized as the head of the family. Members of the family studied under their relatives, at least in the lower-level courses.

Many of the *majalis* mentioned above were associated with families and were used to strengthen their status, as was the case with the four families who descended from Khidr al-Jinaji: the Kashif al-Ghita', Al Radi, Al Khidri, and Al 'Aliyar. One means of perpetuating the elite status of various families common throughout the Middle East was the forging of marriage alliances among them, as among the Jawahiri and Bahr al-'Ulum clans. However, since most 'ulama' were immigrants who came alone to the shrine cities, the extended family played a less important role for them than the patronage relationship.

Class and ethnicity

The importance of the interpersonal links in the shrine cities over-shadowed but did not negate other social classifications such as class and ethnicity. The consolidation of Usulism as the dominant school in Shi'ism had a profound impact on the structure of the 'ulama' community, dividing it into two groups, of mujtahids and low-level 'ulama' respectively. As the 'ulama' population grew in the course of the nineteenth century, the mujtahid group itself came to be divided into an elite and a larger group of junior mujtahids. The rank-and-file 'ulama' were middle- and low-ranking teachers, prayer leaders in the numerous mosques in the shrine cities, preachers (*wa'iz* pl. *wu'az*), narrators of the Karbala' tragedy (*dhakirin, rouzekhans, ta'ziyakhans*), or providers of other religious services.[34]

The 'ulama' in general, and those in the shrine cities in particular, never formed a class since their various roles situated them in different positions *vis-à-vis* the market and created significant socio-economic gaps within their ranks. Likewise, uniform economic action did not constitute the criterion of admission to their ranks nor characterize their role in society. Consequently, tensions between lower-level and senior 'ulama' were a common phenomenon in the Ottoman religious estab-lishment. In Iran, such resentments were among the important causes for the attraction of the Shaykhi and Babi movements.[35]

Such problems were less significant in the shrine cities, as indicated by the relatively limited appeal of Babism among Usuli students there.

The uniqueness of the two cities lay in the narrow socio-economic gaps between teachers and students and in the openness of the community regarding upward social mobility. Except for some members of the Bahr al-'Ulum and Tabataba'i families who were accused of corruption in their handling of the Oudh Bequest, no cases are known which parallel the wealth of Hujjat al-Islam Shafti or the corruption of Muhammad Taqi Najafi (Aqa Najafi d. 1914), the chief mujtahid of Isfahan. On the contrary, at least several of the mujtahids in the shrine cities were renowned for their poverty and asceticism. Only when there was a significant decline in the flow of donations as was the case in 1908–10, and when students felt they were being treated unfairly by their teachers, did rancor appear. This change also reflected the emergence of a collective student identity as a pressure group with its own interests, thereby straining the patronage relationship.[36]

The hereditary nature of many religious posts in Iran enabled mujtahids of dubious scholarship to succeed to prominent positions, while lower-level 'ulama' felt that their way upward was blocked. This phenomenon was less common in the shrine cities due to the centrality of teaching and scholarship in the attainment of high status, which required sons of mujtahids to build their reputations on their own merits. Talented students, regardless of their social origins, had a better chance of attaining prominence than incompetent sons of renowned fathers. The "mujtahid dream," according to which every gifted student could become a mujtahid, played a role similar to the "American dream" in mitigating resentments among high- and low-level 'ulama'.

The nineteenth century witnessed the emergence of the "Shi'i inter-national" centered in the shrine cities, which brought together in unprecedented numbers 'ulama' from far-flung parts of the Muslim world.[37] The largest groups were Iranians, both Persians and Turks, Arabs from Iraq, Lebanon, Bahrayn, and al-Ahsa', as well as Indians and even Tibetans.[38]

The unifying power of religion, however, did not eliminate ethnic differences even before the rise of nationalism. However, unlike other international centers of learning, such as al-Azhar in Cairo, the immi-grants, primarily the Iranians, rather than the natives formed the majority and the dominant faction within the community of 'ulama' in the shrine cities.[39]

The gathering of individuals from diverse places sharpened the sense of otherness, and enhanced ethnic and regional consciousness, as was reflected even in the addition of place of origin to the name. In new unfamiliar territory and society, be it the shrine cities or al-Azhar in Cairo, immigrant students or 'ulama' sought support and amity from those closest to them. Quchani's account illustrates this point. In Sabzivar and Mashhad, the leading centers of learning in Khorasan, students were grouped according to their local origin in Khorasan. In Najaf, on the other hand, local origin partly gave way as a major point of reference in favor to larger notions of identity, for example, Khorasanis within the broader Iranian group. During his first months in Najaf, Quchani was greatly assisted by a group of more senior Khorasani students, who constituted the inner group of Akhund Khorasani's study circle. However, facing Turkish students, the Persians from various regions in Iran closed ranks. This was also the case with the Lebanese students, regardless of regional differences that existed in Lebanon.[40]

Ethnic divisions were apparent even in the smaller 'ulama' community at the beginning of the nineteenth century. Whereas Karbala' was predominantly Iranian, Najaf retained a more mixed character. However, when Bahr al-'Ulum died, he appointed Iranians as executors of his will and ordered that a fellow Iranian, Mahdi Shahristani from Karbala', lead the prayer at his funeral. Likewise, in his polemicist reply to Muhammad al-Akhbari, Ja'far Kashif al-Ghita' stressed his own origins from "the Arab (Bedouins) inhabitants of Iraq."[41] On the other hand, at that time classes were mixed, and Ja'far Kashif al-Ghita' enjoyed senior status among mujtahids from all groups.

The community of 'ulama' in the shrine cities experienced continuous growth from a few hundred at the beginning of the nineteenth century to about 6,000 in 1907 in Najaf alone, thanks to the influx of students and other migrants mostly from Iran, who, according to a sample I have discussed elsewhere, outnumbered the natives by slightly more than five to one (905 to 166). Almost 65 percent of the migrant Iranian students were of non-clerical origins, coming from all segments of society.[42] A better sense of these data is given by a comparison with Dar al-Funun, the most important college in Qajar Iran, which was founded in 1851. Unlike the shrine cities, Dar al-Funun was designed primarily for members of the Qajar elite, and the number of students during the first forty years reached about 1,100.[43]

The Arab groups from Iraq and Lebanon grew at a slower pace because of their predominantly tribal and rural home constituencies. A typical tribe in Iraq or village in Lebanon rarely needed or could sustain more than one 'alim at a time. In Iran the situation was markedly different. Whereas the turmoil of the eighteenth century depleted the ranks of the 'ulama', the return of stability, as well as lavish Qajar patronage during the early part of the nineteenth century, enabled or even attracted many young men to enter the ranks of the 'ulama', filling a vacuum in both the urban and rural regions of Iran. The Iranian economy could sustain a growing number of 'ulama' through endowments and donations from the merchant communities. Moreover, religion played a major role in Iranian society, to a much greater extent than in Iraq, thus creating a genuine demand for 'ulama'. The recruitment of students from all social strata, as well as the openness of the community which offered upward social mobility to talented youths, consolidated the 'ulama''s links with all sectors of Iranian society.[44]

As the numbers of 'ulama' grew, so the ethnic factor became more significant. When students migrated to the shrine cities, they tended to study first under teachers from their own region. *Ahl biladihi* (people of his country) was the term used regarding a certain student from Bahrayn. Muhsin al-Amin, for instance, recalled how he decided not to join a certain course, because there were only a few 'Amili students there. Several leading mujtahids used to hold separate classes for Arab and Iranian students.[45]

Ethnic relations influenced patterns of travel and study. Arab students overwhelmingly studied in Najaf throughout the nineteenth century, and only a few of them came to the Iranian-dominated community of learning in Karbala'. Fewer still traveled to Iran. It is a tribute to Shirazi's greatness as a teacher and patron that he managed to attract a large number of Arab students from Najaf to Samarra'.[46]

Social and poetry circles often corresponded to ethnic and regional divisions.[47] The Shi'i biographical sources rarely provide information on marriages. However, from the data available it appears that marriages between 'ulama' families were mostly conducted among members of the same ethnic group. Inter-ethnic marriages were mostly between promising disciples and daughters of the teacher.[48] The tendency to marry within one's own ethnic group and the constant influx of immigrating 'ulama' perpetuated ethnic divisions, almost completely precluding either the Arabization or the total Iranization of the 'ulama' society in the shrine cities as had happened for instance in Safavid Iran, where the Arab 'ulama' were Iranized. Yet, members of at least three prominent Iranian families – the formerly Azeri Najaf clan, and the Persian Bahr al-'Ulum and Jawahiri clans – were Arabized by the twentieth century.[49]

The competition for funds sharpened ethnic rivalries, particularly when Iranian donors often restricted the beneficiaries to members from their own region or ethnic group.[50] With almost every donation sent from Lucknow to the shrine cities during the 1830s and 1840s, the Indian mujtahids emphasized the need to allocate special funds to the Indians residing or studying in the shrine cities, implying that the Indians were not getting their fair share.[51] Likewise, the Turkish students of Shaykh Hasan Mamaqani argued that it was his duty to provide for the Turks first, since most of the money he received had come from Turks. They complained that Persian and Arab mujtahids distributed stipends only among members of their own groups. Mama-qani, however, rejected their demand as incompatible with the Shari'a.[52]

Housing was divided according to places of origin from the beginning of the century. Mulla Muhammad Iravani, one of the leaders of the Turkish faction, built a special madrasa for Turkish students following their complaints of discrimination by the Persians. Even Indian and Kashmiri students did not live in the same madrasas. In al-Azhar, by comparison, the ethnic division was more formal, as resident halls (*riwaq*, pl. *arwiqa*) were assigned to members of different ethnic groups, each with its own *naqib* or shaykh.[53]

Arabs and Indians resented Iranian domination of the shrine cities. During an argument with Muhsin al-Amin a Lebanese student once declared that "there was no need for *'ilm al-usul* and it was sufficient to refer to the *akhbar* since the *akhbar* are Arab and we are Arabs." Hirz al-Din, for instance, lamented that ever since the Iranians came to dominate Najaf, Arab mujtahids did not get the respect they deserved from their Iranian colleagues.[54]

Ethnic divisions were more evident in the realm of popular religion. Even narrations of the Karbala' tragedy and the 'Ashura' processions, the most powerful symbol of Shi'i belief and collective sorrow *vis-à-vis* outsiders, were conducted separately. The style of recitation and the language used by the *rowzekhan* differed according to the specific ethnic composition, geographic origin, and class attributes of the participant audience.[55]

Iranian predominance in Najaf was evident even in the use of Persian terms by Arab students in daily speech. Upon his return to Lebanon from Najaf in 1298/1880–81, Shaykh Musa Sharara introduced to his country the weekly mourning sessions (*majalis al-ta'ziyya*) that had been practiced in Iran. A less somber influence was his introduction of the Iranian samovar into the Lebanese village. Iranian 'ulama' had to learn literary Arabic as the language of the Qur'an and religious sciences, and most mujtahids wrote their major works in Arabic. But the Iranians did not bother to learn colloquial Arabic. By the mid-twentieth century many Iranian mujtahids had difficulty in communicating in Arabic.[56]

The importance of ethnic differences notwithstanding, its conse-quences should not be exaggerated. The majority of senior mujtahids had students from all groups, and it would be wrong to speak of total separation in social life.[57] Nor does a correlation between ethnicity and political conduct appear during the nineteenth century. The rise of

nationalism at the beginning of the twentieth century and the emergence
of modern states in the aftermath of World War I accentuated the ethnic
and national divisions in the Shi'i world and the community of
'ulama'.[58]

Clientalism and finance[59]

The economic base of the community of learning in the shrine cities was
very different from that of the Sunni Ottoman religious establishment,
and even from that of Shi'i Iran, in the relatively minor significance of
landed endowments (awqaf), and of direct governmental support by
way of salaries or grants.[60] The main sources of income for the shrine
cities were contributions from the believers, primarily through their
networks of patronage, a fact which had significant ramifications on
various aspects of the life of the 'ulama' and their community.

The absence of significant waqf property in the shrine cities was
caused by several factors. For obvious reasons, the Sunni government in
Baghdad established awqaf to benefit the Sunni 'ulama' but not the
Shi'is. Wealthy landowners in Iran could establish awqaf, but in Iraq
government control hardly extended to the countryside, which was
dominated by the tribes throughout the century. Consequently, landowning by urban dwellers and with it the ability to set up awqaf was
confined to "the vicinity of the main towns and in the areas irrigated by
lift or perennial canals where the tribes had disintegrated."[61] Religion
among the tribes who had converted to Shi'ism in the course of the
century was non-doctrinal, and the devotional urge to establish awqaf
was lacking. Tribal leaders preferred to sustain the local sayyids, who
helped them dominate their tribes, rather than set up awqaf for the
'ulama' in the shrine cities, and the tribesmen themselves were too poor
to establish awqaf.[62] Under these circumstances, the main source of
revenue for the 'ulama' in the shrine cities was donations by believers,
which came in several forms:[63]

The first source was the obligatory religious dues of the Imam's share
(sahm-i Imam) i.e. one half of the fifth (khums) of the annual income
which every Shi'i owed to the Imam, and alms (zakat).[64]

The second category was composed of three voluntary types of
payment: The first was the "right of inheritance" (haqq al-wasiyya) or
the more popular term, the "third" (thulth), from the heritable property
of deceased persons, and was usually designated for a certain religious
purpose with the mujtahid acting as a trustee. The most famous one was
the Oudh Bequest, established in 1825 by Ghazi al-Din Haydar, king of
Awadh, from the interest of a loan granted to the East India Company,

and was administered by the British. The bequest, which began to operate in 1849, channeled more than six million rupees to Najaf and Karbala' during the first fifty years of its operation.[65]

The second type of voluntary funds (*sawm wa-salat*) was a fee paid by believers to the mujtahids to arrange prayers and fasting, usually by a student, on behalf of deceased relatives for periods that varied according to the amount paid. The annual fee which Shi'is paid at the turn of the twentieth century ranged from three to six Turkish pounds (£2.14s–£5.8s). The third type took the form of a vow in return to recovery from sickness or deliverance from danger.

The third category of funds channeled to the shrine cities consisted of contributions donated to the shrines directly, which did not reach the 'ulama'.

The economic base of the community of 'ulama' was not secure at the beginning of the nineteenth century, and even senior mujtahids, such as the Bahr al-'Ulum family, reportedly suffered destitution. Consequently, mujtahids often had to travel to Iran to solicit contributions since networks of patronage for the transfer of funds had not yet been established. A major source of income at the period was the "Indian Money," sent by the rulers of Awadh to the shrine cities.[66]

The flow of funds to the shrine cities increased considerably with the consolidation of networks of patronage in Iran beginning from the 1840s. Murtada Ansari reportedly received about 150,000 or 200,000 tumans a year (£66,000–88,000) at a time when the entire annual revenue of the Iranian government was estimated at ranging between 3,200,000 tumans (£1.6 million) in 1851–52 to 4,900,000 tuman (£1,970,000) in 1867–68.[67] His various disciples and successors also received considerable amounts. Muhammad Fadil Sharabiyani reportedly distributed T£4,000 (about £3,240) a year among his students. Unfortunately, it is impossible to calculate from the available sources the yearly amounts reaching the shrine cities.[68] These remittances enabled various mujtahids to build several madrasas to house their students and bolster their own positions.

The reliance on charity compelled the 'ulama' of the shrine cities to cultivate close relations with the two major sources of donations: the Bazaar community in Iran and also government officials. The 'ulama' had to be attentive to the wishes of the donors, sometimes to the point of being led by them in political and even doctrinal issues. In addition, the unstable nature of donations as compared to landed *awqaf* made funding an object of incessant preoccupation and constant rivalry among mujtahids.[69] At the same time, whereas *awqaf* were occasionally appropriated by the state, as in Egypt and the Ottoman Empire, the broad base of the donor pool could not be controlled by any government, thereby sheltering the 'ulama' from depredations by the latter.

The visiting of the shrines of the Imams played a major role in the socio-economic development of the shrine cities as a whole, and of the community of 'ulama' in particular. The visits provided an opportunity for personal contact between the mujtahid and his followers, and served as an important channel for soliciting donations from the believers. They also supplied the platform for the dissemination of ideas in the case of the Shaykhi movement. Pilgrims' donations became a source of serious competition among the mujtahids who were helped by their disciples in this purpose. Low-level 'ulama' and students could earn money from pilgrims by undertaking to recite prayers on their behalf, and by providing various religious services such as praying at funerals and arranging temporary marriages (zawaj mut'a).[70]

Overall, the pilgrimages and the extensive "burial industry" of pious Shi'is in the cemeteries of Najaf and Karbala' were the major mainstay of the local economy of the four shrine cities, which was largely geared to catering to the needs of pilgrims.[71]

Students and low-ranking 'ulama' received stipends from their teachers, sometimes from several teachers simultaneously. Quchani says that Akhund Khorasani's students, who were among the poorest in Najaf, received only 3 tuman (about 12 shillings) a year in addition to bread rations. Though Quchani received an additional 18 tumans (£3.12s) a year from Hasan Mamaqani, he was still constantly short of money. According to Pirzadeh, Habiballah Rashti's students received a minimum stipend of 180 Kran a year (about £5.2s) and an additional 26 Kran (14–15 shillings) for each year of study.[72] Considering that in 1908 one loaf of bread cost 1.24 piaster,[73] these stipends amounted to the bare minimum, and the Shi'i sources are full of descriptions of the poverty of many students and would-be mujtahids.

In addition, many resident 'ulama' and students earned their livings by serving as rouzekhans, copying books, and providing various religious services. Only a few 'ulama' owned land, chiefly those who came from landowning families.[74]

The peculiar nature of the financial basis of the community of learning influenced the nature of its clientalism by holding the balance of mutual dependence between the mujtahid-patron and his student-client. In the absence of secured income from awqaf, the students were totally dependent on stipends from their teachers. Concurrently, the mujtahids needed a large following among students in order to dispatch them as agents and representatives to various Shi'i communities to serve as the crucial link between their teacher and the Bazaar community, to collect religious dues, and refer new students to him. Dependence here switches sides in favor of the students.

The organization of learning

Learning, the *raison d'être* of the community of 'ulama' in the shrine cities, was both influenced by and in its turn shaped the pattern of interpersonal ties. The Shi'i structure of learning which evolved during the nineteenth century was the product of centuries of Islamic tradition, both Sunni and Shi'i, but it was also in some ways unique. To understand it better, it is necessary to place Shi'i learning within the larger historical context of Muslim learning.

The first madrasas devoted to the study of hadith and law were established in the second part of the eleventh century. The madrasa provided the physical structure for instruction and, unlike earlier institutions, a secure source of income to sustain the teachers and students, based on charitable foundations (*awqaf*).[75]

In his numerous writings on Muslim education George Makdisi stresses the structured nature of studies in the madrasa compared with the earlier institutions. This development was manifested in a distinct body of teachers and students, a fixed curriculum, and a system of certification.[76] Other scholars, however, have shown that the madrasa itself did not monopolize Islamic education, since much serious legal and religious instruction took place outside its walls in individual study circles (*halaqat*). More importantly, Islamic education remained fundamentally an informal enterprise revolving around the teacher–student relationship.[77]

The process and precise period in which a fixed curriculum of study was established in higher Muslim learning is a matter of debate among historians. According to Makdisi such a curriculum was in place by the twelfth century, while Chamberlain defers its existence to as late as the fourteenth century. In the more structured Ottoman system, specific books were read in each madrasa according to its position in the Ottoman hierarchy.[78] A similar uncertainty applies to Shi'i learning, but by the middle of the nineteenth century, and probably earlier, a three-staged Shi'i curriculum was already practiced in the shrine cities as well as in all the major centers of learning in Iran. The great resemblance between this structure and the one described by Makdisi for the medieval madrasa suggests that it was established even earlier.

The subjects and modes of study in Shi'i learning were heavily influenced by the archetype of the Sunni institutions and were divided into "transmitted sciences" (*'ulum naqliyya*) and "rational sciences" (*'ulum 'aqliyya*), which were based on observation by the senses and deduction. There were, however, several basic differences between the two sects. Most important was the prominence given to the study of *usul al-fiqh* due to the central role of ijtihad in Shi'ism.

The first stage of study – the *muqaddamat* (preliminaries) – lasted between three and five years, in which studies focused on achieving a firm knowledge of Arabic as well as basic concepts of logic and rhetoric. Optional subjects included mathematics and astronomy.

The second stage, *sutuh* (surfaces), lasted an average of three to six years. *Fiqh* and *usul al-fiqh* were the two main topics of study. There were also higher-level courses of logic and grammar. Each subject had its own specific universally accepted texts, which were read successively. Classes in the first two stages were usually held in small groups of one to three students, who would choose their teachers. The latter were mostly students at higher levels or experts in specific fields who rarely advanced in the 'ulama' hierarchy.

While the texts at the *muqaddamat* stage remained unchanged for several centuries, new works in *usul* and *fiqh* written during the nineteenth and twentieth centuries were incorporated into the Shi'i curriculum indicating the continuing vitality of Shi'i learning during that period. In the absence of overall regulatory bodies, books were introduced individually by teachers and were accepted gradually by unwritten consensus. As teachers and students moved from one center of learning to another so did the various books, thereby cementing the unity of Shi'i learning all over the Muslim world.[79]

The highest stage of learning, the *dars al-kharij* or *bahth al-kharij*,[80] was aimed at the attainment of ijtihad. Courses at this level were given by senior mujtahids on topics in *usul* or *fiqh* of their own choice. The teacher did not use specific books but discussed the various questions and issues, citing opinions of different 'ulama' and adding his own comments and criticism. Most classes were held at the shrine courtyard (the *sahn*), in mosques, or at the mujtahids' homes.[81]

Students enjoyed considerable freedom in choosing their teachers. Ordinarily, passage from one stage to another depended upon completing reading the required book. But students could leave a teacher before getting an *ijaza* (diploma) or before the teacher finished reading the book. There was no fixed number of years for education, and students could continue their studies for as many years as they liked. The would-be Iraqi minister Fadil al-Jamali likened Najaf to a great "fountain to which anybody could go and drink of its learning as much as he could and as long as he cared."[82]

This flexibility in Shi'i learning enabled any mujtahid to set up his own classes. All that was necessary was a following among students and a minimal financial basis to support them. This practice encouraged competition among teachers and ensured a certain degree of quality in teaching. However, the teacher's scholarly qualifications were not always the decisive factor in determining the student's choice. As with institutions of higher learning in the West, more mundane considerations sometimes played an important role in their preferences, rather like the pursuit of stipends by students in earlier periods. Quchani, a sympathetic insider in the community, criticized most students for going wherever money and connections were attainable. Akhund Khorasani, for one, refused to distribute money among his students for the first three years of his independent career in order to ascertain that they had indeed come to his classes for the sake of learning alone.[83]

The mode of teaching in the shrine cities with its heavy emphasis on oral recitation and memorization was no different from other places and times in the Muslim world. Mujtahids employed student rapporteur (*muqarrirun*) to take notes during the lectures. Frequently, the *muqarrir* repeated the lecture to the students after the master had already given it, like the *mu'id* in medieval Sunni classes. Often such students were the most promising ones, who would later emerge as independent teachers themselves.[84] Present-day Shi'i sources still use such terms as "read [a certain book] aloud to" (*qara'a 'ala*) the teacher; "engaged in study" (*ishtaghala*) or "graduated" (*takharraja*) from his teacher, in the same contexts and meanings as in the medieval sources. This continuity was not due to the belated introduction of print in the shrine cities,[85] but rather to the continuous cultural emphasis on the intensive, personal interaction of the student with the teacher, which remained in effect in the twentieth century as well.[86]

Present-day Shi'i sources praise the free lecture atmosphere which was expressed in lively debates and disputations between students and teachers. Legal disputations (*munazara*, or *majalis al-jadl*) between students and mujtahids or among the students themselves, both in class and outside it, have always played an important role in religious schooling. The art of disputation required the student to memorize as extensive a list as possible of the disputed questions of law and have ready answers to them, as well as to possess the dialectics of disputation. More important, the disputation provided the student with the opportunity to prove his eligibility as a scholar and enabled the mujtahids to assess the students' achievements. Al-Sadr, for instance, tells of an arrangement he had with his teacher, Muhammad Taqi Shirazi in Samarra', which lasted for twelve years, for a daily meeting and disputation.[87]

Public disputations were also an arena for elucidating legal questions and establishing informal ranking among mujtahids. When Abu al-Qasim Qummi came to Najaf, the 'ulama' of the town chose Jawad al-'Amili to debate with him the question of the proof of absolutely preponderant supposition (*hujjiyat al-zann al-mutlaq*). Shaykh Jawad's victory in the debate was perceived not only as his own, but of the entire Najaf community.[88]

Ideally, students could raise questions and make objections to their teachers' statements, provided they abided by the ethical code of the profession, that is, they neither challenged the teacher's authority or status nor questioned basic or essential religious truths. Everyday practice, however, did not encourage independent thinking and originality. In several instances, teachers reacted unfavorably to students who dared to argue too much, even going so far as to expel them from their classes.[89]

In contrast to the Sunni scholarly approach, the philosophical tradition in Shi'ism remained unbroken well into the nineteenth century, and was taught in the shrine cities, probably because of its importance for ijtihad.[90] However, as guardians of orthodoxy, whose primary task was the training of jurists (*fuqaha'*), the 'ulama' of the shrine cities often maintained a hostile attitude toward the teaching of philosophy.[91]

As a result of this inconsistent approach, philosophy teachers did not enjoy high status in the shrine cities. Shaykh Muhammad Baqir Istihbanati, a leading teacher of philosophy in Najaf at the turn of the twentieth century, used to complain that by acquiring the reputation of a *hakim*, which is associated with "carelessness, irreligiosity and lack of learning," he had been suffering from "seclusion, poverty, afflictions and debts," while teachers of *usul* and *fiqh* were universally respected. Frustrated, he eventually left Najaf and settled in Shiraz.[92] Indeed, the leading nineteenth-century Shi'i philosophers remained in Iran, and students who wanted to specialize in philosophy did not come to the shrine cities.[93]

The culmination of the process of learning at the *dars al-kharij* stage was the attainment of *ijazat ijtihad*, which authorized the student to exercise ijtihad (independent judgment) in pronouncing specific legal rulings. It was wider in scope than the Sunni *ijaza*, which merely certified that the student had read a certain text and was authorized to teach it. The Shi'i *ijaza* combined the two medieval *ijazat* of issuing *fatwas* (*ijazat al-ifta'*) and teaching.[94] It resembled the medieval Damascus practice in which teachers granted *ijaza* to their disciples not for a specific book but when they deemed the disciple ready to represent a body of knowledge in a variety of fields and to exemplify it to other carriers.[95]

An additional *ijaza*, somewhat less prestigious, was the *ijazat riwaya* in which the teacher gave the student permission to transmit Traditions (*hadith, akhbar*) in his name. Through the chain of transmitters, the *ijazat riwaya* created a direct link between the recipient and the Imams, thereby enhancing the 'ulama''s charisma. Unlike the *ijazat ijtihad*, *ijazat riwaya* were also given to 'ulama' who were not direct disciples of the teacher primarily as a token of esteem. In fact they could be given to other 'ulama' of equal or senior status.[96]

As in the medieval period, the diplomas were not issued by the madrasa as an institution but by the teacher as a personal matter between himself and the student, marking perhaps the culmination of and providing a formal stamp to the patronage ties that existed between them. Consequently, the higher the prestige of the teacher, the greater the value of the *ijazat* he gave. Hence also the usefulness for students to get as many such diplomas from as many teachers as possible.

There were no standard academic prerequisites for the attainment of the *ijaza*, nor did it depend on the number of years a student had spent studying under his teacher. Present-day Shi'i sources praise the traditional schooling, compared with western systems of education, for achieving academic excellence without the recourse to examinations, or other coercive means.[97] They explain that the evaluation of a student took place over a long period and was based on his performance in the numerous disputations he held with his teachers and colleagues. Such a system, they assert, prevents cheating or favoritism due to kin or friendship.[98]

In contrast, Muhsin al-Amin, who studied in Najaf at the end of the nineteenth century and entertained some reformist tendencies,[99] found some faults in these practices, complaining that many students skipped the *sutuh* level courses and rushed to the *dars al-kharij* in order to attain the mujtahid rank as soon as possible. Teachers could not prevent unqualified students from attending their classes because of the lack of examinations or other procedures and because they competed for students among themselves. Non-Arabs were not sufficiently proficient in Arabic, a serious handicap considering the importance of that language in Islam, and the fact that all textbooks were written in Arabic.[100]

These abuses notwithstanding, for most students studies in the shrine cities were an arduous process which lasted many years during which very many of them languished in poverty. Even after obtaining the long-sought *ijaza*, they still had to labor hard in order to attain recognition, status, or wealth.

A major indication of the hardships endured by the students is the fact that only a small minority attained *ijazat ijtihad*. The majority ended their studies somewhere along the way and either returned home or were dispatched by their teachers to serve as low-level 'ulama'. Some others remained in the shrine cities as low-level teachers.[101] Only those 'ulama' who sought to focus on learning and teaching remained in the shrine cities. Those who were more interested in other fields of clerical activity, such as judgeships, and providing religious services to the Bazaar, or those who did not excel in their studies, returned to Iran. Indeed, throughout the nineteenth century, the 'ulama' of the shrine cities had the reputation of greater spirituality than their counterparts living in Iran.

Describing medieval Damascus, Chamberlain noted the ideal of learning as involving exposure to many fields of education, including the many non-Shar'i sciences. That was also the case with the clerical notables – landowning notables who controlled many of the religious and judiciary institutions in Safavid Iran. By the nineteenth century, the education that students acquired in the shrine cities focused mainly on *fiqh* and *usul*, although it did include arithmetic and Greek astronomy. In other words, the professionalization of the 'ulama' in both the Sunni and the Shi'i communities, which had started during the late medieval period, and went on through the Ottoman and Safavid periods, was accompanied by a narrowing of their cultural horizons. It also affected their attitude toward heterodox groups which emerged from their own ranks.[102]

In conclusion, the various characteristics of the community of learning that evolved in the shrine cities during the nineteenth century can be seen as causes and effects of each other. It was a social structure that was heavily influenced and shaped by centuries-old traditions of Muslim learning in conjunction with the situation of a minority under an unfriendly government. Consequently, the multitude of circles of study and the cultural *majalis* that emerged in the shrine cities were all the fruit of local initiative from below, without the Ottoman or Iranian governments playing any role in administering them, and with only limited financial support by the Qajars.

Concurrently, the growing population of scholars and students coming from different ethnic groups, geographical regions, and social classes formed an amorphous but not necessarily fragile system of socialization and social control based on unwritten rules and conventions. Those who deviated or seemed to endanger the authority of the 'ulama' or of the leadership were marginalized or even suppressed, sometimes violently.

The key element in the community was the patronage tie between teacher and student, which extended beyond the period of study into networks of patronage encompassing the various Shi'i communities in the Middle East. Patronage ties superseded without annulling class and ethnic differences, and enabled the teachers to maintain their authority over the students. Students were almost totally dependent on their teachers for their livelihood, accommodation, and even for their future employment among the various Shi'i communities. Concurrently, the teachers and aspirant religious leaders needed their students as their links to their constituencies.

This need was particularly visible in the field of finance. The flow of funds and the entire financial administration in the shrine cities were never managed under one roof regularizing aid to the students. Rather it was a diffused system centered around individuals, who took care of their own proteges. Because of the absence of an overall system, extracting a living depended on each student's ability to fend for himself. This became a major preoccupation for both teachers and students, and a source of rivalry among mujtahids, who vied for leadership.[103]

Finally, the dominance of informal interpersonal relations was a central feature of the structure of learning as students were free to choose and change their teachers at will. While a three-stage learning process was practiced there were no fixed rules as to movement along the various stages. The *ijaza* was a personal matter between the teacher and the student, symbolizing the culmination of their patronage ties, without any fixed rules as to the time for granting it or the precise criteria of the knowledge required. While such a system was open to abuses, the community of learning in the shrine cities appeared less affected by them compared with the Ottoman hierarchy, and created a system based largely on merit, as will be shown in the following chapters.

2   Leadership in the age of multiple centers

Leadership by consensus

The 1985 constitution of the Islamic Republic of Iran states that during the Occultation of the Imam "governance (*vilayat*) and leadership of the community (*umma*) devolve upon the just and pious *faqih* (jurist) who is fully aware of the circumstances of his age, courageous, resourceful and possessed of administrative ability; and recognized and accepted as Leader by the majority of the people."[1]

In what ways does this stipulation for the Leader (*rahbar*) differ from the actual historical type of religious leadership that emerged during the nineteenth century? Was the leadership at that time truly purely spiritual as opposed to the more politicized and mundane type advocated by Khomeini? What are its unique features compared with Sunni religious establishments? How did religious leaders emerge in a community of learning in the absence of state supervision from above or any regulatory bodies from below?

In the following four chapters I shall analyze the evolution of Shiʻi religious leadership in three concentric circles: the local one in each shrine city; leadership in Iraq; and finally in the entire Shiʻi world. I will trace the centralization of Shiʻi leadership to Najaf from a multiplicity of centers, and the shift from local, initially Arab, mujtahids to immigrants in that town. In examining the various ways in which mujtahids consolidated their leadership positions, we will see that only those who were able to combine scholarship with financial resources as well as widespread networks of patronage managed to secure prominent leadership, although none of them achieved completely unchallenged authority, and none made any effort to formalize the appointment and authority of leaders. Finally, I will analyze the various prerequisites for the attainment of status and leadership in Najaf and Karbala'.

Following the reinstatement of Usulism in the shrine cities, Bihbihani was acknowledged as the leading mujtahid in the Shiʻi scholarly community. His death in 1791 and the settlement of his disciples in Iran and the shrine cities opened a new era in the quest for Shi'i leadership.

The reinstatement of the religious establishment in Iran following the Qajar accession to power created a religious elite, but not a formal hierarchy. The 'ulama' who carried out the roles of Shaykh al-Islam (head of religious court) and Imam Jum'a (prayer leader in a chief mosque) in nineteenth-century Iran formed an official religious leadership in every town. But the state was neither able nor willing to set up a formal hierarchy encompassing the entire country. Moreover, the nominations to these posts were often made in recognition of a mujtahid's position and influence as a religious authority in his own town, and not all holders of such posts enjoyed the status of exemplars. In the shrine cities, however, such official posts did not exist, and religious leaders owed their authority to other factors.

As mentioned above, the notion of acknowledging or even yearning for the leadership of one mujtahid of superior knowledge appeared at the time, but it was not fully articulated. It affected each locality or center of learning rather than Shi'ism as a whole. Consequently, the first half of the nineteenth century was characterized by a multiplicity of centers of learning and leadership. While we could speak of a certain hierarchy of deference among mujtahids, there was no explicit subordination to one leader at that period.

The question of leadership in the shrine cities emerged immediately after Bihbihani's death. Since both towns housed more mujtahids than did any other Iranian center, which usually hosted only one or two senior mujtahids, the need to determine some informal ranking was more urgent. At the same time, the Shi'i, and particularly the 'ulama' community, needed communal leaders to represent their interests *vis-à-vis* the unfriendly Sunni government in Baghdad.

The first mujtahid recognized as Bihbihani's undisputed successor in the shrine cities and in the Shi'i world was Muhammad Mahdi Tabataba'i Bahr al-'Ulum (d. 1212/1797–98). He had been one of the first students to switch from Yusuf Bahrani's teaching and join the *usul* classes of Bihbihani, who was also married to his father's sister. Bihbihani showed his preference for him by calling him "my spiritual son." His noble descent from a leading 'ulama' family in Isfahan in the Safavid period which was related by marriage to the famous Muhammad Taqi Majlisi (d. 1070/1659) ensured him great respect in the shrine cities and Iran as well as close relations with Isfahan.[2]

While most mujtahids specialized in one scholarly field, Bahr al-'Ulum demonstrated mastery in various scholarly endeavors. In recognition of his superiority his colleague Ja'far Kashif al-Ghita', although a senior mujtahid at the time, attended his classes for six months "for the sake of its blessing."[3] Bahr al-ʿUlum's spiritual authority was acknowledged in Iran as well, although more with reverence than actual subordination. Even Mirza Muhammad al-Akhbari, a staunch opponent of the Usulis, studied under him and described him as "the rarity of his time; upon his leadership the entire community was in agreement."[4]

According to his modern biographer, Bahr al-ʿUlum established a semi-formal leadership structure by assigning a specific task to each of his colleagues. Jaʿfar Kashif al-Ghitaʾ was responsible for *fatwas, taqlid,* and organizational duties. Husayn Najaf was appointed the prayer imam and representative of Bahr al-ʿUlum, while Sharif Muhyi al-Din was responsible for judgeship and litigation. Muhammad Mahdi himself acted as supreme leader of the community.[5] This arrangement, however, did not outlast him. Nor is there any evidence that he sought to perpetuate it for future generations. A similar pattern, however, in which the disciple responsible for *fatwas* succeeded his master appeared later in the century.[6]

While it was informal, the type of leadership that emerged during Bahr al-ʿUlum's period was aided by the final suppression of other religious alternatives, particularly Sufism. Throughout the history of Shiʿism, an alternative trend of thought developed parallel to the scripturalist doctrine of the ʿulamaʾ. Heterodox ideas in Shiʿism stressed the existence of esoteric forms of religious knowledge as well as symbolic practices attained by non-rational and intuitive modes of understanding. They also stressed the eschatological aspects of religion.[7]

There are quite a few similarities between Sufism and mainstream Twelver Shiʿism. Yet precisely these similarities, which might have presented an alternative to orthodoxy, bred an antagonism among the ʿulamaʾ toward the Sufis. In addition, the ʿulamaʾ feared the messianic undertone in Shiʿi Sufism. Parallel to the emphasis on rational and deductive reasoning in Usulism, the very concept of General Deputyship contained elements of non-rationality from which Usulism, at least in practice, could not escape, since they fulfilled a spiritual need which was not satisfied by the development of Usuli rationalism. Judgments were achieved not only by mere rational effort, but also by an intuitive and "illuminative" perception.[8] Hence, the crux of the ʿulamaʾ's opposition to the Sufi revival was the question of spiritual authority.[9]

A propensity toward mysticism had existed among several leading mujtahids following the rise of Usulism. The most prominent was Muhammad Mahdi Bahr al-ʿUlum himself, who attempted to combine intuitive illumination (*kashf*) with reason (*ʿaql*). His mystical leanings, which included seclusion at the al-Kufa mosque near Najaf where he reputedly reached the stage of *fana'* (immersion in God), only added to his charismatic aura among the ordinary believers. Thus he was reputed to have actually seen the Hidden Imam, among other miracles attributed to him. The difference between Bahr al-ʿUlum and other mujtahids like him and the Sufis was that they acted individually and did not endow their acts with any new doctrinal elaboration, which might have posed a threat to the ʿulamaʾ establishment.[10]

Hence, when Sufi missionaries of the Niʿmat Allahi order came to Karbalaʾ some time after 1792 and managed to convert to their cause several ʿulamaʾ, including one mujtahid, ʿAbd al-Samad Hamadani, they were quickly declared heretics. Unlike the mystically inclined mujtahids, the Sufis posed a direct challenge to the establishment by threatening to draw members from its ranks and challenging its authority. Therefore they had to be confronted head-on. The ʿulamaʾ of Karbalaʾ appealed to Bahr al-ʿUlum to lend his signature to the *takfir*, to give it greater authority. But, according to Sufi sources, Bahr al-ʿUlum was sympathetic toward the Sufi activists, and arranged for them to leave the shrine cities unharmed.[11]

The expulsion of the Sufis from Karbalaʾ was part of a larger campaign conducted in Iran, which culminated with the killing of the leading Niʿmat Allahi missionaries there. In addition to inciting the mob to lynch Sufi activists, the ʿulamaʾ solicited the support of the Iranian rulers against their religious rivals.[12]

The hostility of the Shiʿi ʿulamaʾ toward Sufism stands in sharp contrast to the more reconciliatory attitude of their Sunni counterparts. In this sense the ʿulamaʾ of the shrine cities, working in unison with their colleagues in Iran, acted as a "church" in the sociological sense, that is a dominant religious establishment intolerant toward dissent and heterodoxy. As such they were willing to resort to the assistance of the state with the political price that such a move entailed. Paradoxically, this church-like conduct may have stemmed from a deep sense of insecurity, the result of centuries of Sunni persecution and from inferiority *vis-à-vis* the Sufis who had enjoyed greater popularity in the past. In other words, while behaving like a church, the ʿulamaʾ did not seem to be entirely freed from the mentality of a former minority sect.

With Bahr al-ʿUlum's death, his colleague and disciple Jaʿfar Kashif al-Ghitaʾ emerged as the leader of the community of learning in Najaf. Although Husayn Najaf was regarded by some as the appropriate successor, he was overshadowed by Shaykh Jaʿfar, who combined scholarship and greater assertiveness as a leader.[13] Shaykh Jaʿfar established his scholarly preeminence with his book *Kashf al-Ghitaʾ ʿan*

Khafiyyat Mubhamat al-Shari'a al-Gharra', which was regarded as the most important *fiqh* work up to that time. The methodology of *usul* used in the book dominated studies in Najaf during the first half of the century.

In that book, and in a treatise on Jihad, Shaykh Ja'far further developed the concept of the *niyaba 'amma* as a collective duty and privilege of the 'ulama', equating obedience to the 'ulama' with obedience to the Imam.[14] While focusing on the collective aspect of *niyaba 'amma*, Kashif al-Ghita' advanced the concept of a single mujtahid who would have a greater authority among the 'ulama'. Saying that the declaration of Jihad during the absence of the Imam is the responsibility of the mujtahids, he added that "it is incumbent to give preference to the most learned (*afdal*), or to him who is given permission by [the Imam]."[15] Presumably he had himself in mind as that most learned mujtahid.

Although there were several leading mujtahids in Iran who enjoyed more or less equal veneration at the time, Kashif al-Ghita' claimed preeminence among them, describing himself as "paramount shaykh of all the Muslims" (*shaykh mashayikh al-Muslimin*). His seniority was indeed recognized by several of the leading mujtahids of Iran, and by Fath 'Ali Shah's chief minister, 'Isa Qa'im Maqam, who described him as "the shaykh of the mujtahids" (*shaykh al-mujtahidin*). He was also the first mujtahid to be mentioned as "deputy of the Imam" (*na'ib-i Imam*).[16] During the early part of the nineteenth century the mujtahids of the shrine cities had not yet established networks of patronage of disciples and agents. Thus when Shi'is in Baghdad sought a mujtahid who would serve as their local leader, they appealed directly to Muhammad 'Ali Al Sharaf al-Din, and not through Kashif al-Ghita'. It was Muhammad 'Ali who sought his teacher's permission to go to Baghdad.[17]

Leadership in Karbala' following Bihbihani's death was exercised by two of his disciples, Mirza Mahdi Shahristani and Sayyid 'Ali Tabataba'i. A descendant of an 'ulama' family whose prominence went back to the Safavid period, Mirza Mahdi was one of the first students to join Bihbihani's courses. Notwithstanding this, he remained close to Yusuf Bahrani's Akhbari approach to *fiqh*.[18]

For lack of data, it is difficult to determine Mirza Mahdi's status in Iran, but his prestige in India may serve as an indicator. During the 1780s he spent several years in Delhi and Allahabad, where he enjoyed the patronage of Begum Sahiba Mahall, the widow of the Mogul emperor Muhammad Shah. In later years he was the recipient of the "Indian Money" in Karbala'. He continued to maintain close ties with India, providing assistance to Indian pilgrims and students. The use of the "Indian Money" for public projects also enhanced the status of his family as communal leaders for more than one generation.[19]

Following Mirza Mahdi's death Sayyid 'Ali Tabataba'i emerged as the foremost religious leader in Karbala'. Like his cousins of the Bahr al-'Ulum family, he combined honorable descent, discipleship under Bihbihani, and scholarly achievements to ensure his leadership in Karbala'. His book, *Riyad al-Masa'il*, was an important application of the new Usuli methodology in *fiqh*. He succeeded Mahdi Shahristani as the recipient of the "Indian money", using part of it to buy several houses to establish as *waqf* for students and scholars, an essential measure for patronage building.[20]

While Muhammad Mahdi Bahr al-'Ulum was alive the mujtahids of Karbala' apparently recognized his superiority of learning and seniority, but were not directly subordinated to him.[21] In their own towns they were the paramount leaders. However, following his death, some tension developed between Sayyid 'Ali Tabataba'i and Kashif al-Ghita', who viewed the former with a certain contempt. Their rivalry also stemmed from tensions between sayyids and ordinary mujtahids as reflected in a remark by Kashif al-Ghita' on the differences between the two groups, and from rivalry between the two centers of learning. After Kashif al-Ghita''s death, Sayyid 'Ali was recognized as the leading mujtahid in the shrine cities. He had a following in Sind, Hindustan, and Iraq, but Iran, where local mujtahids held sway, is not mentioned as accepting his authority.[22]

As part of his efforts to establish his own dominance Sayyid 'Ali tended to undermine or even persecute potential rivals among the mujtahids. He denied the scholarship (*fadl*) of 'Abd al-Samad Hamadani, who was one of Bihbihani's most senior disciples, ostensibly because of his turning to Sufism. Likewise, he denied the justice ('*adala*, another prerequisite for ijtihad) of Asadallah Tustari, who was finally forced to leave Karbala' and settle in Kazimayn.[23]

Sayyid 'Ali's death in 1231/1815–16 marked the passing of the first generation of Bihbihani's students as religious leaders in the shrine cities. An important point in assessing their achievement is that the four mujtahids mentioned above headed 'ulama' dynasties which were to play an important role in their respective towns throughout the nineteenth century. Similar dynasties were very common in Iran primarily because of their control of the Shaykh al-Islam and Imam Jum'a posts. In the shrine cities, however, no other dynasties enjoyed similar status. The emergence of these dynasties added another dimension to the competition for leadership between the established families and immigrant mujtahids.

Following Sayyid Ali's death, his son Sayyid Muhammad returned to Karbala' from Isfahan where he had acquired reputation as a leading expert in *usul*. While Sayyid Muhammad maintained religious leadership in Karbala', he encountered competition from his father's former disciples. Tunikabuni claims that on his death bed Sayyid 'Ali Tabataba'i had extracted a promise from his two leading disciples, Muhammad Sharif Mazandarani Sharif al-'Ulama' (d.1246/1831) and 'Abd al-Karim Iravani not to challenge his son's leadership. However, after attending Sayyid Muhammad's classes for a while, Sharif al-'Ulama' refused to be "the ornament of someone else's *majlis*" and set up his own study circle. In other words, his allegiance to the father did not extend to the son. Gradually most students left Sayyid Muhammad to join Sharif al-'Ulama''s class. Iravani, who set up his own circle, failed to keep the students with him and eventually left Karbala' for Qazvin.[24] Tunikabuni attributes Iravani's failure in Karbala' to two factors: whereas Sharif al-'Ulama' was an investigative (*muhaqqiq*) scholar, Iravani lacked the same edge and was merely meticulous (*mudaqqiq*). In addition, as a Turk he had difficulties, compared with his Persian counterparts, in attracting Persian students. While the ethnic factor was already evident at that early stage, Tunikabuni does not mention financial support for the students as a factor.[25]

Upon Sayyid Muhammad's death, Sharif al-'Ulama' was regarded as the foremost teacher in Karbala'. Leadership in Karbala' now passed to mujtahids who had immigrated from Iran. Since he concentrated on teaching, Sharif al-'Ulama' wrote only one treatise but justified himself by saying that whatever his students would write could be viewed as his own. However, mastery in teaching was not always identical with leadership, as is shown by his acceptance of Mahdi Tabataba'i's lead in the struggle against the Shaykhi leader Ahmad Ahsa'i.[26]

Leadership and the 'ulama' of Iran

The renewed stability brought to Iran by the Qajars at the beginning of the nineteenth century prompted many of Bihbihani's disciples to return to their home countries. After the chaos of the eighteenth century they filled a vacuum in the religious and urban leadership, playing a crucial role in the spread of Usulism in Iran. Some of these mujtahids, most notably Abu al-Qasim Qummi, enjoyed the patronage of Fath 'Ali Shah and the Qajar elite. Within two decades many of the once poor graduates of the shrine cities amassed great wealth and became locally dominant figures.[27]

One indication of the new prominence of the various Iranian centers is the pattern of travel among students of the shrine cities. Traveling for the sake of learning has always been extolled in the Islamic tradition. This noble custom persisted well into the modern period when young boys left their homes and journeyed great distances to acquire knowledge in the shrine cities. The shrine cities had always attracted students from all parts of Iran as well as from important regional centers of learning in Iran or India.[28] However, with the emergence of the new Iranian centers, a small number of students traveled to them after a period of study in the shrine cities indicating their belief in the equal status or even superiority of teachers such as Abu al-Qasim Qummi and Ahmad Naraqi.[29]

On the other hand, the respect accorded to Ja'far Kashif al-Ghita' by Fath 'Ali Shah, by Qajar notables, and by people from all classes attests to his prestige in Iran at that time. It was he, rather than any Iranian mujtahid, who undertook to represent the Usulis and contest Mirza Muhammad al-Akhbari's attempt to revive Akhbarism in Iran. Likewise, he and Sayyid 'Ali Tabataba'i of Karbala' were the first mujtahids to whom Fath 'Ali Shah appealed to declare Jihad on the Russians. Very few Arab 'ulama' residing in the shrine cities would enjoy similar prestige in Iran thereafter.[30]

Yet the fact that Kashif al-Ghita' frequently traveled to Iran in order to collect donations suggests that he did not have a network of subordinate 'ulama' or agents there. Moreover, although many of the leading mujtahids in Iran had been his students or were younger than he, they did not regard themselves as his subordinates. Relations between master and disciple at that period were more of reverence than subordination, once the latter had left the shrine cities.

Kashif al-Ghita''s complex relations with Muhammad Baqir Shafti illustrate this point. During a visit to Isfahan he protested to Shafti and to Ibrahim Karbasi concerning their reluctance to recognize and support his disciple and son-in-law, Muhammad 'Ali Hizarjaribi, who was then living in Isfahan. Although both had been his disciples, they now regarded themselves as leaders in their own right and no longer felt allegiance to Kashif al-Ghita' nor heeded his demand.[31]

Fath 'Ali Shah's appeals to Mirza Abu al-Qasim Gilani in Qum, Mulla Ahmad Naraqi of Kashan, Mir Muhammad Husayn Khatunabadi, the Imam Jum'a of Isfahan and Sayyid Muhammad b. 'Ali Tabataba'i, who was then residing in Isfahan, to declare Jihad on Russia in 1813 indicates the diffused nature of the collective religious leadership and the Qajar perception that the Iran-based mujtahids were at least equal to their colleagues in the shrine cities. While the shrine cities retained their lead as the centers of learning, political influence was shared by several mujtahids, most of whom resided in Iran.

Sayyid Muhammad Tabataba'i's influence in Iran reached its peak when he led the 'ulama' campaign to pressure Fath 'Ali Shah to declare a Jihad against Russia in 1826. Complaints from the Shi'is in Russian Azarbayjan against Russian repression were sent to him in Karbala', indicating to his status in those regions. He traveled to Iran alone, mobilizing there the great bulk of the 'ulama' movement to press for Jihad against Russia. When Sayyid Muhammad arrived in Tehran, the British officer Willock wrote, a vast number of people went to meet him. "They kissed the litter, kissed the ladder by which he ascended to it, and collected the dust which had the impressions of the mule's feet that bore him."[32] How much this reception was due to Sayyid Muhammad's own personality or to the fact that he was a saintly mujtahid from the distant shrine cities is, of course, unclear.

Shi'i sources give conflicting assessments as to Sayyid Muhammad's standing compared with his Iran-based counterparts.[33] The discrepancies reflect the diffusion of leadership and the broader phenomenon whereby mujtahids from the shrine cities enjoyed greater reverence from ordinary believers and lower-level 'ulama' in Iran than from senior mujtahids who wished to establish their own independent leadership.

One of those who stood on a par with Sayyid Muhammad was Hujjat al-Islam Muhammad Baqir Shafti. Early in his career Shafti challenged the prestige of the shrine cities even as centers of learning, when he claimed that during his six months of study under Qummi he had learnt more than during all the years he had spent in the shrine cities.[34] Sayyid Muhammad Tabataba'i himself conceded that while he recognized Shafti's authority, he doubted whether Shafti acknowledged his, thereby pointing to the challenge presented by Shafti, and to the diffused nature of the Shi'i leadership. Shafti was also among the first mujtahids to assume the lofty title Hujjat al-Islam.[35]

In addition to effectively dominating life in Isfahan, Shafti enjoyed wide authority throughout Iran and even parts of India, where he sent his disciples following requests from Indian Shi'is. Thus when a group of believers in Nur in northern Iran came out against the local mujtahid, Mirza 'Ali Nuri, they appealed to Shafti and not to the mujtahids of the shrine cities to declare him a sinner (fasiq).[36] On the other hand, local mujtahids, who resented Shafti's ascendancy or did not have strong local support, could seek backing from the shrine cities in order to bolster their position. When Mulla Muhammad Taqi Baraghani was in the minority regarding a certain ruling, his opponents asked Shafti for a fatwa and Shafti too ruled against him. However, as Sayyid Muhammad was the "universally accepted" mujtahid at the time and Baraghani's former teacher and patron, Baraghani asked him to issue a *fatwa* on the matter in order to obtain his endorsement *vis-à-vis* Shafti.[37]

Likewise, when Baraghani excommunicated the Shaykhi leader Ahmad Ahsa'i in 1822, he sought the support of the Tabataba'i family in Karbala', realizing that his own stature outside Qazvin could not ensure sufficient impact for his move. This phenomenon would become more common in later periods, both reflecting and contributing to the leadership status of the shrine cities. At the time, however, the excommunication issued by Mahdi Tabataba'i and other leading mujtahids of Karbala' did not have a widespread effect in Iran. Particularly significant in this context was the refusal of Shafti and Karbasi to join it.[38]

Sayyid Mahdi Tabataba'i's effort in 1249/1833 to induce Muhammad Shah to deprive the Jews in Iran of their status as *dhimmis* is another indication of the differences in power between the mujtahids of the shrine cities and of Iran. Sayyid Mahdi sought to obtain Shafti's support for his campaign, but Shafti refused, a fact that helped the shah to reject the demand. Clearly offended, Sayyid Mahdi remained in the Shah 'Abd al-'Azim mosque, where the 'ulama' of Tehran often visited him to pay their respects, while merchants and notables provided him with food. Even the shah had to come to show his respect, but Mahdi refused to come out to greet him.[39] In other words, whereas reverence was accorded to the mujtahids of the shrine cities, their colleagues in Iran wielded the actual political influence.

The domination of the Kashif al-Ghita' family in Najaf

The death of Ja'far Kashif al-Ghita' ended the consensus over religious leadership in Najaf. The two most prominent candidates for the succession were Musa, Kashif al-Ghita''s eldest son, and his son-in-law, Asadallah b. Isma'il Tustari. Kashif al-Ghita' himself groomed his sons to succeed him. Whenever he took his second son 'Ali with him on his journeys to Iran, Musa used to substitute for him in Najaf. In addition, Ja'far declared Musa as the most learned in *fiqh* alongside himself. Unlike most disciples, Musa was permitted to have his own independent *dars al-kharij* while his father was still alive, in demonstration of his senior status.[40]

In order to avoid a struggle for leadership the 'ulama' of Najaf asked an outsider, Abu al-Qasim Qummi, who was visiting Najaf at the time, to recommend or designate the leader. Qummi put a series of questions to the leading mujtahids to examine the scope of the scholarship. After reading the answers, he gathered the 'ulama' in the *sahn* of 'Ali's shrine, and declared Shaykh Musa the exemplar "as he is the most learned."[41] As an indication of the bitterness of the rivalry or of his disappointment, Asadallah left Najaf and settled in Kazimayn.

The story reveals several significant points: the attempt to settle the question by one decision and the urge to avoid a struggle show that the idea of one religious leader for the community of learning was already deeply rooted at the time. On the other hand, the appeal to Qummi was an ad hoc measure, not followed by any attempt to establish a mechanism that would provide a permanent solution to the problem. The appeal also reflects a recognition of Qummi's seniority or superiority, but points to the desire and need of Najaf to have its own leader. Although selected by Qummi, Shaykh Musa was not subordinated to him, but acted as an independent leader.

Qummi used the term "supreme exemplar" (*marja' 'amm*), but again applied it only in the local context and not for the Shi'a as a whole. In other words, there was a discrepancy between the ideal notion of supreme leadership and the reality in which each center had its own leadership. Superiority in knowledge was regarded as the leading criterion for *marja'iyya*, although it was applicable only in the local context. Consequently, and as will be shown throughout the century, lineage alone was insufficient to ensure *marja'iyya* for sons of prominent exemplars in Najaf and Karbala'. In contrast to Iranian cities, where leadership status was often hereditary and based on control of an administrative post, in the shrine cities personal scholarly reputation was absolutely essential.

In Najaf, Shaykh Musa followed Muhammad Mahdi Bahr al-'Ulum's model in appointing judges and prayer imams. Like his father, he engaged in communal and religious leadership, completing, for instance, the wall around Najaf that his father had started to build.[42] During his visits to Iran, he enjoyed Qajar largess. Yet he had fewer followers in Iran compared with Sayyid Muhammad Tabataba'i of Karbala'. Arab 'ulama' were clearly at a disadvantage in gaining a mass following in Iran.[43]

Musa, who was titled Sultan al-'Ulama', enjoyed effective authority only in Najaf, al-Hilla (where his family originated), and some tribal regions. Although Kazimayn was a less prestigious center, it had its own religious leaders. Many of the Shi'is in Suq al-Shuyukh in the Muntafiq region in Iraq as well as in Ahsa' and Qatif followed their own local leaders. Moreover, Musa's unsuccessful efforts to heal the growing rift between the Usuli community and Ahmad Ahsa'i indicate the limits of his own leadership and of the institution itself within the amorphous structure of the 'ulama' establishment.[44]

When Shaykh Musa died in 1241/1825–26 a prolonged and open struggle over leadership broke out between the Kashif al-Ghita' family, headed first by 'Ali b. Ja'far (d. 1252/1836–37) and subsequently his brother Hasan (d. 1262/1846) on the one side, and Muhammad Hasan Najafi, the author of *Jawahir al-kalam* (hereafter Najafi), on the other. Najafi had studied under Ja'far Kashif al-Ghita' and under his son Musa, and remained loyal to them both as long as they lived. However, since a master–disciple allegiance was restricted to the teacher, he refused to extend it to other members of the Kashif al-Ghita' family and made a bid for the leadership. The rivalry, which largely corresponded to the ethnic division between Arabs and Persians in Najaf, extended beyond the city. It was one more indication of the rise of Najaf as the center of religious leadership for the entire Shi'i world. Shaykh 'Ali enjoyed an initial advantage since he had the support of a solid faction led by the four families descended from his grandfather Khidr al-Jinaji, as well as of other Arab 'ulama' who had been disciples of his father, of his brother Musa, and himself. Shaykh 'Ali's supporters organized a public prayer in Imam 'Ali's shrine in which he served as the prayer imam, in order to establish his leadership by a symbolic gesture. So incensed was Muhammad Hasan Najafi by this act that he compared it with the notorious gathering at the *saqifa* (portico) of the Banu Sa'ida. The original Saqifa gathering was held immediately after the Prophet's death in 632 CE, resulting in the election of Abu Bakr as the caliph by the companions of the Prophet and the frustration of 'Ali's claim to the succession. Ever since then it has been regarded by Shi'is as the epitome of unjust usurpation of leadership and denial of a rightful succession. Najafi's intention was not missed by the Kashif al-Ghita' supporters who replied that they had indeed appointed 'Ali, affirming their allegiance to both the Imam 'Ali and Shaykh 'Ali.[45]

In addition to his rivalry with Najafi, Shaykh 'Ali was briefly challenged by his younger brother Hasan, who claimed to be the better jurist of the two. 'Ali agreed to leave Najaf in order to avoid a quarrel that would harm the family's interests during their contest with Najafi. However, as most of the students preferred 'Ali, and joined him in Karbala', Hasan was forced to admit his brother's leadership.[46] The story, even if fabricated, points to the problem of determining superiority in scholarship. The criterion in this case was popularity among the students, which is not identical with evaluation of scholarship, or status among other mujtahids. Various contemporaries rank Hasan, and not 'Ali, as one of the leading figures of the Bihbihani school in *usul*.[47] Age was another factor in determining the seniority between the brothers.

Shaykh 'Ali, whose expertise was *fiqh*, was known by his book as the

Sahib al-Khiyarat and as the "third *Muhaqqiq*."[48] An instance of his status may be seen in the following story. Ibrahim Qazvini, the leading mujtahid of Karbala', and his personal rival Muhammad Husayn Isfahani, author of *al-Fusul* (d. 1254/1838–39), issued opposing rulings on a certain case. As a way out of the dispute, and acknowledging Karbala''s inferiority *vis-à-vis* Najaf, the matter was referred to Shaykh 'Ali, who backed Qazvini, with the rest of the 'ulama' following suit.[49]

The competition for students was a major arena for the rivalry between Shaykh 'Ali and Najafi. The growth of the number of students in Najaf increased the importance of the ethnic factor,[50] giving Najafi the Persian a clear advantage over the Kashif al-Ghita' family. Ethnic preferences notwithstanding, Shaykh 'Ali did have Iranian students, most notable among them Murtada Ansari, and some following in Iran itself. In addition, he dispatched his students to Lebanon to serve as local 'ulama'.[51]

In patronage building, however, Shaykh 'Ali was completely outdone by Najafi. I was able to trace only one case in which he was requested by a delegation from an Iranian town, Rasht, to send them a spiritual guide (*murshid*). In response, he sent 'Abdallah b. Abu al-Hasan al-Jiba'i al-'Amili. The fact that he dispatched an Arab suggests that either he had few Iranian disciples, or that he was not skillful in handling Iranian constituents. Since students could attend the classes of various mujtahids, 'Abdallah consulted with Najafi, his other mentor, whether or not he should go. Not surprisingly, Najafi advised him against going, presumably because he was reluctant to lose a bright disciple and help his rivals promote a following in Iran. Shaykh 'Abdallah, however, eventually decided to go to Iran.[52] Apparently, there were some rules or limits in the competition for religious leadership, as Najafi did not try to lure away 'Abdallah to become his own representative in Rasht.

The 1246–47/1830–32 cholera epidemic was reportedly an important landmark in the struggle for leadership. Fleeing the outbreak, Shaykh 'Ali left the town while Najafi stayed. Upon his return, 'Ali found that "aside from a few people" the great majority now recognized the leadership of Najafi. One should not ascribe too much weight to such an explanation, since, as will be shown subsequently, Najafi established his religious leadership throughout the Shi'i world by other means. Yet the epidemic could have had some significance in the local context. Although many 'ulama' tended to escape from the shrine cities during epidemics, it is conceivable that by leaving, Shaykh 'Ali manifested a failure of leadership, which drew people away from him. It is also possible that the epidemic hit the Arab faction much harder than the Iranians. The Khanfar clan, which was allied with Al Kashif al-Ghita' and lost three of its members, may have been an example of a wider phenomenon.[53] Alternatively, by going away 'Ali may simply have left the stage free for Najafi to consolidate his leadership.

When Shaykh 'Ali died in 1252/1837 and his brother Hasan returned to Najaf from al-Hilla in order to succeed him, Najafi's position was already paramount. Hasan Kashif al-Ghita' had attained ijtihad at the early age of twenty, and later established himself as one of the leading contemporary jurists. His book *Anwar al-faqaha* is regarded as one of the important works of *fiqh* written at the time.[54] Notwithstanding his scholarship, Shaykh Hasan had to share the religious leadership with Najafi. According to Khunsari, he was the foremost in jurisprudence among the mujtahids, and he was held in higher esteem than Najafi by the Arab 'ulama'. His study circle was the biggest in Najaf. However, in the spheres of issuing rulings and judgments, as well as in emulation by believers outside Iraq, Najafi superseded him.[55] The distinctions made by the biographical dictionaries on the relative status of the two mujtahids delineate the different aspects of religious leadership: scholarly writing, issuing of rulings, and day-to-day guidance of the believers.

Whereas Shaykh Hasan was more influential in Najaf, he lacked a network of support or a following among lay believers outside the city. Nevertheless, the Ottoman governor Najib Pasha's invitation to Shaykh Hasan to head the Shi'i delegation to the trial of the Babi activist Mulla 'Ali Bastami in 1844 implicitly recognized him as the head of the Shi'a in Iraq.[56]

Concurrently, the handling of the "Indian Money" and the intensive correspondence between Najaf and the mujtahids of Awadh, both carried on by Najafi alone, are further indications of Shaykh Hasan's limited influence outside Iraq. Control of these funds also consolidated Najafi's leadership. While the Kashif al-Ghita' clan retained its prominence in Najaf throughout the nineteenth century, they were never able to regain the status they had enjoyed during the first half of the century.

In Karbala', meanwhile, the struggle for leadership had two dimensions: one among the Usuli mujtahids and the second between the Usuli mujtahids and the Shaykhi movement, which was founded on the teachings of Ahmad Ahsa'i (d. 1826) and his successor Sayyid Kazim Rashti (d. 1259/1844). Ahsa'i believed that the major source of all his knowledge stemmed from the Imams themselves. Such intuitive knowledge, which he termed *kashf* or *mukashafa* (hence one of the movement's names, *kashfiyya*), was superior to the mujtahids' use of discursive reasoning. Hence he rejected the mujtahids' judgments as humanly fallible and denounced *taqlid*. He also propounded the doctrine of the "Perfect Shi'i": rare beings, specially guided by the Imam, who act as authoritative examples for the faithful, thus forming a chain of authority bypassing the mujtahids.[57]

Following his studies in the shrine cities, Ahsa'i spent most of his life teaching and traveling in Western Iran. He attracted a following there mainly from the middle and lower ranks of 'ulama', local merchants and officials, and various members of the Qajar family. Ahsa'i's teachings and saintly figure appealed to public yearnings for a spiritual religious leadership which, by its purity and otherworldliness, could stand above temporal or "orthodox" authority, and the more worldly minded image of many Usuli mujtahids.[58]

Although Ahsa'i criticized the 'ulama' he did not openly dissociate himself from mainstream Shi'ism. However, the scope of orthodoxy and pluralism in Shi'ism narrowed down significantly following the victory of Usulism in the eighteenth century. Consequently, the combination of doctrinal challenge and popular appeal aroused hostility among various Usuli mujtahids both in the shrine cities and in Iran. After having been excommunicated by Mulla Muhammad Taqi Baraghani, the Imam Jum'a of Qazvin, in 1238/1822, Ahsa'i decided to go to Karbala'. By the time he reached the town, he faced a hostile reception of 'ulama' led by Sayyid Mahdi b. 'Ali Tabataba'i, who convened a meeting of 'ulama' that declared Ahsa'i a *kafir* (infidel). The Shaykhis claimed that Mahdi even spent large amounts of money to ensure that the declaration was accepted by the masses.[59]

Several 'ulama' went so far as to denounce Ahsa'i to the governor in Baghdad, Da'ud Pasha, claiming that Ahsa'i had slandered the first three caliphs in his writings, probably in the hope that he would be executed or at least deported from Karbala'. Again such conduct is typical of a "church-like" establishment which seeks to destroy dissent by resorting to the state. Out of fear of Mamluk reaction so shortly after the 1824 Mir-Akhur rebellion Ahsa'i left Karbala' for Mecca, but died on the way in Dhu al-Hijja 1241/July 1826.[60]

Prior to his death, Ahsa'i designated his disciple Sayyid Kazim Rashti as his successor. Such nomination, which was common among Sufis, was rare among mujtahids. It was probably deemed necessary in view of its charismatic nature, since Rashti was being named as the direct recipient of the body of knowledge derived from the Imams and through them from God.[61]

At the time of his death, Ahsa'i's position was still that of a respected member of the mujtahid elite despite the excommunication pronounced against him, as he made no attempt to set up a separate school within Shi'ism. The reaction of the mujtahids of the shrine cities to Ahsa'i and his teachings varied greatly, indicating that pure theological considerations were not the crux of the matter. Rather, the mujtahids' attitudes were largely determined by perceptions of the threat to their collective authority, by personal relations with Ahsa'i or his opponents, and by personal aspirations for leadership. Nor did the opposition to Ahsa'i stem from the hostility of long-established families to an immigrant 'alim, since his defenders and opponents belonged to both groups.[62]

The consolidation of Rashti's leadership in Karbala', and his more systematic efforts to propagate Shaykhi ideas, united the amorphous body of Ahsa'i's followers into a distinct school and movement. The commitment of Rashti's students to the Shaykhi teachings and movement was markedly deeper than the attachment to Shaykhism among many of Ahsa'i's disciples in Iran which did not always go beyond personal admiration for him.[63] The pilgrimage to Karbala' helped the Shaykhis to spread their ideas beyond the scholarly community. Overall, the Shaykhi movement evolved and acted as a "sect" intent on conquering the larger Usuli community, the "church."

The formation of the Shaykhis as a movement gave greater grounds to the animosity of the Usulis, and gradually, the vast majority of the mujtahids in the shrine cities joined the anti-Shaykhi front. A significant landmark in this process was the shift in 'Ali Kashif al-Ghita''s position from that of mediator to opponent. His early position and that of most other 'ulama' in Najaf who did not accept Mahdi Tabataba'i's excommunication of Ahsa'i reflected both Najaf's sense of superiority vis-à-vis Karbala', and the amorphous nature of the Shi'i leadership in general. Concurrently, reflecting Shaykh 'Ali's status, it was his opposition to Rashti that turned the majority of the 'ulama' of Najaf against the Shaykhis.[64]

In turn, this hostility further contributed to the consolidation of the Shaykhi community. The various doctrinal objections raised against the Shaykhis became secondary to the more important issue of the basis of authority: individual charismatic as opposed to collective and more legal-traditional. The disagreements over the relation between exoteric (*zahir*) and esoteric (*batin*) interpretations of the scriptures reflected the deeper objection on the part of the mujtahids against bringing the esoteric factor of religion within reach of the common man, preferring it to remain the domain of the elite alone.[65]

The scholarly community of Karbala' gradually became polarized between the two factions, and for the ten years after Mahdi Tabataba'i's death in 1249/1833, the Shaykhis were harassed by Usuli followers, and several attempts were made on Rashti's life. Defending his views, Rashti compared the persecution of the Shaykhis by their opponents to the Shi'is' sufferings under the Abbasid caliph al-Mutawakkil.[66] The 'ulama' of Najaf, who had been neutral in the dispute, were gradually drawn into the struggle against the Shaykhis. The Usuli persecution in the shrine cities, however, did not curb the spread of Shaykhism in Iran.[67]

Overall, however, the struggle against the Shaykhis had the effect of better defining the collective authority of the Usulis by setting them against a common rival and by drawing clear boundaries *vis-à-vis* "the other." The community's external boundaries were thus clearly established.

Despite the persecution, Rashti managed to establish himself as one of the two urban religious leaders in Karbala', helped by his amicable relations with the government in Baghdad. The other leader, Ibrahim Qazvini (d. 1264/1847–48), emerged as the most prominent Usuli mujtahid following Sharif al-'Ulama''s death in 1246/1830–31. Qazvini acquired his reputation through his book *Dawabit al-usul*, and according to his disciple and partisan, Tunikabuni, he had more students and was more prominent in Iran than Najafi.[68]

Control of the "Indian money" played an important role in the struggle for leadership in Karbala'. In addition to supporting students, the funds that were used for public projects enabled Qazvini and Najafi to mobilize the support of merchants, craftsmen, and, to a limited extent, even members of the urban gangs.[69] Thanks to his prestige as a scholar and communal leader, Rashti managed to obtain the position of distributor of the "Indian Money" for two years during the early 1830s, but lost it to Ibrahim Qazvini when the mujtahids of Awadh turned against Shaykhism. With Qazvini as distributor, the Shaykhis were deprived of any share in the money and only the insistence of the Indian mujtahids mitigated that discrimination.[70]

Qazvini's control of the "Indian Money" helped him to attract a large number of students, and to discriminate against his personal enemies. Other mujtahids in Karbala', such as Sayyid 'Ali Naqi Tabataba'i and 'Abd al-Husayn, the son of Qazvini's rival Muhammad Husayn Isfahani, had to appeal directly to Lucknow and ask for an allowance.[71]

Qazvini's use of the Indian funds for self-aggrandizement elicited resentment in Karbala' and probably in Awadh as well. The insistence from Awadh on receipts and detailed reports on the progress of the various public works, as well as the prodding that Indians receive their fair share of the funds, reflect a suspicion of irregularities in handling the money. While the Shi'i biographical dictionaries are disinclined to dwell on such issues, discontent over corruption is explicit in the British correspondence. Concerned with the implications for the British reputation in Iraq and Awadh, the British political agent in Baghdad reported that he had been repeatedly requested by "the heads of the Sheeah population of this Pashalic" to bring to the notice of the British governor-general of India and the king of Oudh "the gross misapplication" of the "Indian money". "It is stated and generally believed," he added, that only "a very small portion" of these funds had been "appropriated to the purpose of charity" as they had been designated. "So notorious" has been the handling of the funds by the mujtahids, he concluded, that British credibility had suffered from its association with the distribution.[72]

The 1840s marked the shift from Karbala' to Najaf as the major center of learning for Iranians, and consequently as center for universal Shiʿi leadership. A sample of 'ulama' of the shrine cities, which I have used elsewhere,[73] demonstrates that whereas 136 migrant Persian students attended the *dars al-kharij* in Karbala' until that period, 135 did so in Najaf. Subsequently, however, 461 migrant Persians attended the *dars al-kharij* in Najaf, compared to only 86 in Karbala' (some students attended these lessons in both towns). The move to Najaf was even more accentuated among the Turkish students. Up to the 1840s twenty of them studied in Karbala' and eighteen in Najaf, whereas in the subsequent period the number of *dars al-kharij* students in Karbala' declined to ten and those in Najaf rose to ninety.[74]

According to Tunikabuni the shift occurred in two stages: the first followed the death of Sharif al-ʿUlama' Mazandarani in the 1830/31 cholera epidemic, which coincided with the early career of Muhammad Hasan Najafi. Tunikabuni claims, however, that Ibrahim Qazvini of Karbala' had more Iranian students than Muhammad Hasan Najafi, and that only after his death in 1264/1848 did his students move to Najaf to study under Najafi.[75] An equally important factor in the shift to Najaf was the bloody rebellion of the Shiʿi population in 1843 and the occupation of Karbala' by the Ottomans. The siege and subsequent repressive measures prompted both mujtahids and disciples to leave the town.[76]

Overall, leadership during the first part of the nineteenth century was characterized by several patterns. The first is the multiplicity of centers both in Iran and in the shrine cities, none of which had outright superiority. On the personal level the leadership was diffused among several often rival mujtahids. While some of them enjoyed prestige and some authority outside their towns, none of them, except Bahr al-ʿUlum, enjoyed universally unchallenged recognition. Whereas the leaders in the shrine cities enjoyed greater prestige as scholars, their colleagues in Iran had greater political and social power. Both communities of 'ulama', in the shrine cities and Iran, increasingly adopted less tolerant attitudes toward their religious opponents. In the shrine cities themselves, Karbala' was dominated by Iranian mujtahids, Najaf by Arabs. However, whereas the Tabataba'i family lost its preeminence to others, mostly immigrant mujtahids, the Kashif al-Ghita' family enjoyed clear supremacy during that period. Both, however, were now facing the growing challenge of Muhammad Hasan Najafi as the emerging leader of Najaf.

3   Monopolization of leadership of Najaf

The leadership of Muhammad Hasan Najafi

Certain scholars describe Muhammad Hasan Najafi as the first universally recognized supreme exemplar in the Shi'i world, citing statements
to that effect from various Shi'i biographical dictionaries, but disagree as
to the exact date on which he attained his position.[1] However, it seems
that these assertions misstate the point, as due to the amorphous
structure of the Shi'i religious establishment none of the three leading
nineteenth-century exemplars – Najafi, Ansari, and Shirazi – enjoyed
absolutely undisputed authority, and each had rivals who challenged
their supremacy.

Rather, I would argue that the 1830s and 1840s, and particularly
Najafi's leadership tenure, represent a qualitative change in the nature of
religious leadership in the shrine cities and the entire Shi'i world. It is
during this period that the consolidation of widespread networks of
patronage extending from the shrine cities to Iran is clearly discernible,
and when mujtahids from the shrine cities are mentioned as explicitly
sending their disciples to Iran to serve as their representatives. Najafi
himself represents a change from his predecessors and contemporaries
in his conscious and apparently methodical efforts to build a patronage
network as the basis for his leadership.

The change in the relationship between the shrine cities and Iran-
based scholars was probably due to a generational change in Iran.
Graduates of the late eighteenth and early nineteenth centuries entered
a vacuum in Iranian religious leadership, and maintained an independent status vis-à-vis the teachers of the shrine cities. This was not the
case with those who followed them. The second generation of graduates
felt less secure vis-à-vis major Iranian authorities such as Shafti and
Karbasi and therefore needed or sought the backing of their teachers
from the shrine cities.

Conceivably, complementary loose networks of patronage existed in
Iran at the time, some of them originating from the shrine cities and

others from regional Iranian centers. The case of Mahdi Kujuri illustrates this point. While teaching in Shiraz, he was informed that Karbasi of Isfahan had endorsed another 'alim in Shiraz. Worried about his own position, he asked his former teacher, Ibrahim Qazvini, to declare his support for him in order to enhance his status in the town.[2]

Another reason for the change was the increasing importance of the popular image of the mujtahids of the shrine cities as pious and otherworldly spiritual leaders compared with their more worldly counterparts in Iran. Such resentment against the Iranian mujtahids, which was manifested in the appeal of the Shaykhi and Babi movements, apparently prompted Iranian communities to appeal directly to the mujtahids of the shrine cities to send them their representatives.[3] In face of such a mood, low-level 'ulama' in Iran probably preferred to stress their links with the shrine cities rather than with local mujtahids in Iran.

The growing competition for students among mujtahids in the shrine cities increased their dependence on donations from Iran. Under such circumstances, the old ways of raising funds without any organization or by going to Iran personally were no longer adequate, and the establishment of networks of patronage became more urgent than ever before. Among these active mujtahids, Najafi was the most skillful in building networks of patronage. It cannot be merely an aberration caused by the particular nature of the available sources, or pure coincidence, that there are many more references to his activities in this regard than to those of any of his contemporaries.

Najafi's new type of leadership was the result of several processes both in Iran and in the shrine cities. During the early 1840s several of the leading Iranian mujtahids died within a short space of time without leaving notable successors, and so facilitating Najafi's ascendence to prominence almost by default.[4] The shift from Iran to the shrine cities was due to the Iranian mujtahids' failure to produce a second generation of students, probably because of their greater emphasis on the administration of justice and communal affairs.

The 1840s also witnessed the final stage in the shift from Karbala' to Najaf as the leading center of learning for Iranians. The combined impact of the 1843 Ottoman occupation of Karbala' and Qazvini's death, which led to a migration of students to Najaf, created a temporary vacuum in Karbala', as none of Qazvini's disciples or the members of the Tabataba'i family had sufficiently high stature to stand on a par with Najafi and the other mujtahids in Najaf. This vacuum, and the prominence of Najafi and subsequently of Ansari, firmly consolidated the superiority of Najaf for the rest of the century.

In addition, Najafi established his leading position in his own right, thanks to a combination of several qualities which enabled his rise to scholarly and communal religious leadership.[5] He excelled as a student under Ja'far Kashif al-Ghita', who wanted to despatch him to Isfahan, but he refused to go, following the advice of Jawad al-'Amili that a promising future awaited him in Najaf. Apparently, he sensed that the shrine cities would always have the edge over Iranian towns as centers of learning.[6] Najafi acquired his great reputation thanks to his *Jawahir al-kalam fi sharh shara'i' al-Islam*, which he completed in 1254/1838–39 after more than twenty-five years of work. The book became the most popular work of reference in *fiqh*, so much so that despite the high price of manuscripts even ordinary believers obtained copies. It remained one of the most important of *fiqh* books well into the twentieth century.[7]

The extensive correspondence conducted during the 1830s and early 1840s between Najafi and the two leading mujtahids of Lucknow, Sayyids Muhammad and Husayn Nasirabadi, demonstrates the importance of the book in consolidating his position. It is unclear whether Najafi sent his book on his own initiative or complied with the request of the Awadh mujtahids. Be that as it may, once the first volumes arrived in Lucknow, they were greeted with enthusiasm, and requests for more copies and additional volumes repeatedly followed. On one occasion the Indian mujtahids designated Rs.1,000 for *Jawahir al-kalam* out of Rs.3,000 sent to Najaf for purchasing various scholarly works.[8] Ibrahim Qazvini, who resented Najafi's ascendancy, sent his *Dawabit al-usul* to Lucknow in order to enhance his own status in India. However, while his book was received with gratitude, it elicited less enthusiasm than *Jawahir al-kalam* and did not produce the same requests for additional copies.[9]

Thanks to his scholarly reputation Najafi was able to attract a growing number of students even while his rivals were still alive. Biographical entries on various 'ulama' show a pattern according to which students, both Arab and Iranian, first studied under members of the Kashif al-Ghita' family and later joined Najafi's classes.[10] The Kashif al-Ghita' family exerted much effort in promoting close relations with the neighboring tribes, and in cultivating young tribal students. Nevertheless, Najafi was able to attract students from that stronghold as well. He also invited to his classes promising students from other towns, such as the future mujtahid Muhammad Husayn al-Kazimi.[11] Even Hujjat al-Islam Shafti, who had established Isfahan as a rival center to the shrine cities, sent his son Asadallah to study under Najafi, thereby acknowledging Najafi's scholarly eminence.[12]

Najafi's efforts to expand his teaching circle led to accusations of being too lenient in issuing *ijazat ijtihad*. Muhammad Shah Qajar (who had little sympathy for the Usuli mujtahids) ridiculed him, saying that he had a dye-house of ijtihad (*masbaghat ijtihad*), in which he dyed his students and then sent them to Iran. Khunsari, his contemporary, estimates the number of students whom he recognized as mujtahids as more than sixty.[13]

Patronage building was the essential complement to teaching in acquiring religious leadership, and Najafi surpassed any other mujtahid in this endeavor. As part of his efforts, he used to delegate to his students the authority to judge on his behalf (*al-qada' bil-taqlid* or *bil-wikala*) thereby consolidating the function of *marja'iyya* and attaching them to himself.[14] The case of his disciple Muhammad Hasan Al Yasin is instructive in demonstrating his care for his proteges. Although Kazimayn was dominated by two mujtahid families, Al Asadallah Tustari and Al Shubbar, Najafi sent his disciple Muhammad Hasan Al Yasin as his representative there.[15] When his followers in Baghdad continued to send their religious dues directly to him and not through Al Yasin, Najafi refused to receive the money and reprimanded them for failing in their duties toward his former disciple. Al Yasin reciprocated by refusing the efforts of his former mentors, the Kashif al-Ghita' family, to woo him to their side.[16]

These intensive efforts at patronage building aroused resentment in other mujtahids, especially the Kashif al-Ghita's, and some other Arab mujtahids in Najaf, as well as Ibrahim Qazvini in Karbala'. Tunikabuni, for instance, claims that Najafi refused to endorse rulings issued by Qazvini or recognize the ijtihad of his students, thereby downgrading Qazvini's scholarship. Only when many of Qazvini's students moved to Najaf in order to join his own class did Najafi agree to acknowledge their ijtihad. Qazvini, for his part, procrastinated in sending the share of the "Indian money" allotted to Najaf.[17] The antipathy between the two was probably enhanced by the fact that Qazvini had studied under 'Ali Kashif al-Ghita' and maintained friendly relations with his family.

While extending his patronage to Iran, Najafi took active measures to enhance his alliances with some of the respected 'ulama' families in Najaf itself. Most notable was his support of the Bahr al-'Ulum clan, which had been impoverished since the death of Mahdi Bahr al-'Ulum in 1211/1797, but still retained considerable respect.[18] In his correspondence with the mujtahids of Awadh over financing the cleaning of the Hindiyya canal, Najafi found it sufficiently important to arrange for an allowance to be sent to the Bahr al-'Ulums. The close relationship between the two families was cemented by teaching and marriage alliance.[19]

Whereas 'Ali Kashif al-Ghita' refrained as much as possible from issuing *fatwas*, out of pious caution (*ihtiyat*), Najafi devoted considerable attention to this activity.[20] The flow of questions was essential in promoting and maintaining close contact between the mujtahid and his followers, and might have been one of Najafi's considerations in emphasizing this part of his duties.

Concurrently, Najafi did not shy away from tarnishing the reputation of his rivals, as can be seen from his treatment of Muhsin Khanfar, a close supporter of the Kashif al-Ghita', who had himself harbored leadership ambitions. In order to undermine Muhsin's position Najafi accused him of supporting Shaykhism, thus prompting many of Muhsin's students to leave him. Among the few who remained loyal to Shaykh Muhsin were the brothers Sayyid Muhammad and Sayyid Hashim Al Rizavi Hindi, but Najafi wooed them to his side giving Sayyid Muhammad an *ijazat riwaya* and marrying his daughters to the two brothers.[21]

The combination of great scholarship and skill in building patronage and alliances facilitated the rise of Najafi to eminence in the shrine cities and in Iran that was markedly different from that of his predecessors, as is shown by the unprecedented lofty titles attributed to him by the various biographical sources.[22]

Two cases demonstrate Najafi's leadership and the new relationships between the shrine cities and Iran. In 1264/1847–48 Mirza Muhammad Sadiq Rizavi Mashhadi requested and received "permission" from Najafi to serve as the custodian of the shrine in Mashhad, even though the appointment was actually made by the shah.[23] Presumably his status within his custodian family or with the shah was not sufficiently secured and Najafi's support was seen as helpful. Perhaps it was an attempt to equate Najafi's endorsement with that of the shah.

In his biography of Sayyid Husayn Nasirabadi of Lucknow, 'Abbas Shushtari wrote that Sayyid Husayn allowed the deputation of judicial authority (*al-istinaba fi al-qada*'), which was then a minority opinion. However, when Najafi advocated the same view in his *Jawahir al-kalam*, the other Awadh 'ulama' changed their position, accepting such a deputation as permissible. In contrast, Shushtari adds, Sayyid Husayn never changed his mind on major questions of law. The story both demonstrates the authority of Najafi and of the institution of *marja'iyya*, but also their limitations. Deference to Najafi as the most learned exemplar was probably more common among lower-ranking mujtahids in North India and Iran than among senior mujtahids.[24] The leading mujtahids of Awadh, while not regarding themselves as subordinate to him, did express their appreciation by sending him copies of their scholarly works.

As befitting his position and wealth, Najafi reportedly assumed a bearing of pomp and majesty, wearing a large diamond ring and a sumptuous turban, with a large retinue following him.[25] Such conduct stood in sharp contrast to the asceticism required and expected of the mujtahids. It did not escape criticism.[26]

In his writings on the question of general deputyship (niyaba 'amma), Najafi included the administration of justice, the management of people's affairs (al-nizam), the holding of political office (al-siyasa), the collection of taxes, and the management of the affairs of minors on behalf of the just ruler. Concurrently, he did not fully agree with Bihbihani's assertion that the jurist was more capable of establishing the rule of justice than any other member of the Shi'a. What emerges from his opinion is that "enjoining the good" provides the moral-religious justification for the existence of government in Islam.[27]

While affirming the authority of the jurist, Najafi opposed the incumbency of the Friday prayers during the Occultation. Although he accused those mujtahids who ruled in favor of the incumbency of "love of leadership (ri'asa) and earthly rule (saltana)," he was clearly in the minority.[28] The Friday prayers were too entrenched at that time among the Shi'a in Iran and India, and the interests of too many 'ulama' from all ranks were served by their administration, for them to be abolished by his opposite ruling. In other words, his effective authority was limited in face of a consensus of most 'ulama'.

In addition to the limitations of his spiritual authority as the exemplar, Muhammad Hasan's leadership was challenged by several Najaf mujtahids. Following Hasan Kashif al-Ghita''s death in 1262/1846, his nephew Muhammad b. 'Ali assumed the leadership of the family, and "the religious leadership of the Ja'fari community (ta'ifa) turned to him."[29] Even if exaggerated, these claims indicate that the Kashif al-Ghita' family exerted itself to maintain its bases of support and did not reconcile itself to Muhammad Hasan's religious leadership. Radi Al Khidr al-Jinaji, a cousin of the Kashif al-Ghita' family, who attended Najafi's dars al-kharij, used to provoke him during his lectures. Following one such incident, he was forced to leave Najaf and live with his tribal relatives until Najafi's death.[30]

A few other Arab mujtahids, most notably Khidr b. Shallal al-'Afakawi, also made a bid for marja'iyya. Eventually, however, they had to acknowledge Najafi's religious leadership.[31] In Iran, Hujjat al-Islam Asadallah Burujirdi (d. 1281/1864) claimed superiority of knowledge for himself. Further, in some of the stories of Ansari's disciples, there are suggestions that he was superior to Najafi, as some disciples joined Ansari's classes after having been disappointed by Najafi.[32]

While there was never any unanimity regarding Najafi's *marjaʿiyya*, his leadership marks a turning point in the development of that institution. He was the first Iranian to assume paramount leadership in Najaf after almost half a century of hegemony by the Kashif al-Ghita' family and of Arab 'ulama'. Likewise, he was the first mujtahid to establish a widespread patronage network in Iran and gain direct influence in that country, setting a pattern to be followed by others. Concurrently, he was the last native of Najaf to enjoy such status in Iran.[33] Henceforth, Iranian immigrants would dominate the shrine cities. These changes paralleled and arose from the growth of the 'ulama' population, from the increasing number of immigrants, and from the shift of Iranian students from Karbala' to Najaf.

The leadership of Murtada Ansari

The Babi accusations that the 'ulama' had usurped the Imam's authority and had mired themselves in excessive worldliness challenged the foundations of the religious establishment in Iran. One may even speculate that the trauma of the Babi threat enhanced conservative inclinations within the community of 'ulama'. To ascertain this, however, would require further research into their writings.

As the leading exemplar in Najaf, Muhammad Hasan Najafi understood the need for the 'ulama' to brace themselves against the Babi challenge. Originally, he had aspired to have his son, 'Abd al-Husayn, as his successor, describing him as such in a letter to Lucknow.[34] Najafi's plan was accepted by many of the first-ranking 'ulama' in Najaf, indicating a support for hereditary leadership. In addition, it reflects his own status, as he believed that he could determine the leadership for the next generation. Hence the surprise when on his deathbed, in the presence of the assembled first-rank 'ulama' of Najaf, he designated Murtada Ansari as the supreme exemplar after him.

Although Ansari had been recognized as a distinguished scholar he was not considered a candidate for supreme leadership.[35] Najafi probably realized that in facing a threat to their authority the 'ulama' needed a leader whose scholarly credentials would be beyond dispute, and whose personal qualities of piety and asceticism would overshadow the charismatic figure of the Bab. He may also have feared that the designation of his son would be viewed as too partisan or factional and would not gain universal acceptance at a time when the 'ulama' could not afford an internal struggle for the succession. Furthermore, Najafi apparently realized that appointing his son would enhance the perception of the mujtahids as an entrenched elite closed to newcomers, a situation which was resented by many of those lower-ranking 'ulama' who had joined the Babi movement. The designation of a successor was unprecedented among the orthodox 'ulama'. Ahmad Ahsa'i had nominated Kazim Rashti as his successor, but that was essentially a charismatic appointment. Significantly, even if Najafi had indeed wanted to institutionalize the nomination of a successor and make it the prerogative of the preceding leader as some historians surmise,[36] he did not formulate his procedure as a rule for future cases, and it was not repeated.

Initially, Ansari pursued a cautious course, inviting the chief mujtahid of Mazandaran and his former classmate from Karbala', Mulla Sa'id Barfurushi Sa'id al-'ulama' (d.1270/1853–54) to assume the leadership in Najaf on the grounds that he was more knowledgeable in the law. Sa'id al-'ulama' had attained prominence among the 'ulama' and maintained friendly relations with Nasir al-Din Shah largely thanks to his vigorous persecution of the Babis during the uprising in Tabarsi (1848–50). He declined Ansari's offer, arguing that although he had indeed been more knowledgeable during their studies, he was subsequently mostly engaged in public affairs while Ansari had been teaching and writing and was, therefore, more qualified for the role.

Ansari's offer might have been motivated by personal hesitation to undertake the responsibility of leadership, or else it was a shrewd move to diffuse a potential source of opposition.[37] He may have preferred an outsider who would not be identified with any of the factions in Najaf. Alternatively, he may have appealed to Sa'id al-'ulama' precisely because of his anti-Babi reputation, which was seen as necessary during the conflict with the Babis. On the other hand, Mazandarani's reply reflected the notion, to take Amanat's phrase, of the need for the 'ulama', in view of the Babi challenge, to shift back from the market place to the madrasa and to emphasize scholarship rather than public activism as the basis of leadership.[38]

Whatever opposition there was to his leadership, Ansari established his preeminence throughout the Shi'i world thanks to a combination of several personal qualities and accommodating circumstances. In his background and personality Ansari could unify the various factions among the 'ulama', and respond to the aspirations of the populace for a new type of spiritual leadership. Coming from Dizful, a region with a mixed Perso-Arabic culture, Ansari had an advantage over his predecessors, whose authority was largely, but not exclusively, confined to their ethnic group. Teaching in both languages, he could bridge the ethnic divide between Arabs and Iranians and emerge as "the joinder of the two seas and the point of approval of the two groups." The fact that he was not Najafi's disciple, but had studied under 'Ali Kashif al-Ghita', facilitated his acceptance by the two factions.[39]

While most mujtahids mastered one scholarly field, Ansari excelled in both *fiqh* and *usul*. He established his scholarly fame by reconstructing the methodology of *fiqh* (*usul al-fiqh*) and by the founding of a new school in *usul* which has dominated Shiʻi learning to the present day. By Ansari's time, the field of *usul al-fiqh* was divided into two major branches: semantic (*lafzi*), which dealt with the rules of reasoning concerning the Qur'an and Traditions; and procedural (*'amali*). Detailed studies on the semantic principles had already been written by Ansari's time, while the procedural field was hardly developed. Ansari's main contribution was development of the procedural principles (*al-usul al-'amaliyya*) as a separate and clearly structured field.[40]

In his treatise *Fara'id al-usul* Ansari set out the three categories in which legal rulings can be deduced. In the first part of the work he dealt with the determination of legal norms with certainty (*qatʻ*), i.e. cases where unambiguous norms can be found in the textual sources and when there is no need for the employment of reason. The second part examines the determination of such norms through "valid conjecture" (*zann muʻtabar*), that is cases where reason is employed to create binding legal norms.[41]

The third and last part, which represents Ansari's main contribution, deals with cases of doubt (*shakk*) where neither guidance in the written sources nor any indication of the probability of a correct answer exists. With reference to these cases Ansari formulated four guiding and interrelated procedural principles which are organized dialectically. When the mujtahid faces a question concerning a religious duty (*taklif*) with several possible solutions, he must look for a precedent. If there is one, then the principle of continuance (*istishab*) should apply. If there is none, he should determine whether the doubt concerning the duty is primary (*shakk ibtida'i*), i.e. when no known legal obligation exists concerning the duty itself. In such a case, the principle of exemption (*bara'a*) may be adopted. However, if the doubt is only secondary, i.e. not referring to the general principles or truths but only to a specific detail or case, and there is such a known obligation, but several options exist, then all of these options must be followed according to the principle of caution (*ihtiyat*). If it is impossible to follow all the options, then the principle of choice (*takhyir*) applies, and one option should be chosen.[42]

Ansari's contribution enabled mujtahids to extend the area of law to any matter where there was even a possibility and not just a probability of being in accordance with the Imam's guidance. It thus enabled them to broaden the jurisdiction of their own profession into wider spheres of human activity, thereby further advancing the professionalization of the 'ulama'. The great bulk of works in *usul* after Ansari was devoted to the elucidation and elaboration of the principles he had set. More than eighty-four commentaries (*sharh*, pl. *shuruh*) were devoted to *al-Fara'id*, rendering it one of the most commented-upon works in Shi'i law.[43] As it was deemed by his contemporaries as bringing to maturity the process begun by Bihbihani, it earned him the title "seal of the mujtahids" (*khatim al-mujtahidin*).[44]

Ansari's new methodology, which made *usul* more accessible to students, came to dominate the madrasa curriculum even in his lifetime. As was the case with the earlier leading scholarly works, the dissemination of such books was carried out by the voluntary popular choice of students who became independent teachers, without any formal decision. Only a few Arab mujtahids, most notably Radi Al Khidr al-Jinaji, adhered to the old approach. Their reluctance to adopt the new methodology was motivated more by conservatism than by factional considerations, since the younger members of the Kashif al-Ghita' family who studied under Ansari did adopt the new approach.[45] Shaykh Radi himself admitted that he never read Ansari's *Fara'id* because he was afraid they would lead him to doubt his own knowledge.[46]

Ansari's contribution to the study of *usul* resulted also in the birth of a new school in *fiqh*. Ansari himself demonstrated the application of his methodology in his *fiqh* book *al-Makasib*, known also as *Kitab al-matajir* (Earnings), which dealt with commercial law. As was the case with Bihbihani earlier, his disciples elaborated and applied the new methodology to all branches of the law.[47]

Ansari's distinction in *usul* and *fiqh* made him the most sought-after teacher in Najaf for both Iranians and Arabs, who numbered in the hundreds.[48] His popularity as a teacher was also due to his reputation as a master who looked after his students.[49] He was further aided by the vacuum in the religious leadership in Iran following the passing of the previous generation of mujtahids.

As the leader of the community Ansari reached an agreement in 1852 with the British consul Rawlinson on the mode of distribution of the Oudh Bequest funds in Najaf, seeking a balance between the various groups in the community: junior mujtahids, low-ranking indigent 'ulama', Persian and Arab students, the custodians of the shrines, and the poor. Apparently, Ansari had the final word on the actual recipients, thereby enhancing his authority in the community.[50]

Shi'i sources universally acclaim Ansari as a just distributor, whereas his successors were constantly accused of favoritism and corruption.[51]

Some dissatisfaction must have existed during Ansari's time, but his reputation as an ascetic and his generally undisputed leadership probably prevented it from coming out in public. By contrast, complaints against Sayyid ʿAli Naqi Tabataba'i, the distributor in Karbala', abounded throughout his tenure.[52]

In 1860, Ansari withdrew from the distribution.[53] The British sources do not explicitly give his reasons, but several modern Iranian sources, projecting later developments on to the past, assert that when Ansari realized that the bequest was a British ploy to buy influence among the 'ulama', he decided to withdraw.[54] Regardless of the validity of Ansari's suspicions, which do not seem to have been justified at the time, the step conforms with his aversion to politics and contacts with temporal powers.

Ansari's reputation for asceticism, otherworldliness, and piety provided the orthodox establishment with a badly needed contrast to the excessive worldliness of various mujtahids in Iran, and a counterweight to the Bab's otherworldly figure. This image earned Ansari wide recognition outside the community of 'ulama' since it responded to a widespread public yearning for a morally reformed leadership. Even the Sufis contended that he was a marjaʿ for the masters of maʿarif-i ilahi (Islamic theosophy).[55] In the past, charismatic figures such as the Niʿmat Allahi Sufi Nur ʿAli Shah, Ahmad Ahsa'i, and the Bab had attracted such yearnings. But when all alternative heterodoxies had been effectively suppressed, they were channeled to Ansari. An important manifestation of Ansari's status as the most eminent mujtahid and a figure of public reverence was the flow of donations and the fifth from all over the Shiʿi world, which he reportedly used for religious and charitable purposes.[56]

As the leading mujtahid of the time, and to stave off the Babi threat, Ansari sought to enhance religious teaching in Iran itself, particularly in the smaller towns. According to his biographer he ordered the religious dues from such towns to be spent on schooling there rather than be sent to Najaf. In addition, he set up a network of 'ulama' in various Iranian cities who taught his works and rulings.[57] Students from his home town Dizful were a sizable group among them.[58]

Probably in response to the Babi challenge to the authority of the 'ulama', Ansari sought to systematize the concept of emulation of the mujtahids and specifically that of the supreme exemplar.[59] In his treatise Sirat al-najat (The path to salvation), Ansari declares that emulation of a mujtahid is a religious duty. Only when the believer performs some ritual act with the proper intention and in accordance with the view of a living mujtahid is this act valid.

The believer must emulate the most learned living mujtahid of his time, but should two mujtahids be found equal in their knowledge of the law, it is permissible to emulate either one. In such a case, other qualities – piety, caution, and dependability – should decide between the two. The more pious and cautious of the two, or the more dependable, should be emulated. Knowledge, however, remains the primary criterion.

Ansari allowed the emulation of a less learned mujtahid only under specific conditions. For instance, if the supreme exemplar prefers not to rule on a certain issue, but another mujtahid had given a ruling on it, and when the believer has a general knowledge that the two are in agreement on the issue. In essence, then, the believer may emulate a less learned mujtahid only when in doing so he is ultimately emulating the supreme jurist. On the whole, Ansari subordinated the ordinary believers to the mujtahids. He in fact narrowed the designation of the most learned mujtahid to the 'ulama' and not the believers.

In a way, Ansari set the basis for an informal hierarchy within the religious establishment, since junior mujtahids are to be emulated only if they act in agreement with the exemplar or in effect accept his authority. Such rudimentary hierarchy, however, was not fully stratified and lacked any middle ranks. The supreme exemplar himself was dependent on the acknowledgment of the junior mujtahids. Ansari's elaboration on the change of allegiance from one to another was possibly due to the emergence of a universally recognized leadership during his time which drew followers from all Shi'i regions, compared with earlier periods, when leadership had a more local basis.

The mechanism for designating the supreme exemplar was the most problematic part of Ansari's concept. He defines the "most knowledgeable" (a'lam) mujtahid as the "one who is more skilful in deducing God's law and comprehending it from the lawful evidence." Yet for the recognition of such quality the "testimony of a single just man who is one of the people of insight is sufficient."[60] It is a subjective and extremely loose criterion, which does not even require certainty. The two other criteria, piety and justice, are similar in this respect. Such a mechanism does not preclude the emergence of several competing exemplars, as indeed would happen repeatedly in Shi'ism.

Although he systematized the concept of the supreme spiritual leadership, Ansari was cautious in exercising it himself. His image of otherworldliness was enhanced by his reputed prudence (ihtiyat) in the issue of legal rulings and his aversion to politics. The ruling elite in Iran responded favorably to this attitude in donations and grants to Najaf. Ansari's quietism, however, did not mean cooperation with or endorsement of the government.[61]

In addition, Ansari neither sought nor achieved absolute centralization of the 'ulama' establishment in his time. Two examples of his reluctance to impose his authority are his refusal to endorse the anti-Baha'i assembly organized by 'Abd al-Husayn Tehrani in Najaf in 1863 and his refusal to come out against the Oudh Bequest even though he himself withdrew from its distribution. None of these decisions had any impact on other mujtahids, demonstrating the limited applicability of the authority of the exemplar.[62]

Ansari's nomination by Najafi and his own scholarly supremacy notwithstanding, his leadership was not accepted immediately or without reservations in Najaf, particularly by the well-established 'ulama' families. With some bitterness, Sharif b. 'Abd al-Husayn Jawahiri wrote years later to Mirza Hasan Shirazi that had it not been for his grandfather, no one would have spoken in such glowing terms of Ansari.[63] Sayyid Husayn b. Rida Bahr al-'Ulum declined a request by a group of 'ulama' to head the Najaf community of learning and assume religious leadership (zi'ama diniyya) following Najafi's death.[64] More significant was the attitude adopted by the Kashif al-Ghita' family, which had never fully acquiesced in Najafi's leadership, and was not inclined to abandon its aspirations after his demise. Many of Ansari's opponents turned to Muhammad b. 'Ali Kashif al-Ghita', who had previously challenged Najafi, to become the new leader.[65]

When Shaykh Muhammad died in 1268/1851–52, his brother Mahdi assumed the leadership of the Kashif al-Ghita' clan and sought to expand its base of support. As part of his efforts to reconcile the Arab and Persian 'ulama', Ansari appointed Mahdi as a sub-distributor of the Oudh Bequest among the Arabs, delegating to him, according to Arab biographical sources, many of the communal issues pertaining to the Arab 'ulama'.[66] By accepting such a role Mahdi ostensibly acknowledged Ansari's leadership, but neither he nor his followers gave up his aspirations. Visiting Najaf in 1273/1856–57, Adib al-Mulk was told by a "respectable person" that Ansari's position was merely due to his control of the "Indian money" while Mahdi was superior to him in learning and scholarship.[67]

True to his image, Ansari did not court Iranian officials visiting Najaf. In contrast, both 'Ali Bahr al-'Ulum and Mahdi Kashif al-Ghita' actively wooed Iranian pilgrims. Both visited Adib al-Mulk to show their respect and win him to their side. In addition, Mahdi exerted much effort to send his disciples to Iran. Adib al-Mulk, who was also invited to Mahdi's majlis, recounts a conversation that sheds vivid light on the struggle for leadership. During the conversation, Mahdi claimed that 200 out of the 2,100 students in Najaf had attained ijtihad, but none of them was an Iranian. He challenged the Iranians to present those among them deserving ijtihad. He also ignored a plea by one of the participants not to send any more of his representatives to Iran, as their presence there had become a source of quarrels.[68] It is unclear whether this strife erupted between supporters of Mahdi and Ansari, or with local 'ulama' who resented the newcomer's competition. Shaykh Mahdi, however, did not comply with the request.

Mahdi's active efforts to attract Iranian students were resented by his Arab students, who felt discriminated against in the distribution of stipends. A delegation of students extracted a commitment from Hajj Muhammad Salih al-Kubba, the wealthiest Shi'i merchant in Baghdad, to distribute a large amount of his own funds among the Arab students. Their pressure and that of other Arab dignitaries convinced Mahdi's cousin Radi Al Khidr al-Jinaji to return to Najaf in a bid to assume the leadership of the Arab faction. Mahdi's efforts bore fruit, and he acquired a following in parts of Iran and in Iraq.[69] In comparison, Iran-based mujtahids did not challenge Ansari. In addition to his scholarly superiority, Ansari was helped by the Iranian 'ulama''s awareness of the need to remain united behind one leader in the face of the Babi threat.

Overall, the identity and background of the three aspirants for leadership discussed above reflect a shift of power from local families to immigrant mujtahids. Local families continued to maintain leadership status and influence as urban notables and in controlling circles of learning. But local prestige did not provide a decisive advantage in obtaining leadership in Iran.

Ansari's leadership consolidated Najaf's position as the leading center of learning for the rest of the nineteenth century as shown by its role in the career of Iran-based 'ulama'.[70] As noted above, the 'ulama' in Qajar Iran were divided into two major groups, the first consisting of government appointees, the Shaykhs al-Islam and Imams Jum'a, while the second comprising independent 'ulama' engaged in teaching, litigation, and religious administration.

Studies in the shrine cities added to a mujtahid's prestige and authority, but were neither essential nor sufficient in and of themselves for the attainment of a high post by members of the established families. A survey of all the families of Shaykhs al-Islam and Imams Jum'a in Iran is beyond the scope of this study, but several cases will demonstrate this mixed picture. Of the various members of the Khatunabadi family, who served as Imams Jum'a of Isfahan and subsequently of Tehran, only three are recorded as having studied in the shrine cities.[71]

A similar pattern is discernible in the families of the religious functionaries of several other towns.[72] The Shaykhs al-Islam of Isfahan, on the other hand – Asadallah b. Hujjat al-Islam Shafti, and subsequently Muhammad Baqir b. Muhammad Taqi Isfahani and his own son Aqa Najafi – all studied in the shrine cities. This mixed record is due to the fact that religious posts, like most of the positions in the Iranian bureaucracy, were hereditary. Consequently, the family's social position and relations with the authorities were at least as important for retaining a particular post under their control as the level of education of its members.

In comparison, studies in the shrine cities had become almost a *sine qua non* for the attainment of high status in the religious hierarchy for the great majority of 'ulama' of the second group, who were not all government appointees, particularly in the case of first-generation 'ulama'.[73] However, exceptions to this pattern were also to be found: Mulla Asadallah Burujirdi Hujjat al-Islam (d. 1281/1864) studied under Abu al-Qasim Qummi in Qum, yet established himself as one of the leading scholars in Iran. With the centralization of scholarship and religious leadership in the shrine cities during the second half of the century, study there became even more important than previously for the attainment of status in Iran. The five leading mujtahids of Tehran in the latter part of the nineteenth and the early twentieth centuries had all studied in the shrine cities.[74]

In contrast, travel to several centers of study was not customary among students in the shrine cities, especially natives of the two towns. Nor was it deemed especially important. Apparently, most students regarded studies in the shrine cities as sufficient for the acquisition of knowledge and status. It is also possible that teachers did not encourage their students to travel for fear of disrupting the crucial patronage relationships and of losing disciples to their rivals.

Those few Arabs and Persians who studied in Kazimayn were largely natives of the town who belonged to the leading 'ulama' families there; they came to Najaf and Karbala' in order to complete their education. Kazimayn had never been more than a local religious center for Baghdad and its immediate environs. Yet a certain rivalry did exist between it and the two principal shrine cities.[75]

The relatively small number of students who came to the shrine cities after attending the *dars al-kharij* in Mashhad and Tehran, and the fact that most of those who did so came from adjacent regions, suggest that the latter two cities were primarily regional centers of learning. Moreover, the fact that the majority of Iranian students came directly to the shrine cities after completing the initial stages of learning in their home districts points to the coexistence of several complementary networks of studies and patronage in Iran. Apparently, most students who had completed their studies in Mashhad, Isfahan, or Tehran did not come to the shrine cities. Hasan Quchani, who studied in Najaf at the turn of the twentieth century, recalled how he had written to his friends who were studying in Isfahan, urging them to come to Najaf because the standard of teaching was higher there.[76] The fact that he had to urge his friends to come suggests that it was not self-evident for students at the *dars al-kharij* level in Iran to study in the shrine cities.

The leadership of Muhammad Hasan Najafi and Murtada Ansari marked the unprecedented concentration of authority and influence under a single mujtahid. It also marked the final shift from Iran to the shrine cities and the rise of Najaf to undisputed center of learning and leadership of the Shi'i world. Their leadership tenure also marked the overshadowing of the Arab mujtahids by Iranians. Najafi was the first Iranian in forty years and the last native of Najaf to achieve supreme leadership, while Ansari was the first immigrant to achieve that status. In addition to their personalities this shift also reflected the demographic changes within the 'ulama' community, particularly the increasing number of immigrants from Iran. While Najafi was a *sayyid* and belonged to a respectable 'ulama' family in Najaf, Ansari came from a humble 'ulama' family in Dizful. In other words, his clerical origins did not play a major role in ensuring his prominence.

Their different personalities notwithstanding, both leaders combined all the necessary prerequisites for supreme leadership. Both were eminent scholars, whose books left a lasting impact on the Shi'i curriculum. Concurrently, both were great teachers and skilled patrons who invested conscious effort in cultivating students and in dispatching them as their agents among the various Shi'i communities. Both also formed close links with the Bazaar community, which financed their enterprise. Whereas Najafi cultivated friendly relations with Qajar officials, Ansari shunned this association, indicating that the political factor did not play a decisive role in their status.

While achieving unprecedented stature neither of the two remained unchallenged by rivals, although none of the latter seriously threatened their position. Likewise, neither of them could impose his views against a consensus of the 'ulama', thus reflecting the inherent weakness of their institution. The informal nature of the institution of leadership remained unchanged.

4   Diffusion, centralization, and politicization

The post-Ansari succession

While Ansari embodied in his own person the model for a single supreme exemplar, his conduct and writings on the matter did not prevent a renewed struggle for power in Najaf after his death in 1281/ 1864.[1] Several sources claim that Ansari had pointed to Mirza Hasan Shirazi as his designated choice and, like Muhammad Hasan Najafi before him, he had instructed the 'ulama' to follow his preference. Shirazi had already acquired renown as a student under Najafi, who had praised him in a letter to the governor of Fars as "the light of our eyes" and as an "absolute mujtahid" (*mujtahid mutlaq*) with a great future awaiting him.[2]

However, whereas Najafi's wish had decided the succession in his time, Ansari's did not have a similar effect, which casts doubt on whether he had explicitly nominated Shirazi. Most sources declare that Shirazi, Mirza Habiballah Rashti, and Hasan Najmabadi were Ansari's favorite students.[3] At the time of Najafi's death there was no one to challenge Ansari's scholarly credentials seriously. By contrast, Ansari's long tenure as leader led to the emergence of a new generation of mujtahids, none of them with a clear superiority over the others. The relatively large number of contenders reflected the growing size of the 'ulama' population in Iran and the shrine cities. The fact that the struggle was held in Najaf demonstrates the town's undisputed status as the leading center of learning in the Shi'i world.

In addition to personal rivalries, the importance of ethnic and regional affinities in forging loyalties was enhanced with the growth of the 'ulama' community. Struggles for leadership took place within each ethnic group, and among mujtahids from different ethnic groups. It is possible, therefore, to speak of three tiers of mujtahids: those who were emulated in their city or home region, those whose fame was limited to their ethnic group, and those whose reputation spread throughout the Shi'i world.

Arab–Iranian divisions had been a permanent feature in the shrine cities, but the post-Ansari succession added a new dimension with the emergence of the Turkish-speaking 'ulama' as a separate faction.[4] An additional division was that between the disciples of Ansari and other mujtahids, who now had the opportunity to make a bid for the leadership.

The biographical sources give contradictory accounts of the influence that the various senior Arab and Persian-speaking disciples exercised. Ansari's Persian disciples – among them Habiballah Rashti, Hasan Ashtiyani, Aqa Hasan Najmabadi, and Mirza 'Abd al-Rahim Nahavandi – opted for a leader from among their own. They met at Rashti's house and recognized Shirazi as the most learned (afdal), who would be given precedence in prayer and teaching. Citing Hasan Ashtiyani, Tehrani claims that Shirazi declined the offer, arguing that he was not fit to take care of the needs of the people, a statement which emphasizes the social rather than the spiritual nature of the religious leadership. Instead, Shirazi proposed Ashtiyani as the leader, but the latter flatly refused. Shirazi's refusal may have been sincere. But, in view of his skills as a patron and faction leader, it was more likely designed to force Ashtiyani to declare support for him publicly and defuse a potential challenge to his leadership. Ashtiyani subsequently left for Tehran where he emerged as a powerful mujtahid.[5]

The Turkish-speaking 'ulama' chose Sayyid Husayn Kuhkamara'i as their leader, declaring him the most learned. The conflicting claims of greater scholarship made by the two opposing factions show up the weakness of Ansari's concept of designating the supreme exemplar. The emergence of the Turkish faction was due to a growing feeling of discrimination in the distribution of funds and housing. It was combined with a sense of confidence produced by a growing number of students and by adequate financial backing from Turkish-speaking areas. Thus, despite its smaller size, the Turkish faction reportedly enjoyed greater esprit de corps than the larger Persian group.[6]

Thanks to his writings and teaching Kuhkamara'i established himself fairly quickly as a leading teacher and a widely emulated exemplar. The Shi'i sources disagree on the strength of the following that Kuhkamara'i and Shirazi had among students in Najaf, and on the relative influence each enjoyed in the first years after Ansari's death. Kuhkamara'i had greater support in the Turkish-speaking Shi'i regions, but was also emulated in several Persian-speaking regions in Iran. At that stage Shirazi had a following only in Persian-speaking areas.[7]

A minority of the Arab 'ulama' followed each of the two Iranian leaders. The majority, however, followed Arab mujtahids, who had previously been eclipsed by Ansari. Mahdi Kashif al-Ghita' enjoyed an advantage over other mujtahids, as he had already been an established leader with his own network of disciples. He expanded his following to the Caucasus and important Iranian cities such as Tehran, Tabriz, and Isfahan in addition to various towns and tribal areas in Iraq. In order to expand his influence in Iran, Mahdi had his *Risalat 'amal* translated into Persian. Likewise in 1284/1867–68 with money sent to him from Qarabagh in Azarbayjan he built two madrasas, both called *al-madrasa al-Mahdiyya*, in Najaf and Karbala' respectively, to house his students. Building a madrasa provided the mujtahid and his family with a long-lasting asset to attract students.[8]

Mahdi's cousin Radi Al Khidr al-Jinaji, as well as Muhammad Hasan Al Yasin, who held the leadership in Baghdad during Ansari's lifetime, also expanded their bases of support in Iran and Iraq.[9] A sharper rivalry surfaced between the Kashif al-Ghita' family and Muhammad Husayn al-Kazimi, Najafi's disciple and son-in-law, who had been building his own following. Al-Kazimi had a following in Baghdad, Kazimayn – his birthplace – and their environs, as well as in Basra. He even sent his disciple Sayyid 'Ali Shinawa Watut to Hilla, the traditional stronghold of the Kashif al-Ghita' family. As he was Lebanese by origin, he enjoyed an advantage in attracting students and donations from Lebanon, although it was of peripheral importance at the time. According to al-Amin (himself Lebanese) the "leadership of the Imamiyya in the Arab lands" devolved to him.[10]

The rivalry came into the open after Mahdi's death in 1289/1872–3. Claiming superior status, al-Kazimi refused to come to the prayer led by Ja'far "al-Saghir" (the little), the new head of the Kashif al-Ghita' clan. A group of students forcibly dragged him to the mosque to acknowledge Ja'far's leadership.[11] In addition, al-Kazimi encountered the hostility of local urban notables. In 1294/1877 members of the newly created municipal council had him detained by the Ottomans for several hours. He was released following pressure by the 'ulama' and because of the Ottoman fear of riots. Both groups may have been allied with the Kashif al-Ghita'.[12] It is unclear whether the Kashif al-Ghita' clan initiated these activities against al-Kazimi, but what emerges is that leadership struggles were not purely of the academy, and that scholarship was not the only way to acquire high status.

On the whole, however, Arab mujtahids were less successful in attracting Iranian students and followers than Iranian mujtahids in attracting Arabs. In addition to a certain sense of superiority among Iranians *vis-à-vis* Arabs, the main reason for that difference lay in the greater financial resources Iranians enjoyed thanks to their closer links with the Bazaar communities in Iran. The Arab tribes in Iraq, by comparison, never provided the similar financial support so necessary for leadership.

The leadership of Muhammad Hasan Shirazi

Mirza Hasan Shirazi gradually enhanced his prestige during the 1860s, but the turning point in his career was the visit by Nasir al-Din Shah to the shrine cities in 1287/1870. Shirazi was the only mujtahid who refused to welcome the shah in public, or to visit him as a mark of respect. His defiance or his manifest indifference to potential favors from the shah earned him lasting admiration in Najaf among all groups. Shirazi's efforts to help the urban poor and needy students during the 1871 famine further elevated him above other mujtahids in Najaf.[13]

Shirazi's growing fame intensified the struggle for leadership in Najaf. Feeling constrained there and unable to expand his network of support and classes, especially because of Habiballah Rashti's growing fame as a teacher, Shirazi decided in 1874 to leave Najaf and settle in Samarra'. Not notifying anyone of his intention, he traveled first to Karbala', ostensibly on a visitation, and arrived in Samarra' in late Sha'ban. He chose these dates so that he could stay there for the whole of Ramadan, keeping the door open to return to Najaf should his endeavor fail. After Ramadan, he informed his students of his decision to settle in Samarra'.[14]

According to Dawlatabadi, Shirazi ruled out Karbala' as a place for residence as it was dominated by Hasan Ardakani and Zayn al-'Abidin Mazandarani. Although Kazimayn had no Iranian mujtahid, it was dominated by Muhammad Hasan Al Yasin. In addition, it was too close to Baghdad, and was unlikely to attract Iranians, who wanted to be away from direct Ottoman control. Samarra', on the other hand, had no Iranian mujtahids, but had the shrine of the Tenth and Eleventh Imams, 'Ali al-Hadi and Hasan al-'Askari, which would attract pilgrims and provide an important source of revenue. The location of the famous cellar (sardab) where the Twelfth Imam reputedly went into Occultation was a major factor in Shirazi's considerations, designed to bestow on him some of the charisma of the Imam.[15]

Initially only a few of his students followed Shirazi to Samarra' and lack of funds was his most serious problem. Gradually, their numbers grew to more than a hundred at any given time. He reportedly had close to three hundred students who attained ijtihad, and boasted that his circle of study was superior to Ansari's, which included students from all levels. Moreover, a pattern was gradually established whereby students moved from Najaf to Samarra'.[16] What explains this success?

Ironically, Shirazi was the one mujtahid who came closest to the status of supreme exemplar as envisaged by Ansari, even though his superiority in knowledge was problematic if scholarly writing is the criterion. Unlike Najafi and Ansari, Shirazi wrote relatively little, mainly commentaries on Ansari's works, and none of his compositions acquired the renown of those of his predecessors.[17] In a revealing remark, Shirazi's former classmate Mirza Habiballah Rashti reportedly said that of Ansari's three distinguished qualities he (Rashti) had inherited superiority of learning (a'lamiyat), while Shirazi had succeeded to Ansari's worldly leadership (ri'asat). As for his piety, Rashti added, Ansari took it to his grave.[18] Rashti's denial of exemplary piety for himself and Shirazi may have been intended to contrast Ansari's idealized figure with the realities of his own time, or to criticize Shirazi and the type of leadership he represented as somewhat incompatible with piety.[19] The distinction Rashti drew between learning and leadership, which was repeated by various contemporary sources, reflects a division of labor within the 'ulama' establishment and the difference between his own status and Shirazi's.[20]

When Ashtiyani reportedly rejected Shirazi's offer to be the leader following Ansari's death, he added that the leadership required a person with "comprehensive qualities, smart and well-versed in politics (siyasat-madar) and in [public] affairs," implying that these qualifications were the decisive criteria for Shirazi's selection.[21] Some of those who had attended the meeting regarded Hasan Najmabadi as the greater jurist. However, he was deemed as too ascetic to be qualified for leadership, an interesting reason which indicates the dissonance between the ideal and practical requirements for the post.[22] On the whole, Shirazi owed his position as the most prominent leader of his time to qualities other than scholarship alone, primarily to his great skills in building networks of patronage and his links with the Iranian Bazaar.

Unlike Ansari, who shunned issuing fatwas, Shirazi laid a greater emphasis on that field of activity. Several sources stress the fact that questions and petitions flowed to Samarra' from all corners of the Shi'i world, and that Shirazi took great care to answer them personally. Considering the number of mujtahids to whom he referred fatwas that were sent to him, the projected image and reputation of Shirazi as a leader attentive to his followers' needs is even more important than the actual fact.[23] He sensed correctly that, for the ordinary believer, fatwas and day-to-day attention to communal affairs were more important than the writing of theoretical works on minute details of law.

As a scion of a family of 'ulama' with long-established links to the networks of merchants in Shiraz and southern Iran, Shirazi had an advantage over other mujtahids in attracting merchant support and funds, which he used to expand his patronage network of students.[24] Merchants served as Shirazi's agents in various towns, channeling to him the fifth and other religious dues. In some cases, Shirazi allowed his merchant-agents to invest such funds in trade, and the profits were used to sustain his students. He also set up a trust fund to secretly support and bail out merchants in need.[25]

Shirazi's conduct toward the merchant community differed from that of many mujtahids in Iran. The latter's partiality in judicial proceedings, tendency to take bribes, and irregular conduct as trustees of *awqaf*, as well as hoarding and speculation in grain, gave rise to constant complaints by merchants. The lack of hierarchy in the Shar'i judicial system, which enabled mujtahids to issue rulings and then overrule them after receiving bribes, prompted many of the merchants to support the elevation of one mujtahid to a superior status in order to give his rulings greater weight. Residence in the shrine cities served as a proof of otherworldliness and honesty, which seemed to be lacking in Iran. In that sense Shirazi was the ideal candidate.[26] Improved transport resulting in the growth of pilgrimage to the shrine cities, and the installation of telegraph lines in Iraq and Iran facilitated communications with the shrine cities and the centralization of authority there.

Close relations with the merchant community resulted in an annual flow of tens of thousands of tumans to Samarra'.[27] Shirazi used the funds to expand his patronage of students and 'ulama' in the shrine cities and in Iran.[28] He reportedly dispatched to his agents lists of needy 'ulama' in various cities and towns to whom funds were to be given. Even while residing in Samarra', Shirazi provided financial support to 'ulama' and students in Najaf enabling him to maintain his influence in the rival center.[29] When Shi'is in Kashmir and Tibet appealed to him to send them teachers, Shirazi brought to Samarra' about a hundred students from both places at his own expense. He appointed teachers and translators and issued special stipends for them.[30] In addition, he extended his patronage to poets, both Iranian and Arab, who exercised an important influence on public opinion.[31]

Shirazi was also aided by the death of rival mujtahids such as Mahdi Kashif al-Ghita' in 1293/1876 and Husayn Kuhkamara'i in 1299/1881–82. Like Najafi before him, Shirazi sent his own representatives to towns where local 'ulama' families enjoyed longstanding authority, such as Kazimayn and Isfahan.[32] Moreover, he also obtained recognition of his authority from several locally established 'ulama' families in various towns in Iran.[33] These cases reflect another aspect of the preference of the Iranian merchants for a unified universal leadership centered in the shrine cities. Apparently, these 'ulama' needed to bolster their local prestige by acquiring the backing of a distinguished exemplar from the shrine cities.

Shirazi's position was also recognized by the Qajars. The shah himself accepted the insult he had received from Shirazi with good grace and if he bore a grudge he did not or could not afford to express it publicly.[34] The Qajars probably preferred Shirazi, who at that stage shunned politics, to the more politically minded and aggressive mujtahids of Tehran such as Mulla 'Ali Kani and subsequently Mirza Hasan Ashtiyani.

The 1891–92 tobacco protest, against the monopoly awarded the British Regie company on the sale of tobacco in Iran, elevated Shirazi to unprecedented authority over both ordinary believers and the entire religious establishment in Iran and Iraq. It transformed him from the preeminent and most influential mujtahid among other leaders into the acknowledged head of the 'ulama', whose authority was accepted by most other exemplars. Equally important, it added the political dimension to this authority for the first time since the 1826 declaration of Jihad. In that respect he surpassed Ansari, whose leadership was spiritual only. Throughout the tobacco protest the merchants, the 'ulama', and the radical members of the intelligentsia, each group for its own reasons, sought to increase Shirazi's involvement. Shirazi's correspondence with the shah regarding the concession indeed reflected his concern for the fate of the merchants and their trade.[35]

Although Shirazi was not the one to initiate the ban on tobacco as long as the concession remained valid, his intervention proved to be decisive. The first rulings banning tobacco came from Isfahan. But, reflecting the decline of Isfahan as a major religious center, these calls had only local impact.[36] The fact that none of the Iran-based mujtahids had authority beyond their own cities reflected the higher status enjoyed by Shirazi, and also prompted appeals to the more eminent leader in the shrine cities. In contrast to the ruling in Isfahan, the ruling issued by, or attributed to, Shirazi had universal impact throughout Iran.[37] Whether or not Shirazi himself wrote the famous ruling, or merely approved in retrospect the version written by Hasan Ashtiyani, is less important to the question of leadership than the fact that Ashtiyani needed to use Shirazi's name, and it was the latter's reputation that assured its universal acceptance.[38]

Only three mujtahids defied Shirazi's ruling: Sayyid 'Abdallah Bihbihani, a personal rival of Ashtiyani; Sayyid 'Ali Akbar Tafrishi, and the royalist Imam Jum'a of Tehran, Zayn al-'Abidin Khatunabadi, who refused to acknowledge the superiority of the Najaf mujtahids. Most mujtahids and emulators regarded Shirazi's prohibition as an "ordinance (*hukm*) binding on all Shi'is rather than a legal opinion (*fatwa*) binding only on the mujtahid's emulators."[39] Bihbihani, on the other hand, claimed that a *hukm* applied only to the plaintiff and the defendant, while a *fatwa* applied only to emulators. Since he was a mujtahid, Bihbihani argued, he was not bound by it.[40] Bihbihani's reasoning seems to reflect, in addition to personal rivalries, an advocacy for the traditional diffused leadership among the 'ulama' and an opposition to the idea of one supreme exemplar who would have juridical authority over other mujtahids and consequently endanger their independent status.

While the tobacco affair enhanced Shirazi's authority it also reflected its limitations. In December 1891, the 'ulama' of Tehran insisted on obtaining Shirazi's approval for any compromise proposal by the shah. However, only a few months later, when the crisis had passed its peak, splits appeared in the unified 'ulama' front. Ashtiyani was willing to compromise and end the boycott on smoking following the shah's pledges to annul the internal tobacco monopoly, ostensibly relying on Shirazi's original ruling. Although Shirazi himself took a tougher stand, he was unable to impose his views on Ashtiyani.[41] The inherent obstacles to a clear hierarchical authority within the 'ulama' establishment were far from overcome.

It was lay reformers rather than 'ulama' who consistently sought to transform Shirazi into the supreme leader of the Shi'a with binding authority in order to use the emerging type of religious leadership against the Qajars and against foreign intervention in Iran.[42] The success of the tobacco protest further convinced the radicals of the need to rely on the power of the 'ulama' in their own struggle to bring about change in Iran. Mirza Malkam Khan, Jamal al-Din Asadabadi "al-Afghani," and Mirza Aqa Khan Kirmani in the opposition newspaper *Qanun* were the most explicit in their designs for Shirazi. Kirmani proposed elevating Shirazi into a sort of a Shi'i pope, who would lead the 'ulama' to confront and overthrow the shah's tyranny. The radicals' ideas, however, had greater impact on the Iranian government, which hastened to denounce them to Shirazi as dangerous and irreligious agitators, than on the mujtahid himself.[43]

The tobacco affair further elevated Shirazi's popular status. Visiting Samarra' in 1308/1891, Muhsin al-Amin described the town as so packed with pilgrims that special permission was needed to enter it. As a manifestation of his unique status, Shirazi was termed the Renovator (*mujaddid*) of the fourteenth Hijri century.[44]

Shirazi and Najaf

Although Najaf lost students, pilgrims, and funds to Samarra', it did not lose its status as the leading center of learning for the Shi'i world during the height of Shirazi's fame. While Shirazi established himself as the leading exemplar in Samarra', the various mujtahids in Najaf continued to compete for students and funds among themselves.

The 'ulama' of Najaf did not form a united front against Shirazi to protect the status of their town partly because some of them maintained close relations with him, but equally important, because of the individualistic structure of teaching and leadership. Only rarely and at times of extreme crisis, as was the case during the Babi challenge, did the 'ulama' of the shrine cities act collectively. Shirazi's departure for Samarra' was not as serious a threat as the Babi affair.

Visiting Najaf around 1301/1883–84, Hajji Sayyah described the attempts of students of the competing mujtahids to lure pilgrims to their teachers, so that they (the students) would benefit from their donations. "What miracles they attribute to their master," he exclaims, "and what slander they heap on the others who are his rivals."[45] Quite a few 'ulama' themselves were uncomfortable with the intensity of the competition. When 'Ali b. Husayn al-Khaqani was asked to compare his contemporaries with 'ulama' of earlier generations, he replied that the earlier 'ulama' had been "Imams," while the present ones were "kings," that is excessively engaged in worldly affairs.[46]

Among the mujtahids in Najaf, Mirza Habiballah Rashti emerged as the most prominent teacher and scholar. As one of Ansari's favored disciples, he was regarded as equal or second only to Kuhkamara'i as a teacher. After the latter's death in 1299/1881–82, Rashti came to be known as the "leader of the learned" in Najaf. His classes were the largest and were attended by both Arab and Iranian students, among them many of the mujtahids of the following generation. As mentioned above, various 'ulama' and his own disciples claimed his superiority over Shirazi.[47] However, in contrast to Shirazi, Rashti was renowned for shunning the leadership role because of his great piety, or more correctly, his unsuitable disposition. He was also famous for his aversion to issuing *fatwas*. Consequently, he was emulated by relatively few people.[48]

The Turkish-speaking faction did not dissolve following Husayn Kuhkamara'i's death, indicating that the ethnic split had become firmly institutionalized in the shrine cities. Two of Kuhkamara'i's former disciples emerged as rival leaders: Hasan Mamaqani and Muhammad Iravani. Mamaqani, who had been responsible for issuing *fatwas* in

Kuhkamara'i's court, regarded himself as the rightful successor. However, while Kuhkamara'i was on his deathbed, as Mamaqani's son asserts, "devilish people" (*shayatin al-nas*) intervened, and caused a rift between Mamaqani and Kuhkamara'i. Consequently, in what is implied as a designation by the teacher, Iravani was the one who succeeded to Kuhkamara'i's circle of study, while Mamaqani set up his own indepen-dent class.[49]

Emulation in the Turkish-speaking areas was now divided between the two Turkish rivals and Shirazi, who expanded his network following Kuhkamara'i's death. Iravani was also emulated in India and parts of Iraq. Following Iravani's death in 1306/1888–89, Mamaqani consolidated his position as a first-rank mujtahid, gaining the alle-giance of the majority in Azarbayjan and the Caucasus as well as in Rasht, Tustar, and the Shi'i community in Istanbul.[50] In other words, the networks of patronage and with them the constituencies of the various leaders fluctuated and were reshaped with the death of each senior mujtahid.

Another important group in Najaf was composed of Shirazi's former disciples and other mujtahids who recognized his leadership. Most prominent among them were Mirza Husayn Khalili, Muhammad Taha Najaf, Muhammad Kazim Akhund Khorasani, and Muhammad Kazim Yazdi Tabataba'i.[51] Although originally from Tabriz and supported by mujtahids from northern Iran, the Najaf family had become Arabized and Muhammad Taha himself came to be recognized as one of the leading Arab mujtahids in Najaf.[52] Muhammad Taha's followers asked Shirazi to refer *fatwas* to him as well as to Husayn Khalili, in order to enhance his reputation as a protege of the great leader. Since Shirazi did not know him, Muhammad Taha came to Samarra' where he gave a sermon in order to impress Shirazi and gain his approval. At a later stage, Muhammad Taha Najaf brought some of his own students to Samarra' to be given *ijazat ijtihad* by Shirazi himself.[53] Such relations of semi-subordination to a mujtahid where previous direct teacher–disciple relationships had not existed were not common in the community of learning. They stemmed from the need of junior mujtahids to acquire widespread recognition and backing from their superiors in a period of intense competition, and reflected Shirazi's growing influence.

The case of Hadi Tehrani (see above), who was excommunicated in 1303/1885–86 reflects the extent but also the limits of Shirazi's power in Najaf.[54] As early as six years before the tobacco protest, Habiballah Rashti, who initiated the excommunication, took care to obtain Shirazi's support for such an extreme step. Concurrently, Arab 'ulama' headed by Muhammad Husayn al-Kazimi and the Turkish mujtahid Muhammad Iravani defended Hadi Tehrani, thereby indicating their independence or even defiance *vis-à-vis* Rashti and Shirazi.[55]

In Karbala' too Shirazi's superiority was not undisputed. In 1892 a British envoy, Major Jennings, sought to persuade Zayn al-'Abidin Mazandarani of Karbala' to accept Sayyid Muhammad Baqir Tabataba'i as the distributor of the Oudh Bequest on the grounds that Shirazi himself supported him. Mazandarani replied angrily: "Muhammad Hasan has nothing whatever to do with Karbala'. *I am (man khodam)* the Mujtahid here" (original emphasis).[56] Mazandarani's sense of confidence was not without foundation. When Jennings enquired among local mujtahids, notables, and ordinary people about the relative status of mujtahids in Karbala', the general consensus was that "the two great mujtahids of first rank, and far above all others were ... Sherazi of Samarra', and Shaikh Zain-ul-'Abidin of Karbala'." Whereas Iranians placed Shirazi above Mazandarani, Arabs "regard the latter as equal, or just a tiny bit the bigger of the two."[57]

In conclusion, although Shirazi wielded influence and authority as no other contemporary mujtahid had done, his superiority was never unanimously and universally acknowledged. He himself was cautious not to attach doctrinal justification to his superior status. Nor did he elaborate Ansari's concept of the supreme exemplar, particularly in its problematic point of designating the most learned mujtahid.[58] His own position did not fundamentally change the diffused structure of the religious establishment or of the institution of leadership itself. The widespread authority he had gained was personal and limited to himself alone. It did not survive as an institution.

Leadership in the post-Shirazi period

Shirazi's abstention from institutionalizing a single-headed leadership is best manifested in the disintegration of his own learning complex in Samarra' after his death in 1312/1895. Of the three senior disciples – *aqtab* (Poles) as they were called – whom he had appointed as teachers in his circle of study, only Muhammad Taqi Shirazi remained in Samarra'. The two others, Isma'il Sadr al-Din Isfahani and Muhammad Fashariki, as well as most students, went back to Najaf or Karbala'. A group of Shirazi's followers adhered to his son, Mirza 'Ali (d. 1355/ 1936), who had remained in Samarra'. But as in other cases, descent alone was insufficient for the attainment of leadership.[59]

The disintegration of the community of learning at Samarra' was due to the disappearance of the major or even only unifying factor that had held the disciples together, the one master, Shirazi, and the personal allegiance each student owed to him. An additional factor was the decline of pilgrimage following Shirazi's death. Shirazi's personal fame was sufficient to attract pilgrims even though Samarra' was relatively far from Najaf and Karbala', the principal pilgrimage sites. The prestige of his disciples, at least in the initial period, was insufficient for that purpose. Shirazi personally overshadowed Najaf, but the latter had the advantage of a wide choice of teachers with whom Samarra' could not compete. Ottoman hostility and pressures also contributed to Samarra''s decline.[60]

With Shirazi's death Najaf regained its superiority as the major center of learning and leadership for the Shi'i world. As in the period following Ansari's death, the community of 'ulama' was far from unified under one exemplar. The increasing number of mujtahids, each of whom was able to consolidate his own network of disciples and followers, diffused the leadership structure.

The relative ranking among mujtahids and personal relations among them at the turn of the twentieth century can be inferred from two *fatwas* signed by several mujtahids,[61] and by Marine's report, a rudimentary British poll conducted in May 1902 in order to establish which mujtahids were eligible to benefit from the Oudh Bequest.[62] The order of precedence of the mujtahids in these documents reflects the relative interplay between scholarship, patronage, and the image of piety in the determination of status. An additional factor that became more important in this period was involvement in Iranian politics, which reflected the eminence of certain mujtahids, and consolidated it even further.

The upper echelons of the 'ulama' of the shrine cities were divided into two tiers. The first was composed of ten or eleven mujtahids who enjoyed wide acclaim and recognition from their peers, some of them in Iran as well. The second was made up of ten to fifteen mujtahids whose reputation did not extend beyond their home towns. Four mujtahids from the first group – Mirza Husayn Khalili Tehrani, Muhammad Fadil Sharabiyani, Hasan Mamaqani, and Muhammad Kazim Khorasani – who were described by both the Qajars and the British as "the four great Mujteheds" played an important role in the mobilization of public pressure against the excessive corruption and pro-Russian policies of the Qajars prior to the Constitutional Revolution.[63]

Modern Shi'i sources state that following Shirazi's death Khorasani emerged as the "supreme exemplar" for the Shi'i world.[64] Yet this statement stands in sharp contradiction to the relatively low ranking that his peers accorded him in Marine's report and in the *Libas-i Taqva fatwa*. The discrepancy lies in the gap between the ideal of determining spiritual leadership and the reality of 'ulama' politics.

As a scholar, Khorasani was probably the most important mujtahid at the time thanks to his book *Kifayat al-usul*, which developed Ansari's work, and which superseded Qummi's *Qawanin al-usul* as the standard text of the *sutuh* level to the present day. Hitherto, the "sources of *fiqh*" i.e. the Qur'an, Traditions, consensus (*ijma'*), and reason (*'aql*) were regarded as the subject matter of *usul*. Khorasani extended it to any general topic related to any of individual *usul* problems by further developing the principles of procedure (*usul 'amaliyya*).[65]

Khorasani's long-term impact on the study of *usul* explains why later Shi'i sources regarded him as the supreme exemplar after Shirazi above his colleagues whose writings did not always outlast them. His higher ranking in the *fatwa* published in Tehran and greater appreciation in Karbala' suggest that scholarship was more visible from a distance, whereas personal rivalries played a more important role among mujtahids in the same town.

Khorasani had remained in Najaf following Shirazi's departure for Samarra', apparently acting as Shirazi's representative in Najaf. According to al-Kazimi, Shirazi had groomed him for the succession and referred *fatwas* to him. He was recognized as the unquestionable master of *usul* even before Sharabiyani's death, and had a large number of students, of whom more than 120 were universally acknowledged (*musallam*) mujtahids.[66] The number is the more remarkable considering the very low stipends he gave them. However, his failure to build a large network of agents and raise funds affected his leadership position.[67] Evidently, scholarship alone was not sufficient for the attainment of supreme leadership.

Kazim Yazdi's case also demonstrates the complexities of leadership in Najaf. Yazdi's book *al-'Urwa al-wuthqa* was probably the most important *fiqh* work written at the turn of the twentieth century. It replaced *Najat al-'ibad* by Najafi, and is still being taught at the *sutuh* stage of Shi'i learning. At the beginning of their careers as independent teachers Yazdi was overshadowed by Akhund Khorasani, but he gradually emerged as the leading *fiqh* teacher in Najaf. His reluctance to intervene in politics at the beginning of the century rendered his position in Najaf less important. However, unlike Khorasani who would become his future rival, Yazdi was more skillful in attracting funds and building patronage networks. Consequently, he would emerge as the most important exemplar during the later stages of the Constitutional Revolution until his death in 1919.[68]

Unlike Khorasani and Yazdi, Mirza Husayn Khalili did not write much. His writings did not circulate in Najaf, and none were published except for a commentary on Najafi's *Najat al-'ibad*. According to several sources, Shirazi used to refer *fatwas* to Khalili in cases when he was too prudent to issue them himself. Yet, following Shirazi's death he was regarded by many as an "absolute leader" (*ra'is mutlaq*) and head of the community of learning in Najaf. He did show great skill in building networks of patronage and had a large following in Iran, Iraq, India, and Lebanon.[69]

Muhammad Fadil Sharabiyani (d. 1322/1904–05) was one of Kuhkamara'i's leading disciples, and attained leadership status after the death of Muhammad Iravani in 1306/1888–89. He gradually climbed in seniority, first within the Turkish group and subsequently in the larger Shi'i community following the deaths of Muhammad Husayn al-Kazimi and Shirazi. He had a large following in Azarbayjan, northern Iran, the Fars region, parts of Khuzistan, Iraq, and even India. Sharabiyani was one of the leading *usul* teachers in Najaf, with about150 students registered in his payroll.[70]

Sharabiyani surpassed Hasan Mamaqani – his senior in years – as a politically influential mujtahid. The disparity in their position was aptly explained by Arthur Hardinge, the British ambassador in Iran, who said that Mamaqani "was in no sense a man of the world."[71] In addition to his political influence in Iran, Sharabiyani established good relations with the Ottomans. Aside from Mamaqani, the three other mujtahids had built several madrasas in Najaf, indicating both the increasing flow of funds to the town and the importance of this act for the attainment of leadership status.[72]

Seeking to give greater effectiveness to their political stand, the mujtahids of Najaf had "unanimously appointed Sharabiyani as their head in all matters relating to their ... objections against the Shah of Persia."[73] This development was highly significant in view of the traditionally diffused and informal structure of leadership among the 'ulama', and only the worsening crisis in Iran could have led them to pursue such a course of action. It should be noted, however, that Sharabiyani's election was limited to the political sphere, and did not endow him with special authority in doctrinal matters. In other words, he was not elected as the supreme exemplar. Equally important, the nomination was only for a limited term, and the political developments of the constitutional period only exacerbated the divisions among the 'ulama'. The other senior mujtahids did not play a prominent political role at the time.

Arab and Indian mujtahids were clearly inferior to their Iranian counterparts. Whereas no Indian mujtahids appear on the two *fatwas*, those who are mentioned in Marine's report were pointed out mostly by fellow Indians and not by Iranians. Likewise, no Arab mujtahids, except for Muhammad Taha Najaf, were mentioned by Marine or in the *Libas-i Taqva fatwa*. Muhammad Taha Najaf's name appeared only after four Iranians in Nuri's *fatwa*, determined primarily by Iranian mujtahids who tended to look down on their Arab colleagues. The other Arab mujtahids who signed the *fatwa*, all members of long-established families, were placed at the bottom of the list.

Several points are worth mentioning on both ranking and interpersonal relations among the mujtahids as revealed by Marine's report. The way each mujtahid acknowledged or denied the ijtihad of his colleagues demonstrates the weaknesses and arbitrariness of the system. There was no clear criterion determining true scholarship while subjective considerations such as personal rivalries and jealousies played too great a role in their evaluations. Accordingly, the reputation of fewer mujtahids from Karbala' transcended the boundaries of their town, or the broad ranks of the 'ulama'.

Personal piety was explicitly mentioned by many, particularly the laymen, as a leading consideration in ranking mujtahids. Ja'far b. 'Ali Naqi Tabataba'i, for instance, acknowledged Khorasani as a first-rank mujtahid in Najaf, but cautioned that he was "not to be trusted." Likewise, he raised charges of corruption against his cousin, Muhammad Baqir, with whom he competed for the distribution of the Oudh Bequest. Sayyid 'Abd al-Husayn, custodian of the Imam Husayn shrine in Karbala', said that only two mujtahids – Isma'il Sadr al-Din Isfahani and Muhammad Taha Najaf – had "worked for God." Such a factor explains the low status of Husayn Mazandarani, who had been openly despised by some of his father's admirers as a "scoundrel" and as a lecher back in 1892.[74]

Age was an important consideration for many mujtahids in naming others, indicating a reluctance to support younger upstarts, and perhaps explaining the lower ranking of Akhund Khorasani and Kazim Yazdi. When Hashim Qazvini, for instance, named other mujtahids, he said explicitly that those he named were older than himself and he could, therefore, acknowledge them. Several mujtahids distinguished between recognition by the 'ulama' and by the laity. Ja'far Tabataba'i said of both Isma'il Sadr al-Din and Husayn Mazandarani that they were not regarded as mujtahids "except by the people," which was deemed less worthy than recognition by fellow mujtahids.

Shi'i religious leadership during the last third of the nineteenth century was characterized by a diffusion among several scholars and with the emergence of Samarra' under Mirza Hasan Shirazi as a rival center to Najaf. This process, which reflected the weaknesses of Ansari's concept of the supreme exemplar, was largely caused by the inflation in the number of senior mujtahids, none of whom achieved scholarly recognition above and beyond his peers. In addition, the ethnic factor became even more important with the emergence of a Turkish faction in addition to the Persian and Arab. Overall, the Iranian immigrants retained or even enhanced their dominance in Najaf. In Karbala' too, the local Tabataba'i and Shahristani families were surpassed by the immigrant Ardakani and Mazandarani.

Shirazi's rise to prominence was due more to his skills as a teacher and patron and to his close links with the Bazaar community in Iran than to pure scholarship. While Shirazi's complex of learning (hawza) in Samarra' seemed to overshadow Najaf for a while, the latter remained the most important center, as it retained its nature as a community of learning rather than a one-man enterprise. As with his predecessors Najafi and Ansari, Shirazi's authority was never universally undisputed, and he did not seek to attach doctrinal justification to his authority.

The other element that became more important at the beginning of the twentieth century was open involvement in Iranian politics. While political activity was a one-time venture for Shirazi, it became more a prevalent feature during later periods.

5   Determinants of status and leadership

The madrasa in medieval Damascus, and implicitly in other cities as well, it has been argued, was not designed to produce elites, but on the contrary served as an instrument of the elites to reproduce themselves and preserve their power. The evolution of the Ottoman system definitely supports that conclusion since high positions were monopolized by a small number of families.[1]

The Shi'i community of learning during the nineteenth century, like almost any other educational system in the world, enabled the clerical elite to reproduce itself and preserve its high status. Yet, it seems to me that the Shi'i learning system in the shrine cities was based first and foremost on merit rather than on ascriptive factors. It thus served as an important channel for upward social mobility and for recruiting new elements into the clerical elite in Iran and Iraq. I will elucidate these points by examining the relative weight of the various components – ascriptive and attained – that determined status and influence in the community of learning, particularly among the mujtahids. In addition, I will examine the mechanisms of elite control.

In medieval Muslim society a man's worth was often described in the terms of *nasab* and *hasab*. *Nasab* is genealogy, "the influence of a man's pedigree on his condition, whereas *Hasab* refers to honor acquired through deeds."[2] Both *nasab* and *hasab* as well as their general meanings survived within the 'ulama' society well into the nineteenth century. In his *ijaza* to Mahdi Shahristani, for instance, Bihbihani praises Mahdi as possessing "excellent and exalted *hasab* as well as lofty [and] elevated *nasab*." Likewise, the marriage between the children of two Lebanese 'ulama' in Najaf was described as joining the "distinction of *nasab* to the loftiness and eminence of *hasab*."[3] It is unclear, however, whether the differentiation between the two terms did not become blurred in the course of the centuries.[4]

The importance of *nasab* in the shrine cities is attested by the care with which genealogies were preserved and referred to as well as by the continuing prominence of certain families even though not all their members were first-rank mujtahids. Another example of high status earned by descent is Muhammad Husayn al-Kazimi's apology to his student, Shaykh Ahmad Jawahiri, a grandson of Muhammad Hasan Najafi, following an argument between the two, because of Ahmad's ancestry.[5]

In medieval Muslim society a person could acquire the *nasab* of his patron, although several generations had to pass before the transfer of *nasab* was regarded as complete. Adoption of a more respectable *nasab* was possible during the eighteenth and nineteenth centuries too, although this was primarily through marriage. The most prominent example of such a practice was the adoption of the *nisba* Shahristani by Mirza Mahdi's son-in-law, Muhammad Hasan Husayni Mar'ashi.[6] As in earlier periods, a distinguished *nasab* compelled a person to live up to the level of his ancestors, or else he might be accused of squandering it. When the mid-ranking 'alim Husayn b. 'Ali Al Mahfuz al-'Amili boasted of his family's *nasab*, he was admonished that it was no concern of his, and that his duty was to study and be like his ancestors.[7]

Still as in the medieval period, in the absence of bureaucratic and "natural" social hierarchies, the acquisition of status and prestige was the outcome of competitive struggle or of implicit "negotiations" among 'ulama' over honorifics and symbols of seniority. Fame rather than title was the marker of social capacity.[8]

Among the many ways to negotiate and determine status, a common one was by appointing a prayer leader (*imam jama'a*), symbolizing leadership status. Even the location where one served as a prayer imam became a symbol of status, as praying at the shrine courtyards (*sahn*) was more prestigious than an ordinary mosque. Thus, when Muhammad Iravani, the leader of the Turkish faction, died in 1306/ 1888–89, his rival Hasan Mamaqani, who had served as a prayer leader at another corner of the shrine court, took Iravani's place, thereby demonstrating that he had succeeded him in his leadership position.[9]

The not uncommon attendance of mujtahids at the *dars al-kharij* of their colleagues was another sign of appreciation and acknowledgment of superiority. Ranking was established or recognized by order of visits among mujtahids. An 'alim who was the first to visit a colleague signaled a recognition of his host's superior status. Returning the call showed reciprocity or a certain act of grace by the more distinguished visitor.[10] The social and scholarly *majalis* too were important arenas for determining relative status. Questions such as who attended whose *majlis*, the number of participants, and the order of seating were important signals of status.[11] The order of signatories in a joint ruling was a symbol of seniority and occasionally a source of bitter disputes among mujtahids.

In a scholarly community naming a scholar by a book he had written was one of the most respectable of honors. The most famous mujtahids were often identified by their books rather than by their names, as was the case in the Jewish rabbinate.[12] An even greater honorific was naming entire families after the founder's book, such as the Kashif al-Ghita' or Jawahiri clans. A mujtahid's fame was also measured at the time of his death by the number of communities in which markets were closed and *Surat al-Fatiha* read in commemoration. The most distinguished mujtahids had markets closed and *fawatih* read in their memory throughout Iran and the Shi'i communities of India. Mirza Hasan Shirazi's funeral which passed from Samarra' via Karbala' to Najaf drew thousands of tribesmen who fought among themselves for the privilege of carrying or passing his bier marking his elevated status.[13]

While there was no official hierarchy among the mujtahids, the marked increase in their numbers which eroded the value of the *ijazat ijtihad*, and the competition for leadership, led to the creation and assumption of titles that were intended to signal a certain hierarchy. The first to adopt the title Hujjat al-Islam wal-Muslimin (Proof of Islam and the Muslims) were the Iran-based mujtahids Muhammad Baqir Shafti in Isfahan and Asadallah Burujirdi in Burujird, who both claimed *marja'iyya*. The appearance of this title first in Iran was probably due to the greater intensity of political and financial concerns there which made it more useful for mujtahids to assume it.[14] It is unclear precisely when mujtahids in the shrine cities adopted that title, but it was used to refer to Abu al-Qasim Tabataba'i of Karbala' as early as 1884.[15]

By the end of the nineteenth century all senior mujtahids in the shrine cities had assumed the title of Hujjat al-Islam. By the beginning of the twentieth century Mirza Husayn Khalili was described by the loftier title of Ayatallah (*fi al-'Alamayn*, God's sign in the world) in addition to Hujjat al-Islam.[16] The rapid spread of the title Hujjat al-Islam suggests that it was due to the initiative of the mujtahids themselves rather than a spontaneous act by emulators. In the absence of regulatory bodies and mechanisms who would officially confer such a title, its assumption was a product of tacit negotiations between the mujtahid who coveted it and his peers who could accept or reject it, or between the disciples and followers who honored their exemplar and others in the community.[17] Both titles reflect the self-perception of the 'ulama' as well as the image they sought to project to their emulators as the embodiment of Islam, maintained by their very presence.

Leadership

In addition to the various means of acquiring or determining status, the struggle for leadership had its own rules and prerequisites. *Nasab*, as well as other ascriptive characteristics such as ethnicity, clerical descent, and local roots were important contributors to status in the community of learning. However, an examination of the leadership ranks based on the sixty-nine senior mujtahids in the shrine cities during the century will show that none of these attributes were necessary or sufficient conditions in themselves for the attainment of high status. Rather, as I have illustrated in the previous chapters, scholarship and the ability to form widespread patronage ties were the crucial elements.[18]

As was the case with the increase of the entire 'ulama' population in the shrine cities during the nineteenth century, the growth in the mujtahids' ranks was mainly due to migration from Iran. Whereas during the first half of the nineteenth century native Iranian mujtahids in Najaf outnumbered the immigrants by eight to four, the situation was radically inverted thereafter. During the second half of the century immigrant Iranians outnumbered native mujtahids by sixteen to four. Overall, migrant Iranian mujtahids (both Persians and Turkish speakers) outnumbered the native-born Iranians in Najaf by the ratio of twenty to twelve due to the consolidation of Najaf as the leading center for the entire Shi'i world at the expense of the Iranian centers. The relative stagnation of Karbala' is reflected by the fact that native Iranian mujtahids slightly outnumbered the immigrants throughout the century.[19] The ratio between natives and immigrants among Iraqi mujtahids (eleven to three), is inverse to the one among Iranians, and they will be discussed separately.[20]

Being an immigrant without the support of a family network in the shrine cities, then, was not an obstacle to the attainment of high status. The four immigrant Persian mujtahids who studied in Karbala' during the first half of the nineteenth century were all first-rank mujtahids. Moreover, Hasan Ardakani, and particularly Zayn al-'Abidin Mazandarani, both migrants, had a greater following in Iran during the second half of the century than the various members of the long-established Tabataba'i and Shahristani families.

This trend was even more visible in Najaf, where the most prominent mujtahids during the second half of the century, such as Murtada Ansari, Mirza Hasan Shirazi, Fadil Sharabiyani, Akhund Khorasani, and Kazim Yazdi, were all immigrants. During that period members of the native Bahr al-'Ulum family did not enjoy the same status inside or outside Najaf. It is very likely, therefore, that family connections in their home towns helped the immigrant mujtahids to consolidate networks of patronage and leadership status in Iran.

The greater availability of higher education in the cities helps explain the 60 percent (eighteen out of thirty) share of urban-born mujtahids among the immigrants compared with less than 15 percent of urban dwellers for the entire Iranian population during the nineteenth century. In addition, such mujtahids enjoyed an advantage, in attracting students from their home cities, over those who came from villages or small towns, in view of the tendency of students to come first to a teacher from their own region. Likewise, there was greater likelihood that a mujtahid from a city would enjoy greater financial support and emulation in his place of origin, which would provide him with a better starting position for consolidating a support network. On the other hand, the presence of village-born mujtahids – at least eight out of thirty – indicates the openness of the establishment to gifted men from humble backgrounds.[21] Muhammad Baqir Bihbihani and Mirza Hasan Shirazi seem to have been the only senior mujtahids who came from well-connected 'ulama' families in Iran. There is no information on the other mujtahids.

Concurrently, birth in the shrine cities was not necessarily an obstacle to attaining high status in Iran. Husayn Najaf at the beginning of the nineteenth century, and even more so Muhammad Hasan Najafi in mid-century, had large followings in Iran. The same could be said at the end of the century of Hasan Mamaqani, who had spent most of his life since early childhood in the shrine cities.

Sayyids were more heavily represented among the Persian mujtahids – 58.7 percent (twenty-seven out of forty-six) – than among the general Persian 'ulama' – 34.9 percent (325 out of 932) of the 'ulama' population in the shrine cities. In addition, they were more heavily represented among the Persians than among Turkish and Iraqi Arab mujtahids – 58.7 percent, 17 percent, and 7 percent respectively.[22] The mujtahids who were both sayyids and descendants of clerical families constituted about 33 percent of the entire elite group (twenty-three out of sixty-nine). In other words, there was a sizable group of 'ulama' families of sayyid origin in Iran, going back to Safavid or even earlier times, for example the Tabataba'is and Shahristanis, who managed to preserve senior status for generations. It is likely that their sayyid lineage was helpful in preserving their prominence throughout the years. On the other hand, sayyid extraction did not necessarily indicate originally high social status. Kazim Yazdi, for instance, was a sayyid, but also a peasant's son.

Notwithstanding its importance, sayyid lineage was neither a necessary nor a sufficient condition for the attainment of high status.

Murtada Ansari, Zayn al-'Abidin Mazandarani, 'Ali and Husayn Khalili, and Akhund Khorasani, to name a few mujtahids, as well as four out of the five Turkish mujtahids, were not sayyids. Yet these mujtahids enjoyed higher status than the Bahr al-'Ulum, the Tabataba'i, and Shahristani sayyid families. The distribution of sayyid mujtahids along time does not indicate a significant change in numbers during the century. Interestingly, during the 1970s all the six senior supreme exemplars in Iran were sayyids, reflecting a certain closure of ranks.

Clerical descent too was neither a necessary nor sufficient condition for high status. It was, however, an important contributing factor, as shown by the higher ratio of descendants of clerical families among the Iranian mujtahid elite compared with the larger Iranian 'ulama' population in the shrine cities, about 70 percent and about 40 percent respectively. Among the immigrant mujtahids the descendants of clerical families amounted to about 45 percent.[23]

The high percentage of mujtahids of clerical descent was largely due to the tendency of sons to follow their fathers' occupations in traditional societies as well as to the advantage in life that people from a more educated and wealthier background enjoy in any society. Sons of prominent mujtahids received a better education than recent migrants from villages, already at the lowest levels of their instruction. More importantly, they could get *ijazat ijtihad* from their fathers with greater ease and at a younger age than newcomers, and suffered less from the financial constraints that beset many new students. Marriages among leading 'ulama' families also helped sons of prominent mujtahids to attain high status.

The share of Iranian mujtahids of non-clerical origin rose from about 16 percent (four out of twenty-four) during the first half of the nineteenth century to about 41 percent (twelve out of twenty-nine) during the second half. This increase correlates with the growing percentage of immigrant mujtahids compared with those born in the shrine cities in the course of the century. As the overall 'ulama' population grew toward the second half of the century, it became easier for mujtahids of non-clerical origin to attain high status, while the importance of the local established families declined.

The numbers of mujtahids descended from clerical families may seem at first glance high enough to justify the notion of an elite reproducing itself, and counter the claim of a religious establishment largely based on merit. However, it was more open than the Ottoman system, in which almost 86 percent of the muftis who held the office of Shaykh al-Islam in both the pre-Tanzimat and the Tanzimat periods came from clerical families. During the 1703–1839 period eleven 'ulama' families dominated the position of Shaykh al-Islam in the Ottoman Empire, with only a few exceptions. In contrast, five of the nine Shaykhs al-Azhar during the nineteenth century were born in villages, indicating a low-class origin.[24] Apparently, institutions of learning – Sunni and Shiʻi – were more open to talent than were the administrative positions.

Moreover, the importance of clerical descent as a determinant of status would be misleading without taking into account the ranking within the community of learning itself. True, several of the founding families of the community of learning, such as the Bahr al-ʻUlum, Tabatabaʼi, and Shahristani, retained high status throughout the century. However, not all the members of these renowned ʻulamaʼ families achieved such status on their own account. Of the twenty-six members of the Bahr al-ʻUlum family, on whom I had data, only six could be counted among the elite, and not all of these were first-rank mujtahids. The same was true of other local families. Likewise in Karbalaʼ Zayn al-ʻAbidin Mazandarani was of non-clerical origin, but enjoyed greater prominence than members of the Tabatabaʼi and Shahristani families.

In contrast, while only two of the eight native mujtahids of Najaf were of non-clerical origin, they were of the three first-ranking mujtahids of that group. Likewise, of the five Iranian mujtahids of non-clerical origin who migrated to Karbalaʼ, three were first rank. In comparison, only five out of the eleven native mujtahids of clerical descent in Karbalaʼ were first rank. Again, a greater number of ʻulamaʼ of non-clerical origin attained first-rank status during the second part of the century, commensurate with the growth of the entire ʻulamaʼ establishment.

Even clerical descent by itself is too general a term for assessing its importance for status without taking into consideration the position of the mujtahid's family within the clerical community. Compared with the Bahr al-ʻUlum, Shahristani, and Tabatabaʼi families, the clerical descent of Murtada Ansari and Hasan Ardakani could not have been significant for their position as both came from small provincial towns, Dizful and Ardakan. Similarly, Akhund Khorasani's father was a minor preacher. All these mujtahids attained greater prominence than members of established ʻulamaʼ families thanks to their superior scholarship.

The composition of the small group of Arab mujtahids was markedly different from that of the Iranians, indicating the greater importance of ascriptive rather than acquired factors in the determination of status among the Arabs and the more closed nature of the Arab elite. On the other hand, the size of the Arab group may be too small to make any meaningful statements. The difference between the Arab faction, which was dominated by the Kashif al-Ghitaʼ clan (eight of the fourteen Arab mujtahids in the sample), and the Iranian is probably due to the recently converted tribal constituency in Iraq which did not provide a large number of mujtahids, and to the smaller size of the Arab community which enabled the Kashif al-Ghita' clan to maintain its influence among the Arab 'ulama'.

The dominance of the Kashif al-Ghita's led to a situation in Najaf whereby natives outnumbered Arab immigrant mujtahids by a ratio of eleven to two. Likewise, descendants of 'ulama' outnumbered those of non-clerical origin by a ratio of eleven to three. Yet, Muhammad Husayn al-Kazimi, the rival of the Kashif al-Ghita' family, was the son of a poor artisan from Kazimayn. His case suggests that only very gifted Arab scholars of humble background could attain high status. On the other hand only one Arab mujtahid was a sayyid, in sharp contrast to the Persian group.

Dynasties of religious leaders were less common and less important in the shrine cities than in Iran or Awadh. The Bahr al-'Ulum, the Tabataba'i, and Kashif al-Ghita' families were exceptional in holding a leadership position for several generations. An important factor in their status was a certain aura that surrounded their founders during the formative period of Usulism. The major source of influence of the Bahr al-'Ulum and Tabataba'i was the "Indian Money" and subsequently the Oudh Bequest, which became their hereditary possession. They thus controlled an independent and permanent financial resource, necessary for the maintenance of leadership regardless of true scholarly status. Yet even the two Iranian families belonged to the second tier of leadership for most of the period, and their authority hardly exceeded the shrine cities. Likewise the Arab Kashif al-Ghita' family kept its position mainly within the Arab faction and at times was overshadowed by other Arab mujtahids.

Local 'ulama' dynasties in Iran managed to perpetuate their leadership status largely thanks to their control over the posts of Shaykh al-Islam and Imam Jum'a. Succession within the family was a common feature in the Iranian bureaucracy, and religious administration was no different in that respect. Succession within the family was also common in Sufi orders, where masters could appoint their sons as their successors, and bestow their charisma upon them. In some places, such as Egypt, such practices required the approval of the ruler.[25]

An additional reason for the longevity of dynasties in Iran and in the Sunni world was control of awqaf. Describing the situation in Cairo under the Mamluks, Berkey noted that the tendency for – and later the provisions in endowment deeds allowing – sons to inherit the fathers' teaching posts contributed to a restriction of social movement and the

concentration of career opportunities in the hands of particular families.[26] The situation in the Ottoman Empire was not much different.
The importance of controlling madrasas for the perpetuation of leadership and patronage is demonstrated by the few *awqaf* that existed in the
shrine cities, such as the madrasas held by the Kashif al-Ghita' and
Tabataba'i clans. It also explains the efforts of the leading mujtahids at
the turn of the twentieth century to establish their own madrasas.

However, due to the scarcity of *awqaf* in the shrine cities, they were
less important than patronage, which provided the aspiring leader with
the essential link to the ordinary believer, particularly the bazaaris in
Iran who financed the entire community. Whereas fathers could pass on
endowed chairs to their sons, in the absence of large-scale *awqaf* they
could not pass on to them their popularity as teachers and their
networks of patronage, which had been forged on a personal basis.
Consequently, in the absence of *awqaf*, every mujtahid had to attract
students and forge his own patronage networks based on his merits as
scholar and teacher. Descent from an illustrious father then, although
helpful, was not sufficient. Consequently, in quite a few cases, sons of
notable mujtahids chose to leave the shrine cities and settle in Iran since
they failed to establish sufficiently high status based on their own
merits.[27]

The tendency of fathers to grant *ijazat* to their sons at an early age is
often described as a corruption of the system. Chamberlain rejects the
notion of corruption, arguing that this practice was designed as an
essential strategy implemented by the elite in order to reproduce itself.[28]
Such phenomena were not absent from the shrine cities and the Iranian
religious establishment as shown by those mujtahids who granted their
sons *ijazat ijtihad* while they were only young children.[29] Moreover,
various mujtahids granted *ijazat* with lenience as part of their efforts to
build patronage networks in their bid for leadership. However, as far as
the available sources tell, the purchasing of *ijazat* with money by
unqualified persons, which plagued the Ottoman religious establishment, did not exist in the shrine cities.[30]

While serving the interests of the elites, these irregular practices were
frowned on by contemporaries who saw them as an abuse of the
intended goal of religious education and as harming the 'ulama''s
prestige among their constituencies.[31] They also led to growing tensions
within the stratum of the 'ulama' itself between members of the elite
and lower-ranking 'ulama', both in the Ottoman Empire and Iran.
Hence, their usefulness is not beyond question.

Moreover, the *ijazat ijtihad* itself was not sufficient for acquiring
widespread recognition. Theoretically, certain additional conditions

were necessary for a jurist to qualify as an "absolute mujtahid" (*mujtahid mutlaq*) or a fully qualified (*jami' al-sharayit*) mujtahid. These qualifications were command of Arabic grammar and syntax, of *fiqh*, of legal opinions (*fatwas*), and of the consensus (*ijma'*) on legal and doctrinal issues. In addition, the mujtahid needed to have a fair knowledge of Qur'anic exegesis (*tafsir*), hadith and biographies of its transmitters (*'ilm al-rijal*), logic, and theology (*kalam*). The partial mujtahid (*mutajazzi'*) would be qualified to express authoritative opinions only on the specific subject of his expertise. However, from the beginning of the nineteenth century there was a growing trend toward denying the validity of the "partial ijtihad" and restricting the validity of ijtihad to the "absolute mujtahid." This had the effect of lowering the status of those who had mastered only one or two branches of religious studies and of obliterating formal stratification among the mujtahids.[32] Once again, all these criteria were rather vague and open to conflicting judgments.

The Muslim *ijaza* system in general, and the Shi'i *ijazat ijtihad* in particular, played an important role in the professionalization of the Shi'i 'ulama'. The restriction of practicing *ijtihad* to holders of the *ijaza*, as well as the sharp distinction and subordination of the followers to the mujtahids, acted as a strategy designed among other things, "to limit and control the supply of entrants to an occupation in order to safeguard or enhance its market value."[33] In other words, there is a universal tendency among professions to raise the minimum standards of entry as increasing numbers of potential candidates attain the formerly scarce qualifications.

An additional aspect of professionalization was the development of a code of ethics (*akhlaq*) of the group, which was a subject of study, and was supposed to guide the conduct of the aspiring mujtahids. The *ijaza* also signaled that the student abided by the professional ethic of the 'ulama', such as piety, asceticism, and justice.[34]

The consensus emerging in the nineteenth century that the attainment of the status of mujtahid required recognition by other mujtahids in addition to the *ijazat ijtihad* corroborates Chamberlain's statement regarding an elite regulating entry to its ranks, but could also be seen as an attempted remedy against possible abuse.[35] On the one hand, an *ijaza* given by a renowned mujtahid was more likely to be accepted by other mujtahids as the first step in joining the elite. Concurrently, even if the Shi'i elite had wished to close its ranks to newcomers, as was the case during certain periods in the Ottoman Empire, it lacked the mechanisms to do so. Single mujtahids could deny recognition to colleagues of humbler origins in order to bar their entry to the ranks of the elite. But the diffused nature of the teaching system and of the leadership as well as the lack of bureaucratic and clear hierarchical organization undermined the effectiveness of such individual acts, as other mujtahids could always give their recognition.[36] This was largely due to the system of patronage upon which the prestige and influence of each mujtahid depended, which required the expansion rather than the restriction of teaching and the cultivation of younger mujtahids, thereby ensuring the inclusion of newcomers.

Concurrently, this very practice of requiring recognition by one's peers inhibited the entry of mediocre sons of distinguished fathers to the elite's ranks. In the more bureaucratized Ottoman system an *ijaza* was the key to an administrative position, and an ignorant judge could rely on his deputies to carry out his religious functions. Conversely, in the shrine cities where teaching and the issuing of rulings were the main occupation of the 'ulama', an unqualified holder of an *ijaza* could not attract students or serve as a source of emulation for ordinary believers. On the other hand, the true greatness of a mujtahid of low social origins would eventually be recognized by at least some of his peers.

The unavoidable conclusion, then, is that scholarship measured primarily by the written works of a mujtahid was the absolutely necessary prerequisite for the attainment of leadership status. Thus written works, the most important criterion for measuring scholarship in the community of learning, had two goals, as is true of western universities: the increase of knowledge, or in the specific case of the shrine cities, the development of Shi'i law; and a more subtle agenda, of establishing the scholar's status and fame among his peers.

The most popular genre since the tenth/sixteenth century (i.e. under the Safavids) was in the form of commentaries (*sharh* pl. *shuruh*) and glosses (*hashiyya* pl. *hawashi*) on important works. Prior to the sixteenth century commentaries engaged mostly in clarifying vague words or passages. After that, however, they were elaborated into lengthy interpretations and critiques.[37] Several of these commentaries achieved fame as leading works in their own right. Such form of writing established the continuity of law as each generation built upon its predecessors' work. In addition, in a society that honored tradition it was easier for a scholar to present his contributions and innovations in the form of commentary on his predecessors rather than as a purely original work.

Legal works often appeared as compilations of lecture notes (*taqrirat*) which students wrote and the mujtahid polished. Such practices went as far back as the fourth/tenth century and continued well into the twentieth. The use of lecture notes as the basis for books might have added to the difficulties of producing clear texts. Hence the need for repeated commentaries and glosses to clarify them. It is possible that the condensed style of juridical works was also influenced by the difficulties of reproducing written works in the pre-printing age, although a major reason for that style was to make memorization easier.[38]

The prevalent publication of lecture notes (*taqrirat*) raised the problem of authorship and academic status. Theoretically authorship of the new book, in which lecture notes played an important role, was determined by the amount of original input invested by the student.[39] However, as in other fields of Muslim learning, such decisions had no clear-cut definitions, but were dependent upon peer consensus. In addition to the question of intellectual honesty and integrity, the establishment of authorship had important implications for the question of status and leadership. As such, it was sometimes a source of tension between teachers and their disciples. Two cases in point are *Dawabit al-usul* and *Bushrat al-wusul* written respectively by the two prominent mujtahids Ibrahim Qazvini and Hasan Mamaqani. Whereas Qazvini's teacher, Sharif al-'Ulama' Mazandarani, was not too happy about his student's act, Sayyid Husayn Kuhkamara'i praised Mamaqani's work, and recommended it to his students.[40]

Only 'ulama' who had distinguished themselves in *fiqh* and *usul* emerged as leaders. Experts in genealogies (*'ilm al-rijal*), ethics (*akhlaq*), or other auxiliary fields could not attract a sufficient number of students and establish networks of patronage. Most mujtahids tended to specialize in these two fields as shown by an analysis of the subjects of the works written by sixty-nine leading mujtahids of the shrine cities. *Fiqh* works constituted 62.3 percent of the titles in the survey, and *usul* 22.5 percent, altogether amounting to 84.8 percent. Scholarly works in eleven other fields, mainly auxiliary sciences, constituted only 15.2 percent.[41]

Mujtahids who dealt with *fiqh* enjoyed an advantage over their colleagues (or rivals) who were mainly experts in *usul*, although there are exceptions to this rule. As a subject dealing with the methodology of law, *usul* was regarded as a difficult field, targeting a limited audience – that of the 'ulama' themselves. This may have been the reason why Arab mujtahids did not venture into this field during the second part of the century probably because of their smaller constituency. In contrast, works on commercial and civil law had greater applicability to low-ranking 'ulama' and students. Therefore, those who sought a large following preferred to produce more works in this field.

Among the most prominent examples of this trend are Muhammad Hasan Najafi who achieved greater prominence thanks to his *Jawahir al-kalam* than Ibrahim Qazvini did with his *Dawabit al-usul*. Akhund Khorasani, the greatest Usuli of his time, had fewer supporters than

Kazim Yazdi, author of the *fiqh* compendium *al-'Urwa al-wuthqa*. Shirazi, who wrote very little and was mainly engaged in issuing *fatwas*, is perhaps the best example of this phenomenon. Ansari, on the other hand, is the most prominent exception in view of his pioneering role in *usul*, but he too broke a new path in commercial law with his *al-Makasib*. Ansari's pivotal role in the development of *usul* and *fiqh* did not lead to a significant increase in major works on *usul*. The thirty-four mujtahids who had preceded Ansari or were his generational cohorts wrote forty-nine works on *usul*. The thirty-six mujtahids who came after him wrote fifty-seven such works, constituting a 16 percent increase.[42]

In comparison, there was a greater increase in the production of works on *mu'amalat* (laws concerned with worldly affairs) from fourteen during the period up to Ansari to forty-four thereafter, or an increase of 214 percent. Nine of these works were commentaries on Ansari's *al-Makasib*.[43] The growing integration of Iran into the world economy raised new problems for Iranian merchants and required new rules of conduct. The attention Ansari paid to the links between trade and questions of purity, i.e. dealings with new commodities or with foreigners, were probably intended to find suitable legal answers in these new circumstances.[44] *Al-Makasib* and the upsurge in books on *mu'amalat* probably reflected an awareness by the 'ulama' of their constituents' needs. Responding to the demand for works on commercial law was a good way for aspiring mujtahids to establish their reputation among the Bazaar community and thereby expand their base of support.

A less important factor in the attainment of a leadership position was being a disciple to a prominent mujtahid. Former students of Murtada Ansari constituted the largest group of competing leaders during the third quarter of the nineteenth century. Likewise, Habiballah Rashti's students 'Ali Nahavandi (d. 1322/1904) and 'Abdallah Mazandarani (d. 1330/1912) were less prominent than Hasan Shirazi's students at the beginning of the twentieth century, to cite just a few examples. It could be argued that brilliant students would anyway go to the most notable teachers, but there is more to it. An *ijaza* given by a greater mujtahid was more prestigious and could open more doors to his students than other *ijazat*. Discipleship under a great mujtahid enabled the aspiring mujtahid to meet more students who might later become his own, and also prospective followers once he became a contender for leadership.

Governments played only a limited role in determining leadership status. An appeal by the shah to a certain mujtahid to produce a ruling on a certain issue, or an Ottoman decision to work with a certain mujtahid as a mediator, often bolstered the latter's position. This could also be a sign of an already-established superior status, as was the case with Fath 'Ali Shah's appeal to Ja'far Najafi and Sayyid 'Ali Tabataba'i. Sunni rulers could elevate low-ranking or even unsuitable 'ulama' to the top of the pyramid. In contrast, due to the different base of authority and status of the mujtahids, rulers in the Shi'a world could appeal only to mujtahids who had already enjoyed a prominent position among their colleagues or constituents. Otherwise their rulings and cooperation would be ineffectual.

As shown repeatedly in the previous chapters, the acumen of building networks of patronage was a necessary condition, though insufficient by itself, for establishing a leadership position. Access to funds was of course a corollary need in this context. However, excessive preoccupation with money could sometimes harm the mujtahid. Thus, during a visit to the shrine cities in 1883 to inspect the conduct of the Oudh Bequest's distributors the acting British resident, Tweedie, acquired the impression that "the acceptance by them of this mundane care and duty, formed in the eyes of many, a lamentable defection from the type of character proper to them," to be regarded as first-rank mujtahids.[45]

In the absence of a formal structure and formal procedures in the shrine cities, mujtahids attained leadership in a variety of ways. Nomination and designation by another senior mujtahid, such as Murtada Ansari by Muhammad Hasan Najafi, was the least common. Occasionally, teachers groomed several of their disciples to serve as future leaders by appointing them responsible for issuing *fatwas* in their courts, but without officially pronouncing them as their successors.[46] On several occasions, mujtahids were nominated or elected by their peers for leadership. Often this nomination was expressed in the ceremonial act of appointing them as prayer leaders. Most often, however, mujtahids consolidated their leadership only after a prolonged process of scholarly activity and patronage building which earned them recognition by followers and peers, usually winning wide acclaim only in old age. In such an informal system, leaders could not be "deposed" by their counterparts. At most we can speak of relative decline of influence or stature *vis-à-vis* their colleagues.

In that sense leadership in the shrine cities resembled Jewish rabbinical leadership in the diaspora. As was the case with the mujtahids, the authority of great rabbis outside their own communities was not based on any official, formal appointment or position, but on their scholarly fame and personal prestige. The source of their authority and symbol of their status was their religious seminary (*yeshiva*) in which they taught and produced disciples, cultivating intimate patronage ties similar to those in the shrine cities. Many of the disciples, themselves communal rabbis, further extended their teacher's authority. In both the Shi'i and

Jewish cases, status was largely based on scholarship and patronage. The Shi'i and Jewish leaders were dependent on communal support and recognition and not on state offices or control of endowed property, which prevented them from being closed elites: "He who says organization says oligarchy," was Robert Michels' sober conclusion. In both cases, the Shi'i and the Jewish, the structure of leadership was amorphous and informal, and, therefore, not oligarchic. Likewise, in both cases, leaders were always challenged by rivals.[47]

The individualistic nature of leadership and teaching as well as the constant need of mujtahids to vie for students and for financial resources bred personal rivalries, and inhibited cooperation among them. Whatever cooperation there was appeared generally at a time of severe external threat to the collective leadership of the 'ulama' in society, as was the case with the Babi movement, or to the Islamic nature of Shi'i countries as during the tobacco protest. Such cooperation for a specific goal was usually short lived, as it was basically defensive and negative in nature, i.e. against a common threat. It was more difficult to obtain a consensus in support of a specific cause among persons with diverse opinions and interests, as events in the Constitutional Revolution would show.[48]

The continuous rivalries among mujtahids over the hearts and purses of their followers undermined their effective independence, forcing them at times to toe their supporters' line. The 1843 rebellion in Karbala' was the most striking example of the 'ulama''s failure as leaders when they were unable to impose their authority on their supposed followers. On other occasions, such as the tobacco protest, the 'ulama' were more often prompted into action by their followers, who also determined the goals of the struggle, than the initiators of such actions themselves.[49]

The British historian Malcolm and the Iranian chronicler Hidayat described, with some exaggeration, the power of the 'ulama' as greater than that of the shah.[50] Yet the 'ulama' were often unable to overcome popular customs as is indicated by the failure of Mirza Hasan Shirazi's *fatwa* prohibiting the practice of flagellation and the shedding of blood in Husayn's memory.[51] The reform-minded mujtahid Hibat al-Din Shahristani went even further in pointing out the 'ulama''s weakness vis-à-vis their followers. He criticized the lack of intellectual integrity among 'ulama', accusing them of saying different things to their students and in their works from what they preached in public because they "fear the anger of the ignorant masses."[52]

Shahristani's criticism raises the question of the prevalence of popular disenchantment with the 'ulama' among the lay public. The biogra-

phical dictionaries and other sources produced by the 'ulama' themselves disregard such issues, for obvious reasons. Indirect evidence is
disclosed by the popular appeal of the Babi movement in Iran, which
rejected the authority of the 'ulama'. The popular proverb comparing
the difficulty of becoming a human being (*adam shodan*) with the relative
ease of becoming a mulla suggests that such feelings were not very rare.
The receptivity among the Iranian public to anti-clerical writings by
radical lay reformers is the most important indicator of such feelings
during the latter part of the century. But this issue requires much
further research, beyond the scope of this study, before any meaningful
conclusions can be reached.

Parallel to the widespread competition for influence and leadership
among mujtahids, its more mundane aspects created a certain sense of
uneasiness among various mujtahids. Throughout the nineteenth
century there were great scholars who shunned leadership because they
lacked the worldly qualifications it required. Muhammad Taha Najaf,
for instance, reportedly pointed to the burden of leadership as one of the
three afflictions he had suffered in his life.[53]

The shortcomings of the institution of religious leadership as it
developed during the nineteenth century raises the question why the
system of informal diffused leadership endured for so many generations.
The inherent conservatism of any establishment, let alone a religious
one that espouses traditionalism, is only part of the explanation. The
diffused nature of leadership served the interests of a great many
mujtahids, who under these circumstances enjoyed greater freedom in
exercising power, and who were, therefore, reluctant to be subordinated
to one supreme leader. In addition, the inherent divisions among the
'ulama' made it difficult to reach a consensus on the matter, or for one
mujtahid to enforce such a system, as long as the 'ulama' lacked central
institutions and organizations to enforce such a change. This may be the
reason why the first attempt to organize a formal Shi'i hierarchy came
only after the 1979 revolution in Iran when reasons of state required
new modes of action, and when the 'ulama' had the power of the state to
carry them out.

Leadership among the 'ulama' moved along two major parallel
processes. First was centralization, manifested by the relative decline
of the various Iranian centers and of Karbala' parallel to the emergence of Najaf as the undisputed center of learning, and the rise to
unprecedented prominence of individual mujtahids there. All this,
however, without eliminating the diffused nature of the religious
establishment.

The shift in the status of the various centers of learning was determined by a variety of causes. Government support in the form of generous *awqaf* could provide an important basis for attracting scholars and students alike, as was the case in early nineteenth-century Qum. Political instability or outright government oppression could seriously undermine a center, as was the case in Karbala' after the 1843 rebellion. The economic or physical infrastructure of a town was often an essential, though not a sufficient, condition for the rise of centers. Shrine cities such as Najaf and Karbala' in Iraq or Mashhad and Qum in Iran had an initial advantage since they constantly attracted pilgrims who provided the necessary donations to the 'ulama'.

Overall, however, the personality of the individual teacher was the key element. Kashan, Qum, and Burujird flourished as centers of learning during the first part of the century, but since they each revolved around one distinguished mujtahid, there was a decline after their respective deaths. Isfahan dwindled from a national to a regional center and lost students to the shrine cities following the deaths of Shafti, Karbasi, and Muhammad Taqi Isfahani. Students who attended the *dars al-kharij* in Iran during the second half of the nineteenth century did so before coming to the shrine cities, recognizing the superior status of the latter.[54] The importance of the individual teacher is evident in the case of Samarra'. Mirza Hasan Shirazi turned it into a flourishing center, without support from the shah, but after his death his circle of study disintegrated and Samarra' lost its importance.

Najaf and Karbala' experienced similar fluctuations in prestige and status. Yet, because of their aura of sanctity, they constantly attracted more scholars and students, as well as financial support from ordinary believers. In addition, the centrality of teaching in the shrine cities compared to greater emphasis on the administration of justice or on politics in the Iranian centers ensured the steady recruitment of newcomers from all geographical regions and social strata and in consequence the formation of a community of scholars rather than one-man-shows in both towns.

The second long-term theme in the history of Shi'i religious leadership during the nineteenth century was the pendulum movement, to use Amanat's phrase, between the madrasa and the marketplace,[55] that is between leaders primarily engaged in scholarship and teaching, and those involved much more in public, political, and economic activity. This pendulum movement was influenced by personalities but also by the external political and social circumstances which favored on occasion leaders from each trend. However, even the greatest scholars were forced to enlist funds and establish patronage links. In other words, the stipulation of the modern Iranian constitution regarding the desired qualities of the Leader did not mark a major break from the actual historical model.

Up to the Constitutional Revolution, the politics of leadership in the shrine cities were largely affected by interpersonal relationships and rivalries. Ideological, doctrinal, or political differences played a secondary role in most cases in determining leadership. During the revolution, however, political attitudes and doctrinal differences regarding politics became a major factor in the configuration of leadership both in Iran and the shrine cities. This new element also marked a change in the role of the 'ulama' as communal leaders, which is the subject of the following chapters.

Part 2

The 'ulama' between the Ottomans and the Qajars

6   The shrine cities, the Mamluks, and Iran

In his testament and will, Ayatallah Khomeini called upon the 'ulama' "not to isolate yourself from and not be indifferent to the problems of society," particularly elections. He also criticized those clerics "who were fooled" by politicians "and considered taking part in the affairs of the country and Muslims as beneath their station."[1]

The 'ulama' of the shrine cities were certainly not "fooled" into believing that communal and social affairs were "beneath their station." Yet, in view of their particular circumstances, the roles they did play were quite different from the excessive politicization advocated by Khomeini.

As communal leaders, the 'ulama' of the shrine cities were active in several interrelated arenas. The most important of these was the political triangle formed with the Qajars in Iran and the Mamluks and subsequently Ottomans in Baghdad, in which the relations between any two of the parties affected the third one as well. Although during the years 1747–1831 the pashalik of Baghdad was ruled by Mamluk officers of Georgian origin, they were an integral part of the Ottoman system, and their relations with the Shi'is cannot be separated from the broader Ottoman perspective.[2] Therefore, whereas most scholars discussing the Shi'i 'ulama' have focused on the Iranian arena, this study seeks to examine the 'ulama' of the shrine cities in the broader perspective of both contexts and their impact on each other.

The question of 'ulama'–state relations in Qajar Iran has produced two historiographical approaches. The earlier one, represented mainly by Algar and Keddie, regards these relations as inherently confrontational. The second trend, advocated primarily by Arjomand and Amanat, views them as much more multi-faceted and complex.[3] And indeed, they were sometimes characterized by tension between segments of the 'ulama' and the Qajars over the 'ulama''s political role, as well as over Qajar policies, which seemed to various 'ulama' detrimental to Shi'i Islam. At the same time, there was a commonality of interests whereby leading 'ulama' granted the Qajars implicit and often explicit religious legitimacy during certain periods of the nineteenth century in return for Qajar preservation of Iran as a Shi'i state and for supporting the 'ulama' financially. On occasions, the two parties cooperated against heretic revolutionary movements such as Babism.

Several scholars have viewed the location of the shrine cities outside the reach of the Qajar state as a source of power for the 'ulama' in Iran.[4] Such a perception seems to be a backward projection based on the conduct of various mujtahids during the Constitutional Revolution, and it overstates Mirza Hasan Shirazi's role in the 1891 protest movement against the tobacco concession.

As I intend to show, it would be more plausible to argue that being Shi'is under a hostile Sunni rule the 'ulama' were often in need of Iranian and British patronage against oppressive measures imposed from Baghdad. Such dependence led many of them to adopt a more quietist attitude toward the Qajars than their colleagues in Iran during most of the nineteenth century.

In their turn, relations between the 'ulama' and the Sunni government in Baghdad – both under the Mamluk officers until 1831 and under the more centralized Ottoman rule thereafter – were shaped by several factors. The bitter rivalry with Iran, going back to the Safavids, aroused continuous Ottoman fears of Iranian designs to regain control of the shrine cities. These apprehensions were exacerbated by Iranian claims during the Safavid and Qajar periods that the shah should be the protector of Shi'i interests in Iraq, particularly in the shrine cities. As a result, the Ottomans[5] regarded the Shi'i population, and especially the 'ulama', as potential or actual agents and allies of Iran.[6] The various attempts among the Shi'is in general and the 'ulama' in particular to avoid conscription and payment of taxes increased Ottoman suspicions. As part of the old Sunni–Shi'i rivalry, the Ottomans never granted the Shi'is the official status of an independent religious school (*madhhab*) or community (*millet*). Concurrently, while resenting the growing Iranian presence in the shrine cities and often taking measures to restrict it, the Ottomans sought to extract the maximal revenue from the growing pilgrimage to the shrine cities. Hence, they never went too far in their anti-Shi'i measures.

The weakness of the central government and the sparsity of the population in the countryside exposed Iraq to continued tribal migrations and invasions from the Arabian Peninsula. The last movement of the kind ended in the years 1795–1805 with the migration of parts of the 'Anaza and the Shammar. Henceforth, the tribes, mostly organized in loose confederations under paramount shaykhs, comprised the bulk of the population in southern Iraq. Throughout the eighteenth and nineteenth centuries the central government struggled with the tribes over control of the countryside, mainly security of the trade routes, and over taxation.[7] The propagation of Shi'ism by the 'ulama' among the tribes increased the government's suspicions of them. Presumably making an analogy with the cooperation between the Sunni 'ulama' and the government, the Ottomans regarded the Shi'i missionary activity as part of Iran's effort to draw the tribes to its side.[8]

The tribal domination of the countryside and the gap between the local Arabic-speaking population and the foreign, Turkish-speaking governors prevented the central government from exerting effective control over the shrine cities. Within that constellation, the 'ulama' functioned as urban notables, or as a mediating elite between the central government and the population. The political influence of the notables rested on two mutually dependent factors: first, they had to possess "access" to authority, and so be able to "speak for society or some part of it"; second, they had to have some social power of their own which was not dependent on the ruler and gave them a position of accepted and "natural" leadership. Their actions were typically intended to preserve the delicate balance between government and society and not to act as opposition to the government, as then they would lose their access to it. The politics of notables, according to Albert Hourani, is characteristic of societies "ordered according to relations of personal dependence." In addition to the vertical linkages between dependent groups and the government, notables also formed horizontal factions, which competed with one another for influence in their society and with their foreign rulers.[9]

The relations between the Shi'i 'ulama' and their Sunni counterparts in Iraq were mostly characterized by antagonism, as might be expected from the standard-bearers of two rival religious sects. Yet, as members of a minority sect which seeks to overcome the majority group, various Shi'i 'ulama' attended the classes of leading Sunni jurists in Baghdad, and demonstrated command of Sunni law. A few even received *ijazat* from Sunni 'ulama'.[10]

Another factor, which played a secondary role within the triangle, was the British presence, often mediating between the 'ulama' and the Sunni government in Baghdad. Lacking a strong land army, the major British interest in the region was to preserve the Ottoman Empire and Iran as buffer states against Russia or any other power that might endanger their Indian empire. This strategy, which originated with Napoleon's invasion of Egypt in 1798, came to be known as the Great Game. As they became aware of the 'ulama''s power to mobilize mass public action in Iran, the British wanted to reduce friction between the two states which was likely to arise out of persecution of Shi'is in Iraq. Their growing economic interests in both countries required obtaining the goodwill of such an important social stratum as the 'ulama'. The 'ulama''s goodwill also served British relations with the Shi'i kingdom of Awadh. Finally, during the second part of the century, the British sought to protect the interests of their Shi'i Indian subjects who lived in the shrine cities.[11] In addition to resorting to British mediation to offset various unfriendly Ottoman policies, the 'ulama' relied upon them to transfer funds from the kingdom of Awadh during the first part of the century. Subsequently, as the British administered the funds of the Oudh Bequest, their links with the mujtahids became even closer.

The interaction between the aspects discussed above positioned the 'ulama' in the peculiar situation of being members of a persecuted group in Iraq, and simultaneously part of a dominant religious hieroc- racy in Iran. In other words, in Iraq they were in the position of a religious sect that does not accept the legitimacy of the surrounding dominant culture of the socio-political environment in which it exists, here that of the Ottoman Empire. Concurrently, they were close to the church end of the continuum as far as their status in Iran was concerned, being members of a dominant religious establishment which suppressed any opposition to its authority, and by and large accepted the sur- rounding system of the Qajar state.[12] As I intend to argue, this duality helps explain some of their activities throughout the century such as their quietist attitude toward the Qajars, and their unfriendly if sub- missive posture *vis-à-vis* the government in Baghdad.

As the following chronological survey will show, Mamluk policies toward the Shi'is and the shrine cities were inconsistent due to the fluctuating weight of the various factors outlined above. In 1780, Suleyman Pasha "the Great" made a pilgrimage to the shrine cities as a gesture of goodwill but also to demonstrate his authority.[13] Toward the end of the century, however, presumably due to Suleyman's old age and the weakening of Mamluk power, the shrine cities, although "the two wealthiest towns in the province, did not bring revenues to the Pasha of Baghdad."[14] However, at some time between Suleyman's rule and the early 1820s the Mamluks did manage to resume the collection of taxes at least from Karbala'.

The Mamluks' tolerance toward the practice of Shi'i devotional rites was largely a function of their military power. Visiting Karbala' in 1803, Mirza Abu Talib Khan observed that the *sabb va rafd* (cursing and disavowal of the first three caliphs) is prevalent in the shrine cities. The Mamluks, he added, "although they cannot endure the sight of Shi'is in other places and spit on them," tolerate such actions in the shrine cities because of their fear of Iranian reprisals. In other towns, primarily Baghdad and Basra, the Shi'is were denied free exercise of their religion. Suleyman Pasha himself did not hesitate to provoke the Shi'is when he confiscated an iron ring suspended from the tomb of the Shi'i shrine at Tauk, where reputedly Imam Husayn had been buried for a while, on the grounds that it "would be useful to his mules."[15]

The Wahhabi raids on Karbala' and Najaf beginning in 1801 demonstrate the interaction between the three actors of the 'ulama'– Ottoman–Qajar triangle. Professing absolute monotheism and seeking to purify Islam, the Wahhabi movement which emerged in the Najd during the second half of the eighteenth century regarded the Shi'i reverence of the Imams as tantamount to polytheism. On the day of Ghadir Khumm 1215/April 21, 1801,[16] a Wahhabi force of about 12,000 warriors led by Amir Sa'ud b. 'Abd al-'Aziz attacked Karbala'. The Mamluk garrison fled, leaving the Wahhabis to plunder the town unopposed. Although Karbala' was partially deserted because many inhabitants had gone to Najaf to celebrate the holiday, the Wahhabis massacred some 5,000 people. One of the most prominent victims was 'Abd al-Samad Hamadani, a leading disciple of Bihbihani. In addition, the Wahhabis desecrated the shrines of Husayn and 'Abbas and looted their treasures.[17]

In addition to the heavy loss of life, the Wahhabi raid dealt a violent blow to the town's economy. Visiting Karbala' shortly after the raid, Mirza Abu Talib Khan said that many of the wealthy merchants had emigrated to Iran or India. Those of his relatives who had remained were impoverished and broken. Many 'ulama' also emigrated.[18]

The Shi'is were quite helpless against the Wahhabi menace, and their feelings are visibly reflected in their poetry. Two poets, Hajj Muhammad Rida Al Azri al-Tamimi and Hashim al-Ka'abi, described in emotional terms the massacre of women and children. Both depicted the tragedy as another recurrence of the murder of Imam Husayn and denounced the Wahhabi doctrine. In contrast to Sunni poets, such as 'Uthman b. Sanad al-Basri al-Wa'ili, who lavishly praised the Mamluks for their fight against the Wahhabis, the Shi'i poets avoided all mention of the Mamluks. Rather, they implicitly expressed their resentment toward Mamluk inaction by calling on their fellow Shi'is to avenge the blood of the martyrs and imploring the Hidden Imam to return and bring justice to his followers.[19]

Wahhabi brutality and Mamluk inaction caused an uproar in Iran. Fath 'Ali Shah wrote a sharp letter to Suleyman Pasha, laying the responsibility for the massacre on his incompetence. The shah threatened to send an army against the Wahhabis and Baghdad itself should the pasha fail to punish Saʿud. In addition, he demanded the recovery of the prisoners and treasures captured by the Wahhabis. Seeking to appease the shah, Suleyman Pasha promised to provide compensation for the life and property lost, and undertook to stand fast against the Wahhabis.[20] To demonstrate his serious intentions, he executed the local commander of Karbalaʾ and dispatched troops to pursue the Wahhabis, but to no avail.[21]

Out of weakness, Suleyman had to negotiate with the Wahhabis to ransom the prisoners. Initially the Wahhabis demanded 1,000 pieces of gold as blood money for each of their own casualties, but eventually settled for 500. Suleyman even accepted the proposal by the British political agent, Harford Jones, to recommend that the Porte should enable Suleyman to sign a defence alliance with Iran against the Wahhabis, but nothing came of this idea.[22]

To avoid further complications with Iran, Suleyman removed the treasures of the shrine of Najaf to Kazimayn. Distrustful of the Mamluks, and possibly in reply to Sayyid ʿAli Tabatabaʾi's request for help, Fath ʿAli Shah sent 500 Baluchi families from southeastern Iran to settle in Karbalaʾ and defend it. The Baluchis remained loyal to the shah through about half his reign, but subsequently mixed with the local brigands in exploiting the population. Fath ʿAli Shah also began to build the fortress and wall of Karbalaʾ but did not complete it. Sayyid ʿAli Tabatabaʾi managed to complete the wall with money received from Awadh.[23]

Following their success in Karbalaʾ, the Wahhabis continued to raid southern Iraq and especially Najaf. In 1806 they launched their largest raid on Najaf, but encountered stiff resistance, led by Jaʿfar Kashif al-Ghitaʾ who mobilized both students and urban brigands. He also encouraged his disciple Jawad al-ʿAmili to write a risala on the necessity of defending Najaf.[24]

After the Wahhabi raids Shaykh Jaʿfar initiated the building of a wall around the town, obtaining donations from Qajar notables, among them the sadr-i aʿzam Muhammad Hasan Khan Isfahani. Jaʿfar also acted as a communal leader in providing protection and mediating between the population and the rulers. Thus he alone paid a tax of forty tighar (about eighty tons) of food levied by the Mamluks on Najaf.[25] Such a type of urban leadership was conspicuously lacking in Karbalaʾ during the same period. Presumably the Iranian ʿulamaʾ in Karbalaʾ were not as rooted in the town as Shaykh Jaʿfar was, or lacked his ability.

Shaykh Jaʿfar's emergence as an urban leader ignited a prolonged power struggle between his family and the local sayyid elite headed by the Milali family. The division of urban society into two rival factions, which were composed of extended personal-based networks of patronage, and the rise of urban gangs, had been common phenomena in Middle Eastern cities since the Middle Ages. This segmentation of society emerged as a mechanism for providing communal and personal security for members of a community in response to the absence of permanent governmental authority in frontier situation, or where the formal government was invested with very little legitimacy. As in the tribal system, injustice caused to an individual was seen as a wrong perpetrated against the group. The division of society into two segments preserved a social equilibrium which prevented one faction from totally subjugating the other.[26]

Like their medieval predecessors the 'Ayyarun, the gangs in the shrine cities, generally referred to as *luti*, *awbash* (riff-raff) or *yaramaz* (worthless in Turkish) assumed a Mafia-like character. They set up a structure of authority parallel to the government based on extortion rackets, exploiting both residents and pilgrims. The relations between the gangs and the urban elites in the shrine cities, as in other places and periods in the Middle East, were characterized by mutual fear and tenuous cooperation. In medieval Syria, for instance, Mamluk emirs used the gangs in their own factional struggles. In many cities gangs enjoyed the cooperation of notable-class bosses, who protected them from the government. At other times gangs terrorized and plundered the population, alienating the Sunni 'ulama'. Ordinarily, each gang controlled a certain city quarter, "protecting" the people of their own neighborhood from government officials and rival city quarters. Cooperation between gang members and 'ulama' was widespread in Iran, with the former serving as the executive arm of the latter in collecting the fifth and carrying out rulings. Bihbihani reportedly used urban brigands in his struggle against Akhbari followers in eighteenth-century Karbala'.[27]

Early nineteenth-century Najaf was divided between two gangs, the Shumurt controlling the Mishraq and Buraq neighborhoods, and the Zukurt, who numbered about a hundred men and controlled the 'Amara and Huwaysh neighborhoods.[28] Shi'i sources trace the emergence of the two gangs to the 1806 Wahhabi raid, although they are more likely to have been an older phenomenon. The various accounts of the origins of the rivalry between the two gangs are less important than the light they shed on the 'ulama''s relations with the gangs and with dominant sayyid families at the time.[29]

Class differences were an important factor in the gang and factional rivalry in Najaf. The Shumurt were allied with the Milali family, which had held the custodianship of the Imam 'Ali shrine since the beginning of Ottoman rule in Iraq and occasionally the local governorship as well. The Milalis served as the tax-farmers of Najaf and were responsible for billeting government troops in the town, two roles that gave them considerable power. Other people associated with the Milalis in the context of the gang rivalry were also wealthy landowners. The Zukurt, headed by 'Abbas al-Haddad (the blacksmith), were associated with the poor, and were allied with the Kashif al-Ghita' clan.[30]

An additional source of conflict was the refusal of the Milalis and their associates to abide by Shaykh Ja'far's rulings. Shaykh Ja'far used the Zukurt to enforce his decisions, and on one occasion in 1228/1813 the latter killed Sayyid Mahmud al-Rihbawi, a wealthy landowner and relative of the Milalis, who refused to appear before Shaykh Ja'far's court.[31] The refusal reflected a deeper rivalry over the actual source of authority in Najaf, the 'ulama' or the older elite.

The Milalis held the Kashif al-Ghita' family responsible for the killing. The Shumurt gang, therefore, began a campaign of harassment against them and their supporters among the 'ulama', which eventually forced Shaykh Musa Kashif al-Ghita' (Shaykh Ja'far died seven months after Sayyid Mahmud's death) to leave Najaf for Kazimayn. In response, the Zukurt assassinated Mahmud al-Milali in 1230/1814-15. Suleyman Milali succeeded his father as governor and custodian, and Najaf was now torn by the struggle. When 'Abbas al-Haddad appealed for support to the Mamluk governor in Baghdad, Da'ud Pasha, Da'ud dismissed Suleyman, and appointed 'Abbas as the governor, presumably seeking to increase his own influence in Najaf by weakening the powerful local magnates.[32]

'Abbas proved to be an efficient local governor. He fortified the town, encouraged agriculture, and restored a measure of security. In 1231/1816, however, fighting resumed between the two gangs. Since 'Abbas had also ceased paying the annual tax to Baghdad, the acting Mamluk governor Sa'id Pasha dispatched troops to Najaf to remove him.[33] In his al-Tuhfa al-gharawiyya, Shaykh Khidr b. Shallal recounts the terror of the people during the second fitna (strife) between the "Zukurt pagans (tughat) and the Shumurt sinners" in Ramadan 1231/July 1816. The 'ulama' were divided on which course of action to take. Many escaped to the neighborhoods controlled by the Shumurt, even though the latter had abused the "shaykh of the community," Kashif al-Ghita', and his supporters. Some 'ulama', fearing destruction by the Mamluk troops, informed them of the whereabouts of members of the Kashif al-Ghita' clan in the 'Amara neighborhood. The Mamluk commander ordered his men to attack the 'ulama' who remained in that neighborhood, and the latter took up arms. When the troops failed to defeat the 'ulama' and their allies, their commander lured 'Ali Kashif al-Ghita' (Musa was in Kazimayn at the time) to a meeting to discuss a settlement. But when Shaykh 'Ali and his cousin came they were arrested. As a precondition for their release, the Mamluks demanded from the 'ulama' that all members of the Zukurt and their 'ulama' supporters leave the 'Amara neighborhood. After pressure from the 'ulama', the Zukurt submitted temporarily and left the neighborhood, which was pillaged by the troops.[34]

Shortly afterwards, however, the town again rebelled, with the 'ulama' and the Zukurt cooperating in defeating the Shumurt and forcing the Mamluk governor to leave. According to Shaykh Khidr, Shaykh Ibrahim al-Jaza'iri organized attacks on the Mamluks, "inflicting fear in the camp of Yazid," until the troops finally left the town.[35] Taking advantage of the governor's engagement in a tribal rebellion, 'Abbas al-Haddad again refused to recognize Baghdad's authority. In 1234/1818 Da'ud Pasha dispatched troops to Najaf, who managed to overcome the Zukurt. 'Abbas was killed by one of his own men, and Muhammad Tahir al-Milali was appointed as governor.[36]

The rivalry between the Milali and Kashif al-Ghita' families ended after the reassertion of direct Ottoman rule in Iraq. Mulla Yusuf, who was both custodian and governor at the time, executed several members of the Zukurt after he had promised them safe passage following one of the numerous clashes between the two gangs. The 'ulama', headed by Shaykh Muhammad b. 'Ali Kashif al-Ghita' (d. 1268/1851–52) apparently appealed in 1255/1839–40 to the governor to dismiss Mulla Yusuf. The governor obliged, presumably because he saw the opportunity to weaken a powerful local magnate and tighten Ottoman control of the town.

The governor offered the post of custodian to Shaykh Muhammad, who accepted it. Several months later, however, Shaykh Muhammad resigned, proposing his deputy, Rida Al Rufa'i, as the new custodian. He probably preferred to maintain his independence as a mujtahid to becoming an appointed official under a Sunni government. While the Rufa'i family held the custodianship well into mid-twentieth century and became one of the wealthiest and most influential families in Najaf, they went on cooperating with the Kashif al-Ghita' faction. The dismissal of the Milali clan, therefore, marked a turning point in the local power struggle in Najaf, in which the 'ulama' gained the upper hand and assumed the urban leadership.[37]

Control of local government and taxation were the leading points of contention between the local elite of Karbala', composed of landowning sayyid families, and the Mamluks. At the beginning of the nineteenth century, the local Karbala' officials, from the governor to the custodians of the shrines and the local mufti, were all Sunnis appointed by the pasha.[38] Following a weakening of Mamluk rule during the second decade of the century, the local elite managed to seize control of most local positions. Although a governor was sent from Baghdad, the local notables, primarily the Naqib al-Ashraf (head of the descendants of the Prophet) and the functionaries of the shrines, held the real power in Karbala'. Unable fully to control them, the governor could only play off the various families against each other to enhance his own influence. The local notables were allied with and assisted by urban brigands.[39]

Relations between Karbala' and the governor, Da'ud Pasha, deteriorated in 1241/1825–26. Taking advantage of the war between the governor and Iran, both Hilla and Karbala' ceased to pay taxes to Baghdad. Da'ud subdued Hilla, but had greater difficulties with Karbala'. According to a later source, the Naqib al-Ashraf Sayyid Husayn Al Darraj arranged the murder of the local Mamluk governor. When Da'ud was informed of the murder, he warned the 'ulama' to leave the town, since he intended to punish Karbala'. In other words, he distinguished between the 'ulama' and the lay elite. Indeed, many of the 'ulama' did leave Karbala', as their interests did not always conform with those of the local elite and their general inclination was more quietist.[40]

Da'ud besieged Karbala' for eighteen months but could not subdue the town. In 1244/1828–29 he agreed to a compromise negotiated with Sayyid Mahdi Qazvini and Musa Kashif al-Ghita of Najaf, under which the town paid a tax of 10,000 piasters a year instead of the 35,000 he had originally demanded. Sayyid Husayn was arrested and brought to Baghdad, where he was jailed until the naqib of Baghdad, Sayyid 'Ali al-Kilani, interceded on his behalf. Da'ud, however, did not enter Karbala' and the town maintained its semi-independence until 1843.[41]

'Ulama' and Qajars in the early nineteenth century

The relations between religion and state in Qajar Iran ranged from a cooperation of convenience existing together with ideological division between a hierocracy and the rulers, to periods of tension and hostility. Unlike the Safavids, the Qajar dynasty lacked charismatic legitimacy based on alleged descent from the Imams and as the heads of a Sufi order. Rather, they sought to establish their legitimacy on the basis of patrimonial concepts of kingship and justice and on their role as defenders of Islam, as well as on religious sanction by the 'ulama'.

The interest of Fath 'Ali Shah in securing a firm *de jure* basis for the legitimacy of Qajar rule, and the doctrinal interest of the 'ulama' in the removal of inconsistencies between Shi'i doctrine and the principles of legitimacy of the Safavid era, according to Arjomand resulted in a "separation of political and hierocratic domination."[42] Various writings by the 'ulama' accepted the compatibility of the patrimonial theories of kingship and justice with Twelver Shi'ism, asserting that "the blessing of the Hidden Imam came to be bestowed upon the king as a *temporal ruler*" (original italics).[43] While relegating political power to the monarch, the 'ulama' sought and largely succeeded in monopolizing all manifestations of organized religion under their control, thereby emerging as the dominant "church" in Iran able to suppress possible heterodox sects.

Fath 'Ali Shah cultivated friendly relations with the 'ulama' by providing generous endowments and financial allotments to individual members by commissioning various religious works, and by expressions of personal piety and submission to the 'ulama'. When mujtahids from the shrine cities came to Iran they were greeted with the utmost reverence by the shah and the Qajar elite, and were given large amounts for charity. When Fath 'Ali Shah needed the support of the 'ulama' in his 1813 war against Russia, he appealed to Shaykh Ja'far Kashif al-Ghita' and Sayyid 'Ali Tabataba'i, as well as to mujtahids in Iran. Significantly, however, the bulk of the funds channeled to the shrine cities was given to the upkeep of the shrines rather than to support the learning establishment.[44] Such a policy had the double advantage of publicizing the shah's piety among the thousands of pilgrims without too much enhancing the power of the 'ulama'.

His patronage of the shrine cities notwithstanding, Fath 'Ali Shah's main efforts were aimed at the 'ulama' in Iran, particularly Mirza Abu al-Qasim in Qum. After Qummi's death, Isfahan under Hujjat al-Islam Shafti and Ibrahim Karbasi attracted the greatest Qajar concern.[45] The preferential treatment of Qummi stemmed from his quietist approach to politics and his willingness to legitimize the shah's rule. It was also motivated by the shah's perception that the mujtahids in Iran were more important politically than those residing in the remote shrine cities. While the mujtahids of the shrine cities may have enjoyed reverence as scholarly sages, their colleagues in Iran emerged as powerful urban magnates thanks to their close contacts with the bulk of Shi'i believers, their control of the judiciary, their growing financial resources, and the weakening of central control in the provinces. Hujjat al-Islam Shafti's arrogant encounters with Muhammad Shah in Isfahan reflect the growing confidence of the Iranian mujtahids in their dealings with the Qajars during the second quarter of the nineteenth century. Such defiance, however, did not necessarily mean that the Iran-based mujta-hids opposed the Iranian state. The same Shafti supported the shah's foreign policy regarding the 1838 Herat crisis in his correspondence with the British minister.[46]

The common belief among the 'ulama' of the shrine cities that they needed and could rely on the Qajars is demonstrated by the case of the Asafiyya canal which was dug in 1775 with funds given by the nawwab of Awadh, Asaf al-Dawla. In 1817 the nawwab Ghazi al-Din Haydar wished to reopen the silted canal. The governor, well aware of the political and ecological effects of the reopening of the canal, in view of the tribal turbulence caused by the Hindiyya canal, attached too many conditions to the project. Asking for British assistance, the nawwab cited an 'alim who had returned from the shrine cities asserting that the pasha would comply with British pressure. More importantly, the 'alim "was convinced that all the religious characters at Kerbela and Nejef who are greatly respected by Fath 'Ali Khan the King of Persia and by the Prince Muhammad 'Ali Khan would exert their instant influence" on the two to have the project accomplished. The nawwab was certain that the Qajars "would second the holy persons in an affair like this regarding the faith" and apply the necessary pressure on the Ottomans and Mamluks. The nawwab concluded that in case of the governor's intransigence, he would appeal to the 'ulama' to use their influence with the Iranians.[47] Either the British did not apply the necessary pressure, or the nawwab exaggerated the 'ulama''s influence in Iran, for the canal had to wait more than thirty years before it was reconstructed. However, the perception of both the 'alim and the nawwab of the relations between the shrine cities and the Qajars is significant.

The reverence the mujtahids of the shrine cities enjoyed in Iran was not missed by the Mamluks. In 1221/1806 Ja'far Kashif al-Ghita' was sent (according to another version he offered his services) by the governor, 'Ali Pasha, to meet the Iranian army advancing toward Baghdad. His mission was to secure peace and the release of Ottoman prisoners of war. Shaykh Ja'far succeeded after an Ottoman envoy had failed in a similar mission. By complying with Ja'far's requests, the shah presumably wanted to demonstrate his piety. Alternatively, it may have been easier for him to end the war ostensibly at Shaykh Ja'far's request. Shaykh Ja'far repeated his mediation in 1227/1812. When hostilities broke out again in 1234/1818 in the Baban region of Kurdistan, Aqa Ahmad Kirmanshahi, a mujtahid resident at Karbala', mediated between Suleyman Pasha, the governor of Baghdad, and Muhammad 'Ali Mirza, the eldest son of Fath 'Ali Shah, who served as governor of Kirmanshah.[48]

In 1237/1821–22 Shaykh Musa Kashif al-Ghita' performed the same role, mediating between Sa'id Pasha and Muhammad 'Ali Mirza. According to the family chronicler, his precondition for mediating was the return of the treasures of 'Ali's shrine from Kazimayn to Najaf. The Mamluks accepted this condition, and in 1239/1823–24 the treasures were brought back to Najaf. Following the success of his mission Musa earned the title "the peacemaker between the two states." As an expression of gratitude and recognition of Musa's influence, Da'ud Pasha, who had been one of the prisoners of war released in 1237/1821–22, granted the Kashif al-Ghita' family ownership of the village al-Basira.[49] With the launching of the Tanzimat in 1839, which meant *inter alia* the professionalization of the Ottoman foreign ministry, employment of the Shi'i 'ulama' as envoys and mediators ceased, thereby shutting off a source of influence with the government.

Taking advantage of the 1821 agreement, and of Shaykh Musa's mediation, Shaykh Nassar b. Sa'ad al-'Abbasi organized the first open *majlis ta'ziyya* (mourning sessions) in Najaf, which had hitherto been prohibited by the Mamluks due to their anti-Sunni connotations. He was gradually followed by other 'ulama'. In Baghdad, however, the Shi'is still had to perform the *majalis ta'ziyya* in cellars for fear of Mamluk retribution.[50]

While the Mamluks sought the help of the 'ulama' whenever it seemed useful, they did not change their basic attitude toward the Shi'is. When Suleyman Aqa Irbili, the governor of Hilla, suspected that Shaykh Musa Kashif al-Ghita' had been responsible for the ferment in the town (some time between 1824 and 1826), he expelled him. The poet Salih al-Tamimi, who wrote some verses expressing the anger the Shi'is felt at the humiliation of their leader, was forced to retract them when summoned to Da'ud Pasha. Likewise, Da'ud executed the maternal uncle of the Kashif al-Ghita' brothers for alleged disrespect toward the Sunnis, even though Shaykh Musa himself enjoyed "the greatest respect and veneration" in his court.[51]

The 'ulama' and the conversion of the tribes

A major factor that shaped the relations between the 'ulama' and the central government in Baghdad was their role in converting most tribes in south-central Iraq to Shi'ism. Yitzhak Nakash has shown that the consolidation of Shi'ism as a majority religion, following the conversion of the bulk of the tribes, took place only since the late eighteenth century and continued well into the nineteenth century. Previously Shi'ism in Iraq had been predominantly confined to the cities, where only a small minority of the population lived, and only a few tribes had adopted Shi'ism, as was the case among the Tayy during the fifteenth century.[52] The massive tribal conversion after the late eighteenth century was due to two factors: the great dislocation within tribal society as a result of an intensive and prolonged process of sedentarization which lasted through the late eighteenth and nineteenth centuries; and the energetic missionary activity by the Shi'i 'ulama', or "the Rafidi devils" who frequented the tribal areas, in the words of the Sunni chronicler al-Haydari.[53]

The opening in 1803 of the Hindiyya canal which brought water to Najaf from the Euphrates enabled the cultivation of wide areas between Karbala' and Najaf and attracted several tribes to settle there. Concurrently, the Hindiyya drained the Shatt al-Hilla waterway, which irrigated a rich agricultural area. This caused the ruin and disintegration of the semi-sedentarized tribal communities on its banks, and drove them to move toward the Hindiyya and clash with those tribes who had already moved there. Sedentarization was expanded after 1831 as a result of the Ottoman policy aimed at settling the tribes and transforming them into pacified tax-paying cultivators.[54]

The settlement process diversified the tribal economy and sharply stratified tribal society. Oppressed by their shaykhs, and by the increasing taxation of the Sunni government, the tribespeople were receptive to Shi'ism with its messages stressing government oppression and tyranny. Equally important, sedentarization, and its consequent weakening of tribal structure and solidarity, created a crisis of identity as well as a sense of displacement and alienation among the tribespeople.[55] The significance of the crisis caused by sedentarization is further shown by the fact that the purely nomadic tribes remained Sunnis.

Moreover, while the nomads' ties with the urban centers were predominantly confined to trade, sedentarization exposed the tribespeople to the more concerted cultural influences of the urban center, a process already observed by Ibn Khaldun in the fourteenth century. By adopting the religious customs or by taking part in the religious life of the nearby town, the tribespeople acquired a new sense of identity and affiliation and a new sense of self-respect.

The shrine cities had a particularly strong radiating power, in addition to trade, in their capacity as pilgrimage centers with each of these factors enhancing the other. In addition, the cities were the home of the conscious and intensive missionary activity of their 'ulama'. This activity, which strove to draw the tribespeople nearer, strengthened these new feelings of affiliation with a new community.[56]

The proximity of sedentarized settlements to the shrine cities or other urban centers was a crucial factor in determining whether the tribes adopted Shi'ism or remained Sunnis. The weakness of the central government enabled the Shi'i missionaries to propagate their message freely near the shrine cities or further south in Iraq. They also had an advantage due to the low number of Sunni 'ulama' and the poor state of Sunni learning in the pashalik. They did not enjoy the same freedom of action closer to Baghdad, which exerted a different type of cultural influence. Consequently, tribes who settled along the Hindiyya or south of Najaf by and large converted to Shi'ism, with the exception of a few branches, while tribes who moved more to the north were less likely to convert. The importance of the geographical factor is particularly visible in the case of branches of the same tribe or tribal confederacy, which each took a different religious path according to the location of their settlement.[57] Overall, the conversions brought about a major historical change in Iraq by transforming the Shi'is into a majority of the population, a change that would have profound socio-political ramifications in the twentieth century.[58]

The motivation of Shi'i missionary zeal could be attributed to several causes. In addition to the desire to consolidate the status of the shrine cities as regional centers, the 'ulama' probably hoped that conversion to Shi'ism would reduce tribal revolts and raids on pilgrims which threatened the economic basis of the cities. It is less likely that they hoped the conversion would substantially increase the channeling of religious dues to the cities, in view of the abject poverty of most tribespeople. They probably realized that peasants in Iraq would not be more generous donors than peasants in Iran or Lebanon. It is true, however, that the demand for religious services by the tribespeople did promise some income to the 'ulama'.[59]

The traumatic Wahhabi threat to the shrine cities may have reinforced the 'ulama''s resolve to convert the tribes as a counterweight to the invaders, as suggested by Nakash. However, the process had begun long before the Wahhabi raids. Thus the Khaza'il had already become Shi'is in the early part of the eighteenth century. Two other indications of earlier conversions are Khidr b. Shallal (d. 1255/1839–40), one of the leading contenders for religious leadership during the late 1830s, who came from the 'Afak tribe, and the mother of Hasan Kashif al-Ghita' (b. 1201/1786) who belonged to the leadership family of the Jaliha tribe.[60] In other words, the conversion of the tribes was part of the missionary zeal that characterized Shi'ism for centuries.

Religious and psychological motives and factors are not popular among some historians, but I would argue that the major motivating force for this missionary activity was the entrenched sect-like mentality of the Shi'i 'ulama'. It is the urge of the minority sect that has suffered persecution and restriction by the dominant majority to spread and proselytize its message among the larger group and conquer it from within. In earlier periods, the same urge prompted the Shi'is to produce a vast literature advocating Imam 'Ali's claim to the Prophet's succession, and fervent anti-Sunni polemics. Even during the Safavid period when they were in a dominant position, the Shi'i 'ulama' did not relent in their proselytizing efforts, resorting even to persecutions of religious minorities.[61]

In nineteenth-century Iraq the 'ulama' pursued their missionary activity in numerous levels. Shi'i 'ulama' often engaged their Sunni counterparts and Ottoman officials and even Jewish rabbis with polemical disputations in order to prove the superiority of their sect. Not surprisingly, according to Shi'i sources, they always had the upper hand, leading to the conversion of their rivals to Shi'ism. Shi'i 'ulama' were also actively proselytizing among ranks of the Ottoman Sixth Army and the police force. The Ottomans believed that the 'ulama' were urging the soldiers not to use arms against the Shi'is, thereby rendering them unreliable. The publication of anti-Sunni tracts well into the late nineteenth century is another indication of the sectarian drive.[62] It is likely that the victory of Usulism, which enhanced the 'ulama''s religious status and facilitated a greater and more active role for them in society, further invigorated their drive to convert the tribes.

The conversion process was gradual and prolonged as it did not involve any formal act, but rather the adoption of Shi'i practices. The Shi'i missionaries encouraged the visiting of the shrines, the cult of Shi'i saints, and the rituals of the commemoration of the slain Imam Husayn. As Nakash demonstrates, they adjusted Shi'i rituals to conform with Arab ideal attributes of manhood and tribal styles of celebration.[63]

Ja'far Kashif al-Ghita', to take one example of missionary activity, conducted periodic tours to propagate Shi'ism among the tribes and enhance his ties with their shaykhs. As part of this effort, he himself married the daughter of the Banu Jaliha leader and gave his own daughters to tribal chieftains. During such trips he also used to recruit promising youths to study in Najaf under his patronage.[64]

Agents (mu'mans) sent by the mujtahids to the tribal areas (some of whom were members of the tribe who had been recruited to study in the shrine cities) played an essential role in the conversion process. The agents performed basic religious services such as marriage contracts and divorce. Initially, a certain rivalry developed between these agents and the tribal sayyids, who fulfilled important religious and social functions in the tribes, even though they lacked formal religious education. One measure of the agents' success can be seen by the willingness of tribespeople to allow the mujtahids as early as the 1820s to impose Islamic punishments, the *hudud*, instead of the traditional tribal codes of law. Students from tribal areas who studied or served as the link between their tribes and the 'ulama' occasionally received lands from their tribes.[65] In other words, the networks that tied the tribes to the 'ulama' contained two intertwined layers which cemented the ties between the two groups.

Nevertheless, as late as 1887 Hajji Pirzadeh described the distaste several mujtahids and custodians of the shrines felt toward the conduct of the tribespeople at the shrine in Najaf, who used to litter and defile the place. Various 'ulama' even considered preventing the tribespeople from entering the shrine courtyard, but were allegedly prohibited from doing so by Imam Husayn who appeared in their dreams, thereby providing a solution to the problem of the tribespeople's ritual impurity (*najasa*).[66]

Overall, however, the 'ulama' used the visiting of the shrines to cement Shi'i communal solidarity among the tribespeople, tightening their links to the shrine cities. The 'ulama' apparently sought various means to consolidate their ties with tribal leaders through marriage, correspondence, and visits to the cities.[67] Politically, however, relations between the tribal leaders and the 'ulama' were not always smooth during the nineteenth century. The series of tribal rebellions in 1849, 1852, 1863–66, 1878–83, and 1899–1905 were not religiously motivated, but erupted from opposition to government taxation, conscription, and from attempts to break the power of the shaykhs, causes that were common to both Sunni and Shi'i tribes.[68] Although many of the Arab 'ulama' were of tribal origin, there are no data to show that they acted as spiritual leaders in any of these rebellions or declared any of them to be a Jihad.[69] In other words, there is no evidence for a political alliance between the 'ulama' and tribal leaders against the Ottomans.

Traditional political quietism since the time of Imam Ja'far (d. 765) and the problematics of declaring Jihad against Sunni Muslims, as well as political realism, were the major motives behind the 'ulama''s conduct.[70] Moreover, since these rebellions disrupted pilgrimage, the burial traffic and trade, which were essential to the sustenance of the community of learning, the 'ulama' probably shared the government's view of the need for security and order. Consequently, they typically acted as intermediaries between the tribal leaders and the government. On the other hand, Shi'i tribespeople sometimes extended support to revolts in both towns against the central government. In addition to religious solidarity, this support was apparently motivated by kinship ties between 'ulama' and tribespeople and by mutual resentment against the central government.

In combining the roles of urban notables, religious propagators, and mediators between the tribes and sedentarized society, the 'ulama' played a key role in the process of Shiʻi community formation in Iraq. This community consisted of multiple groups, tribal and urban, bound by ceremonial and economic exchange. Ceremonialism, or the visiting of the shrines in the Shiʻi context, functioned both to define the local groups as in the towns and also to create and maintain regional intergroup relations. In the following century, during World War I, some mujtahids sought to further develop this community into a political one as well.[71]

7 The 'ulama' and the reassertion of direct Ottoman control

Mamluk rule in Iraq ended in 1831 when Sultan Mahmud II, as part of his effort to modernize and centralize the Ottoman Empire, sent an army headed by 'Ali Rida Pasha to restore direct central rule over the pashalik. Gravely weakened by a devastating plague which had almost ruined the entire country, Baghdad capitulated to the Ottoman armies, and Da'ud Pasha was sent to an honorable exile in Anatolia.

The restoration of direct Ottoman rule marked the beginning of the Tanzimat (Ottoman reforms) period in Iraq. The main goal of the Tanzimat in the Arab provinces of the Ottoman Empire was to take over under central control the various autonomous social, religious, and economic organizations into which subjects of the empire had been organized and to forge an Ottoman patriotism that would supersede more parochial identities. These policies would play a decisive role in shaping the relations between the 'ulama' and the central government throughout the nineteenth century.

Iraq's geopolitical and demographic structure rendered the process more difficult and slower than in other Ottoman provinces. The government's first priority was to submit to its authority the various semi-independent centrifugal forces in the country. These efforts coincided with and in their turn facilitated greater western economic penetration into Iraq, a growing demand for local agricultural products, and an increase in imports of finished goods.[1]

Whereas the Sunni population of Baghdad preferred the local Mamluk rulers to direct Ottoman rule from Istanbul, the Shi'is, who resented Da'ud Pasha's harsh policies, felt that they could only gain by the Mamluks' demise. Shi'i notables from Baghdad sent a seven-member delegation to 'Ali Rida Pasha's camp in Mosul prior to his arrival at Baghdad complaining about their ill-treatment by Da'ud, particularly the prohibition on mourning sessions (majalis ta'ziyya). 'Ali Rida Pasha promised not only to permit the ta'ziyya and 'ashura' processions, but to attend them himself.[2] While Da'ud was on his way to Istanbul, Shaykh Hasan Kashif al-Ghita' asked the Shi'i poet 'Abd

al-Husayn Al Muhyi al-Din to compose a panegyric for 'Ali Rida and to
dispatch it to Istanbul to counter panegyrical poetry written in favor of
Da'ud Pasha by the Sunni poet 'Abd al-Baqi al-'Umari.[3]

As a member of the Bektashi order, which honored the twelve Imams,
'Ali Rida Pasha fulfilled his promises. He abolished restrictions on Shi'i
religious rites and various exorbitant fees levied on Shi'i pilgrims to the
shrine cities.[4] 'Ali Rida's tolerance was also due to Ottoman fear of
intrigues by Muhammad 'Ali of Egypt, who had been continuously
sending letters to various towns in Iraq, including the shrine cities. The
British resident Taylor felt "obliged to point out the growing desire of
the people for the Government of Muhammad 'Ali." After their loss of
Syria to Muhammad 'Ali, the Ottomans regarded him as a greater threat
in Iraq than alleged Iranian subversion.[5] A more important cause,
however, was 'Ali Rida Pasha's general weakness as a governor and
inability to impose effective control over his pashalik. Whereas the semi-
independent Da'ud Pasha had sent Istanbul an annual tribute of 2,000
purses, 'Ali Rida Pasha could not muster even that amount.[6]

'Ali Rida Pasha's weakness was most evident in Karbala'. Some time
after his arrival in Baghdad he sought to appoint an Ottoman governor
for the town, but the gangs either drove away or murdered the
appointee. In the summer of 1835 'Ali Rida planned to subdue the
town, but eventually backed down, feeling too weak to occupy it, and
perhaps also because he feared Iranian reaction. Recognizing his own
weakness vis-à-vis the local notable–gangs coalition, 'Ali Rida Pasha was
forced to appoint Sayyid 'Abd al-Wahhab Al Tu'ma, the custodian of
the shrines, as the local governor and as the tax-farmer for the town.
Moreover, when he demanded the right to perform a pilgrimage to the
shrines in 1841 in order to assert symbolic Ottoman sovereignty (itself a
sign of his weakness), the gang leaders consented provided that he
would be escorted only by a small bodyguard of no more than ten to
fifteen people. Opting for the lesser humiliation, 'Ali Rida returned to
Baghdad without performing the pilgrimage.[7] Ever since the 1824
rebellion, Karbala' functioned as a "self-governing semi-alien republic,"
whose real power brokers had been the gangs, with 'Abd al-Wahhab
serving as the titular governor. In 1842 there were fourteen gangs in
Karbala', ranging from 60 to 400 members each, amounting altogether
to 2,000–2,500 men, which extracted protection money from both
residents and pilgrims. Many of the gang members had been criminals,
and debtors from all over Iraq, as well as deserters from both the
Ottoman and Iranian armies. Ibrahim al-Za'frani, of mixed Iranian-
Arab and lower-class origin, headed the largest gang, composed mainly
of Arabs. His main rival, Mirza Salih, who was the leader of the minority

Iranian faction, presents an interesting case of an 'alim–notable–gang
leader. The third leader, Muhammad 'Ali Khan, head of the Baluchi
gang, was allied with Mirza Salih.[8]

Mirza Salih's father was an 'alim in Karbala' and the grandson of
Mirza Majd al-Din Muhammad, the *mutawalli* of the Madrasa Mansur-
iyya in Shiraz, while his mother was the daughter of Sayyid 'Ali
Tabataba'i, the late leading mujtahid of Karbala'. Mirza Salih himself
married into the aristocratic family of the late "ra'is ul-umara' of India."
He studied under his maternal uncle, Mahdi Tabataba'i, and under
Ibrahim Qazvini. According to Tehrani he was a popular teacher who
had assumed "religious leadership" in Karbala'. He was known to be
very strict on "enjoining the good" and "because of one of his religious
reforms (*islahat*), the *fitna* of 1258/1843 broke out." The "Persian
Account" regards him as one of the town's notables.[9]

The relations between the gangs and the 'ulama' were tenuous and
complex. The divisions between Usulis and Shaykhis played into the
hand of the gang leaders, who were regarded as crucial allies in the
struggle. Consequently, the 'ulama' themselves were often victims of the
gangs. Unlike their counterparts in Iran, they seemed to have had little if
any control over the gang leaders. Al-Za'frani, for instance, used to
extort from Ibrahim Qazvini the religious dues he had received, and his
men humiliated Qazvini in front of his students. Qazvini sought the
protection of Mirza Salih, while al-Za'frani declared himself to be a
supporter of Kazim Rashti. According to the British resident "the
Moolahs" were among the various groups of inhabitants who had
occasionally appealed to Baghdad to relieve the town of the menace of
the gangs.[10] Sayyid 'Abd al-Wahhab, the governor, paid money to
al-Za'frani as protection against Mirza Salih and the Persian faction.

In September 1842 a new governor, Muhammad Najib Pasha, arrived
in Iraq. He had been known as a conservative who opposed giving too
much away to minorities and as an advocate of centralized government
control. Establishing direct Ottoman rule in the shrine cities was one of
his first priorities. Consequently, on October 23 he set off for Musayyib
on the Euphrates, ostensibly to oversee repairs of the Hindiyya canal, for
which money had been donated by the king of Awadh. Najib sent to
Karbala' for provisions, and announced his intention to visit Imam
Husayn's shrine. In return the urban leadership sent him a token
amount of provisions, adding that he would be admitted to the town
with only four or five bodyguards, while his main force should remain
outside. Najib was incensed by the reply, and demanded that Karbala'
accept an Ottoman garrison.

Najib, who was determined to reassert Ottoman rule over the town, by force if necessary, was well aware of the consequences of his actions on Iranian–Ottoman relations. He, therefore, wrote to the British, French, Russian, and Iranian consuls informing them of his plans to subdue Karbala'. In explaining his reasons Najib stated that in view of the hostile feelings between the Ottomans and Iran, he could not, in a case of war between the two countries, "leave in his rear a populous town, containing many Persians, and governed by a set of lawless vagabonds . . . [who] defied the Sultan's authority, with a powerful tribe of Arabs close at hand ready to assist them in case of emergency."[11]

Najib accused the gang leaders of an open rebellion against Ottoman authority stressing, after the fact, that unlike other Ottoman dominions, the *khutba* (sermon) in the sultan's name, the symbol of his sovereignty, was not read in Karbala' and Najaf. Likewise, he rejected the right of the Iranian government to interfere in the affairs of Karbala' by virtue of the large number of Iranians residing there, claiming it was the hereditary possession of the sultan, who could do with it as he pleased. The sanctity of Karbala', he maintained, should not "be reason for the great concourse of Persians at Karbala'," since "these shrines are also revered by all Mussulmans." Najib also emphasized the brutality and crimes committed by the gangs against the innocent population and even against the 'ulama', arguing that "in accordance with the dictates of religion and the law" he had to put an end to this oppression.[12]

Following the initial confrontation between Najib Pasha and the town's leaders, negotiations took place in order to avoid further fighting and bloodshed between the Ottomans and the inhabitants. However, when all attempts to reach an agreement failed in mid-December 1842 due to the uncompromising stance of both sides, Najib Pasha imposed a siege on Karbala'. After several clashes and shelling of Karbala', the Ottoman troops managed to force their way into the town on January 13, 1843.

Sunni–Shi'i animosities played an important role in aggravating the crisis, and bolstering the intransigence of the gang leaders and their supporters among the lower classes. The population, and the 'ulama' in particular, did not regard the Ottoman government as legitimate and felt no allegiance to it. Moreover, the 'ulama' had good reasons to fear Ottoman control over the town as it could (and in fact did) lead to restrictions on Shi'ism and the 'ulama''s freedom of action. The advent of the millennium of the Imam's Occultation in the year 1260/1844–45 also heightened religious feeling as is evident in the subsequent emergence of the Babi movement. Rumors that the shah was about to send an army of 20,000 troops to rescue Karbala' also added to the self-confidence of the defenders. Describing the intense religious emotions involved, Farrant reported that, "when one party showed the slightest appearance of yielding to the Pasha's orders, some chief of the other party stepped forward and reminded them of their faith, and asked them if they wished to become the slaves of the Soonies." The priests (the 'ulama' or custodians of the shrines), he added, did all in their power to excite the people to fight, telling them that God was on their side, and that death was better than the Sunni rule. Consequently, "townspeople appeared daily on the walls cursing the Soonies, their prophet, and the Sultan, and lavishing all the abuse they could account."[13]

The 'ulama', who did not fight, repaired damages to the town's wall, and according to Farrant, "prayed in the Mosques encouraging and exciting the people telling them it was a religious war." On one occasion when "all had nearly agreed to the Pasha's proposition," the custodian of 'Abbas' shrine got up in the assembly, and "dashing his turban to the ground, exclaimed do you call yourselves Sheeah, and talk of giving up the town and your wives to the infidels outside?" It should be mentioned, however, that the officials of the shrines were not 'ulama' and stood to lose considerably should the Ottomans take the town and seize control over the shrines, as in fact eventually happened. Their interests and those of the 'ulama' were not always in harmony.

The elite of mujtahids did not share the general enthusiasm so it is not possible to speak of a unified stand by the 'ulama' in the affair. The Shaykhi leader, Sayyid Kazim Rashti, played a key moderating role both in Karbala' and in the negotiations. Unfortunately for him, he had very little power over his supposed ally and client, Ibrahim al-Za'frani. During various meetings held by the besieged urban leaders, Rashti "pleaded with them to accept Najib's terms," but to no avail. Moreover, he was often "abused and threatened" for his stance. Clearly, the mujtahid–gang alliance was tenuous and neither party felt obliged to support the other.

The Usuli–Shaykhi enmity and Rashti's personal rivalry with Ibrahim Qazvini undermined his efforts. Undoubtedly, Rashti's rivals feared that his success in the negotiations would enhance his position in the town thereafter. According to his disciple Karim Khan Kirmani, "however much the noble Sayyid endeavored to dampen the fire of this rebellion through conciliation and forbearance, his opponents declared that they would rather see their women and children prisoners in the hands of the Turks than to have this dispute settled by him." According to Zarandi, the Usuli 'ulama' incited the people to attack the Ottoman forces in order to thwart Rashti's efforts.[14]

Ibrahim Qazvini's position was more ambiguous. He took a far less active role than Rashti in the negotiations, and his supporters opposed Rashti's moderate stance. Yet he himself, in addition to some of his students, left Karbala' as the siege began and found refuge in Kazimayn which was under firm Ottoman control. From Kazimayn he tried to mediate a compromise with the help of the Iranian consul, but to no avail. In other words, he found Sunni rule less threatening than gang rule and was unwilling to lend his support to their cause. His personal secretary did stay in Karbala'.[15] In a letter to Lucknow Sayyid 'Ali Naqi Tabataba'i described those who stayed in the town as "the poor" and "miserables," which may suggest that he and his family were not among them.[16]

Apparently, a generational gap or a divergence between senior and lower-ranking 'ulama' is largely responsible for the different responses of the 'ulama' to the rebellion. The mujtahids may have been more cautious and more willing to adopt a quietist political approach than their disciples, and they did not regard the gang rule in Karbala' as greatly preferable to Ottoman rule. The fact that no senior 'alim is mentioned by the biographical dictionaries as having been killed in the battle and the ensuing massacre may also indicate such a gap. Local Shi'is interrogated by Colonel Farrant mentioned differences between natives and migrants, implying perhaps that the latter had been less ardent in preserving Karbala''s independence.[17] This divergence points out to the inherent weakness of the Shi'i leadership and to its failure in this case. Neither one of the mujtahids could impose his views on the population and brigands.

When the Ottomans broke into Karbala', frightened inhabitants fled to the houses of Sayyid Kazim Rashti and the exiled Qajar prince, Zill al-Sultan, as well as into the two shrines which had been designated as sanctuaries by Najib Pasha. Rashti's house was so full that people spilled into the courtyard, where more than sixty people were crushed or suffocated to death in the panic. Before the battle began, the Ottoman troops had been promised financial rewards for every head or ear of a *luti* they would bring. Consequently, when the troops arrived at the shrine of 'Abbas and were shot at, discipline broke down and soldiers spread throughout the town, looting and killing indiscriminately. A massacre in Husayn's shrine was stopped only at the intervention of the Ottoman commander Sa'dallah Pasha, who had hitherto given his troops a free hand. After thorough inquiries, Farrant estimated the loss of life at 3,000 inside the town, and 2,000 tribespeople outside the walls. Iranian sources claimed that as many as 30,000 people were slain. Ottoman losses were estimated at 400, an indication of the fierce resistance they encountered. Arab tribespeople who had fought alongside the gangs now joined the plunder, their tribal tradition superseding their religious solidarity.[18]

Najib Pasha came to Karbala' on January 18, and went to pray at Imam Husayn's shrine to show his religiosity. He appointed an Ottoman officer as governor while an assistant *qadi* (judge) and a *khatib* were dispatched from Baghdad, signifying the end of Karbala''s semi-independence. Most of the leaders of the Karbala' rebellion, the former governor Sayyid 'Abd al-Wahhab as well as the gang leaders, were captured by the Ottomans, but subsequently pardoned. Mirza Salih was taken to Istanbul but was released following the intercession of Nasir al-Din Shah. He migrated to Tehran where he later emerged as an important mujtahid.[19]

From Karbala' Najib proceeded to Najaf to assert Ottoman authority there. Having witnessed Karbala''s fate, the town did not offer any resistance. A delegation headed by Hasan Kashif al-Ghita' went to negotiate Najib's entry to the town indicating that the 'ulama', rather than the custodians of the shrine, were perceived as better mediators between the population and the government. Shi'i sources give a glorified version of Hasan's proud encounter with Najib, which cannot be verified. Significantly, he played on the ramifications of a forcible occupation of Najaf on Ottoman–Iranian relations as a major argument to dissuade Najib from employing force. Upon entering the town, Najib prayed at the shrine, but could not keep himself from uttering sarcastic remarks about Imam 'Ali and the Shi'is. While visiting the shrine he was escorted by Muhammad Hasan Najafi, presumably keeping a balance between the two rival mujtahids.[20]

Najib appointed an Ottoman officer as governor of Najaf. Since the local sayyid elite had been allied with the Shumurt gang, he appointed the Zukurt leaders as tax-farmers for Najaf. The new tax-farmer added "by force and torture of imprisonment, a hundred thousand Shamis to the usual tax" levied on the town. In addition the Zukurt persecuted their Shumurt rivals with a vengeance.[21] Ironically, due to the bloody Ottoman suppression, Karbala' seemed to have suffered less from the menace of the gangs than Najaf for the rest of the century.

The bloodless occupation of Najaf was misleading as it spared the urban gangs from destruction. In 1852 a rebellion of the Shumurt and the Zubayd broke out in Najaf. Seeking to split Wadi Bey, paramount shaykh of the Zubayd and tax-farmer of the Hindiyya region, from the gang, the governor, Namik Pasha, asked for the intercession of the "Sheeah priesthood." He offered Wadi Bey and his men the "most honorable terms" if they would evacuate the town. The "chief Priest," as Rawlinson called him, intervened in order to avert bloodshed and "by

his holy character persuaded the rebel chief to accept terms of accommodation." Though the tribal forces abandoned the town, when the
Ottoman troops entered Najaf fierce fighting erupted, with heavy loss of
life for the population and troops. The two gangs were forced to leave
the town temporarily, but were not subdued.[22]

As soon as Najib's intentions to take Karbala' by force were known,
the Iranian government asked the British to dissuade him from attacking
Karbala', accusing Najib of "determined disregard" for Iranian feelings.
In addition to genuine fear of possible profanation of the shrine, the
Iranian government was deeply worried for its domestic credibility and
prestige in view of such provocations.[23] The news of the sack of Karbala'
caused both grief and rage in Iran. Hujjat al-Islam Shafti, for instance,
exerted pressure on Muhammad Shah to declare war on the Ottomans
by threatening to raise himself an army of 20,000 men against Najib.
Iranian rage in 1843 exceeded that which followed the Wahhabi attack,
since the perpetrators were the traditional Ottoman enemies rather than
an extremist tribal sect. Under pressure, the shah made some threats
against the Ottomans, which were mainly designed to show that he was
doing something.[24] Iran did demand indemnification for the property
belonging to its subjects, a written Ottoman apology and condemnation
of the massacre as well as the dismissal and punishment of Najib Pasha.

The British ambassador in Istanbul, Sir Stratford Canning, feared
that the sack of Karbala' would undermine the Iranian–Ottoman
negotiations on border demarcation that were being held in Erzerum
and, even worse, would lead to a religious war. At the time Britain was
seeking to bring about a reconciliation between the two hostile Muslim
empires so that both could serve as an effective buffer against Russian
encroachment southward.[25] In a rare and a surprising case of agreement
both Canning and the Russian ambassador exerted pressure on the
Ottomans to comply with at least some of the Iranian demands.

Following extensive diplomatic activity between the Iranians, Ottomans, and the British, an agreement was reached.[26] The Porte consented to allocate "a suitable sum . . . to the relief of the sufferers at
Kerbela." Likewise, it agreed to address a letter to the Iranian *Sadr-i
A'zam* in which it would "declare its disapproval of the late expedition
against Kerbela, its regret at the occurrence as unauthorized and
unreasonable, and . . . its sorrow for the effusion of blood which
ensued." Najib Pasha was instructed to "repair the Shrines at Kerbela,
to administer his province with equity, to protect the Persian subjects
there, and particularly the pilgrims from Persia." He was also threatened
with dismissal should a similar affair take place.[27]

While Iranian honor may have been redeemed, nothing was done to alleviate the suffering of the true victims. Colonel Farrant admitted that it was extremely difficult to verify the numerous claims made by many Iranians for the loss of considerable property. The Ottomans, however, did not even make the slightest effort. When the British consul raised the issue in April 1846, Najib responded that indeed 200 purses (100,000 piasters) had been allocated by the Porte, but blamed his *defterdar* (chief treasurer) for the lack of any action in that regard. As three years had passed since the massacre, during which the population underwent significant change, and in view of the difficulties of verifying the claims for lost property, Najib proposed to give a certain amount to Sayyid Ibrahim Qazvini "either as a benefaction to the shrine, or for charitable distribution among the indigent pilgrims." However, as late as 1850 Najib had not provided one piaster to the victims, and there is no indication that he or any other governor did so afterwards. Since Iran renounced its own claims for compensations as part of the second Erzerum Agreement of 1847, he felt no pressure to do anything.[28]

The bloody Ottoman repression did not bring about a long-term change in the social structure of Karbala', although the dominant notable sayyid class may have been weakened compared with the 'ulama'. A few months after the rebellion, Colonel Farrant reported that the town had returned to normal life and that many of the "respectable" residents rejoiced at the expulsion of the gangs.[29] According to the "Persian account" many merchants and 'ulama' emigrated to other cities or even to Iran and India shortly after the Ottoman occupation. Pilgrimage did decline for a while after the rebellion, but recovered fairly quickly. In fact 1260/1844–45, the millennium of the Twelfth Imam's Occultation, witnessed a record number of pilgrims, due to the heightened messianic expectations in the Shi'i world. While the rebellion was an important cause of Karbala''s decline as the major learning center, the city retained its status as the preferred pilgrimage site for the Shi'is and consequently remained a flourishing market town.

The rebellion and its bloody outcome exacerbated Sunni–Shi'i animosities in Iraq, with Najib Pasha labeled "Yazid," the most notorious Shi'i epithet, equating him with the hated Umayyad caliph who was responsible for Imam Husayn's death. Shi'i poets, probably expressing prevalent feelings among the Shi'is, implored the Mahdi to return and relieve his people from oppression. One poet, Salih al-Kawwaz, called upon the Mahdi to regain the caliphate being held by usurpers, charging the sultan with occupying a place that was not his. Al-Kawwaz, it might be noted, also used ethnic themes in mourning the fate of the Arabs who are ruled by foreigners.[30]

One minor Usuli 'alim, Mulla Yusuf Astarabadi, arrived at an extremely different conclusion. Enraged and grieved by the death of his son in the massacre, he exclaimed in a letter to India "Would that there were no king (*sultan*) ruling over us, and none over Iran." It is conceivable that Astarabadi's anger at Muhammad Shah's inaction was shared by many other 'ulama'. However, his "rudimentary republicanism," as Cole puts it, does not seem to have been prevalent at the time, considering the 'ulama''s subsequent conduct.[31] More importantly, the modern Karbala' tragedy was seen by many Shi'is as cataclysmic events preceding the awaited appearance of the Mahdi. It heightened messianic expectations in Shi'ism, which were already rising due to the approaching millennium of the Occultation of the Twelfth Imam, and apparently facilitated the acceptance of the Babi claims at least within the Shaykhi community.[32]

The 'ulama', the Ottomans, and the Babi challenge[33]

The Babi movement, which emerged during the 1840s, posed the most serious ideological and social threat to the Shi'i 'ulama' in Iran and the shrine cities during the nineteenth century by offering a messianic alternative to the established orthodoxy at a time of growing socio-economic difficulties. While the entire history of the relationships between the 'ulama' and the Babi movement is beyond the scope of this study, the encounter in the shrine cities was crucial to the history of the new movement, and marked an important chapter in the 'ulama'–Ottoman–Qajar triangle.

The founder of the Babi movement, Sayyid 'Ali Muhammad, "the Bab" (the Gate), was born in Shiraz on 1 Muharram 1235/October 20, 1819 into a family of merchants. Even in his youth he inclined toward mysticism, and in 1257/1841–42 moved to Karbala' where he spent eleven months. He was influenced there by Shaykhi ideas and in turn left a deep impression on various Shaykhi students there. Sayyid 'Ali Muhammad returned to Shiraz, and resumed his trading activity while engaging in meditation and mystical experiences. During that period he began to believe that he had been chosen for a divine mission, as the Gate to the Imam and as a bearer of a new divine revelation.

The advent of the year 1260/1844–45, the millennium of the Imam's Occultation, combined with evidence of decay and western encroachment on Iran, created the feelings of crisis that usually serve as a fertile ground for millenarian movements. The messianic urge had been particularly strong within the Shaykhi community in Karbala' ever since Rashti made repeated allusions during the last year of his life to the impending *zuhur* (appearance) of the Mahdi after his own death.

Presumably because of such expectations, Rashti refused to nominate a successor to head the Shaykhi community.

Consequently, after Rashti's death on 11 Dhu al-Hijja 1259/January 2, 1844, the Shaykhi community was deeply divided over the succession and its general orientation.[34] A group of Shaykhi students, led by Mulla Husayn Bushru'i, rejected the various contenders for succession in adherence to Rashti's allusions to the coming appearance of the Hidden Imam. They decided to leave Karbala' and retire in prayer and fasting (*i'tikaf*) in the Kufa mosque and wait for the *zuhur*. After spending forty days in *i'tikaf*, they set out for Kirman. Passing through Shiraz, Bushru'i met Sayyid 'Ali Muhammad Shirazi. It was during this meeting that he recognized the Sayyid's claim to be the Promised One, or the Gate (*bab*) to the Imam, and formed the first group of disciples. The meeting and proclamation marked the birth of the Babi movement.

With the coming of the Hajj, the Bab decided to make his claim public and propagate his mission. The Bab planned to go to Mecca and proclaim his mission there and subsequently appear in the shrine cities. He dispatched Bushru'i to Tehran and Mulla 'Ali Bastami to the shrine cities to spread his message before his arrival. The goal of winning over the Shaykhi community and delivering the Bab's message to the Usuli mujtahids was critical for the success of the new movement, making the shrine cities the principal focus of Babi attention.

Bastami arrived in Karbala' in August 1844 carrying the Bab's message to the Shaykhi community, which was still in crisis following Rashti's death. Having converted to his mission a considerable number of Shaykhis, Bastami proceeded to Najaf for the celebration of the *Fitr* (1 Shawwal 1260/October 6, 1844).[35] In Najaf, he presented Muhammad Hasan Najafi with the Bab's writing claiming that his written message *Quyum al-Asma'* had superseded all previous holy scriptures, declaring him to be the only legitimate source of authority in Islam.[36]

Najafi, who had consistently denounced all heterodoxies ranging from theosophy to Shaykhism, "forthwith pronounced Mulla 'Ali a heretic and expelled him from the assembly."[37] Najafi's response in a period of growing intolerance to non-conformism among the 'ulama' was inevitable in view of the audacious challenge to orthodoxy and to the authority of the 'ulama'. His leadership position required him to set an example to all believers. Other mujtahids from Najaf and Karbala' joined him in denouncing the new message as blasphemous. Najafi's sharp reaction was also influenced by the messianic tension in the shrine cities manifested in the record number of pilgrims, 20,000–30,000. The 'ulama' had always feared the consequences of such messianism in view of the past Shi'i defeats.[38]

Although repudiated by the mujtahids, Bastami was successful in spreading his call among low-ranking students, presumably by appealing to their disenchantment with the dry legalistic approach of the traditional Islamic learning. Hostility toward the orthodox style of learning had motivated several of the Bab's early disciples. "Not one warm-hearted man (*ahl-i dil*) has ever come out of a madrasa," Mulla Husayn Bushru'i once declared. "Down with these schools which are house of ignorance."[39]

Evidently alarmed by the new threat, Najafi's supporters, "joining hands with their adversaries," the Shaykhis, seized Bastami and delivered him to the Ottoman government, "arraigning him as a wrecker of Islam, a calumniator of the Prophet . . . and worthy of the penalty of death."[40] In addition to protecting their own interests, the 'ulama' apparently feared that Bastami's messianic preaching would lead to anti-Ottoman agitation and to developments similar to the tragic events in Karbala' the year before.

According to Rawlinson, the arrest "created no great sensation" at first. The outcome of the affair desired both by the mujtahids and the governor was to have Bastami banished to Iran and his book destroyed. However, the Sunni 'ulama', to whom the governor referred the matter, took up the case, "in a rancorous spirit of bigotry."[41] The Sunni court upheld the charge of blasphemy and recommended the maximum penalty of death. Contrary to his earlier conciliatory tone, when he had discussed the affair with Rawlinson, Najib Pasha now approved the verdict. The court's "inveteracy," Rawlinson added, "has enlisted the sympathies of the entire Sheeah sect" in favor of Bastami. The affair became a focal point of Shi'i resentment against the Ottomans and perhaps also at the timidity of the mujtahids *vis-à-vis* the government. As such, it was transformed from an internal Shi'i dispute into "virulent contest between the Soonee [Sunni] and Sheeah [Shi'i] sects" in Iraq.[42]

In addition to exacerbating sectarian enmity, the affair threatened the already tense Iranian–Ottoman relations. As events would show subsequently, the Iranian government proved extremely hostile to the Babi cause when it threatened its own authority. Yet, at the time, it viewed Bastami's trial as an imposition of Sunni jurisdiction over the Shi'i population and a further Ottoman encroachment upon the rights of Iranian subjects in Iraq. The governor of Kirmanshah, Muhibb 'Ali Khan, appealed to Rawlinson to intercede on Bastami's behalf and protest at the improper arrest of a Persian subject "on a mere accusation." He requested that if Bastami's crimes could be proven he should be banished to Iran and punished there.[43] Rawlinson appealed to Stratford Canning, the British ambassador in Istanbul, to pressure the

Porte to revoke the verdict, out of fear of aggravating sectarian animosity and jeopardizing the ongoing Iranian–Ottoman border negotiations. Najib, however, rejected Rawlinson's intercession, arguing that "Persian subjects residing in Turkey are in civil, criminal and religious matters, entirely subject to Ottoman law."[44]

Nevertheless, in order to "give all due formality to his proceedings, and to divest the affair of the appearance of mere sectarian prosecution" Najib adopted an unprecedented measure and summoned a joint Sunni–Shi'i court to decide Bastami's fate.[45] The Shi'i mujtahids faced a serious dilemma whether or not to comply. The execution of Bastami on charges of blasphemy could precipitate similar charges against the Shi'is in the future.[46] On the other hand, they could not defend Bastami's heresy and accept the challenge to their own authority. Furthermore, Bastami's initial success in the shrine cities revealed the difficulty in suppressing the heresy by their own means. Nor could the mujtahids openly defy the governor who had proved his ruthlessness against their community. In addition, in view of traditional Ottoman discrimination against Shi'ism, Najib's invitation of the Shi'i mujtahids implied official recognition of the distinct status of Shi'ism, an opportunity that could not be dismissed. Finally, participation in the trial while preventing an extreme anti-Shi'i verdict could enhance the status of the participants in the Shi'i community.

The Sunni delegation to the trial was headed by the chief mufti of Baghdad, Shihab al-Din Mahmud al-Alusi. Initially a bitter opponent of Shi'ism, he modified his views late in his life and accepted coexistence with the Shi'is as long as they did not threaten the superiority of Sunni law. The other Sunni participants were the Naqib al-Ashraf, fifteen other 'ulama', and the two shaykhs of the Sunni Sufi orders.[47]

Altogether thirteen Shi'i mujtahids participated in the meeting. The Najaf delegation was headed by Hasan Kashif al-Ghita', whose role in sparing Najaf from the fate of Karbala' established him as the leading Shi'i representative vis-à-vis the Ottomans. Ibrahim Qazvini headed the Karbala' delegation, which included the Shaykhi leader, Mulla Hasan Gauhar.[48]

The unprecedented inter-sectarian gathering created a great stir among both Sunnis and Shi'is in Baghdad. The trial began on 4 Muharram 1261/January 13, 1845, six days before the mourning of 'Ashura' and the expected arrival of the Bab in Karbala'. Being aware of the messianic expectations among the Shi'is, and wary of heightened anti-Ottoman agitation, Najib wanted to obtain the necessary ruling before that fateful date.[49]

Both Sunni and Shi'i jurists agreed that the Bab's book, *Quyum* al-asma', was blasphemous and its propagator deserved death, the first time that such punishment was prescribed for adherents of the new cause. However, the jurists disagreed on Bastami's own fate. The Sunnis refused to accept his repentance and disavowal of the book and, therefore, sentenced him to death. The Shi'is accepted it and returned the verdict that he was only guilty of dissemination of blasphemy, and was therefore liable to imprisonment or banishment.[50] Although the joint *fatwa* was dominated by the Sunni point of view, in their attached individual rulings the Shi'i jurists carefully avoided the mention of a death sentence. They merely subjected the author of the book and his followers to the "anger of the all-merciful."[51] Shi'i dilemmas in the trial are reflected in Tunikabuni's description of his teacher, Ibrahim Qazvini, who supported Hasan Kashif al-Ghita"s views, "although he was very fearful and practiced *taqiyya* all along."[52] The final decision on Bastami's fate was referred to the Porte in Istanbul, which instructed Najib Pasha in April 1845 to transfer Bastami to Istanbul. Bastami was sentenced to life labor at the docks, where he died.[53]

Tahirah (or Qurrat al-'Ayn as she had been called in the Shaykhi community), the most senior female disciple of the Bab and a scion of the Baraghani mujtahid family of Qazvin, assumed the leadership of the Babi community in the shrine cities. Tahirah aroused the animosity of both the Shaykhi leadership in Karbala' and of the Usuli mujtahids, as she managed to transmit the Babi message to the Shi'i public in Iraq beyond Karbala'. In her writings, sermons, and public actions, particularly in unveiling herself in public, Tahirah led the Babi movement to the final break with Shi'i Islam. She invited the Usuli mujtahids for a debate, and when none responded, she challenged them to a *mubahala* (mutual execration in the hope of divine arbitration between good and evil).[54] The Usulis were unwilling to take up that challenge either, which might have lent some credibility to a heretic. A mob, which had been incited by her opponents, attacked Kazim Rashti's house where she had resided, and arrested her. To prevent further disturbances, the Ottoman governor detained her, but released her shortly thereafter on condition that she leave Karbala'. Tahirah was brought to Baghdad, and in Rabi' al-Thani 1263/March–April 1847 she was deported to Iran.[55] Tahirah's case demonstrated once again the inability of the Usuli mujtahids to overcome the external challenge to their authority by their own power and their dependence on the government, even a Sunni one, to combat heresy.

In its direct attack on the tenets of orthodoxy and the foundations of the 'ulama' system, as well as in its appeal to the masses, Babism proved to be one of the most serious challenges to the 'ulama"s authority during the nineteenth century. In the shrine cities, however, the closing of ranks among Sunni, Usuli, and Shaykhi leaders sealed its fate.[56] The very nature of society in the shrine cities as centers of orthodoxy precluded a major breakthrough for Babism beyond the circle of the Shaykhi community. The total enmity by the Usuli establishment accelerated, in its turn, the final break of Babism with Shi'i Islam. The focus of Babi activity shifted to Iran and the mujtahids there had taken the lead in the fight against it.

8   The 'ulama' and Ottoman centralization policy

The 1843 Ottoman occupation of Karbala' and Najaf ended the period of semi-autonomy in the history of the shrine cities. Though the Ottomans never achieved complete centralization in Iraq, particularly in the countryside, the cities were subjected to growing Ottoman control. As part of that process, relations between the 'ulama' and the Ottomans grew more fractious, while cooperation was tenuous. This friction was the outcome of several processes. Among them: repressive Ottoman measures against Shi'ism as a religion, intended to abolish the independent authority of the Shi'i 'ulama'; policies that were part of the Tanzimat reforms implemented throughout the empire, some of which presented special problems to the Shi'is, e.g., military conscription and tighter control of the shrines; steps taken against the Iranian community designed to limit its economic power and force the Iranians to accept Ottoman nationality; the personal inclinations of Ottoman officials to enrich themselves as well as to provoke and harass the Shi'is.

In addition to reviewing these processes, I will seek to analyze their impact on the status and political conduct of the 'ulama' in the political arenas in Iraq and Iran, pushing them to cling to their quietist approach. Immediately after the brutal suppression of Karbala', the Ottomans showed total disregard of Shi'i sensitivities by billeting troops in the courtyards of the two shrines. While emotionally painful, this provocation was short lived. A more ominous sign for the long run was the appointment of a deputy *qadi* in Karbala' and Najaf, signifying the state's intention to appropriate all legal activity under its control. For the first time since the days of Da'ud Pasha, in both Najaf and Karbala' the Sunni *khatib* read the *khutba* in the name of the sultan in the shrines. The Shi'is, who were forced to attend the service in the early days after the occupation, were obliged to conform with the Sunni form of prayer and practice religious dissimulation (*taqiyya*). Shi'i demoralization was so deep during that early period that "no one dares pray . . . in the Shi'a form; nor use the seal of the sacred earth of Karbala' in the prostration."

Only toward the end of Muharram did a few persons procure permission to recite this service.[1]

The Sunni *khatib*, however, used to leave the mosque after an hour, and the Shi'is could then pray with their own prayer imams. The reading of the last verse of the Shi'i call to prayer – "and 'Ali [is] the helper-friend of God (*wa-'Ali wali Allah*)" – was prohibited.[2] Prayers in all other mosques were conducted by Shi'i prayer imams. In other words, the Ottomans were more interested in demonstrating their sovereignty than in forcing the Shi'is to abandon the tenets of their religion. Consequently, they did not prohibit the *ta'ziyya* processions despite their anti-Sunni undertone. In 1845, for instance, both Najib Pasha's son, Ahmad Bey, and the governor of Karbala' attended these processions as a sign of goodwill. The Ottomans did prohibit the public *sabb va-rafd* of the first three caliphs, since that was open defiance against Sunni Islam.[3]

The most serious threat to the independence and livelihood of the 'ulama' was the Ottoman policy of abolishing Shi'i legal courts and ensuring the monopoly of the government Hanafi courts. Though orders to that effect were issued immediately after the occupation of Karbala', the Shi'is did not abide by them and continued to resort to their own mujtahids. Consequently, following instructions from Istanbul and at the "urgent instigation" of the newly appointed Sunni *qadi* of Baghdad, Najib wrote to Ibrahim Qazvini in early 1845 expressing his "surprise" and anger that the deputy *qadi* in Karbala' remained idle. He instructed Qazvini to warn his fellow Shi'is that in the future all legal disputes and transactions must be drawn up and registered in the Ottoman *qadi*'s office. Legal documents issued by the Shi'i 'ulama' would be invalid, and "the parties executing or accepting such illegal decisions and all who may abet or connive at such proceedings will be held to be obnoxious [i.e. exposed] to further punishment."[4]

When Rawlinson enquired about the matter, Najib explained that "he considers the long-established reference to the Sheeah chief priest as a mere conventional method of arbitration, and as long as the decision of such courts are given orally and privately, he has no desire to interfere." However, he added, he could not allow the Shi'i 'ulama' "by public execution of written decrees, to arrogate powers which are vested explicitly in the Sultan," and which "can only be legitimately exercised . . . under a special patent or trust."[5]

Indeed when the "Mujtahid 'chief priest' of Kazimayn" dealt with the estate of an Iranian woman who had died without heirs, the Sunni *bayt al-mal* (public treasury), which was supposed to inherit the money according to Hanafi law, notified Najib Pasha of the breach. The governor summoned the mujtahid to Baghdad, and, according to Consul Rawlinson, intended to order "his immediate and ignominious deportation to Persia." Rawlinson persuaded the governor merely to admonish the mujtahid, since punishing him would be regarded by the Iranian court as a "gratuitous religious insult."[6]

Najib's action against Shi'i litigation was not motivated solely by sectarian intolerance. The reorganization of the judicial system was one of the important components of the Tanzimat. As part of the centralization process, the Ottomans could not tolerate the existence of independent non-governmental Muslim courts such as had existed in Iran with their political ramifications of undermining the government's sovereignty and authority. Though they gave the non-Muslim communities judicial autonomy as part of the *millet* system, the Ottomans refused to grant the Shi'is the status of a separate *millet*, as the Shi'is were not *dhimmi*s (protected minorities) according to Sunni law, but sinning Muslims. Granting them an independent *millet* status would be tantamount to their exclusion from Islam, and status as a separate religion.[7] Moreover, by abolishing Shi'i courts the Ottomans could deprive the Shi'i 'ulama' of an important source of revenue and independent power while increasing the revenues of the Sunni court and indirectly of the governor himself.

The British were worried that Najib's measures would aggravate the tensions between Iran and the Ottoman Empire and endanger the Erzerum negotiations. Consequently, they sought to mitigate or delay the application of the order. Najib had no difficulty in telling the British that "he had removed the interdict on Sheeah jurisdiction," but admitted that "the orders to this effect have not been as yet. . . generally promulgated, nor will the Sheeah tribunals probably be established until after the Ramadhan." The interdiction, however, was never revoked.

In 1852 the governor, Namik Pasha, went further, decreeing that neither marriages nor divorces conducted by Shi'i 'ulama' would be recognized as valid in the local courts. The 'ulama' were again warned against any violations. Shi'i law, Rawlinson concluded, was "not only unrecognized throughout this Pashalic, but it is positively proscribed, and to dispense it renders penal."[8]

The case of the inheritance of a British-Indian subject, Muhammad Rida Shirazi, reflects the new division of labor between the Shi'i mujtahids and the Ottoman courts. A certain Muhammad Isma'il was appointed as the executor by a mujtahid in Karbala', but needed the authorization of the Ottoman *qadi* to take possession of the property. The executor of the will appealed first to the mujtahid, probably in order to obtain communal consent and legitimize his claim. The

mujtahid in this case lacked the power to enforce his decision, but the
qadi relied on his ruling.[9] The Ottomans, however, lacked the police
apparatus to effectively enforce their orders and coerce the Shi'is to
resort to Ottoman courts in all cases.

Although they themselves suffered from Ottoman discrimination, the
Shi'i 'ulama' did not recoil from appealing to the Ottomans to act
against dissenters in their own camp. In 1863 Shaykh 'Abd al-Husayn
Tehrani of Karbala' asked the Ottomans to deport the Baha'i leader,
Baha'ullah, from Baghdad. When that failed, he appealed to the shah to
exert pressure on the Ottomans to deport Baha'ullah, reflecting the
mujtahids' dependence on the Qajars.[10]

In June 1845 the acting governor, Ahmad Bey, notified the Iranian
and British consuls of his intention to enforce, after a six-month
transitional period, the Porte's orders that all foreigners possessing land
or houses in the Ottoman dominions would be regarded as Ottoman
subjects liable to all relevant laws. Non-Muslim foreign nationals had
always been prohibited from owning real estate in the Ottoman Empire
and any property they had purchased was registered under the names of
local Muslims. Muslim foreigners could purchase such property and
have it legally registered in the *qadi*'s court.[11]

The governor's proclamation caused great consternation among the
Iranian and Indian communities which were largely concentrated in the
four shrine cities. Acceptance of Ottoman nationality would have meant
the loss of the privileges accorded to Iranian commerce in the treaty of
Erzerum and subjection to all taxes and "duties assessments" that
applied to Ottoman subjects. Worst of all from their point of view was
the threat of conscription to the Ottoman army. On the other hand, if
they tried to sell their property within a short period of time in order to
preserve their nationality, they faced a considerable financial loss, due to
the great numbers of those involved. Rawlinson, who estimated their
numbers as more than 50,000 Iranians holding property worth more
than £1,000,000 and several thousand Indians holding over £100,000
worth of property, believed the loss would amount to two-thirds of the
property's value.[12]

Concerned with the fate of their own subjects in Iraq, the British
exerted pressure on the Porte not to apply the new law retroactively.
Bowing to this pressure, the Ottoman Porte informed the British that
they did not intend to enforce the orders. Najib had to give up his efforts
to apply the measure to the Indian community, but continued his
threats against the Iranians. Based on the Porte's message and on his
own conversations with Najib Pasha, Rawlinson asserted that Najib's
main goal was self-enrichment. Shortly before issuing the order, he

obtained the Porte's permission to raise the fees levied on all real estate transactions to 8.75 percent of their value. While the *qadi* collected 1.25 percent as his fee, the rest was to go to Najib's treasury. The projected sale of such a vast property would have meant a sizable profit of "several thousand purses" for the pasha. Alternatively, should the foreigners accept Ottoman nationality, the pashalik's (and his own) revenues would rise substantially by the imposition of new taxes.[13]

The new measure threatened the 'ulama''s interests both as property owners and indirectly by the harm done to their constituency. According to Rawlinson, thousands of lower-class Iranians, mainly shopkeepers and house owners, decided to return to Iran rather than face Ottoman conscription. Wealthier Iranians could not give up their property so easily. Consequently, at their behest, a delegation of 'ulama' went to Baghdad to seek a settlement with Najib Pasha. The delegation proposed that "as a private conveyance of property, to such an enormous extent, and in so brief a period, is out of the question, the Turkish Government would take the lands and houses off their hands at as low a valuation as the local authorities may think fit to offer." In case of Najib's refusal, the delegates intended to ask for guarantees with regard to those who would accept Ottoman nationality against the loss of their property.[14]

Presumably as a result of the British pressure, Najib postponed the retroactive application of the new law. He may also have understood that a mass migration of Iranians from Iraq would severely affect the pashalik's economy, which depended largely on the pilgrimage to the shrine cities. However, the danger of the retroactive application of the measure remained as a constant threat over the heads of the Iranians, presumably as a means of pressure.[15] In early 1852 the new governor, Namik Pasha, prohibited all masons from helping Iranian proprietors to repair their houses or shops without official permission. The new order was designed to cause Iranian property to deteriorate and be abandoned so that the authorities could appropriate it, or simply as a new means of exacting bribes from the Iranians.[16] Ever since the promulgation of the new measure, Iranian 'ulama' who purchased land in Iraq had had to accept Ottoman nationality. The most prominent case was that of the Bahr al-'Ulum family, which used its control over the Oudh Bequest to acquire land.

Summing up Najib Pasha's treatment of the Shi'is, Rawlinson asserted that "hating equally Christians and Sheeahs, whom he classes together as infidels and strangers," his conduct to the two communities is distinguished by the relative willingness of the Iranian or European governments to allow "greater or lesser latitude for the indulgence of his rancour." The Iranians, he added, "are the objects of an undisguised and undiscriminating persecution," and their grievances "extend over every portion of the body politic and every question of individual right, whether affecting religion, conscience, nationality, property, commerce or personal security."[17]

It should be mentioned, however, that not in all cases did the Shi'i 'ulama' and the Qajars share the same interest against Najib Pasha. When the Iranians submitted complaints to the Ottomans against the governor's ill-treatment of Iranian pilgrims to the shrine cities in late 1843, the agents of Sayyid Ibrahim Qazvini of Karbala' and Shaykh Husun (sic) of Najaf (Hasan Kashif al-Ghita'?) hastened to assure the British consul that the visitors' grievances were relatively few and minor. They added that once they had brought "these grievances to the notice of the Pasha, he had immediately taken measures for their relief."[18] In other words, as the mujtahids were interested in the uninterrupted flow of visitors to the shrine cities, they did not always share the Qajars' desire to use the issue as a political lever in the broader Ottoman–Iranian rivalry.

Increased government revenues was one of the Tanzimat's main goals. Prior to its occupation, Karbala' paid about 70,000 piasters (roughly £700) annually to the Baghdad government. In comparison, in 1259/ 1843–44 alone the Ottomans collected 810,000 piasters (£8,100) from Karbala' and 315,000 piasters (£3,150) from Najaf. A year later they almost doubled their revenues, collecting 1,500,000 (£15,000) and 600,000 piasters (£6,000) respectively.[19] Apparently because the tax collection in Karbala' declined in the following year, the *defterdar* of the pashalik decided in 1845 to farm out the town to the highest bidder.

The "chief mujtahid" (whose name is not mentioned) appealed to Consul Rawlinson for help. The mujtahid argued that the tranquillity in Karbala' since its occupation was mainly due to the "imposition of a fixed and moderate assessment, and to the judicial and liberal conduct of the governor, Sadiq Bey, in realizing the revenue and in preventing unrecognized exactions." He expressed fears that a tax-farmer "under a liability to double or even treble the legitimate revenues, would be obliged to institute fresh taxes, accept bribes, . . . and otherwise oppress the inhabitants." Significantly, the mujtahid warned that should the measure be adopted he "with all the respectable portion of the inhabitants" would emigrate and thus shake the entire economic basis of the shrine cities and with that Ottoman prospects for more revenues.[20]

In reply to Rawlinson's inquiry, the *defterdar* argued that while Karbala' paid only 100 purses (about £500) a year, his task was to increase the government revenues as much as possible, and should anyone offer him 300 purses (£1,500), it was his duty to accept the bid. Najib Pasha proved to be more moderate than his *defterdar* and gained the Porte's assent not to auction off Karbala''s tax.[21] It is unclear whether the Porte feared Iranian reaction or a new rebellion or the threat of the mass exodus of the 'ulama' which could have endangered the pilgrimage to the shrine cities. At all events, the Ottomans did not hesitate to impose illegal taxes on Iranian subjects and pilgrims.

The population in Iraq as a whole, and not only the Shi'is, suffered from the governor's financial policies. Whereas Najib Pasha was granted a farm of the Baghdad pashalik at the assumed gross annual value of 60,000 purses (£300,000), Rawlinson reported in 1848 that he had raised "by ostensible means alone, above 120,000 purses (£600,000)." His other income, accrued from his grain monopoly, from confiscations, fines, presents, "and above all from direct bribes," amounted "at the most moderate calculation" to £1,000,000. Taking into consideration that Da'ud Pasha had sent 2,000 purses annually less than twenty years earlier, and that the pashalik's economy had not experienced a commensurate growth during that period, the increased revenues meant a much heavier burden on the population.[22]

As part of the reforms in the empire, the Ottomans established in October 1838 the Ministry of Endowments (*Nezrat-i Evkaf*), designed to bring all charitable foundations under centralized government control. Whereas in the past trustees (*mutevellis*) held their posts as a hereditary right or were appointed by the local *qadis*, now they were to be appointed by the ministry. More importantly, all surplus revenues of the *awqaf* were turned over to the government's treasury, particularly to the troops of the new army.[23]

The shrines of the Imams and a few madrasas were the major beneficiaries of *awqaf* in the shrine cities. These *awqaf* consisted of orchards, canals, shops, and bathhouses. Prior to the reassertion of effective Ottoman control, the custodians and functionaries (*khadim* pl. *khadama*) of the shrines were nominally appointed by the government. In practice, the custodians enjoyed considerable freedom to spend the *awqaf* revenues as they saw fit. Not surprisingly, then, the Ottoman decision to place all the *awqaf* in the pashalik under state control caused "the greatest discontent" among the Shi'i population and the 'ulama'. True, government control of *awqaf* also increased the dependence of the Sunni 'ulama' on the central Ottoman authorities, but at the same time, these 'ulama' could enjoy government patronage and derive considerable income as *mutawallis* under government supervision even after the establishment of the ministry. The Shi'is, on the other hand, feared that government control would deprive them of the revenues from their own *awqaf*. In repeated appeals to the British consul, the "Sheeah priest-hood" (it is unclear whether Rawlinson means the 'ulama' or the custodians of the shrines), which stood to lose the most from the new measure, complained that Ottoman control of the revenues and expenditure of the Shi'i *awqaf* "would be equivalent . . . to their suppression and would in fact amount almost to a proscription of the faith."[24]

Unlike their handling of the Sunni *awqaf*, the Ottomans did not expropriate or tamper with the shrine treasures, probably because they realized the potential uproar among the Shi'is and in Iran should they expropriate them. Instead, they settled for indirect control over the shrines. An Ottoman supervisor over the *awqaf* was appointed for Najaf and Karbala', but the custodians and attendants of the shrines were not replaced, and drew their salaries from the Ottoman ministry.[25] Officials of the *awqaf* ministry came to the shrine cities periodically, to inspect and register the accumulating treasures, but it is unclear how effective and meticulous these inspections were.[26] The various madrasas too, remained under the control of their Shi'i *mutawallis*. In that sense, even at the height of the Tanzimat the Shi'is still enjoyed greater autonomy than their Sunni counterparts. The Ottomans did draw considerable revenues from the vast burial activity conducted in the shrine cities and administered by the shrine custodians, who took some of the profits for themselves. In important policy matters, however, the custodians were subordinated to the Ottoman government.[27]

During his 1870 visit to the shrine cities, Nasir al-Din Shah wished to examine the register compiled by Musa Kashif al-Ghita' when the treasures of Imam 'Ali's shrine had been returned from Baghdad, and saw that nothing had been taken. The governor, Midhat Pasha, proposed that the treasures be sold and the money used to build a railroad from Iran to Najaf for the pilgrims. The 'ulama' rejected the idea out of hand because of its sacrilegious implications and probably because they did not want to provide the Ottomans with improved means to bring troops to the shrine cities. The custodians and 'ulama' also resisted Ottoman proposals to use the treasures for servicing the pilgrimage or the development of the town itself. Significantly, the Ottomans did not tamper with the treasures even later.[28]

The subordination of the shrines to Ottoman control, in addition to the earlier loss of local governorship, affected the status of the custodians and the local sayyid elite. According to one British traveler, the custodian in Najaf paid the governor £10,000 in 1877–78 in order to purchase his post,[29] an indication both of his considerable income (the Rufa'i family was known as the wealthiest in Najaf) and of some dependence on the governor's goodwill. The 'ulama', on the other hand, maintained their institutional and financial independence from the Ottomans throughout the century. Although far more research is needed on local life in the shrine cities as a whole, the Ottoman measures most likely affected the status of the local lay elite *vis-à-vis* the 'ulama'. It does not seem merely a coincidence that the Ottomans turned to the 'ulama' rather than to the sayyids when mediation was needed with the urban gangs.[30]

It should be remembered however, that the perception of the weakening of the sayyids may be created by the sources, which were written by and for 'ulama'. The local municipalities in both shrine cities were an important power base, held by lay notables. It is conceivable that lay Shi'is acted as tax-farmers for both towns, a post that provided its holder with considerable economic and social power. Access to local libraries and the *sijill* of the local Ottoman *qadis* would probably help to balance the picture.

Sayyid Ahmad, son of the Shaykhi leader Kazim Rashti, played an important role in the appointment of the custodian of Imam Husayn's shrine in Karbala'. A majority of the notables and a large number of the clans (*'asha'ir Karbala'*) led by Sayyid Ahmad, opposed the candidacy of Al Kamuna, the incumbent custodian family. The second party, led by Muhsin Kamuna, was supported by the majority of the Iranians living in Karbala'. Eventually, Sayyid Ahmad's faction successfully lobbied the governor to appoint Sayyid Muhammad Jawad Al Tu'ma as the new custodian. The latter had to pay the *bedel* (fee) of 1,000 Ottoman pounds to obtain the post.[31] Although the 'ulama' seemed to have failed in this particular case, their role as power brokers in local politics is still significant.

The two groups, 'ulama' and Sayyids, were not necessarily at odds with each other. Sayyid Ibrahim b. Isma'il Al Kamuna, for instance, used to transfer a share of the funds donated to the shrines to Murtada Ansari and subsequently to Mahdi Al Kashif al-Ghita'. Both distributors of the Oudh Bequest gave considerable monthly allowances to the custodian families throughout their tenure in office. Sayyid 'Ali Bahr al-'Ulum's daughter even married the custodian Sayyid Jawad al-Rufa'i, indicating the integration of at least some 'ulama' families with the local elite. Sayyid Ahmad Rashti could be regarded equally as a religious leader and as a local notable, as his murder in 1295/1878 by supporters of Al Kamuna indicates.[32]

When the reformer statesman Midhat Pasha was appointed in 1869 to the governorship of Baghdad the pattern of relations between the Shi'i population and the Ottoman government had been largely established. Hitherto, the Tanzimat in Iraq had consisted mainly of governmental efforts to impose central authority over the various local forces in the province, but without any organizational and structural reforms. Midhat Pasha had distinguished himself as the governor of Nish in Bulgaria (1861–64) and, more importantly, as the governor of the newly created and expanded province of Tuna (Danube) in 1864–67, which served as a test case and model of the new Vilayet system for the entire Ottoman Empire. Midhat was sent to Iraq both because of a personal dispute with the grand vizier 'Ali Pasha, and because of the dire state of Iraq, where the implementation of the Tanzimat lagged behind other provinces.[33]

In Baghdad, Midhat made the first concerted effort to implement the new Tanzimat laws in three major fields. He reorganized the provincial administration and gave Iraq its final administrative shape, while extending uniform administration to the countryside. He also began to build several towns in the tribal areas, such as Nasiriyya, to serve as local government and commercial centers, and created a representative provincial council consisting of notables to assist the governor. The composition of the council aroused resentment among the Shi'is, who were not given representation, while special seats were allocated to the Jews and Christians. In 1870 Midhat established new municipal councils whose members were paid, since the previous arrangement had proved to be a source of corruption. He also laid the foundations of secular education in Iraq, affecting mostly the Sunni population of Baghdad.[34]

Midhat's most important long-term reform was the settlement of the tribes, which had been started by his predecessors but was not pursued vigorously. He intended to transform the tribespeople into peasant-owners and encourage the shaykhs to develop vested interests in preserving the political order. For that purpose he sought to provide a regular system of land tenure according to the 1858 Ottoman land law by giving cultivators title deeds to their plots on state lands. He also encouraged the selling of state lands to individual holders and reduced land rent fees. However, as had happened in other places, the lands were registered under the shaykh's name, and the tribespeople were turned into exploited tenants.[35]

Midhat dismissed the governor of Karbala' and several of his subordinates for taking bribes. When he visited Karbala' for that purpose, he initiated the building of a new neighborhood in the town to ease the density in living conditions. It was the first planned neighborhood in Iraq in many years, and the first to have broad streets. Several European travelers praised the new part of Karbala' as an exception in the pashalik, "presenting an almost European appearance."[36]

The 'ulama' and conscription

No measure by the Ottomans and particularly by Midhat aroused as much fear and resentment among Sunnis and Shi'is alike as the introduction of military conscription. The long service and the harsh conditions in the Ottoman army were perceived as almost tantamount to a death sentence for the conscript. The first attempt to impose conscription in Karbala' was made in 1858, but riots ensued and the results were meager.[37] The Ottomans apparently relaxed their attempts to impose conscription until Midhat's arrival. When he reintroduced conscription in the pashalik, disturbances broke out in Baghdad.[38]

In contrast to Sunni madrasa students in the empire, the Shi'i students were not at first exempted from conscription, as the Shi'i system of learning was not under government control, and the Ottomans refused to grant the Shi'i community official status. In addition to the ordinary hardships associated with military service, the thought of serving a hostile Sunni government and the inability to practice one's religion in the army were particularly resented by the 'ulama'. Moreover, they feared that conscription would be used by the Ottomans to harass or discipline 'ulama' whom they regarded as troublemakers, and perhaps even as a tool to undermine the entire Shi'i community of learning.[39]

Two cases illustrate how Ottoman policy regarding conscription drove the 'ulama' into greater dependence on the Iranian government. Shaykh 'Ali Jawahiri, grandson of Muhammad Hasan Najafi, reportedly sought to register his family as Iranian subjects when ordered by the Ottomans to provide a list of his kin eligible for conscription. Muzaffar claims that forceful Iranian intervention was necessary before the governor consented to leave the Jawahiri family and all other 'ulama' who were Iranian subjects in peace. Jawad Jawahiri reportedly warned the Qa'im Maqam that he would have all the Ottoman subjects in Najaf register as Iranians should the latter continue his oppressive policies. Indeed, even Arab 'ulama', most notably the Khalisi family of Kazimayn, had taken Iranian nationality in order to avoid conscription. Muzaffar concludes that the affair boosted the prestige of the Iranian government as protector of 'ulama', adding that Najaf would have suffered much more from Ottoman oppression had it not been for Iranian protection.[40]

More important was Nasir al-Din Shah's personal intervention on behalf of the 'ulama'. During his visit to the shrine cities several Arab and Iranian mujtahids implored him to intercede with the Ottomans to secure exemption for the students. Realizing the opportunity to enhance his own position among the 'ulama', the shah complied with their request. In gratitude, a panegyric was composed for him reflecting the contrast between the 'ulama' of the shrine cities and the less submissive attitude of their colleagues in Iran.[41]

Either following the Shah's intercession or at a later stage after additional Iranian pressure, the Ottomans agreed to exempt Shi'i madrasa students from conscription. According to his family's biographer, Sayyid Muhammad b. Muhammad Taqi Bahr al-'Ulum was recognized as the *ra'is al-mudarrisin* (head teacher) of Najaf, and whoever carried his signed approval that he was a student was exempted from conscription.[42] This recognition was not necessarily in appreciation of Sayyid Muhammad's scholarship, but probably because he was the highest-ranking Iranian mujtahid to have accepted Ottoman nationality. However, the mujtahids could now claim official Ottoman recognition of their status.

The Ottomans suspected that the mujtahids would give false affidavits to release as many people as possible from military service. Indeed, the British sources claimed that the exemption "unduly swells" the students' ranks, and that in the district of Karbala', where it is easy to become a student without going far from home, "the Turks obtained very few recruits."[43] Consequently, the Ottomans required all students to pass an official examination in Baghdad. The mujtahids accompanied their students to Baghdad and brought them back to the shrine cities in order to make sure that they would be treated fairly and not taken into the army by force. While the Ottomans always preferred to deal with mujtahids who had already been recognized as communal leaders, such as members of the Kashif al-Ghita' and Radi families, access to the authorities further enhanced their status as mediator notables.[44] The mujtahid's power to secure an exemption for his student was one more bond increasing the latter's dependence on his master. It is very likely that the popularity of certain mujtahids as teachers grew as a result of this official recognition.

Popular resentment against conscription came into the open in July 1877. Hard pressed in their war against Russia, which forced them to send troops from the provinces to the front, the Ottomans ordered the mobilization of the *Redif* (local reserve troops) in Karbala'. Probably afraid of being sent to the front, the *Redif* mutinied and seized control over the town. Under *Redif* rule anarchy prevailed, with "rival Arab [former tribesmen] factions" fighting each other. Traders and even pilgrims coming to the town were fired upon from the surrounding date groves. The governor, 'Akif Pasha, sent regular troops from Baghdad equipped with artillery, who managed to fight their way into Karbala'.[45]

Having learnt the lesson of 1843, and because they had witnessed the terror inflicted by the gangs in Najaf, the 'ulama' did not support the mutineers. Rather, from the beginning they sought to mediate between them and the government in order to bring about a peaceful end to the rebellion; however, their ability to influence the *Redif* was very limited. Following "admonitions" by the 'ulama', 'Akif Pasha reported, the mutineers ostensibly pledged submission to the Ottomans in return for a promise of government leniency, but shortly afterwards they regrouped in the date groves around the town, raiding caravans and the townsmen.[46] The *Redif* evacuated their positions only after bands of tribal warriors from the 'Anaza and the Banu Hasan who had been called in by the Ottomans arrived at Karbala'.[47] They were more afraid of the tribespeople than of the authorities.

The apparent Ottoman weakness tempted the Zukurt gang in Najaf to rebel. When an Ottoman force reached Najaf from Karbala', the Zukurt retired to Kufa where they prepared to fight. The Ottoman commander, Mir Alay (Colonel) Hajji Bey, appealed to Sayyid 'Ali Bahr al-'Ulum to mediate and secure the Zukurt's surrender. After establishing contacts with the Zukurt and gaining their trust, as Sayyid 'Ali wrote to Consul Nixon, he sent his nephew, the young mujtahid 'Ali Naqi, with a delegation of "'ulama', elders and chiefs of the Hindiyya Arabs" to the gangs. The delegation "brought the rebels into Nejjeff to pray for mercy." They were taken to the barracks "and made to fall upon the hands and feet of Meer Alai, and the Ulema begged pardon for them," which the Ottoman officer granted.[48] According to Geary, who was hosted by Sayyid 'Ali several months after the event, "the mujtahid and the other great men present expressed their entire approval of the action of the Turks in restoring order." Since the arrest of the ringleaders of the disturbances, Sayyid 'Ali and his colleagues stated, Najaf had been tranquil for more than a year.[49]

Sayyid 'Ali's support of the Ottoman action against the gangs was not only due to the fact that he had become a wealthy landowning urban notable anxious for peace and order. It seems that while some 'ulama' recognized the usefulness of an alliance with the gangs, the lack of security in Najaf caused by the constant fighting between them seemed too high a price to bear. Shaykh Rida b. Musa Al Kashif al-Ghita', for instance, was forced to leave Najaf after he had been accused of leaning toward the Zukurt gang, returning only in 1290/1873–74. Sayyid 'Ali Naqi Bahr al-'Ulum was assassinated in Ramadan 1294/September 1877 by a member of the Shumurt while visiting Karbala'. During their clashes gang members sought to seize the shrine of Imam 'Ali, occupation of whose minaret would enable them to control the town. On one occasion, some of the Shumurt seized control over Shaykh Muhammad

Iravani's madrasa, using it as a stronghold from which they shot at their rivals. Under such circumstances, Ottoman control seemed the lesser of two evils. Sayyid Ja'far Al Khorasan, a poet and minor 'alim, went so far as to send a letter to the governor during one of the clashes in 1290/1873–74, in which he elaborated on the destruction caused by the gangs and urged the governor to send his "victorious troops" to Najaf to extinguish the fire of the *fitna* (sedition).[50]

Overall, the mujtahids, particularly those from established local families, consolidated their role as urban notables during the nineteenth century. A few of them could even be described as having been assimilated into the Ottoman system, expressing solidarity with the Ottomans against their European rivals.[51] The Tanzimat, however, widened the differences between the mujtahids and the Sunni 'ulama' and notables elsewhere in the empire. Despite flaws and failures, the Tanzimat brought about significant changes in the Arab provinces of the Ottoman Empire, and in the status of both Sunni and Shi'i 'ulama'. The Ottomans succeeded in imposing their authority on the urban centers, although not on the entire tribal population in the countryside. Even so, however, there were no longer local challenges to their overall authority, as there had been during the eighteenth century.

While the available sources stress the Shi'i plight under the Ottomans, it should be kept in mind that Ottoman policies *vis-à-vis* such an unfriendly element as the Shi'i 'ulama' were less harsh than the centralization policies carried out by many modern states during the twentieth century. In addition, while the 'ulama' were indignant about Ottoman intolerance, they themselves failed to show even a similar degree of tolerance toward religious minorities in Iran itself, during both the nineteenth and twentieth centuries.

The Sunni 'ulama' lost their monopoly over the judiciary and education with the establishment of new court and education systems. Likewise, the Sunni 'ulama', particularly in Syria, opposed but eventually had to accept the extension of legal (though not necessarily social) equality to the non-Muslim minorities. However, by the second part of the nineteenth century they had adjusted themselves to the new circumstances. As the Sunni 'ulama' and Ashraf grew more dependent on Istanbul for their official positions, they increasingly sent their children to secular schools that enabled them to secure high posts in the administration. As such, they were more fully integrated into the Ottoman system, while still retaining their local power. The mismanagement of the 1858 Ottoman Land Law and the integration of the Middle East into the world economy enabled the Sunni 'ulama' to become landowners and join the emerging bureaucratic landowning class in the Arab provinces.[52]

Unlike their Sunni counterparts, the Shi'i mujtahids did not enjoy Ottoman largess. The educational reforms in Iraq did not encroach upon Shi'i education to the same extent as they did upon the traditional Sunni system. Nor were the Shi'i 'ulama' concerned so much with the question of legal equality for non-Muslim minorities. Politically, the Shi'i 'ulama', and here I refer only to the local Arabs, were not integrated into the Ottoman clerical or provincial bureaucratic system but retained their independence. They remained alienated from the official Ottoman culture, being much closer to the Iranian cultural milieu. In other words, the religious divide was more significant than the difference between notables in major urban centers and those from smaller provincial towns. Economically and socially, the shrine cities were part of the larger Ottoman system, but the Shi'i 'ulama' did not join the landowning class to nearly the same extent as the Sunni 'ulama'. Nor did they integrate socially with Ottoman officialdom through marriage, for example, or join the landowning bureaucratic class.[53] Rather, they remained primarily a status group, whose main source of influence was its religious authority, and its ability to mediate between the government and the population.

The 'ulama' and Sultan 'Abd al-Hamid

The 'ulama'–Ottoman–Qajar triangle underwent a certain transformation during the last quarter of the nineteenth century due to changes in Ottoman policy, in Iran itself, and in the relations between the 'ulama' and the two governments. The conclusion of the Ottoman–Iranian agreement on December 20, 1875 put an end to twenty-eight years of dispute over the *ex officio* privileges awarded to the consuls of each country. The Iranians had interpreted this clause as including judiciary powers over Iranian subjects, similar to those given to European consuls. The Ottomans rejected that view for two reasons. European privileges were the result of the capitulations agreements and were perceived as symbols of Ottoman weakness. The Ottomans had no reason to subject themselves to a similar humiliation from Iran. Secondly, non-Muslims who were foreign subjects had no clear status in the Shar'ia since they could not be regarded as *dhimmis*. The Iranians, however, were Muslims subject to the Shari'a, which does not recognize different nationalities among Muslims.[1]

Since the Iranian consuls were always looking for new means to enhance their income as their salaries were usually in arrears, their compatriots living in the shrine cities were not enthusiastic about being subjected to their jurisdiction. In some cases Iranians accepted Ottoman nationality in order to escape from the consuls' "extortion and oppression," which were often attended with corporal punishment and even torture.[2]

The 1875 agreement reflected, in Master's words, a transformation from the geopolitical concept of *umma* to nation by equating Iran's position to that of other foreign powers.[3] The Ottomans gave the Iranian consuls "exclusive authority" over Iranian subjects similar to that of European consuls, except in cases of violation of Ottoman law. Certain powers of assistance and protection in local legal proceedings, however, were reserved to the Iranian representatives. In addition,

Iranian subjects were exempted from taxes levied exclusively on Ottoman subjects.[4] In other words, the agreement relieved the migrant Iranian 'ulama' from the threat of being subjected to the obligations imposed on Ottoman subjects, particularly conscription and taxation.

The accession of Sultan 'Abd al-Hamid to the throne in 1876 marked another change in relations between the Ottomans and the 'ulama'. 'Abd al-Hamid's strategy of ensuring the empire's survival focused on Islam as the ideological cement of the empire, on unity among the Muslim populations of the empire, and on applying pan-Islamic policy abroad.[5]

In Iraq itself, this policy sought to draw the Shi'is closer to the Ottoman cause through various gestures, while safeguarding or even tightening Sunni domination. Although the government did not retract any of its major discriminatory policies, the mere fact that new ones were not introduced meant a certain respite for the Shi'is, and particularly the 'ulama'. In addition, the role of mujtahids as mediators between the population and the government was fully entrenched. Even migrant mujtahids, such as Hasan Ardakani and Zayn al-'Abidin Mazandarani of Karbala' and Fadil Sharabiyani of Najaf, acquired considerable influence with the local Ottoman authorities.[6] As an expression of goodwill and piety toward the Shi'is, 'Abd al-Hamid completed the gilding of the two minarets in 'Ali's shrine, which had been begun by his predecessor, Sultan 'Abd al-'Aziz, in addition to other "munificent largesse to the holy shrines." The Shi'is also perceived the digging of the 'Abd al-Ghani and Hamidiyya canals to Najaf in 1305/1888 and 1310/1893 as an act of benevolence toward their community. In gratitude, Shi'i poets wrote panegyrics in honor of the sultan.[7]

On the local level sectarian animosities between Sunnis and Shi'is aggravated the frictions between the government and the 'ulama'. Descriptions of the mutual contempt and even the hatred prevailing between members of the two sects frequently appear in foreigners' accounts. In one illustrative case, the local Ottoman governor in Najaf "took a pleasure in causing the Sheah Persians to 'eat dirt' at the hands of the infidels" as he escorted his European guests into the shrine despite the evident resentment of the Shi'is all around them.[8]

Mutual antagonism also marked the attitudes of Sunni and Shi'i 'ulama'.[9] Mirza Hasan Shirazi's migration to Samarra' alarmed the Sunni 'ulama' in Baghdad, who feared that the town would be taken over by the Shi'is. Consequently, Shaykh Muhammad Sa'id al-Naqsha-bandi of Baghdad urged the governor, Hasan Pasha, to prohibit Shirazi's residence in Samarra'. The governor appealed for instructions from

Istanbul, but Sultan 'Abd al-Hamid did not want to create another source of tension with the Iranian government, and instructed the governor to deal with the matter peacefully.[10]

Indeed, during the 1880s and 1890s Ottoman officials became deeply concerned at the spread of Shi'ism among the tribes in Iraq, the full extent of which they had not grasped earlier, and which they believed was inspired and financed by Iran. As a remedy to the problem, various officials proposed to establish Sunni madrasas in Baghdad; to send specially trained teachers and 'ulama' to Iraq who would be able "to debate with their Shi'i counterparts," and instill the virtues of Sunni Islam in primary schools. One official proposed to "turn" the influence exercised by the mujtahids, as most of them were Arabs and Ottoman subjects, in the Ottomans' favor. He also proposed the "granting of munificent largesse" to the holy shrines "as had been done in the time of Sultan 'Abd al-Majid."

The most radical proposals were to limit pilgrimage by Iranians; to expel mujtahids and students who "spread seditious ideas"; and to inculcate the notion that it was thanks to the Ottoman caliph that Shi'i Ottoman subjects could flourish and that Shi'i 'ulama' could come to the shrine cities. Significantly, none of the officials made any reference to military action. Some even rejected it as harmful to Ottoman interests.[11] In practice very little came of these discussions. Only one Sunni madrasa was established in Samarra', and it remained active as long as Shirazi was alive. In 1318/1900–01, as part of this policy, the Ottoman government appointed a Sunni notable from Baghdad instead of the local Shi'i sayyids as the *Naqib al-Ashraf* in both shrine cities. Such measures, however, also belonged to a broader policy to edge the local Sunni 'ulama' and sayyids in Iraq out of their positions of independent influence, and fully subordinate them to the government while endowing them with titles, honors, and material privileges.[12]

Shirazi's prominence after the 1891 tobacco affair brought a flow of pilgrims and funds to Samarra', and commercial prosperity to the entire town. In order to promote goodwill among the Sunnis, Shirazi spent considerable amounts on building a new market and a bridge on the Euphrates. Sectarian animosities, however, proved to be more powerful than economic benefits. Shirazi himself aggravated the tension when he refused to rise in respect when the governor paid him a visit. As a demonstration of Ottoman domination and also to curtail the expansion of Shi'i property, the governor initiated building activity on a plot which was a Shi'i *waqf*, adjacent to Shirazi's mosques.[13]

Shortly after the governor's visit an anti-Shi'i riot triggered by a quarrel between one of Shirazi's servants and an Ottoman gendarme broke out in Samarra', on the twelfth day of Ramadan 1311/19 March 1894. A Sunni mob of several hundred people, incited by an Ottoman officer, roamed the streets beating Shi'is with clubs and stones and chanting "It is a fight for the faith, kill the pigs, the *Rafida* sect, the infidels, the sinners." The mob also attacked Shirazi's madrasa, beating and robbing the students. As the Ottoman garrison did not interfere, dozens of Shi'is were injured, and at least two students were killed.[14]

Although order was finally restored and some rioters arrested, many Shi'is fled to Baghdad and Karbala' for several weeks after the affair, fearing more persecution. Shirazi himself considered leaving Samarra', but eventually decided to stay despite the exhortations of a delegation of mujtahids from Najaf who urged him to return to that city. When news of the riot reached Najaf, the markets were immediately shut in protest. The authorities prevented a crowd from setting out toward Samarra'. In Kirmanshah in Iran crowds threatened the life of the Ottoman consul.[15]

According to the French consul, the Porte laid responsibility for the riot on the governor and ordered him to restore order. Based on a conversation with an Ottoman official, the consul concluded that the Porte was genuinely concerned over the riot's adverse connotations for Ottoman–Iranian relations.[16] Under pressure from the Porte and the British consul, the governor dispatched his secretary and another official to Samarra' to investigate the affair. The two officials asked for an audience with Shirazi, seeking to procure from him a written statement expressing his satisfaction with the Ottoman handling of the situation, but Shirazi refused to receive them.

Shirazi's defiance notwithstanding, the governor was clearly wary of the consequences should the mujtahid decide to leave Samarra'. He sought, therefore, to bring about a quick reconciliation between Shirazi and the Sunni public leaders. Despite the exhortations of the Sunni *qadi* of Baghdad not to take any action against the rioters, the governor, in an attempt to appease the Shi'is and the foreign consuls, removed the Qa'im Maqam and *qadi* of Samarra', who had either encouraged the rioters or had given them a free hand.[17]

Hirz al-Din claims that as the governor refused to listen to the complaints of the 'ulama' and did not report the matter to 'Abd al-Hamid, a group of 'ulama' traveled to Iran to inform both the sultan and the shah about the condition of Iranian subjects in the shrine cities. While the shah did not initiate any decisive action, 'Abd al-Hamid took firm measures to settle the affair and punish those responsible. Although Hirz al-Din's claim is somewhat contradicted by the French report, it does demonstrate the 'ulama''s propensity to appeal to the Qajars when they felt seriously distressed. At the same time, the positive portrayal of

'Abd al-Hamid is also of significance, reflecting an awareness or appreciation of his religious policies.[18]

Shirazi too made an effort to defuse the situation by publicly asking the governor to release eight of the detained rioters. He was careful to localize the affair and refused to receive the British consul who visited Samarra', declaring that the riot was an internal Muslim affair in which Britain had no business interfering. Similarly, he declined the offer of mediation made by the Iranian consul, who brought him presents sent from the shah.[19] Subsequently Shirazi issued a statement designed to reconcile all parties, saying that he disapproved of anything happening that may cause "hatred" and "aversion" between Muslims. He implored his brethren to assume "sentiments of affection, love, ... and good behaviour."[20] When Shirazi died in 1312/1895 and his body was transferred to Najaf via Baghdad, the governor and the commander of the Ottoman troops came to pay their respects. According to al-Amin, however, Ottoman hostility was one of the reasons for the decline of the learning center in Samarra' following Shirazi's death.[21]

Most important, however, in the broader context of 'ulama'–Ottoman relationships was the mujtahids' very favorable attitude toward 'Abd al-Hamid's pan-Islamic policy and particularly the efforts to reach a *rapprochement* with Iran. As part of his programme, 'Abd al-Hamid also cultivated a group of Iranian pan-Islamists, most notable among them being Shaykh al-Ra'is, grandson of Fath 'Ali Shah, who corresponded with mujtahids in the shrine cities, attempting to encourage Islamic unity against Europe through support for 'Abd al-Hamid. Such appeals did not fall on deaf ears.[22]

On the local scene the 'ulama' reciprocated by silencing opposition to Ottoman policies. When a certain preacher, Shaykh Ibrahim al-Kashi, openly criticized the Ottomans for imposing levies to finance the building of the Hijaz railway, the leading mujtahids ordered their students to expel al-Kashi forcibly from their classes.[23] Equally important, the changing situation in Iraq would significantly influence the 'ulama''s activity in Iran itself.

The shrine cities and Qajar politics: from quietism to confrontation

The conduct of the 'ulama' of the shrine cities toward Iranian politics was by and large quietist throughout most of the century. A detailed discussion of the political role of the Iran-based 'ulama' is beyond the scope of this study. Yet, if some of the major landmarks in these relations are examined, the minor role of the shrine cities will become evident.

Participation in the efforts of the Qajar elite pro-war faction to pressure Fath 'Ali Shah to wage war on Russia in 1826 was the first political action on the national level undertaken by the 'ulama' of Iran. Sayyid Muhammad Tabataba'i of Karbala' played a key role in this campaign, for which he was titled *al-Mujahid*, but he was the only mujtahid from the shrine cities to do so. Moreover, in order to pursue his efforts, Sayyid Muhammad left the supposedly safer shrine cities and came to Iran, both to mobilize mass support and to apply direct pressure on the shah. Whatever role the 'ulama''s pressure played in pushing the shah into the war, it was inside Iran and not by remote control from the shrine cities.[24] In the aftermath of the war, the 1829 murder of the Russian envoy Griboyedov by a mob in Tehran, which jeopardized the relations between the two countries, was instigated by local 'ulama'.[25]

Quite a few 'ulama' in the shrine cities cultivated friendly relations with the Qajars and other Shi'i rulers. Muhammad Hasan Najafi, for instance, sent his congratulations to Nasir al-Din Shah on his accession to the throne. He also used to correspond with high level Iranian officials. The lofty titles by which Najafi referred to the king of Awadh in his correspondence with the mujtahids there reflect at least a practical understanding of the need to gain the king's favor.[26] Various other 'ulama' dedicated written works to the shah, while several poets wrote panegyrics for him.[27]

Following the British occupation of Bushehr in 1857 'ulama' from most major Iranian cities declared the war against the British a Jihad. Yet no mujtahid from the shrine cities is mentioned among them.[28] The aversion to politics of Murtada Ansari, the religious leader of the shrine cities at the time, must have been a major cause for the inaction of the Najaf 'ulama' in this particular case. Another reason may have been their dependence on the British to offset discriminatory Ottoman measures, which precluded the likelihood of an open confrontation with them. Reluctance to endanger the Oudh Bequest and pilgrimage from India probably also affected various mujtahids.

The competition for leadership and the need to raise funds for the sustenance of the community of learning required various 'ulama' to court visiting Qajar officials. It should be noted, however, that there were always mujtahids who shunned contact with state officials, viewing them as oppressors. Murtada Ansari, for instance, instructed his brother, who was going to Iran, not to return should he receive any presents from government officials.[29] Soliciting funds from officials did not necessarily mean endorsement or approval of that class, but was a pragmatic step. It is very likely that the Qajar preference for Ansari and Shirazi was influenced by their manifest lack of interest in politics.

Nasir al-Din Shah's 1870 visit to the shrine cities demonstrates the working of the triangular relationship discussed above, as well as the difference between the conduct of mujtahids from the shrine cities and their counterparts in Iran. Prior to the shah's visit, the Russian ambassador in Istanbul, playing on Ottoman fears, tried to persuade the Ottomans to prevent it on the ground that it would make the Shi'is look "toward the dynasty of their own religion" and "encourage the ambitious hopes of the Persians." The Porte, however, accepted the British argument that the visit would help to improve the relations between the two countries, and instructed the governor, Midhat Pasha, to treat the shah with the utmost respect. The shah and his huge entourage stayed in Iraq for three months and proved to be a serious drain on the pashalik's treasury.[30]

Upon his arrival at Musayyib near Karbala', Nasir al-Din Shah was greeted by a delegation of 'ulama' headed by the two leading mujtahids of Karbala', 'Ali Naqi Tabataba'i and Zayn al-'Abidin Mazandarani, and the custodian of the 'Abbas shrine, Sayyid Husayn. Mirza Hasan, the kilidar of Husayn's shrine, came to welcome the shah only when he approached the shrine, indicating that he regarded himself of higher status than the previous delegates. In Karbala', the shah's new favorite, the ambassador to Istanbul and shortly thereafter *Sadr-i A'zam*, Mushir al-Dawla, held several meetings with the 'ulama'.[31]

Only one mujtahid, Mulla Aqa Darbandi, reportedly dared show some defiance toward the shah during his visit, when he scolded him for his untrimmed mustache. While the shah was visiting the Husayn shrine, a local preacher, Shaykh Lutfallah, displayed a remarkable degree of flattery when he declared "O Husayn! On the day of Karbala' you asked 'is there a helper' (*hal min nasir*) and no one came to your assistance. Rejoice today, for the helper [i.e. Nasir al-Din Shah] has arrived." The shah broke into a sob and ordered a monthly pension to be paid to the preacher and his children after him.[32]

Coming to Najaf the shah was welcomed at the halfway point by a delegation of 'ulama', among them four members of the Bahr al-'Ulum family. The rest of the 'ulama' and students waited for the shah in Wadi al-Salam on the outskirts of Najaf. On both occasions the shah received the 'ulama' while on horseback, thereby demonstrating his superior status. On the next day he was visited by the leading Arab and Iranian mujtahids. Of all the important mujtahids, the shah noted, only Shirazi refused to come to him. Eventually a compromise was reached and the two met in the shrine courtyard.[33] Shirazi's defiance or manifest indifference to royal favors earned him the admiration of many believers, but among the 'ulama' he was in a minority. As mentioned above, the 'ulama''s main concern in the entire affair was to enlist the shah's help to abolish conscription in the Ottoman army.

A less important issue resolved by the shah's visit was the Shi'i call to prayer. Citing oral testimony, Wardi claims that while visiting Husayn's shrine the shah heard the *mu'adhin* calling for prayer, and noticed that the *adhan* did not include the third (Shi'i) *shahada*, "'Ali wali Allah" ('Ali [is] the friend of God), which had been omitted since the 1843 occupation of Karbala'. The shah implored the *mu'adhin* to include the third *shahada*, and ever since then it was also called in Iraq. It is possible that the shah's visit merely gave the Shi'is the opportunity or excuse to reintroduce the third *shahada*.[34]

The shah made some gestures to promote friendly relations with the 'ulama' by awarding pensions to various (mainly middle-ranking) members.[35] There are no data as to whether the shah offered financial support to any of the leading mujtahids. It is unlikely that the Shi'i sources, which usually glorify their subject matter, would have ignored a rejection of such offers. Years later, in 1893, the shah conferred honorary titles on Sayyid Muhammad Bahr al-'Ulum and on his aide.[36] In comparison, in 1290/1873–74, only three years after the visit, Mulla 'Ali Kani and Mirza Salih Arab led the opposition in Tehran against the reforming *Sadr-i A'zam* Mushir al-Dawla after he had signed the Reuter Concession. No mujtahid from the shrine cities is recorded as having taken part in their campaign.[37]

Mirza Hasan Shirazi's role in the 1891 tobacco protests is often cited as an example of the importance of the shrine cities as oppositional centers. Shirazi himself took action against the monopoly fairly late and only after repeated exhortations by other 'ulama' and the merchants. Even if we discount the argument that the *fatwa* was actually fabricated by a group of merchants in cooperation with Mirza Hasan Ashtiyani, it appeared only in December 1891, after the campaign in Iran was well under way. The shah had began to waver in his position even before its publication, following mass protests in most major Iranian cities.[38]

The appeals to Shirazi from merchants and 'ulama' to intervene in the national struggle reflected the desire for a supreme and unified religious leadership, for which he seemed the most suitable candidate. It did not stem from any perception that his residence in Samarra' would make him immune to pressure from the shah. In fact, before the crisis Shirazi had been known for his lack of interest in politics. Apart from Shirazi the other mujtahids in the shrine cities did not take any hostile action against the tobacco Regie.[39]

Realizing the potential power of the 'ulama', some radical reformers, most notably Malkam Khan and Mirza Aqa Khan Kirmani, sought to draw them into oppositional activity. Various 'ulama' in the shrine cities did discuss the possibility of further oppositional moves, and maintained some contacts with their colleagues in Iran to coordinate their protest. Wary of these activities, the shah sought to induce the Ottomans to secure a pledge from the 'ulama' to refrain from political activity.[40] Shirazi himself did not take part in these consultations. On the other hand, when Nasir al-Din Shah, who wanted to undermine Ashtiyani, asked him to send several Iranian mujtahids whom he trusted to Tehran, Shirazi complied, subsequently despatching Muhammad Rida Qummi and Sayyid Muhammad Tabataba'i.[41] Apparently he did not regard his activity in the tobacco affair as an all-out campaign against the shah.

On the whole, as Bakhash says, the 'ulama' in the shrine cities "remained reluctant to become deeply involved in a serious movement against the government."[42] Some of the reasons for their reluctance were described in a conversation held in Istanbul between Kirmani and Aqa Shaykh 'Ali b. Ja'far, an 'alim from the shrine cities. Writing to Malkam Khan of this conversation, Kirmani reported that the 'ulama' of the shrine cities appeared to fear that "a change in the condition of the monarchy and the government," especially if brought about with the 'ulama''s support, would lead to internal weakness and foreign domination. The 'ulama', Shaykh 'Ali added, were not involved in politics and were incapable of running the government.[43]

The very nature of the shrine cities as scholarly centers largely determined their political quietism. Those who were primarily interested in writing and teaching were more likely to remain in the shrine cities. More worldly and politically ambitious 'ulama' preferred to return to Iran. Three notable examples of this pattern are Hujjat al-Islam Shafti and subsequently Aqa Najafi in Isfahan and Mulla 'Ali Kani in Tehran.[44] Distance from the main arena of political events and from the majority of their constituents was another factor fostering political quietism. It is no coincidence that most mujtahids of the capital Tehran were known more for political and public activity than for scholarly writings. Of the three leading mujtahids in Tehran at the beginning of the twentieth century, 'Abdallah Bihbihani, Muhammad Tabataba'i, and Fadlallah Nuri, only Nuri was known to have taught regularly.[45] Until the introduction of the telegraph in Iraq and Iran during the 1870s, political activism from a distance was extremely difficult. The Qajars were well aware of these facts. Consequently, they used to deport troublemaking 'ulama' to the shrine cities, realizing that they would be less threatening to the government at that distance.[46] At the same time, while the Qajars did not provide financial support on a permanent basis for the 'ulama' in the shrine cities, Nasir al-Din Shah did grant various mujtahids personal stipends, apparently regarding them as apolitical proteges in contrast to their more politicized colleagues inside Iran.[47]

Shirazi's *fatwa* in the tobacco protest marked the beginning of the involvement of the shrine cities in Iranian politics, but was in a way an isolated event. Only during the political ferment leading up to the 1905 Constitutional Revolution was there continuous political involvement by a group of mujtahids from the shrine cities. Several factors are responsible for the change. The bankruptcy of the Iranian government forced it to take loans from Russia at the cost of mortgaging the state's revenues and of allowing Russia a large say in managing Iran's financial affairs. Even apolitical 'ulama' could not remain indifferent to the fear spreading in Iran for the country's independence and Islamic identity. The Iranian Bazaar, the main financial stay of the 'ulama' community, had been losing its control of Iran's exports and even some domestic markets to foreign merchants. It suffered an additional blow with deflation in the years 1900–05, which led to an economic downturn. Artisans were losing their livelihoods, particularly in textile handicrafts due to the competition of European imports. The 'ulama' could not ignore the plight of their major constituencies, which affected them through the decline of religious dues.[48]

The improvement in atmosphere between the mujtahids and the Ottomans made them less apprehensive of using their influence in Iran. Thus, when Shi'is in the Russian-held Caucasus complained of Russian tyranny, the leading mujtahids in Najaf advised their brethren, in a letter intercepted by the Russians, "to apply to Turkey whom they [the mujtahids] will induce to afford the necessary protection."[49]

It is possible that Muzzafar al-Din Shah's timid personality also encouraged the 'ulama' to be more bold. Thus, when Hasan Mamaqani visited Iran in 1903, he reportedly declined the shah's invitation to come to Tehran so that he could wash the mujtahid's feet as a sign of his piety and humility. The "holy man," in Hardinge's words, declined the offer, saying that "he would not defile himself by entering a city polluted by so many Jews and Christians with their shameless unveiled wives and daughters." Likewise, in a conversation with the Iranian consul in Najaf, held in August that year, Sharabiyani reputedly referred to the shah as a "dog," reflecting the monarch's low stature among the senior 'ulama'.[50]

The 'ulama' of Tehran played an important role in the agitation against the second Russian loan. Their appeals to the shrine cities were vital in drawing the latter into the political fray. The impact of Shirazi's *fatwa* persuaded many in Iran that the mujtahids of the shrine cities were the appropriate political leadership in a national crisis.[51] Significantly in this regard, even Iran-based 'ulama' toyed with the idea of appealing to the Ottoman sultan "as the strongest Muslim ruler" so that he would "impress on the Shah" their opposition to his growing subservience to Russia. In other words, the growing western challenge aroused support for Islamic ecumenism, both in the shrine cities and in Iran, which would grow even stronger during the subsequent years.[52]

Two letters sent from Tehran to the mujtahids of Najaf reflect the perceptions and motives of the opposition, and the expectations of the leadership in the shrine cities.[53] One letter, from "a group of distressed Muslims to the leading lights of the Faith," contained themes similar to those that had led to the appeals to Shirazi eleven years earlier. The writers described the misery of the Iranian traders and the threat to Iran's Islamic identity "once we fall into the grasp of Russia." They argued that if the 'ulama' repudiated the loan, the shah and his elite would have to obey them, warning that if the loan would be accepted "Islam disappears," and all power will be taken from the 'ulama'. "To whom can we look save to the heads of the Faith?" they asked. "It is not for us people to address the ruler [lit., *Sultan-i 'Asr*] . . . but the Ulema have power to do so. We felt bound to appeal to you to learn our duty and obey your orders." In addition to recognizing the supremacy of the shrine cities, the petitioners pointed out the weakness of the mujtahids in Tehran caused by internal discord and undesirable intimacy with members of the elite, arguing the need for "one will and one arbiter in regard to the affairs of Islam." [54]

In an uncommon step, forced by the gravity of the situation, the four leading mujtahids in Najaf, Fadil Sharabiyani, Akhund Khorasani, Husayn Khalili, and Hasan Mamaqani, joined hands. They sent several remonstrances to the shah protesting against the employment of Europeans in the government service, which they termed "oppressive," and particularly the two loans "which had placed the . . . monarchy in a position of deplorable dependence upon Russia." They accused government officials of embezzling state funds so that money had to be borrowed from Russia and even then not used for the general good.[55]

Although the 'ulama' failed to thwart the second Russian loan, they did play an important role in mobilizing the public against the policies of the *Sadr-i A'zam*, Atabeg-i A'zam. In his conversations with Hardinge, the latter argued that the disturbances that had erupted in various Iranian cities "were not ordinary or isolated incidents, but were the outcome of an organized movement, whose source was at Kerbela and Nejef."[56]

The political involvement of the 'ulama' of the shrine cities culminated in an excommunication of the Atabeg issued in their name during

September 1903. As with Shirazi's *fatwa* there were doubts whether the document was authentic, although three of the four (Sharabiyani excluded) issued another declaration affirming its validity. It is unclear whether the excommunication played any role in the Atabeg's dismissal since, as Keddie argues, it may have appeared too late to have influenced his fall. Its importance, however, lay in reflecting "the general 'ulama' movement against the Atabeg" which had been a contributory factor to his downfall, and it also acted to prevent his recall to Iran in any official capacity.[57]

If at the earlier stage of the crisis in Iran, the mujtahids sought to exert pressure on the shah by appealing to the Ottoman sultan, the promulgation of the excommunication prompted the Iranian government to employ the same tactic against the 'ulama'. It demanded that the Ottomans put an end to the mujtahids' activity, denouncing the 'ulama' as following British designs. To substantiate its argument the Iranian government described the joint *fatwa* issued by twenty mujtahids from the shrine cities at the end of 1903, prohibiting pilgrimage to Mecca along the Kha'il route due to hostilities between Ibn Sa'ud and Ibn Rashid of Kha'il, as a service rendered by the 'ulama' to the shaykh of Kuwait and his British patrons. The Russians, who had been annoyed at the continuous correspondence between the shrine cities and the Shi'is under their rule, issued a similar demand.[58]

Complying with the pressure, and presumably because they themselves were afraid of any popular movements and revolutionary agitation, the Ottoman grand vizier instructed the governor to warn the mujtahids that they "should not interfere in the affairs of the two governments," otherwise they would be deported to Medina. In addition, the local authorities were instructed to make an inquiry as to the mujtahids' "true aims" and investigate "by what means, methods, or *exterior relations*" (original emphasis) they pursue "such obstructive and offensive steps."[59]

The Ottoman threats appear to have been effective for a while. The 'ulama''s political efforts were also weakened by the death of Sharabiyani in December 1904, whose funeral "all but caused a riot against the Turkish authorities in Najaf in consequence of interference with it by the Turkish sanitary staff." The mujtahids were also persuaded to condemn the Iranian newspaper *Habl al-Matin* of Calcutta which published "what purported to be a correspondence" between several mujtahids and the Ottoman sultan.[60] The excommunication of the Atabeg marked the high point of the shrine cities' 'ulama''s involvement in Iranian politics prior to the outbreak of the Constitutional Revolution.

As was the case with other spheres of communal life in the shrine cities, the political conduct of the 'ulama' during the nineteenth century was not determined by an overall organization or a unified leadership institution. Rather, it was determined by more powerful external circumstances, primarily the fact that the 'ulama' belonged to two socio-political arenas, that of the Ottoman Empire and of Qajar Iran, and by the workings of the Ottoman–Qajar–'ulama' triangle. As the relatively weaker player of the three, the 'ulama' could mostly maneuver between or exert pressure on the two other players in order to protect the interests of their community. Consequently, notwithstanding ethnic differences and the bitter competition for leadership, their conduct as communal leaders was characterized by a high degree of persistence and consensus.

While the Shi'i 'ulama' never accepted the legitimacy of the Sunni Ottoman state, they never came out against it publicly. Moreover, like their Sunni counterparts, they acted as urban notables mediating between the local population and the central authorities. Their only active endeavor which subverted Ottoman interests was their campaign to convert to Shi'ism the tribes of southern Iraq. However, that activity was more the product of a long-term missionary zeal of a sect-like minority seeking to spread its mission among the rival majority than a conscious political effort to undermine the Ottoman state.

The shift from the Mamluks to direct rule from Istanbul brought certain relaxations for the Shi'is in the ritual sphere, but also the loss of their function as mediators between Iran and the Ottoman Empire. At the same time, the Shi'is in general and the 'ulama' in particular were subjected to continuous Ottoman efforts to extract more revenues and subordinate them to central Ottoman judicial and military institutions. Yet, the 'ulama' managed to enhance their position *vis-à-vis* rival social groups, thanks to Ottoman policies, and thanks to their financial independence and the spiritual authority of emulation. Overall, the Ottomans were more tolerant toward the Shi'is than the Shi'i 'ulama' themselves had been toward religious minorities under their control.

At the same time, the 'ulama''s conduct in the Iranian political scene was much more quietist than that of their colleagues inside Iran due to their dependence on Qajar backing to offset various Ottoman pressures and discriminatory measures. Additional factors were the centuries-old doctrine of political quietism (*qu'ud*) *vis-à-vis* Sunni governments and the greater emphasis in the shrine cities on scholarship and teaching than on politics and religious administration than was the case in centers in Iran.

Overall, the 'ulama' of the shrine cities accepted during most of the nineteenth century the division between the political and religious authority in Iran and the need of the *millat* and *dawlat* (community and government) to aid each other.[61] Hence, only major developments in the following two arenas pushed the 'ulama' of the shrine cities toward greater political activism. The first was: progress in Ottoman–Iranian relations as the external pressures on both countries rendered the differences between them of secondary importance. A major factor in this process was Sultan 'Abd al-Hamid's pan-Islamic policy, both in foreign and domestic affairs, which led *inter alia* to a more favorable Ottoman policy toward the Shi'is and the 'ulama' in the shrine cities. The second was the grave economic and political deterioration in Qajar Iran, to which the 'ulama' could not remain indifferent.

Only when the government of Muzaffar al-Din Shah appeared to be incapable of discharging its duty of protecting the realm of Islam, or even likely to betray it, did the mujtahids of the shrine cities, in their capacity as the foremost religious leaders, assume an open role in the opposition. Their vigorous activism was not so much influenced by their Ottoman sanctuary, as presumed by some historians, as by the necessity to respond to the plight of their followers on whom they were heavily dependent, and because they were deemed to be free from the intimate proximity to government circles in Iran. Yet, even while disputing Qajar policies, they did not deny the legitimacy of the Qajar state itself.

Even though the 'ulama'–Ottoman–Qajar triangle appeared to return to its original set-up in 1904, the unfolding of the Constitutional Revolution in Iran transfigured the political arenas in Iran and in the shrine cities, pushing the mujtahids of the shrine cities once more into the political fray.

Conclusion

Two basic questions arise when we come to assess the question of continuity and change in the history of the community of learning in Najaf and Karbala' during the nineteenth century. The first concerns the nature of the changes that took place during this period. Were they structural or merely conjunctural or *événementielle*, that is, did they entail the complete replacement of the systems or units, or were they merely small-scale or intermediate-range changes within structures? Another issue is the relative weight of the external and the immanent causes of the changes that took place during the period under study. I would start however, by delineating major continuities with earlier periods of social patterns and structures.

The formation of the community of learning in the shrine cities represented in various ways the culmination or full fruition of the long-term development of religious institutions in the Muslim world, and in the Shi'i community in particular. The three-stage structure of study in Shi'ism, the mode of learning, and the system of certification had originated in the medieval period and were basically the same as in Sunni centers. Shi'i higher learning attained its final form and differentiation from parallel Sunni education systems after the reinstatement of the Usuli school in the eighteenth century and the placement of ijtihad as a major topic of learning. Likewise, the continuing professionalization of the 'ulama' which had begun in previous centuries was advanced to its highest degree with the triumph of Usulism and the consolidation of the status of the mujtahids as a learned elite distinct from ordinary believers.

Of particular importance was the endurance and centrality of informal interpersonal ties between masters and disciples in the absence of formal organizations and mechanism. Both elements, which had typified Muslim societies in earlier centuries, remained as a central pillar of the Shi'i institutions of learning, permeating almost all aspects of life in the community of 'ulama' well into the twentieth century. The traditional clientalist system was broadened and turned more sophisticated during

179

the nineteenth century with the spread of large networks of patronage closely linking mujtahids and former students both in the shrine cities and throughout the Shi'i world. As in previous epochs, the clientalist system served as a bridge between ethnic, social, and generational differences within the community, but did not annul them. Moreover, the clientalist system in the shrine cities did not attach the 'ulama' to rulers or to government officials as was the case in most Sunni centers of learning.

In its basic components, the financial organization of the community of learning was more complex than previous practice in the Shi'i world. The doctrinal infrastructure for the collection of religious dues, primarily the *zakat* and the fifth, not to mention reliance on endowed property, was well in place before the nineteenth century. The individualistic nature of raising and distributing funds was again deeply rooted in earlier practices. However, the finances of the shrine cities were unique, both in comparison with the past and with contemporary 'ulama' communities. Safavid and Ottoman 'ulama' relied mainly on endowed property and on direct government support as their main source of income and economic power. In contrast, the relatively minor role of *awqaf* in the shrine cities increased the importance of voluntary religious dues from the believers. The flow of funds to the cities increased with the formation of patronage networks in the course of the century. Pilgrimage and burial activity had always played a role in generating revenues for the shrine cities and income for all ranks of the 'ulama'. During the nineteenth century they assumed greater proportions and consequently produced a greater flow of funds.

Parallel to the persistence of earlier patterns, the community of learning in the two shrine cities experienced several important processes of change in the course of the nineteenth century. The most important one was the growth of Najaf from a small community of several dozen 'ulama' at the end of the eighteenth century to a major center of learning comprising several thousand teachers and students a century later. During the early decades of the nineteenth century several centers of learning coexisted or competed among themselves in Iraq and Iran. But by the 1840s the various Iranian centers declined while the shrine cities attracted the bulk of students and emerged as the undisputed strongholds of Shi'i learning and religious leadership. The division between Karbala' as the primary location for Iranians and Najaf for Arabs gave way to the rise of Najaf as the center for all ethnic groups.

The fluctuations in the status of centers of learning were both caused by, and in turn effected, changes in the 'ulama' population in the two shrine cities. The number of 'ulama' of all ethnic groups who resided permanently or just studied in the cities grew continuously throughout the century. The Iranian group, including both Persians and Azeri-Turks, registered the highest increase, largely due to the greater influx of students of non-clerical origins. The tribal human reservoir of the Shi'i community in Iraq could provide, and in turn required, fewer 'ulama' than the more religiously minded urban society in Iran.

The incremental changes in the 'ulama' population were influenced by political and economic circumstances in the shrine cities and in the students' home communities. A prominent mujtahid would attract a larger number of disciples from a variety of regions and ethnic groups, and thereby influence the growth and composition of the student population. The existence of holy shrines, however, gave certain towns a clear advantage in attracting pilgrims and students, beyond the activity of a single mujtahid.

The increase in the number of 'ulama' accentuated ethnic differences by exacerbating competition over funds and domination, and by bringing the smaller ethnic groups to the size of a critical mass which enabled them to organize as factions. The growth of the 'ulama' community extended to the mujtahids as well, causing a certain devaluation of the *ijazat ijtihad*. The inflation in the ranks of mujtahids resulted in the formation of an informal and amorphous hierarchy among the mujtahids manifested in the assumption of the titles Hujjat al-Islam during the 1830s and Ayatallah at the beginning of the twentieth century

Usuli methodology and its application in *fiqh* underwent continuous elaboration and refinement during the first half of the nineteenth century, largely based on the foundations laid down by Bihbihani. New ground was broken in both fields with the writing of Murtada Ansari's *Fara'id al-usul* and Akhund Khorasani's *Kifayat al-usul*. Both these books enabled the mujtahids to elaborate Shi'i law and expand the jurisdiction of the profession to new fields, as shown by Ansari's book on commercial law, *al-Makasib*. Ansari's writings marked the beginning of a new era and school in Usul. However, it would be difficult to describe this development as a structural change, since it did not bring about the complete replacement of the previous system or unit, but only a major advancement built upon it. A byproduct of the ascendancy of Usulism was the lessening of tolerance within the 'ulama' community toward heterodox ideas, as manifested by the church-like persecution of the Sufi, Shaykhi, and Babi movements.

The evolution of leadership too constituted both continuity and change from the past. The theoretical basis for the institution of Shi'i religious leadership, *ri'asa* and *marja'iyya*, had been laid down in the course of the centuries after the Occultation of the Imam, as the 'ulama' appropriated his various prerogatives to themselves. Individual mujtahids had enjoyed preeminence in Shi'i communities in earlier centuries. However, the reinstatement of Shi'ism as the state religion in Iran that followed the victory of Usulism enabled the mujtahids to establish themselves as religious and communal leaders over their constituents much more forcefully than ever before. This development also restored the 'ulama' in Iran and in the shrine cities to the position of a church-like establishment, accepting the social environment surrounding it and suppressing dissident groups from within.

The full doctrine of *marja'iyyat al-taqlid* was articulated only in mid-century by Murtada Ansari. It is difficult to assess the impact of this theory on the actual formation of leadership, since the criteria it set for supreme leadership – superior learning, justice, and piety – were too subjective and therefore difficult to implement. In addition, the theory did not establish any mechanism to elect or appoint the leader. On the other hand, by setting the ideal of the most learned mujtahid, it consolidated the position of those mujtahids who had succeeded in establishing superior status through patronage building and successful teaching. While Ansari himself was averse to politics, his theory helped the 'ulama' to claim a leadership role in communal affairs which verged on the political, particularly by the turn of the twentieth century.

As in other spheres of social organization in the community of learning, Shi'i leadership was largely molded by the traditional informal interpersonal pattern of social relationships in the community of learning. The attainment of leadership status was dependent on three major prerequisites: scholarship; the close ties with the Iranian Bazaar that were necessary to secure a financial basis; and skills in forging patronage relations with students and followers. Scholarship was an essential precondition, but not a sufficient one for establishing leadership. Superior learning could be measured and recognized by the quantity and quality of scholarly writings, which were often a subject of bitter dispute, or by the personal charisma (in the popular sense) of a teacher. Mujtahids who engaged in *fiqh* had the strongest prospect of emerging as religious leaders since their work had a greater relevance to lay constituents and lower-ranking 'ulama'. Experts in auxiliary fields of learning such as ethics or philosophy were less likely to establish the sufficiently wide basis of patronage necessary for leadership.

Leaders were not formally elected by their followers or by any formal body composed of 'ulama'. Nor were they nominated by their predecessors or the state. Rather, they emerged from among the cohort of their classmates and colleagues through a long process of teaching, patronage building, and peer recognition. The individualistic nature of leadership and teaching as well as the constant need of mujtahids to vie for students and for financial resources bred personal rivalries, and inhibited co-operation among themselves. Since they did not hold official posts with coercive means to enforce their injunctions, the authority of the mujta-hids was moral and religious, consisting in validating the religious actions of their followers. Occasionally, however, such authority was limited or even forced the 'ulama' to toe the line of their supposed followers. The legal–traditional nature of mujtahid leadership, which was based on consensus rather than on the appeal of charismatic leaders, is another church-like characteristic of the 'ulama' community. In contrast the heterodox Shaykhi and Babi movements stressed charis-matic leadership, more typical of sects.

During the first third of the nineteenth century religious leadership was diffused among several mujtahids residing in Iran and the shrine cities. Mujtahids of the shrine cities enjoyed reverence in Iran, but their actual authority there was less tangible. The passing of a generation of senior mujtahids in Iran and in Karbala' during the 1840s, following and parallel to the extension of networks of patronage from the shrine cities to Iran, led to the centralization of the leadership in Najaf. The same process marked the shift from the domination of the Arab Kashif al-Ghita' family in Najaf to Iranians, initially to a native of the shrine cities, and subsequently to immigrant mujtahids.

The centralization of religious leadership under a single mujtahid, although never absolute, often lasted for short periods. The diffusion of power among several mujtahids, and a subsequent rise to prominence of one of them, would become a pattern in itself well into the twentieth century. Unlike the religious hierarchy in the Ottoman Empire, leader-ship among the Iranian mujtahids of the shrine cities remained largely open to talented newcomers. Among the Iraqi Arabs religious leadership retained a more hereditary nature, apparently due to the smaller size of the Iraqi 'ulama' community. During the second part of the century, the question of leadership shifted between the unattainable ideal of one single exemplar, and the reality of diffused authority among several leaders.

The major change in the nature of leadership at the beginning of the twentieth century was the introduction of political activity as an important factor in determining the status of a mujtahid. The belief in an unbroken chain of supreme exemplars since the Great Occultation had important ramifications in the twentieth century in justifying the jurists' claim for political authority. Overall, however, once the institu-tions of *ri'asa* and *marja'iyya* took shape they did not undergo structural but only conjunctural changes throughout the nineteenth century. Only with the advent of the 1978–79 revolution in Iran did the leadership institutions undergo complete centralization and formalization with the establishment of the role of the *faqih*, and the various mechanisms for his election, and the nomination of other religious functionaries.

It was in its relations with the outside that the community of 'ulama' witnessed the greatest changes, the most important of which were the shift from Mamluk to direct Ottoman rule, and the conversion of the bulk of the tribes in Iraq to Shi'ism during the first part of the century. The reassertion of direct Ottoman control over Iraq removed various restrictions on Shi'i devotional rites. However, it subjected the 'ulama', both as members of a subordinated sect and as Iranians, to a series of Ottoman policies designed to constrict their autonomy and economic power; most important of these were the restrictions on the independent functioning of their courts. Nevertheless, they still maintained a larger measure of their autonomy compared with the Sunni 'ulama' in the empire. Mujtahids were always part of the urban notability which mediated between the central government and local society. Yet as a result of Ottoman policy which partially weakened the older sayyid elite, they gained in importance and influence. Likewise, the Ottoman occupation of Karbala' and the suppression of the urban gangs in the town put an end to the fragile and fractious relationships between the 'ulama' and the gang leaders there, marking a difference with many other Middle Eastern cities. Concurrently, improved Ottoman control over the countryside and the easing of tension between the Ottoman Empire and Iran encouraged the flow of pilgrims, which was so crucial to the sustenance of the 'ulama'.

By accepting a division of functions between the lay Shi'i ruler and the 'ulama' as political and religious heirs respectively of the Imam, the Usuli school reconciled the longing for the return of the Imam with political reality. In other words, in Iran the 'ulama' as a dominant church-like institution accepted or was even a principal component of the dominant environment and culture. Hence it was willing to legit-imize and at times cooperate with the Qajars on certain issues. More importantly, it resorted to governmental support, even Ottoman, to suppress its religious rivals. Joining the ranks of the 'ulama' promised upward mobility more than anything else to ambitious new recruits. Moreover, the majority of these came from Iran where Shi'ism was the dominant church. In contrast, joining the Shaykhi and Babi movements was a deliberate act often entailing personal sacrifice, characteristic of oppositionary sects.

The legal–traditional nature of mujtahid leadership, based on consensus rather than the attraction of charismatic leaders, is another church-like characteristic of the 'ulama' community. Again, the heterodox Shaykhi and Babi movements were those that stressed the charismatic leadership typical of sects.

In Iraq, on the other hand, the Shi'i 'ulama' did not accept the legitimacy of the surrounding dominant culture. Throughout most of the nineteenth century they regarded the Ottoman government as an illegitimate power, and harbored resentment against the Sunni 'ulama'. Both of these in their turn perceived the Iranian mujtahids as an alien and threatening element. The two factors positioned the 'ulama' as a minority sect *vis-à-vis* the government. The 'ulama''s role as mediators between the Ottomans and the local population did not mean accepting Ottoman or Sunni legitimacy, but reflected the quietist pragmatism of the Shi'i sect. In Iraq the 'ulama' were also engaged in a systematic effort of proselytism among the tribes in order to convert them to Shi'ism. Their missionary activity was a typical sect-like enterprise of a minority group seeking to conquer the majority culture from within, appealing to their constituents' sense of alienation toward the government, and their state of internal crisis and disorientation following sedentarization. Becoming a Shi'a in Iraq was not done for material benefit as would be the case in joining the dominant group, but for other more psychological and political motives.

Finally and most importantly, in persecuting the Sufi, Shaykhi, and Babi movements which posed a challenge to their monopoly of religious leadership, the 'ulama' displayed the distinct characteristics of a ruling church. Significantly, even the 'ulama' in Iraq turned to the Sunni Ottoman state in their struggle against opposition sects. However, such reliance on the state inside Iraq is not necessarily a church-like pattern of behavior, as other minorities have often sought the help of the state in internal disputes.

I would even argue that the intolerance of the Shi'i 'ulama' inside Iran regarding minorities, which was considerably greater than that of Sunni 'ulama' anywhere, was largely the .outcome of a deep-seated sense of insecurity carried over from their distant past as a persecuted sect.

The shift of the 'ulama' toward political activism at the beginning of the twentieth century marked an important change from previous practices or quietism. Their friendlier attitude toward Sultan 'Abd al-Hamid's pan-Islamic policies marked a certain shift in the conduct of the Shi'i mujtahids in the shrine cities from a sect-oriented to a denomination type. This process was further accelerated during World War I, but with the advent of the modern Sunni-dominated state of Iraq, the Shi'i 'ulama' reverted to the status of a sect. This divergence of fates as a persecuted sect in Iraq and a dominant church-like establishment in Iran culminated in the late 1970s with Khomeini's rise to power in Iran and the execution of the leading mujtahid of Najaf, Muhammad Baqir al-Sadr, in 1981.

In their relations with the Ottomans, the Shi'i 'ulama' were mostly reacting to external challenges. In contrast, the conversion of the bulk of the Iraqi tribes to Shi'ism was largely the outcome of concerted missionary effort by the 'ulama', a typical sect-like action. The conversion brought about a profound change in religious, human, and, subsequently, political realities in Iraq. It transformed the Shi'is in Iraq from a minority to a majority of the population, broadening the constituency of believers and increasing the pool of new recruits to the ranks of 'ulama'. The conversion also helped to secure the shrine cities and the 'ulama' from tribal raids. The mujtahids' influence over the tribespeople enabled them to serve as mediators between them and the government, and consequently bolster their standing *vis-à-vis* the Ottomans. The sedentarization and conversion of the tribes also marked a structural change in the history of Iraq, whose full and profound repercussions on the country's political history would unfold during the twentieth century.

The conversion of the tribes marked one type of change in the 'ulama''s relations with an important constituency. Their relations with other constituencies witnessed less profound mutations. The concept of emulation articulated in the eighteenth century and advanced by Ansari's writings established the basic pattern of relations. The spread of networks of patronage reinforced the links between the 'ulama' and their followers, it improved the collection of funds for the shrine cities, and made it easier for the 'ulama' to mobilize their supporters in times of need. Concurrently, however, the financial dependence of the 'ulama' on their followers, the fact that the latter could switch their allegiance among mujtahids, and the absence of coercive means to impose their authority, rendered the 'ulama', particularly those of the shrine cities, dependent on their constituencies and left their power fairly precarious well into the twentieth century. Changing political and economic circumstances drew the 'ulama' of the shrine cities to play a greater role in politics, often ostensibly at the head of various movements, but not necessarily actually leading them, as was the case during the 1905–11 Constitutional Revolution in Iran. Once again, the 1979 revolution transformed those relations by providing the 'ulama' with unprecedented means of coercion, and by depriving the followers of their right to choose the supreme exemplar.

Overall, then, of the three sets of relationships, inside the community of 'ulama', with their lay followers in Iran, and finally with the Ottoman and Iranian states, it was in the latter set that we witness the greater changes during the period under investigation.

The study of change is at the heart of history. Yet persistence and continuity also require examination, as they are as prevalent as change. If we assume the position advocated by Robert Nisbet that structural changes are primarily an outcome of, or response to, external "disruptive" causes, we may understand many of the continuities in the community of learning.[1]

Every establishment, let alone a religious one, inclines to conservatism. The persistence of social structures in the community of learning of the shrine cities, therefore, may be explained by the absence of sufficiently strong external forces and pressures which might intrude and disrupt local institutions and practices. Such an argument is further validated by comparison with the changes the 'ulama' experienced in other Middle Eastern countries. In those cases the main force of change was the growing power and intervention of the state or the ruling colonial power. The Ottoman 'ulama' were subjected to growing state intervention and pressure during the Tanzimat period. Likewise, reforms in al-Azhar both in curriculum and system of certification were forced upon it by the government at the turn of the twentieth century. The 'ulama' establishments in North Africa experienced significant dislocations under the impact of French colonial policy. Similarly, the major changes in the Jewish religious seminaries (yeshivoth) in Eastern Europe were introduced at the beginning of the nineteenth century to combat the rising influence of the Enlightenment on the Jewish communities.

The community of learning in the shrine cities was still spared such challenges, since the Ottomans did not intervene in the internal affairs of 'ulama' society. The Qajars too were unwilling, or rather unable, to subdue the 'ulama' in Iran. The economies of both Iran and Iraq underwent significant transformations during the nineteenth century following their incorporation into the world economy. These changes, however, affected the 'ulama' only toward the end of the century. Likewise, Najaf and Karbala' were less exposed to new ideologies than Cairo or Istanbul.

The internal reforms in Shi'i institutions of learning carried out during the twentieth century were largely defensive measures *vis-à-vis* growing governmental or secular challenges, as was the case in Qum during the 1940s or in Najaf during the early 1960s. External pressures and intervention, however, did not bring about structural change in the institution of leadership as far as practices of selecting leaders and means of exercising authority were concerned. It may well be that external pressures exerted by the Pahlavis in Iran even increased conservatism and opposition to changes among many 'ulama'.

The 1905 Constitutional Revolution in Iran and the 1908 revolution in the Ottoman Empire marked the beginning of a new era in the shrine cities. Both events politicized the 'ulama' to a higher degree than ever before. Both introduced new ideas into the shrine cities, shook the patronage bonds between teachers and students, and introduced new elements to the institution of leadership. Most important, both were attempts to form new types of a more secular nationalist state in the region, and were harbingers of the more formidable challenges which would confront the 'ulama' in the shrine cities and in Iran in the years to come.

Appendix A: Tables

Table 1 Occupational origin of migrant 'ulama'

group:	clerical	other	total	other %
Persians	247	531	778	68.3
Turks	28	99	127	77.9
Iraqis	65	65	130	50
Lebanese	34	16	50	32

Table 2.1 Attendance at *dars al-kharij* by migrant Arab 'ulama'

generational group:	1	2	3	4	5	6	7	8
Najaf	16	7	10	4	26	3	12	33
Karbala'	5	2	1				2	2
Kazimayn	3				1		1	1
Samarra'							8	6

Table 2.2 Attendance at *dars al-kharij* of Arab 'ulama' born in the shrine cities

group:	1	2	3	4	5	6	7	8
Najaf	30	3	15	9	30	8	19	30
Karbala'	1	3	2		1			2
Isfahan							1	
Kazimayn		1		1				1
Qum		1						
Samarra'						1	3	2

Table 3 Ethnic marriages among resident 'ulama'[1]

wife's origin:	Persian	Arab	Turk
'Alim			
Persian	89	12	1
Arab	9	25	
Turk	4	2	3

Table 4 Geographical distribution of migrant Persian 'ulama'[2]

group:	1	2	3	4	5	6	7	8
Iraq–'Ajam (Araq–Burujird–Golpayegan–Khunsar region)								
	1	2	8	2	5	1	9	7
Bihbihan	4			3	4	1	4	1
Gilan	3	2		1	3	5	12	1
Hamadan	1	1	3	2	8	1	9	2
Isfahan	2	1	6	4	7	5	21	16
Kashan	1		3	1	11	1	4	3
Khuzistan	6	3	4	5	18	4	9	5
Kirmanshah	3		1	1	1			2
Mazandaran	6	4	4		5	7	8	9
Khorasan	8		8	1	14	3	22	9
Mashhad	4		3		3	1	2	2
Qazvin	7	4	5	3	11	1	10	5
Qum			3	1	4	1	9	15
Rasht	4		1	1	4	6	14	5
Shiraz	1	2		5	3	11	12	
Tehran	3	3	7	3	15	3	13	16
Yazd	4	4	6	4	10	1	8	4
Zanjan							4	2

Table 5.1 Attendance at *dars al-kharij* by Persian 'ulama'

generational group:	1	2	3	4	5	6	7	8
Karbala':	59	28	38	11	28	17	26	15
Najaf	32	8	54	41	148	52	122	139
Burujird		1			3			
Isfahan	4	6	13	2	11	2	3	2
Kashan	3	1	1		1			
Mashhad	1		1	3	1			
Qum	21				1			
Sabzivar				1				
Samarra'			10	13	117	14	10	
Tehran			1	1	1	3	1	8

Table 5.2 Attendance at *dars al-kharij* by Turkish 'ulama'[3]

generational group:	1	2	3	4	5	6	7	8
Karbala'	13	1	3	3	3	2	2	3
Najaf	8	2	4	4	29	9	18	34
Qum	1							
Isfahan	2		1		1			1
Kaziman				1		1		
Mashhad	1						1	
Samarra'							9	
Tabriz								1
Tehran							1	1

Table 6 Ethnic origin of the mujtahids

ethnic group:	Persians	Turks	Arabs	Lebanese	Total
Najaf born	10*	2*	11		23
Karbala' born	11*				11
Migrants Najaf	17	3	2	2	24
Migrants Karbala'	9	1	1		11

* Both Muhammad Husayn b. Muhammad 'Ali Shahristani of Karbala' and Rida Bahr al-'Ulum were born in Iran while their fathers were temporarily out of the shrine cities. Hasan Mamaqani came to Karbala' as a young child. Socially, all three should be counted as natives of the shrine cities, since their families had already been established in the shrine cities. Henceforth they will be regarded as natives of the shrine cities.

Table 7 Birth place of migrant Iranian mujtahids[4]

	city	town	village	unknown*	Total
Persians	11	5	5	3	24
Turks	1	1	3	1	6
Total	12	6	8	4	30

*It may be assumed that Luftallah Mazandarani was born in a town or a village in Mazandaran. Muhammad Husayn Isfahani was probably born in the village Iywan Kaf near Tehran to a local Qajar governor, and cannot be described as a villager. It is unknown where in Kashmir Murtada Kashmiri was born.

Table 8 Number of sayyids among mujtahids

	Persians	Turks	Arabs	Lebanese	Total sayyids	Total mujtahids
Najaf born	5[10]	[1]	1[11]		6	22
Karbala' born	9[11]				9	11
Migrants Najaf	8[16]	1[4]	[2]	1[2]	10	24
Migrants Karbala'	5 [9]	[1]			5	11
Number	27[46]	1[6]	1[13]	1[2]	30	68

* The overall number of mujtahids from each group is given in parenthesis.

Table 9 Sayyids within the Persian group in the shrine cities

	total	Najaf	Karbala	Mujtahids
Persian	938	175*	98*	46
ssayyids	328	83	54	27
percentage	34.9	47.4	54.5	58.9

*Both numbers refer to those 'ulama' who had settled in either town.

Table 10 Clerical descent among Iranian mujtahids and overall Iranian group population

	overall sample	immigrants overall	mujtahids general	native mujtahids	immigrant mujtahids
Iranians	1071	905	53	23	30
cler-des	416	275	36	20	17
% cler-des	38.89	30.4	69.2	86.9	56.7

Table 1 1 Categories of scholarly works[5]

category	number	%
usul	106	22.5
general *fiqh* works*	77	16.4
mu'amalat	58	12.3
'ibadat	121	25.7
ahkam	31	6.6
iqa'at	6	1.3
polemics	17	3.6
proofs of Imamite	10	2.1
rijal	9	1.9
sciences	8	1.7
tafsir	7	1.5
kalam	7	1.5
grammar	5	1.1
mantiq	3	0.6
philosophy	3	0.6
history	2	0.4
akhlaq	1	0.2
Total	471	100

fiqh works that encompass several categories e.g. *mu'amalat* and *'ibadat*

Table 12 Distribution of scholarly works along time[6]

	general fiqh	mu'amalat	'ibadat	usal	ahkam and iqa'at
Pre-Ansari:[7]	44	14	66	49	13
Ansari and post-Ansari[8]	33	44	55	57	24

Notes

INTRODUCTION

1 Al-Raghib al-Isfahani, cited in Franz Rosenthal, *Knowledge Triumphant: The Concept of Knowledge in Medieval Islam* (Leiden, 1970), 322–24.

2 Steven Humphreys, *Islamic History: A Framework for Inquiry* (Minneapolis, 1988), 173; Ira M. Lapidus, *Muslim Cities in the Later Middle Ages* (Cambridge, Mass., 1967), 107–08.

3 The two other shrine cities, Kazimayn where the seventh and ninth Imams, Musa al-Kazim and Muhammad al-Jawad, are buried, and Samarra', where the tenth and eleventh Imams, 'Ali al-Hadi and Hasan al-'Askari, are buried, will not be included in this study, except when directly related to Najaf and Karbala'.

4 On the concept of the "Shi'i International" see Chibli Mallat, *The Renewal of Islamic Law, Muhammad Baqer as-Sadr, Najaf and the Shi'i International* (Cambridge, 1993), 45–46, 188–89.

5 For the differences between class and status group, see Max Weber, "Class, Status and Party," in *From Max Weber: Essays in Sociology* (New York, 1946; repr. 1958), 180–95.

6 That does not mean of course that there were no women in the shrine cities, but only that the sources hardly mention them except for citing marriages.

7 Ervand Abrahamian, *Iran between Two Revolutions* (Princeton, 1981), 9–37.

8 Among the most notable recent literature on the Sunni 'ulama', see Jonathan Berkey, *The Transmission of Knowledge in Medieval Cairo: A Social History of Islamic Education* (Princeton, 1992); Michael Chamberlain, *Knowledge and Social Practice in Medieval Damascus, 1190–1350* (Cambridge, 1994); George Makdisi, *The Rise of Colleges: Institutions of Learning in Islam and the West* (Edinburgh, 1981). For the more modern period, see Richard C. Repp, *The Mufti of Istanbul: A Study in the Development of the Ottoman Learned Hierarchy* (London, 1986); Madeline Zilfi, *The Politics of Piety: The Ottoman Ulema in the Post Classical Age (1600–1800)* (Minneapolis, 1988); and Christopher Eccel, *Egypt, Islam and Social Change: Al-Azhar in Conflict and Accommodation* (Berlin, 1978).

9 Among the major studies on the Iranian 'ulama', see Hamid Algar, *Religion and State in Iran 1785–1906: The Role of the 'Ulama' in the Qajar Period* (Berkeley, 1969); Abbas Amanat, "In between the Madrasa and the Marketplace: The Designation of Clerical Leadership in Modern Shi'ism," in Said A. Arjomand (ed.), *Authority and Political Culture in Shi'ism* (Albany, 1988);

Said A. Arjomand, *The Shadow of God and the Hidden Imam: Religion, Political Order and Societal Change in Shi'ite Iran from the Beginning to 1980* (Chicago, 1984); Nikki Keddie, "The Roots of 'Ulama' Power in Modern Iran," in Nikki Keddie (ed.), *Scholars, Saints and Sufis: Muslim Religious Institutions since 1500* (Berkeley, 1972); Ann K. S. Lambton, *Qajar Persia* (London, 1988); and various articles by the last two scholars as well as Vanessa Martin, *Islam and Modernism: The Iranian Revolution of 1906* (London, 1987). For the Shi'i 'ulama' in India, see Juan R. I. Cole, *Roots of North Indian Shi'ism in Iran and Iraq: Religion and State in Awadh, 1722–1859* (Berkeley, 1988).

10 Hanna Batatu, *The Old Social Classes and the Revolutionary Movements in Iraq* (Princeton, 1978); Abbas Kelidar, "The Shi'i Imami Community and Politics in the Arab East," *MES* 19 (1983), 3–16; Pierre-Jean Luizard, *La formation de l'Irak contemporain: le role politique des ulemas Chiites à la fin de la domination ottomane et au moment de la construction de l'état irakien* (Paris, 1991); Mallat, *The Renewal*; Yitzhak Nakash, *The Shi'is of Iraq* (Princeton, 1994); and Joyce Wiley, *The Islamic Movement of Iraqi Shi'as* (Boulder, 1992).

11 John Malcolm, *History of Persia*, 2 vols. (London, 1815), II, 432. Both definitions of officials and informal leaders are based on Edward Gross and Amitai Etzioni, *Organizations in Society* (Englewood Cliffs, 1985), 114.

12 Shaykh Zayn al-Din b. 'Ali al-'Amili al-Shahid al-Thani (d. 966/1558) took the concept of *al-na'ib al-'amm* to its logical conclusion in the religious sphere in his *al-Rawda al-bahiyya fi sharh al-lum'a al-dimashqiyya*. Mulla Ahmad Naraqi formulated the notion of *wilayat al-faqih*, vesting the mujtahid with all the power of the Imam in his *'Awa'id al-ayam*. See also *Bulghat al-faqih* by Sayyid Muhammad Al Bahr al-'Ulum (d. 1326/1908), which summarizes the previous discussion on the point. Among the secondary sources, see Arjomand, *The Shadow*; 'Abd al-'Aziz 'Abd al-Husssein Sachedina, *The Just Ruler (al-Sultan al-'Adil) in Shi'ite Islam* (Oxford, 1988); Norman Calder, "The Structure of Authority in Imami Shi'i Jurisprudence" (Ph.D. diss., SOAS, 1980).

13 See such lists in 'Ali Davani, *Zindigani-yi za'im-i buzurg-i 'alam-i tashayyu' 'alama-yi 'aliqadr hadrat-i ayatallah burujirdi* (Qum, 1961), 31–34 and in Sayyid Ahmad Husayni Eshkivari Asaf-Aqa, *al-Imam al-hakim* (Najaf, 1384/ 1964), cited in Michael J. Fischer, *Iran from Religious Dispute to Revolution* (Cambridge, Mass., 1980), 252–54.

14 Said A. Arjomand, "The Mujtahid of the Age and the Mulla-Bashi: An Intermediate State in the Institutionalization of Religious Authority in Shi'ite Iran," in Arjomand (ed.), *Authority and Political Culture*, 80ff.; Arjomand, *The Shadow*, 135.

15 Abbas Amanat, *Resurrection and Renewal: The Making of the Babi Movement in Iran, 1844–1850* (Ithaca, 1989), 41.

16 Aqa Muhammad Baqir Bihbihani, *Risalat al-ijtihad wal-akhbar* (n.p., 1895), 1–20; Mirza Abu al-Qasim Qummi, *Qawanin al-usul* (Tehran: lithograph, 1378/1958), cited in Ahmad Kazemi Moussavi, "The Institutionalization of *Marja'-i Taqlid* in the Nineteenth Century Shi'ite Community," *The Muslim World* 83:3–4 (July–October 1994), 282ff.

17 Juan R. I. Cole, "Imami Jurisprudence and the Role of the 'Ulama': Mortaza Ansari on Emulating the Supreme Exemplar," in Nikki Keddie (ed.), *Religion and Politics in Iran: Shi'ism from Quietism to Revolution* (New Haven, 1983); Amanat, "Madrasa," 102.

18 Amanat, *Resurrection*, 42.

19 Amanat, "Madrasa," 98–101.

20 Amanat, "Madrasa," 99, 101; Arjomand, *The Shadow*, 242–43.

21 For this differentiation see Gross and Etzioni, *Organizations in Society*, 144–45.

22 Hamid Dabashi, "The Sufi Doctrine of the 'Perfect Man' and the View of the Hierarchical Structure of Islamic Culture," *Islamic Quarterly* 30:2 (1986), 118, 121.

23 Algar, *Religion*, 17 and Keddie, "The Roots of 'Ulama' Power" tend to support the confrontational view. Arjomand, *The Shadow*, Martin, *Islam*, and Amanat, "Madrasa," to mention only a few names, advocate the other view.

24 Albert Hourani, "Ottoman Reforms and the Politics of Notables," in Albert Hourani, *The Emergence of the Modern Middle East* (London, 1981), 36–66.

25 Lawrence Stone, "Prosopography," in Lawrence Stone, *The Past and the Present* (Boston, 1981), 45.

26 Rodney Stark and Sims Bainbridge, "Of Churches, Sects, and Cults: Preliminary Concepts for a Theory of Religious Movements," *JSSR* 18 (1979), 117–33; Benton Johnson, "Church and Sect Revisited," *JSSR* 10:2 (Summer 1971), 124–37. For the successful application of this model to Muslim societies, see Cole, *Roots*, 123–27.

27 Etan Kohlberg, "Imam and Community in the Pre-Ghayba Period," in Arjomand (ed.), *Authority and Political Culture*, 37–39.

28 Wilferd Madelung, "Authority in Twelver Shi'ism in the Absence of the Imam," in George Makdisi et al. (eds.), *La notion d'autorité du Moyen Age: Islam, Byzance, Occident* (Paris, 1982), 166; Dennis MacEoin, "Changes in Charismatic Authority in Qajar Shi'ism," in C. E. Bosworth (ed.), *Qajar Iran: Political, Social and Cultural Change, 1800–1925* (Edinburgh, 1983), 154.

29 Hossein Modaressi Tabataba'i, *An Introduction to Shi'i Law: A Bibliographical Study* (London, 1984), 4, 7–9, 23–58; Abu al-Qasim Gurji, "Nigah-i bar tahawul-i 'ilm-i usul va-maqam-i an dar miyan-i 'ulum-i digar," *Maqalat va-barrasi-ha* 13–16 (1352/1973), 27–80; Norman Calder, "Doubt and Prerogative: The Emergence of an Imami Shi'i Theory of Ijtihad," *SI* 70 (1991), 57–78.

30 On the concept of *niyaba 'amma*, see above note 12. On the issue of *zakat*, see Norman Calder, "Zakat in Imami Shi'i Jurisprudence, from the Tenth to the Sixteenth century AD," *BSOAS* 44:3 (1981), 468–80. On the *khums*, see 'Abd al-'Aziz Sachedina, "Al-Khums: The Fifth in the Imami Shi'i Legal System," *JNES* 39 (1980), 276–89, and Madelung, "Authority," 169.

31 Andrew M. Abbott, "Introduction," *A System of Professions* (Chicago, 1988), particularly 22ff.

32 Madelung, "Authority," 169; Calder, "Doubt," 61.

33 Arjomand, *The Shadow*, 211; Moojan Momen, *An Introduction to Shi'i Islam* (New Haven, 1985), 107–08.

34 For the relations between the Safavids and the religious establishment see

Jean Aubin, "La politique religieuse des Safavides," in T. Fahd (ed.), *Le Shiʿisme imamite* (Paris, 1970): 236–45; Arjomand. *The Shadow*, part 2.
35 Arjomand, *The Shadow*, 105–08, 122ff., 178–79; Roger Savory, *Iran under the Safavids* (London, 1980), 238–39; John Chardin, *Voyages de Monsieur le Chevalier Chardin en Perse et autres lieux de l'orient* (Amsterdam, 1709), II, 206–07, cited in Juan R. I. Cole, "Shiʿi Clerics in Iraq and Iran, 1722–1780: The Akhbari–Usuli Conflict Reconsidered," *IS* 18:1 (Winter 1985), 5.
36 MacEoin, "Changes in Charismatic Authority," 158; Said A. Arjomand, "The Shiʿite Hierocracy and the State in Pre-modern Iran, 1785–1890," *Archives européenes de sociologie* 20 (1981), 48.
37 Lawrence Lockhart, *Nadir Shah* (London, 1938), 99–101, 108; R. Shaʿbani, "Siyasat-i madhhabi-yi nadir," *Vahid* 7:9 (1970), 1132–56.
38 For a detailed description of the Najaf conference see ʿAbdallah al-Suwaydi, *al-Hujaj al-qatʿiyya li-ittifaq al-firaq al-islamiyya* (Cairo, 1905); and Rasul Kirkukli, *Dawhat al-wuzaraʾ fi taʾrikh baghdad al-zawraʾ*, trans. M. K. Nawras (Beirut, 1963), 62–63.
39 Cole, "Shiʿi Clerics," 5ff.; Amanat, *Resurrection*, 36. On the ʿulamaʾ from Bahrayn and al-Ahsaʾ, see Juan R. I. Cole, "Rival Empires of Trade and Imami Shiʿism in Arabia, 1300–1800," *IJMES* 19:2 (May 1987), 187ff.
40 Etan Kohlberg, "Aspects of Akhbari Thought in the Seventeenth and Eighteenth Centuries," in Nehemia Levtzion and John O. Voll (eds.), *Eighteenth Century Renewal and Reform in Islam* (Syracuse, 1987), 133–60.
41 Mirza Abu al-Qasim Qummi reportedly studied the "old Usul" in Iran before coming to Karbalaʾ: see Muhammad Baqir Khunsari, *Rawdat al-jannat fi ahwal al-ʿulamaʾ wal-sadat*, 5 vols. (Tehran, 1962) (hereafter *RJ*), V, 369.
42 Kohlberg, "Aspects," 148ff.; Amanat, *Resurrection*, 35.
43 Cole, "Shiʿi Clerics," 15–16; On Aqa Muhammad Baqir, see ʿAli Davani, *Ustad-i kull aqa muhammad baqir b. muhammad akmal maʿruf bi vahid-i bihbihani* (Qum, 1958) and the sources cited there.
44 Cole, "Shiʿi Clerics," 15–16; Davani, *Ustad-i kull*, 128–30, 140–43.
45 *RJ*, II, 95; Davani, *Ustad-i kull*, 143. See Muhammad Sadiq Bahr al-ʿUlum, "Muqaddima," in Muhammad Mahdi b. Murtada Tabatabaʾi, *Rijal al-sayyid bahr al-ʿulum al-maʿruf bil-fawaʾid al-rijaliyya* (Najaf, 1967), 34, who mentions such Usulis. If true, then Bihbihani was not the first Usuli teacher in Karbalaʾ, but rather the first who openly challenged the Akhbaris.
46 Davani, *Ustad-i kull*, 144–45, 165, 195–96.
47 Cole, "Shiʿi Clerics," 20.
48 Amanat, *Resurrection*, 36.
49 Robert Michels, *Political Parties: A Sociological Study of the Oligarchical Tendencies of Modern Democracy* (New York, 1962 repr.), 353, 365; Cole, "Shiʿi Clerics," 20 suggests that the 1772 cholera epidemic harmed the Arab Akhbaris more than the Iranian Usulis, but does not provide direct evidence for his assertion. In addition, the Akhbari–Usuli split did not fully correspond to the ethnic divide, as various important Akhbaris were Iranians, while Bihbihani had Arab students.
50 E. Honigman, s.v., "Karbalaʾ," *EI²*.

51 Hasan al-Amin, *Islamic Shi'ite Encyclopaedia*, 4 vols. (Beirut, 1973) (hereafter *ISE*), VI, 82; Luizard, *La formation*, 143.
52 'Ali al-Bahadili, *Al-Hawza al-'ilmiyya fi al-najaf al-ashraf: ma'alimuha wa-harakatuha al-islahiyya, 1339–1401/1920–1980* (Beirut, 1993), 74.
53 For general surveys of Iraq under the Mamluks see 'Abbas al-'Azzawi, *Ta'rikh al-'iraq bayn al-ihtilalayn*, 8 vols. (Baghdad, 1375/1955), V–VII; Steven H. Longrigg, *Four Centuries of Modern Iraq* (Oxford, 1925); John G. Lorimer, *Gazetteer of the Persian Gulf, Oman and Central Arabia* (London, 1972; repr.), I, 1B; A. K. S. Nawras, *Hukm al-mamalik fi al-'iraq* (Baghdad, 1972); Tom Nieuwenhuis, *Politics and Society in Early Modern Iraq: Mamluk Pashas, Tribal Shaykhs and Local Rule between 1802 and 1831* (The Hague, 1981).
54 Charles Issawi, "Iraq, 1800–1991: A Study in Aborted Development," *Princeton Papers in Near Eastern Studies*, No. 1 (1992), 74; Batatu, *The Old Social Classes*, 16; Luizard, *La formation*, 80; Hala M. Fattah, "The Development of the Regional Market of Iraq and the Gulf 1800–1900" (Ph.D. diss., UCLA, 1986), xii.
55 Arjomand, *The Shadow*, 168–69, 190; Dwight M. Donaldson, *The Shi'ite Religion: A History of Islam in Persia and Irak* (London, 1933), 90, 93–94; Momen, *Introduction*, 119.
56 Donaldson, *The Shi'ite Religion*, 90, 93–94; Sachedina, *The Just Ruler*, 79; Ja'far Al Mahbuba, *Madi al-najaf wa-hadiruha*, 3 vols. (Najaf, 1955), I, 15–16.
57 Nakash, *The Shi'is*, 174; Arjomand, *The Shadow*, 168–69; Donaldson, *The Shi'ite Religion*, 90, 93–94.
58 Yahya Dawlatabadi, *Hayat-i yahya*, 4 vols. (Tehran, 1341s/1963) (hereafter *HY*), I, 77–78; Muhammad 'Ali Pirzadeh Na'ini, *Safarnamah-yi hajji pirzadeh*, 2 vols., ed. Hafiz Farman-Farmayan (Tehran, 1343s), II, 326ff. For the population figures based on the 1905 Ottoman statistics, see Lorimer, *Gazetteer*, II, 2A, 844.
59 For a manifestation of tribal practices see the "Constitution of the Buraq Quarter of Najaf" composed in 1916 in Great Britain, Administration Report, 1918, CO696/1, cited in Nakash, *The Shi'is*, appendix 1. See also the complaint of 'Ali Khaqani, *Shu'ara' al-ghari*, 12 vols., 2nd ed. (Qum, 1988), XII, 457, that "most people of Najaf still live in tribal mentality."
60 In 1785 Aqa Muhammad Khan, founder of the Qajar dynasty, became the de facto ruler of most of Iran, while in 1796 he officially assumed the title of shah.

1 CONCEPT AND ORGANIZATION

1 For such a view, see Chamberlain, *Knowledge*, 4–6, 20, 46–47, 56, 59, 63.
2 Nur al-Din Shahrudi, *Ta'rikh al-haraka al-'ilmiyya fi karbala'* (Beirut, 1990), 73–76. *Hawza* is also used to describe circles of study or a wider complex of study headed by one mujtahid, but this meaning will not be used here. Present-day Shi'i sources use the terms Najaf School (*madrasat al-Najaf*) or even the Najaf University (*jami'at al-Najaf*), which existed briefly in the

early 1960s, to demonstrate its academic equality or superiority to the secular state-sponsored institutions.

3 Several such procedures were introduced in Qum during the twentieth century by 'Abd al-Karim Ha'iri and subsequently by Ayatallah Burujirdi. They were also implemented in Najaf during the early 1960s by Ayatallah Muhsin al-Hakim.

4 Dennis MacEoin, s.v., "Ahsa'i, Shaykh Ahmad," *EIr*; Arjomand, *The Shadow*, 252; Kazim Rashti, *Dalil al-mutahayyirin* (Kirman, 1980), 51–53.

5 *HY*, I, 79–80; Muhammad Mahdi al-Kazimi, *Ahsan al-wadi'a fi tarajim ashhar mashahir mujtahidi al-shi'a* (Baghdad, 1930); Mahdi Bamdad, *Sharh-i hal-i rijal-i iran dar qarn-i 12, 13, 14 hijri*, 6 vols. (Tehran, 1347s/1971), VI, 238–389; Muhsin al-Amin, *A'yan al-shi'a*, 60 vols. (Sidon, 1957), XL, 60–61, and L, 44.

6 Berkey, *Transmission*, 23.

7 George Makdisi, "Madrasa and University in the Middle East," *SI* 32 (1970), 257, 264.

8 James Bill, "Class Analysis and the Dialectics of Modernization in the Middle East," *IJMES* 3 (1972), 422–23; Guilian Denoeux, *Urban Unrest in the Middle East: A Comparative Study of Informal Networks in Egypt, Iran and Lebanon* (Albany, 1993), 30ff.

9 Lawrence Rosen, *Bargaining for Reality: The Reconstruction of Social Relations in a Muslim Community* (Chicago, 1984), 2ff.

10 S. N. Eisenstadt and L. Roniger, "Patron–Client Relations as a Model of Social Exchange," *Comparative Studies in Society and History* 22:1 (1980), 60–69; S. N. Eisenstadt and L. Roniger, *Patrons, Clients and Friends: Interpersonal Relations and the Structure of Trust in Society* (Cambridge, 1984), 48–49; Ernest Gellner, "Patrons and Clients," and John Waterbury, "An Attempt to put Patrons and Clients in their Place," both in Ernest Gellner and John Waterbury (eds.), *Patrons and Clients in Mediterranean Societies* (London, 1977), 1–6, 329–42.

11 On the social need for individuals to establish themselves in as many social networks as possible in two remote Muslim societies of Iran and Morocco, see James A. Bill, "The Plasticity of Informal Politics: The Case of Iran," *MEJ* 27:2 (Spring 1973), 131–51, and Rosen, *Bargaining for Reality*.

12 John Pedersen, s.v., "Madrasa," *EI²*; Berkey, *Transmission*, 34.

13 Marshall G. S. Hodgson, *The Venture of Islam: Conscience and History in a World Civilization*, 3 vols. (Chicago, 1974), II, 210.

14 Husayn Najaf is described as one of Mahdi Bahr al-'Ulum's *khawass* in Mahbuba, *Madi*, III, 417. For Muhammad 'Ali Khunsari, who reportedly had only few *khawass*, see al-Kazimi, *Ahsan al-wadi'a*, 239. See Mulla Muhammad Zaman Mazandarani, who carried out various tasks for Shirazi, in Aqa Buzurg Tehrani, *Nuqaba' al-bashar fi al-qarn al-thalith 'ashar* (Najaf, 1954–68), 792–93. For Ashtiyani, see al-Amin, *A'yan*, XXI, 143. For the medieval *khawass*, see Roy P. Mottahedeh, *Loyalty and Leadership in an Early Islamic Society* (Princeton, 1980), 154–55.

15 *HY*, I, 75.

16 Tehrani, *Nuqaba'*, 638; Hasan Quchani, *Siyahat-i sharq ya zindiganinamah-yi aqa najafi quchani* (Mashhad, 1351/1972), 295, 297, 315.

17 Al-Amin, *A'yan*, XXXII, 72; Hasan al-Sadr, *Takmilat amal al-'amil* (Qum, 1985), 22, 394. For similar descriptions, see Davani, *Ustad-i kull*; Muhammad Sadiq Bahr al-'Ulum, "Muqaddima"; Murtada Ansari, *Zindigani va-shakhsiyati-i shaykh ansari quddisa sirruhu* (n.p., 1960).
18 Quchani, *Siyahat*, 314; Aqa Buzurg Tehrani, *Hadiyat al-razi ila al-imam al-mujaddid al-shirazi* (Tehran, 1984), 73.
19 Quchani, *Siyahat*, 314–15, 312–13; Ja'far al-Khalili, *Mawsu'at al-'atabat al-muqaddasa*, 2nd ed., 10 vols. (Beirut, 1987), VII, 118–20.
20 Quchani, *Siyahat*, 344, 347; Aqa Buzurg Tehrani, *Tabaqat a'lam al-shi'a al-kiram al-barara fi al-qarn al-thalith ba'd al-'ashara* (Najaf, 1954–68), 382, 749–50; Tehrani, *Nuqaba'*, 1405–07; al-Amin, *A'yan*, XVII, 164; Muhammad Hirz al-Din, *Ma'arif al-rijal fi tarajim al-'ulama' wal-'udaba'*, 3 vols. (Najaf, 1964-65), II, 125–28.
21 Mahbuba, *Madi*, I, 324–34; Quchani, *Siyahat*, 460–62; Said A. Arjomand, *The Turban for the Crown, The Islamic Revolution in Iran* (Oxford, 1988), 52–53.
22 'Ali Khaqani, *Shu'ara' al-ghari*, 10 vols. (Najaf, 1954), I, 364–65. All references to Khaqani, unless specifically mentioned otherwise, are from this edition.
23 See, for instance, the al-Nahawi family and Al Bahr al-'Ulum in Mahbuba, *Madi*, III, 450–59 and Hirz al-Din, *Ma'arif*, II, 277–82, III, 217–19; and Muhammad Al 'Anuz Najafi and various members of the Kashif al-Ghita' family in Hirz al-Din, *Ma'arif*, II, 351–52.
24 Hodgson, *Venture of Islam*, II, 214–16.
25 See, for instance, the rupture between Ja'far Kashif al-Ghita' and Sayyid Jawad al-'Amili over the latter's decision to become an independent teacher, probably after Mahdi Bahr al-'Ulum's death. Al-Amin, *A'yan*, XVII, 164.
26 For a typology of such networks, see J. C. Mitchell, *Social Networks in Urban Situations* (Manchester, 1969).
27 While the Sufi network resembled the mujtahid's network in its structure, it could survive its founder if a successor had been designated. Hodgson, *Venture of Islam*, II, 216.
28 See, for instance, the cases of Muhammad Fadil Sharabiyani (d. 1322/ 1904–5), who "inherited" former clients of Muhammad Iravani (d. 1306/ 1888–89), of Muhammad Husayn al-Kazimi (d. 1308/1892), and of Mirza Hasan Shirazi (d. 1312/1895), in Hirz al-Din, *Ma'arif*, II, 372–75; Muhammad 'Ali Mudarris Khiyabani, *Rayhanat al-adab*, 8 vols. (Tabriz, 1967), II, 302; al-Kazimi, *Ahsan al-wadi'a*, 144.
29 Al-Bahadili, *Hawza*, 196–97, citing a public lecture of Ayatallah Muhammad Baqir al-Sadr.
30 Chamberlain, *Knowledge*, 75.
31 For such cases, see the students of Murtada Ansari, Habiballah Rashti, Hadi Tehrani, and Mirza Hasan Shirazi, in Tehrani, *Hadiyat al-razi*, 40; al-Amin, *A'yan*, XX, 96, XL, 60–61.
32 For the collective activity of students in Najaf during the 1905 Revolution and after, see Arjomand, *The Turban*, 52–53; Nakash, *The Shi'is*, 51, 217.
33 Nakash, *The Shi'is*, 246; Luizard, *La formation*, 185; Muhammad Mahdi Asifi, *Madrasat al-najaf wa-tatawwur al-haraka al-'ilmiyya fi-ha* (Najaf,

1964), 27–29. For a list of Arab *majalis* held by families, see Haydar Marjani, *Al-Najaf al-ashraf qadiman wa-hadithan* (Baghdad, 1986), 101–81.

34 Momen, *Introduction*, 203.

35 Uriel Heyd, "The Ottoman 'Ulema and Westernization in the Time of Selim III and Mahmud II," *Scripta Hierosolymitana* 9 (1961), 63–96; Amanat, *Resurrection*, 66.

36 For these tensions, see Nakash, *The Shi'is*, 249.

37 Mallat, *Renewal*, 45–46, 188–89.

38 For an analysis of the ethnic composition of the 'ulama' population, see Meir Litvak, "Continuity and Change in the 'Ulama' Population of Najaf and Karbala', 1791–1904: A Socio-Demographic Study," *IS* 23 (1990), 31–34, 40, 52. The terms "Turk" or "Turkish" appear in the Shi'i sources as defining ethnicity referring here to 'ulama' from both Russian and Iranian Azarbayjan. The term "Persians" is used in this study to distinguish between Persian-speaking and Turkish-speaking Iranians.

39 On the prevalence of migrants over native-born 'ulama' in the shrine cities, see Litvak, "Continuity," 40, 52. On al-Azhar see Eccel, *Egypt, Islam and Social Change*, 295.

40 Quchani, *Siyahat*, 297, 312, 330–31.

41 Mahbuba, *Madi*, III, 421; *RJ*, II, 203.

42 On this growth and occupational origins of the 'ulama', see Litvak, "Continuity," 38ff., and table 1 in the appendix. For an estimate of the community's size in 1907, see Selim Deringil, "The Struggle against Shi'ism in Hamidian Iraq: A Study in Ottoman Counter Propaganda," *WI* 30 (1990), 56.

43 David Menashri, *Education and the Making of Modern Iran* (Ithaca, 1992), 55; Murtada Ravandi, *Sayr-i farhang va-ta'rikh-i ta'lim va-tarbiyat dar iran va-urupa* (Tehran, 1364/1985), 104.

44 Nakash, *The Shi'is*, 46; on the difficulties experienced by Lebanese villagers in supporting 'ulama', see al-Amin, *A'yan*, XL, 39 and XLVIII, 147.

45 Al-Amin, *A'yan* XL, 55; Tehrani, *Kiram*, 528; Hirz al-Din, *Ma'arif*, II, 261–63, and Mahbuba, *Madi*, II, 287.

46 See tables 2.1 and 2.2 in the appendix.

47 Al-Amin, *A'yan*, XL, 257 and XLIX, 25.

48 See table 3 in the appendix.

49 Al-Amin, *A'yan*, XLV, 251–52; Ansari, *Zindigani*, 273; Mahbuba, *Madi*, III, 431–40; Bahr al-'Ulum, "Muqaddima," 139–43, 159–62; Hirz al-Din, *Ma'arif*, I, 32–34; Tehrani, *Nuqaba'*, 457.

50 Tehrani, *Nuqaba'*, 13–14; Quchani, *Siyahat*, 330.

51 Sayyid 'Abbas Shushtari, *al-Zill al-mamdud* (Arabic MS. in the library of the raja of Mahmudabad, Lucknow), fos. 82a–85a, 85a–88b, 95a–100a, 142a–144a, 95a–100b.

52 'Abdallah Mamaqani, *Makhzan al-maghani* (Najaf, 1345/1926), 237–38.

53 Khalili, *Mawsu'at al-'atabat*, VII, 120; Quchani, *Siyahat*, 331–32; Nasser Rabbat, s.v., "Riwak" and J. Jomier, s.v., "al-Azhar," both in *EI²*.

54 See the observation by the British resident Newmarch that the Iranian mujtahids "were prone to think themselves superior to all other Orientals,"

in IGFD P/6652 no. 390, Newmarch to Barnes, September 20, 1902; al-Amin, *A'yan*, XL, 65–66; Hirz al-Din, *Ma'arif*, III, 136–42.

55 Pirzadeh Na'ini, *Safarnamah*, I, 350–52; FO 195/707 Baghdad no. 47, Kemball to Bulwer, September 21, 1862; FO 195/1409 Baghdad no. 33, November 1, 1882; FO 195/1885 Baghdad no. 533/94, Mockler to Currie, October 10, 1895. For an analysis of the differences of themes in Shi'i mourning rituals, see Nakash, *The Shi'is*, 143ff.

56 Al-Amin, *A'yan*, XL, 25–26, 55; XLIX, 26–27; *HY*, 28; Nakash, *The Shi'is*, 261.

57 To cite a few examples: both Persians and Arabs were among 'Abdallah Mamaqani's (d. 1246/1830–31) circle of close friends. When Sadr al-Din Isfahani visited Najaf 'ulama' from all ethnic groups came to see him. Mamaqani is mentioned as attending *ta'ziyya* at the house of Al Kashif al-Ghita', and Habiballah Rashti had Arabs in his *majlis ta'ziyya*.

58 On the growing divisions between Arabs and Iranian 'ulama' in subsequent periods, see Nakash, *The Shi'is*, 76, 85–88, 100–08, 257–58.

59 For an elaborated discussion of this topic, see Meir Litvak, "The Finances of the 'Ulama' Communities in Najaf and Karbala' in the Nineteenth Century," forthcoming in *WI*.

60 On the role of *awqaf* in al-Azhar, see Eccel, *Egypt, Islam and Social Change*, 72, 121–22. On Iran, see Ali Reza Sheikholeslami, "The Patrimonial Structure of the Iranian Bureaucracy in the Late Nineteenth century," *IS* 11 (1978), 204.

61 Salih Haidar, "Land Problems of Iraq" (Ph.D. diss, London University, 1942), cited in Charles Issawi, *The Economic History of the Middle East, 1800–1914* (Chicago, 1966), 164.

62 Nakash, *The Shi'is*, 39–41.

63 For a summary of the various financial resources, see L/P&S/11/165 Reports on Administration for 1918 of Divisions and Districts of the Occupied Territories in Mesopotamia.

64 On the evolution of the two taxes, see Sachedina, "Al-Khums," and Norman Calder, "Zakat in Imami Shi'i Jurisprudence, from the Tenth to the Sixteenth Century AD," *BSOAS* 44:3 (1981), 468–80.

65 For a more detailed review of the Oudh Bequest, see Nakash, *The Shi'is*, 215ff.; Litvak, "The Shi'i 'ulama'," chap. 5.

66 Mirza Muhammad Tunikabuni, *Qisas al-'ulama'* (Tehran, 1378/1967) (hereafter *QU*), 36, 191ff.; al-Amin, *A'yan* V, 24, XLV, 233, XLII, 46. For the Indian money, see Juan R. I. Cole, "'Indian Money' and the Shi'i Shrine Cities of Iraq 1786–1850," *MES* 22:4 (1986), 461–80.

67 Muhammad Hasan Khan I'timad al-Saltana, *Kitab al-ma'athir wal-athar* (Tehran, 1306/1888), 136. For the revenues of the Iranian government, see Arjomand, *The Turban*, 212, table 4.

68 Mamaqani, *Makhzan al-maghani*, 233; Hirz al-Din, *Ma'arif*, II, 374.

69 Ahmad Ashraf, "Bazaar–Mosque Alliance: The Social Basis of Revolts and Revolutions in Iran," *Politics, Culture and Society* 1 (1988), 538–40; Nakash, *The Shi'is*, 231–32.

70 Quchani, *Siyahat*, 327–29; Adib al-Mulk, *Safarnamah-yi adib al-mulk bih 'atabat (dalil al-za'irin) 1273h.q.*, ed. Mas'ud Golzari (Tehran, 1364s/1986),

119; Hajji Sayyah, *Khatirat-i hajji sayyah*, ed. Hamid Sayyah and Sayfallah Gulkar (Tehran, 1346/1967–68), 281.

71 "Sanitary Report, 1916" L\PS\10\23; Nakash, *The Shi'is*, 166, 191; Vital Guinet, *La Turquie d'Asie* (Paris, 1891–95), 202; H. S. Cowper, *Through Asiatic Arabia* (London, 1894), 367; Habib Chiha, *La province de Baghdad* (Cairo, 1908), 180.

72 Quchani, *Siyahat*, 297, 315. Al-Amin, *A'yan* XL, 64. In another passage, however, al-Amin says he lived off three Ottoman pounds for half a year: *ibid.*, XL, 54; Pirzadeh Na'ini, *Safarnamah*, 332.

73 Charles Issawi, *The Fertile Crescent, 1800–1914: A Documentary Economic History* (Oxford, 1988), 476. Unfortunately Issawi does not give prices for the 1890s, when al-Amin stayed in the shrine cities. In 1858 the price of bread fluctuated between 1.25 and 1.5 piasters, and it may be assumed to have stayed within that range in the interim.

74 Al-Amin, *A'yan*, XXXIII, 396; Tehrani, *Kiram*, 184–85; Tehrani, *Nuqaba'*, 792–93, 1209; Hirz al-Din, *Ma'arif*, III, 23–24; al-Sadr, *Takmilat amal al-'amil*, 102.

75 Pedersen, "Madrasa"; 'Abd al-Latif al-Tibawi, "Origins and Character of the Madrasa," *BSOAS*, 25 (1962), 230–31; Berkey, *Transmission*, 7–8.

76 Makdisi, *Rise of Colleges*, 39, 171–80; Makdisi, "Madrasa and University."

77 Tibawi, "Origins," 230–31; Berkey, *Transmission*, 8, 47; Mottahedeh, *Loyalty*, 140.

78 Makdisi, *Rise of Colleges*, 171–80 mentions three levels of study in the medieval madrasa: *mubtadi'* (beginner); *mutwassit* (intermediary); and *muntahi* (advanced). The beginner and intermediary levels probably parallel the Shi'i levels of *muqaddamat* and *sutub*. Halil Inalcik, *The Ottoman Empire: The Classical Age 1300–1600*, trans. N. Itzkowitz and C. Imber (London, 1973), 168–69.

79 On the Shi'i curriculum, see anonymous, "Le programme des études chez les Chiites et principalement chez ceux de Nedjef," *Revue du monde musulman* 23 (June 1913), 271–75; Khalili, *Mawsu'at al-'atabat*, VII, 91–106; *ISE*, IV, 84–85. On *Qawanin al-usul* see *QU*, 94–95; *RJ* V, 372; Aqa Buzurg Tehrani, *al-Dhari'a ila tasanif al-shi'a*, 26 vols. (Tehran, 1355s/1936), VI, 98–102.

80 The term is an abbreviation of *dars kharij al-kitab* (class exceeding the book), which means that the mujtahid does not read a specific book from an assigned curriculum, but whatever he chooses. Asifi, *Madrasat al-najaf*, 11.

81 Momen, *Introduction*, 200–01; al-Amin, *A'yan*, XL, 49–50; *ISE*, IV, 86.

82 Fadil al-Jamali, "The Theological Colleges of Najaf," *Muslim World* 50:1 (1960), 17.

83 Quchani, *Siyahat*, 160, 212–13, 367–69. See similar criticism by Al-Amin, *A'yan*, XL, 55, 324–25; Sayyah, *Khatirat*, 281; Pirzadeh Na'ini, *Safarnamah*, I, 333–34.

84 'Abd al-Hadi al-Fadli, *Dalil al-najaf al-ashraf* (Najaf, 1966), 67; on the role of the *mu'id*, see Makdisi, *Rise of Colleges*, 193–94.

85 The first lithograph printer in Iraq was brought to Karbala' in 1856. The first printing press in Najaf was established in 1909: Abdul-Wahhab 'Abbas al-Qaysi, "The Impact of Modernization on Iraqi Society During the

204 Notes to pages 40–43

Ottoman Era: A Study of Intellectual Development in Iraq, 1869–1917"
(Ph.D. diss., University of Michigan, 1958), 75, 113.

86 Pedersen, "Madrasa"; Berkey, *Transmission*, 21. For the survival of these
practices in twentieth-century Iran, see Fischer, *Iran*, 40–41.

87 Al-Sadr, *Takmilat amal al-'amil*, 17–18; Jamali, "Colleges," 17; Asifi,
Madrasat al-najaf, 6–7; Pedersen, "Madrasa"; Mallat, *Renewal*, 41–42.

88 *RJ*, V, 374; al-Amin, *A'yan*, VII, 92; *QU*, 5.

89 Mudarris Khiyabani, *Rayhanat al-adab*, II, 14; *QU*, 107; Hirz al-Din,
Ma'arif, II, 376–79. Discussing twentieth-century Qum, Michael Fischer,
Iran, 71 remarked that many of the questions students asked reflected "a
concern intermingled with enjoyment of the scholastic game."

90 Nikki Keddie, "Islamic Philosophy and Islamic Modernism: The Case of
Sayyid Jamal al-Din al-Afghani," *Journal of Persian Studies* 10 (1980), 53.

91 For expressions of hostility, see Hajj Zayn al-'Abidin Shirvani, *Bustan
al-siyaha* (Tehran, 1315/1897–98), 463. See also *QU*, 191–93, and
Murtada Mudarrisi Chahardahi, *Ta'rikh-i ravabit-i iran va-iraq* (Tehran,
1351s/1972), 195–96.

92 Quchani, *Siyahat*, 347–48. For similar examples, see Hirz al-Din, *Ma'arif*,
II, 211–14, Nikki Keddie, *Sayyid Jamal al-Din "al-Afghani," A Political
Biography* (Berkeley, 1972), 16.

93 Mulla 'Ali Nuri and his son Muhammad Hasan, and subsequently Jahangir
Khan Qashqa'i in Isfahan: see Tehrani, *Kiram*, 342–43; Muhammad
Mahdi Kashmiri, *Nujum al-sama' takmila*, 2 vols. (Qum, 1397/1977) I,
402; Tehrani, *Nuqaba'*, 344–45; and Algar, *Religion*, 59, 69; Sayyid Abu
al-Hasan Tabataba'i Isfahani Mirza-yi Jelva in Tehran in Mudarris Khiyabani, *Rayhanat al-adab*, I, 273; Mulla Hadi Sabzivari in Sabzivar, in
Murtada Mudarrisi-Chahardahi, *Zindigani va-falsafa-yi hajji mulla hadi
sabzivari* (Tehran, n.d.).

94 Makdisi, *Rise of Colleges*, 270–72.

95 Chamberlain, *Knowledge*, 82–84, 138.

96 Sachedina, *The Just Ruler*, 59.

97 Jamali, "Colleges," 17; Asifi, *Madrasat al-najaf*, 18ff.

98 Mallat, *Renewal*, 42.

99 See his attempt to restrict flagellation during the 'Ashura' processions and
the debate this provoked in Werner Ende, "The Flagellation of Muharram
and the Shi'ite 'Ulama'," *Der Islam* 55 (1978), 19–36.

100 Al-Amin, *A'yan*, XL, 49–50; *HY*, I, 27–28. See similar observations on
al-Azhar in Eccel, *Egypt, Islam and Social Change*, 150–52, 156.

101 See Litvak, "Continuity," 47–49, which shows that 31.4 percent (293 out of
932) of the Persian 'ulama' in the sample used for that study settled
permanently in the shrine cities. A similar ratio of 32.4 (45 out of 139)
existed for the Turks. The real percentage of permanent settlers was
probably less, as most of those who returned to Iran served as low-ranking
mullas, and were unknown to the compilers of the biographical dictionaries.

102 Chamberlain, *Knowledge*, 80–81, 101; Arjomand, *The Shadow*, 127–29.
On the concept of professionalization, see Joan Gilbert, "Institutionaliza-
tion of Muslim Scholarship and Professionalization of the 'Ulama' in
Medieval Damascus," *SI* 52 (1980), 105–35.

103 In 1964 Ayatallah Muhsin al-Hakim established the first roof-organization in Najaf, *al-marja'iyya al-diniyya al-'amma* (the general religious *marja'iyya*), which gave students monthly stipends each according to his social position: see Mallat, *Renewal*, 38.

2 LEADERSHIP IN THE AGE OF MULTIPLE CENTERS

1 Excerpts from the translation published in *al-Tawhid* 3:1 (1406/1985), trans. Hamid Algar, as "Excerpts of the Constitution of the Republic of Iran," in Arjomand (ed.), *Authority and Political Culture*, 376.
2 For his biographies see Bahr al-'Ulum, "Muqaddima"; *RJ*; *QU*, 168–74; Husayn Nuri Tabarsi, *al-Mustadrak 'ala wasa'il al-shi'a* (Tehran, 1318–21/1900–03), 383; al-Amin, *A'yan*, XLVIII, 165ff.; Davani, *Ustad-i kull*, 212–36; and Muhammad 'Ali Mu'allim Habibabadi, *Makarim al-athar dar ahwal-i rijal-i dawra-yi qajar*, 2 vols. (Isfahan, 1958), II, 414–29.
3 Bahr al-'Ulum, "Muqaddima," 67–68; Nuri, *Mustadrak*, 383.
4 Al-Amin, *A'yan*, XLVIII, 165 says he was the unrivaled leader in Iraq, which suggests that he was not so in Iran: Bahr al-'Ulum, "Muqaddima," 48.
5 Al-Amin, *A'yan*, XLVIII, 168; Bahr al-'Ulum, "Muqaddima," 95–97.
6 Hasan Mamaqani was responsible for *fatwas* under Husayn Kuhkamara'i, and Mirza Hasan Shirazi referred questions to other mujtahids as a sign of his preference for them.
7 On the contrast between the two trends, see Amanat, *Resurrection*, chap. 1; Mangol Bayat, *Mysticism and Dissent: Socio-Religious Thought in Qajar Iran* (Syracuse, 1982), 1–35 and MacEoin, "Changes in Charismatic Authority," 165.
8 Amanat, *Resurrection*, 42–43.
9 For the similarities between Sufism and Shi'i doctrines, see Momen, *Introduction*, 208–09.
10 MacEoin, "Changes in Charismatic Authority," 165; Tehrani, *Kiram*, 91; Bahr al-'Ulum, "Muqaddima," 71–72.
11 For an analysis of the Sufi revival during the eighteenth century and the 'ulama''s reaction, see William R. Royce, "Mir Ma'sum 'Ali Shah and the Ni'mat Allahi Revival 1776–77 to 1796–97: A Study of Sufism in Late Eighteenth Century Iran" (Ph.D. diss., Princeton University, 1979); Muhammad Ma'sum Na'ib al-Sadr Shirazi, *Tara'iq al-Haqa'iq*, ed. M. J. Mahjub, 3 vols. (Tehran, 1345s/1966), III, 199–200.
12 Royce, "Ma'sum 'Ali Shah," 87, 135–36, 152–55, 159–60, 173–74.
13 Tehrani, *Kiram*, 434. See for instance the story of how Shaykh Ja'far appropriated money given to Shaykh Husayn by his emulators with the latter accepting this without protest. Muhammad Hirz al-Din, *Ma'arif*, I, 261.
14 Amanat, "Madrasa," 103; "Kashf al-Ghita'" (1317/1899), 394 and *Risala-yi jihadiyya*, Persian MS, Kitabkhanah-yi Astani-i Quds-i Rizavi, Mashhad, No. 123/2343, both cited in Abdul Hadi Ha'iri, "The Legitimacy of the Early Qajar Rule as Viewed by the Shi'i Religious Leaders," *MES* 24:3 (July 1988), 276–77.
15 Ann K. S. Lambton, "A Nineteenth Century View of Jihad," *SI* 32 (1970), 188.

16 *RJ*, II, 200; Muhammad Kalantar, "Muqaddima," in Murtada Ansari, *Kitab al-makasib* (Najaf, 1392/1972), I, 60–66; *Risala-yi jihadiyya*, cited in Ha'iri, "Legitimacy," 276; al-Amin, *A'yan*, XV, 413–16; Hirz al-Din, *Ma'arif*, I, 150–57; Mudarris Khiyabani, *Rayhanat al-adab*, V, 24; Mahbuba, *Madi*, I, 38; *QU*, 107, 191–92.

17 Al-Sadr, *Takmilat amal al-'amil*, 384.

18 Al-Amin, *A'yan*, XLIX, 7–8, citing *Riyad al-janna* and the content of the *Ijaza*; Davani, *Ustad-i kull*, 239.

19 Sayyid Athar Abbas Rizvi, *A Socio-Intellectual History of the Isna 'Ashari Shi'is in India*, 2 vols. (Canberra, 1986), II, 96.

20 Al-Amin, *A'yan*, XLII, 46.

21 See above their appeal for his support against the Sufis.

22 Zayn al-'Abidin Shirvani, *Hada'iq al-siyaha* (Tehran: 1348s/1970), 428; Ahmad Kirmanshahi, *Mir'at al-ahwal jihannamah*, cited in Davani, *Ustad-i kull*, 337; *QU*, 21–23.

23 *RJ*, I, 100, IV, 198, II, 217.

24 Al-Amin, *A'yan*, XLVI, 79; *QU*, 94–95.

25 *QU*, 94–95; Ansari, *Zindigani*, 61–63.

26 *QU*, 115; Tehrani, *Kiram*, 620; Hirz al-Din, *Ma'arif*, II, 298; Ansari, *Zindigani*, 149.

27 Amanat, "Madrasa," 104–07.

28 See table 4 in the appendix.

29 The natural trend would be to travel from the less prestigious centers to those of more renown and not vice versa. A student who regards his teachers as the most learned would be less inclined to look for other teachers.

30 *QU*, 183–98; *RJ*, II, 201–05; Amanat, "Madrasa," 103; Davani, *Ustad-i kull*, 250; Sa'id Nafisi, *Ta'rikh-i ijtima'i va-siyasi-yi iran dar dawra-yi mu'asir*, 2 vols. (Tehran, 1340s/1961), I, 70; Tehrani, *al-Dhari'a*, V, 296.

31 *QU*, 134; al-Amin, *A'yan*, XVII, 164, 168.

32 Willock's dispatch, FO 60/27, July 15, 1826.

33 Al-Amin, *A'yan*, XLVI, 79; Shirvani, *Hada'iq al-siyaha*, 429. Mirza Muhammad Taqi Siphir Lisan al-Mulk, *Nasikh al-Tawarikh*, 4 vols. (Tehran, 1385/1965), I, 215. Rida Quli Khan Hidayat, *Ta'rikh-i rawdat al-safa-i nasiri dar dhikr padshahan-i dawra-yi safaviya afshariya zandiya qajariya*, 10 vols. (Qum, 1399s), IX, 642.

34 *RJ*, II, 100; for Shafti's power in Isfahan and his defiance of the shah, see: *QU*, 135–68; Algar, *Religion*, 59–63; Amanat, "Madrasa," 106–07.

35 Davani, *Ustad-i kull*, 291; *QU*, 125–26. On the significance of the title see above, p. 98.

36 Kashmiri, *Nujum al-Sama'*, I, 62–63; Tehrani, *Kiram*, 259–60; Habibabadi, *Makarim*, I, 117.

37 *QU*, 23.

38 Murtada Mudarrisi-Chahardahi, *Shyakhgari va-babgari* (Tehran, 1345s/1966), 38.

39 *QU*, 124–25. Sayyid Mahdi eventually died in Tehran.

40 Al-Amin, *A'yan*, XLIX, 43; Hirz al-Din, *Ma'arif*, III, 26–29; Tehrani, *Kiram*, 138.

41 Mahbuba, *Madi*, III, 200.

42 *Ibid.*; Tehrani, *Kiram*, 87, 408.

43 Mahbuba, *Madi*, III, 200; Shirvani, *Hada'iq al-siyaha*, 431.

44 Al-Amin, *A'yan*, XXXIX, 79–80; Hirz al-Din, *Ma'arif*, I, 106; Tehrani, *Kiram*, 138; Ansari, *Zindigani*, 389n.; 'Ali b. Hasan al-Bahrani, *Anwar al-badrayn fi tarajim 'ulama' al-qatif al-ahsa' wal-bahrayn* (Najaf, 1960), 316–17; Rashti, *Dalil*, 51.

45 Mahbuba, *Madi* II, 217, III, 169; Hirz al-Din, *Ma'arif*, I, 296; Ansari, *Zindigani*, 301; Khaqani, *Shu'ara'*, VI, 256.

46 *QU*, 184.

47 See Sayyid Muhammad al-Hindi, *al-Nazm al-li'ali*, cited in Tehrani, *Kiram*, 317. See also Modaressi Tabataba'i, *Introduction*, 57 who holds Shaykh Hasan as a greater legal authority.

48 The first two Muhaqqiqs were Ja'far b. Hasan al-Hilli (d. 676/1277) and 'Ali b. 'Abd al-'Ali al-'Amili al-Karaki (d. *c.* 940/1533).

49 *QU*, 16–17.

50 For this growth, see Litvak, "Continuity," 40.

51 Khaqani, *Shu'ara'*, V, 256–57; Mahbuba, *Madi*, III, 170.

52 Tehrani, *Nuqaba'*, 1202–05; Hirz al-Din, *Ma'arif*, II, 16–17; al-Amin, *A'yan*, XVII, 168.

53 Hirz al-Din, *Ma'arif*, II, 12–13; Mahbuba, *Madi*, II, 259.

54 Hirz al-Din, *Ma'arif*, I, 210–17; Tehrani, *Kiram*, 316–20; Mahbuba, *Madi*, III, 147–51; al-Amin, *A'yan*, XXI, 133–38; Modaressi Tabataba'i, *Introduction*, 57.

55 *RJ*, II, 306–07; al-Amin, *A'yan*, XXI, 134; Hirz al-Din, *Ma'arif*, I, 296.

56 On the trial see Amanat, *Resurrection*, 220–38 and Moojan Momen, "The Trial of Mulla 'Ali Bastami: A Combined Sunni–Shi'i Fatwa against the Bab," *Iran* 20 (1982), 113–43; see also chap. 7 below.

57 On the history of Shaykhism see Denis MacEoin, "From Shaykhism to Babism" (Ph.D. diss., Cambridge University, 1979); MacEoin, "Ahsa'i, Shaykh Ahmad"; Amanat, *Resurrection*, 48–69; Bayat, *Mysticism*; Rashti, *Dalil*. On the théoretical aspects of Shaykhism see Henri Corbin, "L'école shaykhie en theologie shi'ite," *Annuaire de l'Ecole Pratique des Hautes Etudes, Section des Sciences Religieuses 1960-61*; Henri Corbin, *Terre celeste et corps de resurrection* (Paris, 1960), 99–174; Henri Corbin, *En Islam iranien: aspects spirituels et philosophiques* (Paris, 1971), IV; Vahid Rafati, "The Development of Shaykhi Thought in Shi'i Islam" (Ph.D. diss., UCLA, 1979); A. L. M. Nicolas, *Essai sur le Cheikhisme*, 4 vols. (Paris, 1910).

58 Amanat, *Resurrection*, 62–65.

59 Al-Amin, *A'yan*, XLVIII, 155ff.; al-Kazimi, *Ahsan al-wadi'a*, 11–12; *QU*, 88–89. Rashti, *Dalil*, 76–83; Nicolas, *Essai*, I, 60; See above Mahdi's efforts to persecute the Jews, which were not supported by Shafti, as an example of his extreme views.

60 Rashti, *Dalil*, 62–64, 76–83; Nicolas, *Essai*, I, 51–56, 60.

61 MacEoin, "Changes in Charismatic Authority," 166.

62 Rashti, *Dalil*, 62–64, 76; Nicolas, *Essai*, I, 51–56; Muhammad Hasan Astarabadi, *Mazahir al-athar*, cited in Mudarrisi-Chahardahi, *Shaykhgari va-babgari*, 30.

63 Amanat, *Resurrection*, 62–63; Bayat, *Mysticism*, 41.

64 Rashti, *Dalil*, 99–101, 118, 115–16, 127–30; Nicholas, *Essai*, I, 21–22.
65 Rashti, *Dalil*, 92, 94, 99–108; 126–27; Bayat, *Mysticism*, 56.
66 Rashti, *Dalil*, 90–104, 130–33; Bayat, *Mysticism*, 41–42.
67 Rashti, *Dalil*, 99–101, 118, 115–16, 127–30; Nicholas, *Essai*, I, 21–22; Amanat, *Resurrection*, 62–63, 67.
68 *QU*, 10; al-Amin, *A'yan*, V, 336.
69 Cole, "'Indian Money'," 472.
70 Cole, "'Indian Money'," 468; On the attitude of Shaykhis to politics and their relations with the Qajars, see Amanat, *Resurrection*, 64.
71 Shushtari, *al-Zill*, fos. 53b–55a, 144a–146a, 172a–174b, 241a–243b; Tehrani, *Kiram*, 710. See also Cole, "'Indian Money'," 471–72.
72 IGFD Political Consultation nos 28–29, June 8, 1844 – Political Agent in Turkish Arabia no. 90, March 21, 1844, cited in Cole, "'Indian Money'," 471–72.
73 Litvak, "Continuity," 53–55.
74 On the Persian and Turkish students, see tables 5.1 and 5.2 in the appendix.
75 *QU*, 10.
76 On the Karbala' rebellion, see Juan R. I. Cole and Moojan Momen, "Mafia, Mob and Shi'ism in Iraq: The Rebellion of Ottoman Karbala', 1824–1843," *Past and Present* 112 (1986), 112–43.

3 MONOPOLIZATION OF LEADERSHIP OF NAJAF

1 Cf. Momen, *Introduction*, 135; 'Ali al-Wardi, *Lamahat ijtima'iyya min ta'rikh al-'iraq al-hadith*, 6 vols. (Baghdad, 1969), II, 84–85; Kazemi Moussavi, "Institutionalization," 280; Abdul Hadi Ha'iri, *Shi'ism and Constitutionalism in Iran: A Study on the Role Played by the Persian Residents of Iraq in Persian Politics* (Leiden, 1977), 64; and Luizard, *La formation*, 139. See also statements by Muhammad Baqir Khunsari, *RJ*, II, 304; Kashmiri, *Nujum al-Sama'*, II, 73; Mudarris Khiyabani, *Rayhanat al-adab*, III, 357.
2 *QU*, 16–17.
3 See for instance the reply by the mujtahid of Kirman to a Babi activist that he would abide by the decisions of the mujtahids of the shrine cities regarding the Bab's claims, in Mirza 'Ali Isfahani, *Bihjat al-sudur*, cited in Kazemi Moussavi, "Institutionalization," 286.
4 Amanat, "Madrasa," 109. Among the deceased mujtahids were Shafti in 1844, Karbasi in 1845, Sadr al-Din 'Amili in 1846, all of them in Isfahan. In Qazvin Sayyid 'Abd al-Wahhab died in 1847, and his rival Mulla Muhammad Taqi Baraghani was assassinated in the same year. In Karbala' Sayyid Kazim Rashti died at the end of 1843 and his bitter opponent Ibrahim Qazvini died in 1847, while Hasan Kashif al-Ghita' died in 1846 in Najaf.
5 Bamdad, *Sharh*, I, 115; *RJ*, II, 306.
6 Al-Amin, *A'yan*, XVII, 164, 168.
7 Modaressi Tabataba'i, *Introduction*, 93; Muhammad Rida al-Muzaffar, "Tarjamat al-mu'allif" in Muhammad Hasan Najafi, *Jawahir al-kalam fi sharh shara'i' al-islam*, ed. 'Abbas Quchani-Najafi (Najaf, 1958), I, 16.

8 Shushtari, *al-Zill*, fos. 90a, 139b, 205a–b, 247a–b.
9 Shushtari, *al-Zill*, fos. 84a–85a.
10 See for example Hirz al-Din, *Ma'arif*, I, 21–23, III, 101–04; al-Amin, *A'yan*, XXII, 379; Tehrani, *Nuqaba'*, 450–51.
11 For such students, see al-Amin, *A'yan*, L, 28; Hirz al-Din, *Ma'arif*, I, 317–18, II, 250.
12 *RJ*, II, 103.
13 *QU*, 103–04; *RJ*, II, 305; al-Amin, *A'yan*, XLIX, 108–10; Tehrani, *Nuqaba'*, 1205; al-Wardi, *Lamahat*, 85.
14 Tehrani, *Nuqaba'*, 1205.
15 See al-Sadr's *Takmilat amal al-'amil*, cited in Mahbuba, *Madi*, II, 132; and Khaqani, *Shu'ara'*, VIII, 383; Tehrani, *Nuqaba'*, 450–51; Hirz al-Din, *Ma'arif*, II, 231–33.
16 Muzaffar, "Tarjama," 17. For other students whom he dispatched see al-Amin, *A'yan*, XXII, 163, Hirz al-Din, *Ma'arif*, II, 304–05; Mirza 'Abd al-Rahman Mudarris, *Ta'rikh-i 'ulama'-yi khorasan* (Mashhad, 1341s/1963), 122.
17 *QU*, 10–11; Shushtari, *al-Zill*, fo. 59b.
18 Sayyid Muhammad 'Ali in *al-Yatima*, cited in al-Amin, *A'yan*, XLIV, 347.
19 Shushtari, *al-Zill*, fos. 95a, 206a–207b, 244b–245b; Bahr al-'Ulum, "Muqaddima,", 132–35; Tehrani, *Nuqaba'*, 581–82; al-Amin, *A'yan*, XLIII, 133.
20 Al-Amin, *A'yan*, XLI, 102.
21 Al-Amin, *A'yan*, XLIII, 176–79, LI, 10–11; Kashmiri, *Nujum al-Sama'*, II, 253.
22 The official Qajar almanac compiled by Muhammad Hasan Khan I'timad al-Saltana, *Kitab al-Ma'athir wal-Athar*, 135–36, described him as the "religious leader of the [Shi'i] nation (*milla*) and religion, the sign of God (*ayat Allah*) and the deputy (khalifa) of His deputy (khalifa) on earth." See also *RJ*, II, 305.
23 See the content of the permission in al-Amin, *A'yan*, XLV, 229.
24 'Abbas Shushtari, *al-Ma'adin al-Dhahabiyya*, Adab 'Arabi MS. 4446, Raza Library, Rampur, fo. 14, cited in Cole, "'Indian Money'," 473–74.
25 Mahbuba, *Madi*, II, 131.
26 Al-Amin, *A'yan*, XLIV, 6; *QU*, 10–11.
27 Muhammad Hasan Najafi, *Jawahir al-kalam* (Tehran, 1392/1972), XXII, 115–56, cited in Sachedina, *The Just Ruler*, 208.
28 Amir Arjomand, *The Shadow*, 236.
29 Al-Amin, *A'yan*, XLVI, 112; Mahbuba, *Madi*, III, 193. Both authors rely on *al-Husun al-mani'a* and *al-'Abaqat al-'inbariyya*, two unpublished manuscripts written by 'Ali Kashif al-Ghita', who was an interested party in this issue.
30 Hirz al-Din, *Ma'arif*, III, 6–8.
31 Tehrani, *Kiram*, 337–38; al-Amin, *A'yan*, XLIV, 5; Mahbuba, *Madi* II, 95.
32 I'timad al-Saltana, *Ma'athir*, 140; Ansari, *Zindigani*, 225; Hirz al-Din, *Ma'arif*, II, 103–06.
33 Hasan Mamaqani had lived in the shrine cities from his childhood, but he never achieved the same status as Muhammad Hasan Najafi. See below, chap. 4.

34 Shushtari, *Al-Zill*, fo. 204.
35 Mahbuba, *Madi*, II, 134; Abu Turab Dizfuli, *Lum'at al-bayan*, cited in Ansari, *Zindigani*, 72-73; Muzaffar, "Tarjama," 19.
36 Cole, "Imami Jurisprudence," 42; Kazemi Moussavi, "Institutionalization," 289.
37 Ansari, *Zindigani*, 84; Amanat, "Madrasa," 114.
38 Amanat, "Madrasa," 112–13.
39 Amanat, "Madrasa," 113; Ansari, *Zindigani*, 72; Kalantar, "Muqaddima," 106; Abu Turab Dizfuli, *Lum'at al-bayan*, cited in Ansari, *Zindigani*, 77.
40 Modaressi Tabataba'i, *Introduction*, 10, 57; S. Murata, s.v., "Ansari, Shaykh Mortaza," *EIr*, II, 103.
41 Arjomand, *The Shadow*, 237.
42 Muhammad Baqir al-Sadr, *Durus fi 'ilm al-usul* (Beirut, 1978), 176; Modaressi Tabataba'i, *Introduction*; Murata, "Ansari Shaykh Mortaza"; Momen, *Introduction*, 187; Roy P. Mottahedeh, *The Mantle of the Prophet* (New York, 1985), 211–12.
43 Among the most important works in *usul* written in the shrine cities and based on Ansari's methodology were: *Mahajjat al-'ulama'* by Hadi Tehrani; *Bushrat al-wusul fi 'ilm al-usul* by Sayyid Husayn Kuhkamara'i; *Bada'i' al-usul* by Habiballah Rashti; *Tashrih al-usul al-kabir* by 'Ali b. Fathallah Nahavandi, and *Ghayat al-mas'ul fi 'ilm al-usul* by Muhammad Husayn Shahristani; Tehrani, *al-Dhari'a*, VI, 152–62; Gurji, "Nigah," 75.
44 Modaressi Tabataba'i, *Introduction*, 57.
45 See 'Abbas and Ja'far "al-Saghir" b. 'Ali Kashif al-Ghita' in al-Amin, *A'yan*, XXXVII, 35 and Khaqani, *Shu'ara'*, II, 45; Tehrani, *Kiram*, 528.
46 Hirz al-Din, *Ma'arif*, I, 237–38; al-Amin, *A'yan*, XXXI, 110. See *HY*, 25, a condescending remark that Ansari excelled in *usul*, a road on which only a few Arabs had made even a little progress.
47 Among the most important books in this category were: *al-Iltiqatat* by Habiballah Rashti; *Misbah al-faqih* by Aqa Rida Hamadani; *al-'Urwa al-wuthqa* by Sayyid Kazim Yazdi, and commentaries on *al-Makasib* by Akhund Khorasani and Muhammad Taqi Shirazi; Modaressi Tabataba'i, *Introduction*, 57–58.
48 Kalantar, "Muqaddima," 131; Ansari, *Zindigani*, 111. See also Litvak, "Continuity," 40, which demonstrates the major increase in the number of students in Najaf during his tenure.
49 Ansari, *Zindigani*, 78ff.; Hirz al-Din, *Ma'arif*, II, 112; Kalantar, "Muqaddima," 131ff.
50 P/437/71 Political proceedings no. 122, June 1867 – Baghdad, Kemball to under secretary of state, India Office, April 7, 1867.
51 IGFD-General P/1026, September 1876, proceedings nos. 47–48; Hirz al-Din, *Ma'arif*, II, 108–09.
52 IGFD-G P/1026, proceedings no. 35 – Baghdad no. 9, Nixon to Thornton, February 14, 1876.
53 IGFD P/437/71 Political proceedings no. 122, June 1867 – Baghdad, Kemball to under secretary of state, India Office, April 7, 1867.
54 Mahmud Mahmud, *Ta'rikh-i ravabit-i siyasi-yi iran va inglis dar qarn-i*

nuzdahum miladi, 8 vols. (Tehran: 1949–50), VI, 1343–44; Isma'il Ra'in, *Huquq-i bigiran-i inglis dar iran* (Tehran: 1347/1968), 104.

55 Shirazi, *Tara'iq al-haqa'iq*, III, 466.

56 Amanat, "Madrasa," 113, 115. When he died, Ansari reputedly left only 17 tumans, the amount to which he was in debt: Abdul-Hadi Ha'iri, s.v., "Ansari Mortaza," *EI²*, supplement.

57 For several such 'ulama', see Ansari, *Zindigani*, 79; Tehrani, *Kiram*, 605–06, 663–64; Hirz al-Din, *Ma'arif*, II, 372–73.

58 See, for instance, his distant cousin Ahmad b. Mubarak who was sent to India, in Hirz al-Din, *Ma'arif*, III, 23n.; Mir Muhammad 'Ali Shushtari-Jaza'iri who was sent to Qum, in Fischer, *Iran*, 109; Mulla Nasrallah Turab Dizfuli who was sent to Khormabad, and Sayyid 'Ali b. Muhammad Tustari, in Ansari, *Zindigani*, 174–75, and 138–39 respectively.

59 The following passage on Ansari's concept is based on Cole, "Imami Jurisprudence," unless specified otherwise.

60 Ansari, *Sirat al-najat*, cited in Amanat, "Madrasa," 99.

61 Amanat, "Madrasa," 112; Ansari, *Zindigani*, 325.

62 Ha'iri, "Ansari, Mortaza."

63 Mahbuba, *Madi*, II, 110–11. Members of the Jawahiri family never regained the first-rank status of their founder, and were mostly second-echelon mujtahids. See Tehrani, *Nuqaba'*, 393, 862, 1519–20; Mahbuba, *Madi*, II, 115; al-Amin, *A'yan*, VIII, 337, XLIII, 227–31.

64 Bahr al-'Ulum, "Muqaddima," 133–34; Khaqani, *Shu'ara'*, III, 216–17.

65 Tehrani, *Nuqaba'*, 435; Mahbuba, *Madi*, III, 193; al-Amin, *A'yan*, XLVI, 113.

66 Mahbuba, *Madi*, III, 206.

67 Adib al-Mulk, *Safarnamah*, 185.

68 Adib al-Mulk, *Safarnamah*, 186.

69 Hirz al-Din, *Ma'arif*, I, 311.

70 The 'ulama' who settled among the tribes in Iraq as well as the majority of the Lebanese 'ulama' constituted the lower echelons of the establishment, and therefore are irrelevant to this discussion. However, even the leading 'ulama' families of Lebanon, such as Al Fadlallah and Shams al-Din, sent their sons to the shrine cities.

71 Tehrani, *Kiram*, 62–64.

72 On the Shaykhs al-Islam of Tabriz, see Mirza Nadir, *Ta'rikh va-jughrafi-yi dar al-saltana tabriz* (Tehran, 1323), 222–27. On the Imams Jum'a of Tabriz, see Tehrani, *Kiram*, 102–03; al-Amin, *A'yan*, XIV, 134; Mudarris Khiyabani, *Rayhanat al-adab*, I, 204; Tehrani, *Nuqaba'*, 287–88, 319–20, 743–44. For Mashhad, see Mudarris, *Ta'rikh 'ulama'-yi khorasan*, 66–69, 91; Tehrani, *Nuqaba'*, 228, 304, 363–64. For Qazvin, see Tehrani, *Kiram*, 808, 773, 327, 721–23; Tehrani, *Nuqaba'*, 164, 711, 1613–14, 1631, 1637. For Sabzivar see Ansari, *Zindigani*, 236–37; Tehrani, *Nuqaba'*, 161, 216. For Japilaq, see Tehrani, *Kiram*, 625; al-Kazimi, *Ahsan al-wadi'a*, 30–41; Tehrani, *Nuqaba'*, 764; I'timad al-Saltana, *al-Ma'athir*, 162. For Khunsar, see Tehrani, *Kiram*, 590–92; Hirz al-Din, *Ma'arif*, I, 229–30, 273; *RJ*, II, 106–10; al-Kazimi, *Ahsan al-wadi'a*, 114–28. For Huwayza, see Hirz al-Din, *Ma'arif*, II, 366–69.

73 Examples during the early nineteenth century include Sayyid Muhammad
Baqir Shafti, Hajj Ibrahim Karbasi, and Muhammad Taqi Aywankafi in
Isfahan; Mirza Ahmad Mujtahid in Tabriz; Mulla Muhammad Taqi Baraghani and his brothers Muhammad Salih and 'Ali in Qazvin; Hajj Muhammad Hasan Qazvini Shirazi, Mirza Ibrahim Fasa'i, and Mahdi Kujuri in
Shiraz; Sayyid Muhammad Qasir Rizavi in Mashhad; and Mulla Muhammad Sa'id Mazandarani in Barfurush.
74 On the background of the three mujtahids – Fadlallah Nuri, 'Abdallah
Bihbihani, and Muhammad Tabataba'i – see Tehrani, *Nuqaba'*, 1193–94;
Bamdad, *Sharh*, III, 96–97, II, 284–89.
75 Al-Wardi, *Lamahat*, I, 22. See also the condescending remarks by an Iranian
merchant living in Karbala' about the people of Hilla in Cowper, *Asiatic
Arabia*, 334.
76 Quchani, *Siyahat*, 324.

4 DIFFUSION, CENTRALIZATION, AND POLITICIZATION

1 Since Najaf was the major arena for leadership struggle, and Karbala' was
relegated to secondary importance, I will not discuss the leadership question
in Karbala'. For details on Karbala', see Litvak, "The Shi'i 'ulama'," chap. 2.
2 Tehrani, *Hadiyat al-razi*, 34–35.
3 Tehrani, *Nuqaba'*, 172, 387, Ansari; *Zindigani*, 234; al-Amin, *A'yan*, XXIII,
268–69.
4 *HY*, I, 25.
5 Tehrani, *Kiram*, 304; Ansari, *Zindigani*, 241–42, 227; Tehrani, *Hadiyat
al-razi*, 40.
6 Al-Amin, *A'yan*, XXIII, 269; *HY*, 25. See for instance complaints by
Turkish speakers of discrimination in housing; Mahbuba, *Madi*, 132. For
the considerable growth of the Turkish-speaking group during and after
Ansari's tenure, see Litvak, "Continuity," 40, 42.
7 I'timad al-Saltana, *Ma'athir*, 148; Tehrani, *Kiram*, 421; al-Kazimi, *Ahsan
al-wadi'a*, 129; al-Amin, *A'yan*, XXVII, 154.
8 Mahbuba, *Madi* I, 130, III, 206; al-Amin, *A'yan* XLVIII, 152; Hirz al-Din,
Ma'arif, III, 96.
9 Tehrani, *Kiram*, 529. Khaqani, *Shu'ara'*, VIII, 383 claims that people turned
to him with *fatwas* following Najafi's death and in emulation following
Ansari's death. The distinction between the two may be explained by
Ansari's refusal to issue *fatwas*.
10 Hirz al-Din, *Ma'arif*, II, 164 and III, 132–33; al-Amin, *A'yan*, XVII, 144,
XLIV, 275.
11 Hirz al-Din, a partisan of the Kashif al-Ghita', claims that "when a spiritual
leader of Al Kashif al-Ghita' died, the people would pray behind the one
whom the family nominated and the latter would be emulated." *Ma'arif*, I,
337–38.
12 Hirz al-Din, *Ma'arif*, II, 338, 250.
13 IGFD P/3996 Proceeding no. 185 – Baghdad no. 82, Tweedie to secretary
of state to the government of India at the Foreign Department, February 12,
1891; al-Amin, *A'yan*, XXIII, 270; Tehrani, *Hadiyat al-razi*, 40.

14 Al-Amin, *A'yan*, XXIII, 270; Ansari, *Zindigani*, 235; Tehrani, *Nuqaba'*, 439; *HY*, I, 27.
15 Both *HY*, 27 and I'timad al-Saltana, *Ma'athir*, 137 mention the *sardab* when referring to Shirazi's move to Samarra'. The fact that two sources, one critical of and the other sympathetic to Shirazi, mention the *sardab* indicates its importance in that context.
16 *HY*, 75; Shirazi, *Tara'iq al-haqa'iq*, III, 564. Tehrani in *Hadiyat al-razi* lists the biographies of close to 360 students; al-Amin, *A'yan*, XXIII, 280, 283.
17 Shi'i biographers sought to justify this anomaly by pointing to Shirazi's great modesty in refusing to elaborate on Ansari's writings, as well as to his heavy load of teaching and engagement in communal affairs. Al-Amin, *A'yan*, XXIII, 282; Tehrani, *Hadiyat al-razi*, 37; Kalantar, "Muqaddima," 141. Ansari's other disciples, however, did not draw the same conclusions from the necessity of modesty.
18 Ansari, *Zindigani*, 85, 225.
19 Amanat, "Madrasa," 116. On the tendency to idealize Ansari compared with his successors, see also Litvak, "The Shi'i 'ulama'," chap. 5, 312–16.
20 Pirzadeh Na'ini, *Safarnamah*, I, 354; al-Kazimi, *Ahsan al-wadi'a*, 131; Hirz al-Din, *Ma'arif*, II, 376–79; Mudarris Khiyabani, *Rayhanat al-adab*, II, 76.
21 Tehrani, *Hadiyat al-razi*, 39. Tehrani himself concedes in his hagiographic book that although one may question Shirazi's superior learning, his preeminence (*awlawiyat*) should be acknowledged.
22 Tehrani, *Nuqaba'*, 389–90; I'timad al-Saltana, *Ma'athir*, 148; Hirz al-Din, *Ma'arif*, II, 103–06; Mahbuba, *Madi*, II, 238–43.
23 See al-Amin, *A'yan*, XXIII, 279; Pirzadeh Na'imi, *Safarnamah*, I, 354; *HY*, 76; and Tehrani, *Kiram*, 605–06 on Shirazi's agent in Mashhad who read his *fatwas* there. Al-Amin adds that occasionally when Shirazi was flooded with petitions and questions his attendants threw them into the Tigris.
24 Amanat, "Madrasa," 116.
25 Tehrani, *Nuqaba'*, 638; al-Amin, *A'yan*, XXIII, 267.
26 *HY*, I, 50–52; Amanat, "Madrasa," 118. See also Nikki Keddie, *Religion and Rebellion in Iran: The Tobacco Protest of 1890–91* (London, 1966), 118, on the popular notion of the incorruptibility of the shrine cities mujtahids compared with their counterparts in Iran.
27 Pirzadeh Na'ini, *Safarnamah*, I, 354.
28 His network encompassed among other places Simnan; Kirmanshah; Shiraz; Muhammara; Mashhad; the Lar region; and Basra: see Tehrani, *Nuqaba'*, 84, 136–37, 441, 621 1511–12, 1262–64; Tehrani, *Kiram*, 605–06; Bamdad, *Sharh-i Hal*, VI, 133–34; «Abbas Qummi, *al-Fawa'id al-ridawiya* (Najaf, 1956), 300; al-Amin, *A'yan*, XXIII, 266–67, XLIV, 153–54; Pirzadeh Na'ini, *Safarnamah*, 376.
29 Al-Amin, *A'yan*, XXIII, 267, 279; Pirzadeh Na'ini, *Safarnamah*, I, 376; *HY*, I, 76; Tehrani, *Nuqaba'*, 60–61. Shaykh Zayn al-'Abidin b. Isma'il Tabrizi Marandi (d. 1340/1921–22) was responsible for distributing financial support to students in Najaf: Tehrani, *Nuqaba'*, 799–800.
30 After Shirazi's death, the project was administered by Shaykh 'Ali Asghar Kashmiri, who came to Kashmir in 1324/1906–07 and became the exemplar there: Tehrani, *Nuqaba'*, 374. British correspondence affirms the presence of

students from Tibet: see FO 195/1841 Baghdad no 237/24, Mockler to Currie, May 5, 1894.

31 Tehrani, *Nuqaba'*, 439–40, 935; al-Amin, *A'yan*, XXIII, 273.

32 Tehrani, *Nuqaba'*, 941, 421; Khaqani, *Shu'ara'*, IV, 211. See below on Shirazi's other agent in Isfahan.

33 Among such 'ulama' were at least two members of the powerful Baraghani family of Qazvin, Sayyid Ishaq b. Muhammad Imam Jum'a and his nephew Da'ud, who maintained their allegiance to him after returning to their home town. Sayyid Muhammad Taqi (d. 1333/1914–15), whose father Hasan Mudarris was a leading *usul* and *fiqh* teacher in Isfahan, was Shirazi's representative in Isfahan. See also 'Ali b. Abu Ja'far Kirmani, whose family held religious leadership in Kirman, and Mulla Muhammad Baqir Tabasi, who returned to Tabas after studying in Samarra' and succeeded his father as a mujtahid in the city. Tehrani, *Nuqaba'*, 132, 251, 711, 188, 1329.

34 Nasir al-Din Shah Qajar, *Ruznamah-yi safar az tehran ila karbila va najaf* (Tehran, 1870), 168, in which he mentions Shirazi's refusal to see him with little comment. He merely describes Shirazi as an ascetic worshipper and a great scholar. See also the description in the official Qajar almanac, *al-Ma'athir wal-athar*, 168 as the one "whose superior status is recognized by other mujtahids," and more importantly, as "the most learned of the mujtahids."

35 On the relations between the merchants and the 'ulama' during the protest, see Feridun Adamiyat, *Shurish bar imtiyaznamah-i rizhi* (Tehran, 1360s/1981), and Amanat, "Madrasa," 116–21.

36 Adamiyat, *Shurish*, 53–54, 74; Keddie, *Religion*, 95.

37 Keddie, *Religion*, 96. Two examples are sufficient to illustrate the impact of Shirazi's name during the affair. The 'ulama' of Mashhad maintained close relations with the shah and joined the anti-Regie activity only reluctantly and after strong popular pressure. Yet they too obeyed Shirazi's ruling. Adamiyat, *Shurish*, 64. Even the Shaykhi community in Kirman obeyed the ruling, declaring that whereas they differed on details of the *Shari'a*, they accepted Shirazi's leadership in political matters. Hasan A'zam Qudsi, *Khatirat-i man ya rushan shodan, ta'rikh-i sadd-i saleh* (Tehran, 1342), 44.

38 Adamiyat, *Shurish*, 77.

39 *Ibid.*; Teymuri, *Tahrim-i tunbaku*, 120, cited in Amanat, "Madrasa," 119.

40 Qudsi, *Khatirat-i man*, 44.

41 Keddie, *Religion*, 114–19.

42 See the letter by Jamal al-Din Asadabadi (al-Afghani) to Shirazi during the tobacco protest, which reputedly prompted the mujtahid to increase his involvement in the affair: Amanat, "Madrasa," 120.

43 Hamid Algar, *Mirza Malkum Khan: A Biographical Study in Iranian Modernism* (Berkeley, 1973), 212–13; Shaul Bakhash, *Iran: Monarchy, Bureaucracy and Reform under the Qajars: 1858–1896* (London, 1978), 329–31.

44 Al-Amin, *A'yan*, XXIII, 272; Tehrani, *Nuqaba'*, 441. On the Islamic tradition of the emergence at the beginning of every century of a great figure who would revitalize religion, see Momen, *Introduction*, 205–06.

45 Sayyah, *Khatirat*, 281. See similar comments by Dawlatabadi, *HY*, I, 78.

46 Tehrani, *Nuqaba'*, 1406.
47 Al-Amin, *A'yan*, XX, 96; al-Kazimi, *Ahsan al-wadi'a*, 131.
48 Al-Amin, *A'yan*, XX, 96; Ansari, *Zindigani*, 226; Tehrani, *Nuqaba'*, 359;
   al-Amin adds that Rashti was famous for devoting an excessively long time
   to the discussion of a single issue, a manifestation of his incapacity for
   leadership. See also the story in Shirazi, *Tara'iq al-haqa'iq*, III, 642 of how
   Zayn al-'Abidin Khatunabadi, the Imam Jum'a of Tehran, abrogated a *fatwa*
   Rashti had issued concerning a disputed plot of land, and issued an opposing
   one, which justified his own claim. None of the Tehran 'ulama' intervened
   in Rashti's favor.
49 Mahbuba, *Madi*, III, 253; Ansari, *Zindigani*, 239; Mamaqani, *Makhzan
   al-maghani*, 239.
50 I'timad al-Saltana, *Ma'athir*, 205; Mamaqani, *Makhzan al-maghani*, 231;
   al-Amin, *A'yan*, XXIII, 266.
51 Hirz al-Din, *Ma'arif*, II, 301–03; for the other mujtahids of the group, see
   below.
52 Al-Amin, *A'yan*, XL, 51; al-Bahrani, *Anwar al-badrayn*, 246–47; Ansari,
   Zindigani, 273; Tehrani, *Nuqaba'*, 963–64.
53 Mahbuba, *Madi*, III, 433; Tehrani, *Nuqaba'*, 963; Khaqani, *Shu'ara'*, VI,
   179–80.
54 *HY*, I, 79–80; al-Kazimi, *Ahsan al-wadi'a*, 136; Bamdad, *Sharh-i hal*, VI,
   238–389; al-Amin, *A'yan*, XL, 60–61, L, 44.
55 Al-Amin, *A'yan*, XL, 61, L, 44; Hirz al-Din, *Ma'arif*, III, 225–28.
56 IGFD-Internal P/4187 Proceedings no. 208, Jennings to Mockler, March
   16, 1892; IGFD-Internal P/4187 Appendix A, Proceedings no. 207 –
   Baghdad, Mockler to secretary to the government of India at the Foreign
   Department, March 23, 1892.
57 *Ibid.*
58 Amanat, "Madrasa," 101, 99.
59 Tehrani, *Nuqaba'*, 261–63, 1564–65; Hirz al-Din, *Ma'arif*, II, 139–40,
   215–17; al-Amin, *A'yan*, XLIII, 297, XLIV, 121–22, XLVI, 195.
60 Al-Amin, *A'yan*, XXVI, 217, For the Ottoman attitude to Shirazi, see
   below, chap. 9.
61 The first one is a joint *fatwa* on "the prohibition of traveling via the
   mountain route to Mecca the Noble," initiated by Fadlallah Nuri, one of
   Tehran's leading mujtahids, in Fadlallah Nuri, *Majmu'a-yi az rasa'il-i,
   i'lamiyaha-yi maktubat-i wa-ruznamah-yi shaykh shahid fadlallah nuri*, 2 vols.,
   compiled by Muhammad Turkoman [Tehran, 1362s], I, 25–38. The second
   fatwa was attached to Jamal al-Din "Wa'iz" Isfahani's treatise *Libas-i taqva*
   (Shiraz, n.d.).
62 Memorandum enclosure no. 5 in IGFD-Internal P/6652 Proceedings no. 70
   – Baghdad no. 390, Newmarch to Barnes, secretary to the government of
   India at the Foreign Department, September 20, 1902. For a discussion on
   the merits and weaknesses of each of these sources for determining seniority
   among the 'ulama' see Litvak, "The Shi'i 'Ulama'," chap. 4.
63 FO 416/16 no. 112, Hardinge to Lansdowne, January 1, 1904.
64 See for instance Davani, *Zindigani*, 33; and Hibat al-Din Shahristani
   "Ayatallah al-khorasani akbar 'ulama' al-din wa-ra'is al-mujtahidin," *al-'Ilm*

2 (1912), 290ff., 309ff., cited in Abd al-Hadi Ha'iri, s.v., "Akhund Khorasani," *EIr*, I, 732.

65 S. Murata, s.v., "Akhund Khorasani: His Importance in Usul," *EIr*, I, 734–35.

66 Mudarris Khiyabani, *Rayhanat al-adab*, II, 16; al-Kazimi, *Ahsan al-wadi'a*, 147; Quchani, *Siyahat*, 330.

67 Quchani, *Siyahat*, 325; Arjomand, *The Turban*, 52.

68 Al-Amin, *A'yan*, XLVI, :207; Tehrani, *Nuqaba'*, 703–04, 860–61. On his role during the Constitutional Revolution, see Arjomand, *The Turban*, 52–53; and Quchani, *Siyahat*, 455-82.

69 Tehrani, *Nuqaba'*, 573–76; Hirz al-Din, *Ma'arif*, I, 276–82; Ansari, *Zindigani*, 248–49; al-Amin, *A'yan*, XXV, 24–33. He is known to have sent representatives to Bombay, Hamadan, Kirmanshah, the Persian Gulf ports, Jisr al-Kufa, Tuwayrij, Kut al-'Ammara. See Tehrani, *Nuqaba'*, 118–19, 264, 267, 632–33, 703–04, 1224–25, 1472–73 1199; al-Kazimi, *Ahsan al-wadi'a*, 257–58, Hirz al-Din, *Ma'arif*, II, 319.

70 Hirz al-Din, *Ma'arif*, II, 372–75; Mudarris Khiyabani, *Rayhanat al-adab*, II, 302; al-Kazimi, *Ahsan al-wadi'a*, 144.

71 Mamaqani, *Makhzan al-maghani*, 231; Hirz al-Din, *Ma'arif*, III, 374; Arthur Hardinge, *A Diplomatist in the East* (London, 1928), 322.

72 Ansari, *Zindigani*, 306; Mudarris Khiyabani, *Rayhanat al-adab*, II, 302; Mahbuba, *Madi*, I, 131, 135–38.

73 FO 416/14 "Memorandum from Muhammad Hassan Mohsin" enclosure 8 in no. 286, India Office to Foreign Office.

74 IGFD-Internal P/4187 Proceedings no. 208, Jennings to Mockler, March 16, 1892; IGFD-Internal P/4187, Appendix A Proceedings no. 207 – Baghdad, Mockler to secretary to the government of India at the Foreign Department, March 23, 1892.

5 DETERMINANTS OF STATUS AND LEADERSHIP

1 Chamberlain, *Knowledge*, 106; Madeline Zilfi, "'Elite Circulation' in the Ottoman Empire in the Eighteenth Century," *JESHO* 26 (1983), 320.

2 For a discussion of the two concepts, see Mottahedeh, *Loyalty*, 98.

3 Tehrani, *Kiram*, 406–08, 552–54, 590; Mahbuba, *Madi*, II, 58, 183; al-Kazimi, *Ahsan al-wadi'a*, 68–75; al-Amin, *A'yan*, VII, 293.

4 Mottahedeh, *Loyalty*, 100 says that the terms were not synonymous for people of later centuries and were sometimes used in the opposite meanings.

5 Al-Amin, *A'yan*, VII, 337.

6 Al-Amin, *A'yan*, XLVIII, 3–9.

7 Tehrani, *Kiram*, 407–08; Mottahedeh, *Loyalty*, 101.

8 See Chamberlain's analysis for medieval Damascus, in *Knowledge*, 148–152; and Rosen, *Bargaining for Reality*, 42. For the Ottoman religious hierarchy, see Repp, *Mufti*, chap. 1.

9 *QU*, 191–92; Hirz al-Din, *Ma'arif*, I, 337–38; Mamaqani, *Makhzan al-maghani*, 231.

10 See *QU*, 116–17.

11 See for instance, al-Sadr, *Takmilat amal al-'amil*, 238.

12 Even the term of ownership describing the author's relation to the book is synonymous in both communities: *sahib al-* and *ba'al ha-*.

13 Compare for instance, the reading of *fawatih* after the death of Muhammad b. 'Ali Kashif al-Ghita' (d. 1851) in Najaf and Hilla, and 'Ali Naqi Tabataba'i in Karbala' and Najaf, with that for Mirza Hasan Shirazi and Muhammad Taha Najaf, who were more senior mujtahids, throughout the Shi'i world: see Bahr al-'Ulum, "Muqaddima," 146; Tehrani, *Nuqaba'*, 964; and Hirz al-Din, *Ma'arif*, II, 35; Kashmiri, *Nujum al-sama'*, II, 153.

14 Amanat, "Madrasa," 104–07; on Qummi's phrase see Mahbuba, *Madi*, III, 200; see also Kazemi Moussavi, "Institutionalization," 296.

15 FO 248/413 Baghdad no. 728, Herbert to Thomson, November 10, 1884. Hasan al-Sadr, *Takmilat amal al-'amil*, 19n. claims that Mirza Hasan Shirazi was the first mujtahid to assume this title in the shrine cities, but does not cite a date.

16 Cf. the *fatwa* on "the prohibition of traveling via the mountain route to Mecca the Noble," in Nuri, *Majmu'a*, 25–38, and the *fatwa* attached to Jamal al-Din "Wa'iz" Isfahani's tract *Libas-i taqva* (Shiraz, n.d.), which sought to promote the consumption of local textiles in Iran.

17 See Mottahedeh, *Mantle*, 241, which gives a vivid description of how titles were adopted or attributed to mujtahids in twentieth-century Iran.

18 The mujtahids were chosen on the basis of number of students, role in key events, and appearance on available *fatwas*. The highly subjective terms first- and second-rank mujtahids are often used by the biographical sources themselves.

19 The small number of Iranian mujtahids in Karbala' renders meaningless any attempt to draw further conclusions.

20 See table 6 in the appendix.

21 See table 7 in the appendix. The birth places of four mujtahids are unknown.

22 See tables 8 and 9 in the appendix.

23 See table 10 in the appendix. As mentioned above, the dominance of the Kashif al-Ghita' family in the Arab faction skewed upward the overall results among the mujtahids.

24 Norman Itzkowitz and Joel Shinder, "The Office of Seyh ul-Islam and the Tanzimat – A Prosopographical Enquiry," *MES* 8:1 (1972), 98–99; Zilfi, "'Elite Circulation'," 586. On al-Azhar, see Haim Shaked, "The Biographies of 'Ulama' in Mubarak's *Khitat* as a Source for the History of the 'Ulama' in Nineteenth Century Egypt," *Asian and African Studies* 7 (1971), 62.

25 Frederick de-Yong, *Turuq and Turuq-Linked Institutions in Nineteenth Century Egypt* (Leiden, 1978), 11, 20.

26 Berkey, *Transmission*, 127.

27 See for instance Muhammad 'Ali Hizarjaribi, whose father Muhammad Baqir was a notable 'alim during Bihbihani's time, in Tehrani, *Kiram*, 174–75 and Davani, *Ustad-i kull*, 196–97; Shaykh Ahmad, Habiballah Rashti's son who settled in Tehran, in al-Amin, *A'yan*, XI, 57–58; Abu al-Qasim, Hasan Mamaqani's son, in Tehrani, *Nuqaba'*, 66; Mirza Abu al-Fadl, 'Ali Nahavandi's son, who migrated to Tehran, in al-Kazimi, *Ahsan*

al-wadi'a, 133; Jawad and 'Ali Asghar, the two sons of Muhammad Iravani, who were both low-level *khatibs* in Karbala', in Tehrani, *Nuqaba'*, 1059–60; and Muhammad Hasan Khan I'timad al-Saltana, *Ma'athir*, 152.

28 Chamberlain, *Knowledge*, 18, 67, 82–84, 138.
29 Al-Amin, *A'yan*, XXIII, 268; al-Sadr, *Takmilat amal al-'amil*, 385.
30 Richard L. Chambers, "The Ottoman 'Ulama' and the Tanzimat," in Keddie (ed.), *Scholars Saints and Sufis*, 34.
31 For such criticism in the Ottoman Empire, see Bernard Lewis, "Ottoman Observers of Ottoman Decline," in Bernard Lewis, *Islam in History: Ideas, People and Events in the Middle East* (Chicago, 1993, new ed.), 212–13, 15; Zilfi, *Politics*, 119–20.
32 Gholam Riza 'Irfaniyan, *al-Ra'y al-sadid fi al-ijtihad wal-taqlid* (Najaf, 1386/1967), 9–22, cited in Amanat, "Madrasa," 125n.; Arjomand, *The Shadow*, 242.
33 Frank Parkin, *Marxism and Class Theory: A Bourgeois Critique* (New York, 1979), 54.
34 Abbott, *Professions*, 7ff.
35 A scholar who attained *ijazat ijtihad* but was not yet widely recognized as a mujtahid was called *mujtahid muhtat* (in abeyance): al-Jamali, "Colleges," 19.
36 Cf. the refusal of Sayyid 'Ali Tabataba'i to recognize the ijtihad of Sayyid Jawad al-'Amili and Asadallah Tustari Kazimi, though the two were universally recognized as brilliant scholars: *RJ*, I, 100, VI, 198, II, 217.
37 Tehrani, *al-Dhari'a*, VI, 7.
38 Al-Amin, *A'yan*, XVII, 171; *QU*, 118. For similar practices in medieval Damascus, see Chamberlain, *Knowledge*, 130n.
39 Al-Amin, *A'yan*, XXIII, 283 claims that Sayyid Jawad al-'Amili, author of *Miftah al-karama*, was the first to publish the *taqrirat* of his teacher Mahdi Bahr al-'Ulum's lectures under his own name. The original version of Khomeini's book *Vilayat-i faqih* or *Hukumat-i islami* was based on such lecture notes.
40 *RJ*, I, 92; Tehrani, *Nuqaba'*, 410. Gurji, "Nigah," 71 attributes *Bushrat al-wusul* to Kuhkamara'i and not to Mamaqani.
41 See table 11 in the appendix.
42 It is impossible to determine on the basis of titles alone whether Ansari influenced the mujtahids of his own group, such as Mahdi Qazvini Hilli. These mujtahids were, therefore, included in the first period.
43 Modaressi Tabataba'i, *Introduction*, 174. For details see table 12 in the appendix.
44 Mottahedeh, *Mantle*, 212.
45 IGFD-External P/3966 Baghdad no. 123, Tweedie to Thornton, March 12, 1890.
46 Bahr al-'Ulum, "Muqaddima," 95–97; Mahbuba, *Madi*, III, 253.
47 Mordechai Bruer, *The Rabbinate in Eshkenaz during the Middle Ages* (Jerusalem, 1976; in Hebrew), 11–13, 18; Jacob Katz, *Tradition and Crisis: Jewish Society at the End of the Middle Ages* (Jerusalem, 1958; in Hebrew), 229; Shaul Shtampper, "Three 'Lithuanian' Yeshivot during the Nineteenth Century" (Ph.D. diss., Hebrew University of Jerusalem, 1981; in Hebrew),

3–5; Menachem Friedman, *The Haredi (Ultra-Orthodox) Society: Sources, Trends, and Processes* (Jerusalem, 1991; in Hebrew); Michels, *Political Parties*.
48 The story of Baqir al-Bata'ihi discussed in chap. 1 above shows rare agreement and joint action among leading mujtahids as opposed to the more common efforts to build personal networks. This cooperation is even more interesting as it did not involve political issues or threats to their collective interests by external forces.
49 For such a view, see Adamiyat, *Shurish*.
50 Malcolm, *History*, II, 432; Hidayat, *Rawdat al-safa-yi nasiri*, cited in Menashri, *Education*, 20.
51 Al-Amin, *Risalat al-tanzih*, cited in Nakash, *The Shi'is*, 156.
52 Hibat al-Din Shahristani, *al-'Ilm* (Najaf, 1911), II, 266–67. Shahristani was famous for his reservations and opposition to the practice of transporting corpses to the shrine cities for burial.
53 Other such mujtahids were Sayyid Husayn Bahr al-'Ulum, Mirza Habiballah Rashti, and Muhammad Isfahani Fashariki.
54 The most prominent examples of such graduates are Asadallah Isfahani, son of Hujjat al-Islam Shafti; Muhammad Baqir b. Muhammad Taqi Isfahani (author of *al-Hashiyya 'ala al-ma'alim*), and his son Aqa Najafi, Mirza Hasan Shirazi; and Muhammad Husayn Na'ini.
55 Amanat, "Madrasa," 123.

6 THE SHRINE CITIES, THE MAMLUKS, AND IRAN

1 Ruhallah Khomeini, *Imam Khomeini's Last Will and Testament* (Washington: Iranian Interest section, Algerian Embassy, n.d.), 34.
2 For general surveys of Iraq under the Mamluks, see al-'Azzawi, *Ta'rikh*, V–VII; Longrigg, *Four Centuries*; Lorimer, *Gazetteer*, I: 1, B; Nawras, *Hukm*; Nieuwenhuis, *Politics*. For the concept of the Mamluks as Ottomans, see Ehud R. Toledano, "The Emergence of Ottoman-Local Elites in the Middle East and North Africa (1700–1900)," in I. Pappe and M. Maoz (eds.), *Essays in Honour of Albert Hourani* (Oxford, forthcoming).
3 See Algar, *Religion*; Keddie, "The Roots of 'Ulama' Power"; Ann K. S. Lambton, "The 'Ulama' and the Constitutional Movement in Iran," in T. Fahd (ed.), *Le Shi'ism imamite* (Strasbourg, 1971), 245–69 for the first approach. See Arjomand, *The Shadow*; Martin, *Islam*; and Amanat, "Madrasa" for the second.
4 See Algar, *Religion*, 165; Keddie, "The Roots of 'Ulama' Power," 226; Ann K. S. Lambton, "Quis Custodiet Custodes? Some Reflections on the Persian Theory of Government," *SI* 6 (1956), 143.
5 The term "Ottoman" here refers also to the Mamluks.
6 Suleyman Pasha expressed such fears during a conversation with Harford Jones, the British agent in Baghdad. See IOL G/29/27 no. 109, April 20, 1800. See also C. H. Imber, "The Persecution of the Ottoman Shi'ites According to the Muhimme Defterleri, 1565–1585," *Der Islam* 56:2 (1979), 245–73, esp. 246–49 on the Shi'is in Iraq.
7 Nakash, *The Shi'is*, 25; Nieuwenhuis, *Politics*, 123–26, 158; Luizard, *La formation*, 66.

8 Carsten Niebuhr, *Travels through Arabia and Other Countries in the East*, trans. Robert Heron, 2 vols. (Edinburgh, 1792), II, 173; 'Abd al-'Aziz Suleiman al-Nawwar, *Da'ud pasha wali baghdad* (Baghdad, 1967), 114.

9 Hourani, "Ottoman Reforms," 36–66; Philip Khoury, "Continuity and Change in Syrian Political Life: The Nineteenth and Twentieth Centuries," *American Historical Review* 96:5 (December 1991), 1375–77.

10 Hirz al-Din, *Ma'arif*, I, 216, II, 51–53; Mahbuba, *Madi*, II, 167–68, III, 162; al-Sadr, *Takmilat amal al-'amil*, 237; Muhammad Mahdi Bahr al-'Ulum even studied in Mecca under Sunni 'ulama': see Bahr al-'Ulum, "Muqaddima," 35–36.

11 Robert Ingram, "Introduction," *In Defence of British India, Great Britain in the Middle East, 1775–1842* (London, 1984). For British interests and policy in Iran, see Firuz Kazemzade, *Russia and Britain in Persia, 1864–1914* (New Haven, 1968); for British policies in Iraq, see Zaki Saleh, *Mesopotamia (Iraq) 1600–1914: A Study in British Foreign Affairs* (Baghdad, 1957).

12 Johnson, "Church and Sect," 127–28; cf. Stark and Bainbridge, "Churches, Sects, and Cults," 124–26.

13 Longrigg, *Four Centuries*, 200. Hasan Pasha made a similar pilgrimage in 1704: al-'Azzawi, *Ta'rikh*, V, 164.

14 J. B. Kelly, *Britain and the Persian Gulf, 1795–1880* (Oxford, 1968), 35. Unfortunately, Kelly does not specify the source for his statement.

15 Mirza Abu Talib Khan [Isfahani], *Masir-i talibi ya safarnamah-yi mirza abu talib khan*, ed. Husayn Hadivim (Tehran, 1352), 401; Niebuhr, *Travels*, II, 189. Cursing the first three caliphs was the litmus test for Shi'i heresy in Ottoman eyes, amounting to a defiance of the Sunni Ottoman sultan. Imber, "Persecution," 245; Constance Alexander, *Baghdad in Bygone Days. From the Journals and Correspondence of Claudius Rich, British Resident in Baghdad 1808–1821* (London, 1928), 120.

16 Ghadir Khumm is the place where, according to Shi'i tradition, the Prophet Muhammad nominated 'Ali as his successor on his return from his last pilgrimage on 18 Dhu al-Hijja. It is the only joyous Shi'i holiday in the year.

17 Kelly, *Britain*, 100; al-'Azzawi, *Ta'rikh*, VI, 145; Longrigg, *Four Centuries*, 217; Abu Talib Khan, *Masir*, 408 puts the number of the dead at 25,000.

18 Abu Talib Khan, *Masir*, 408; Shirazi, *Tara'iq al-haqa'iq*, III, 342–45; al-Amin, *A'yan*, XLVI, 79; Cole, "Shi'i Clerics," 12.

19 Ibrahim al-Wa'ili, *al-Shi'r siyasi al-'iraqi fi al-qarn al-tasi' 'ashar* (Baghdad, 1961), 123–25, 128–29.

20 Siphir Lisan al-Mulk, *Nasikh al-tawarikh*, I, 69; Kelly, *Britain*, 100; Jevdet Pasha, *Ta'rikh-i jevdet* (Istanbul, 1302), VII, 139–40, cited in Nawras, *Hukm*, 58.

21 Al-'Azzawi, *Ta'rikh*, VI, 145; Lorimer, *Gazetteer*, I, 1B: 1286.

22 L/PS/9/6 Baghdad, Jones to Scot, August 12, 1801.

23 Al-'Azzawi, *Ta'rikh*, VI, 145, 217; Lorimer, *Gazetteer*, 2A, 775; FO 195/519, Farrant to Canning, May 15, 1843; Sayf al-Dawla Sultan Muhammad, *Safarnamah-yi mecca*, ed. 'Ali Akbar Khodaparast (Tehran, 1364s/1986), 230.

24 Mahbuba, *Madi*, I, 137; al-Muzaffar, "Tarjamat," 11; Sachedina, *The Just Ruler*, 22.

25 Mahbuba, *Madi*, I, 28, III, 138.
26 Dale Eickelman, *The Middle East: An Anthropological Approach* (Englewood Cliffs, 1989), 131ff.; Steven Caton, "Power, Persuasion, and Language: A Critique of the Segmentary Model in the Middle East," *IJMES* 19:1 (1987), 78–79, 89.
27 Cole and Momen, "Mafia," 116–18 and the sources cited there for typology of gangs. See also Lapidus, *Muslim Cities*, 105, 170ff., which stresses the criminal aspect of the gangs' activity. On the Lutis in Iran, see Willem Floor, "The Lutis – A Social Phenomenon in Qajar Persia: A Reappraisal," *WI* 13 (1971), 103–20; Willem Floor, "The Political Role of the Lutis in Iran," in M. E. Bonine and N. Keddie (eds.), *Modern Iran: The Dialectics of Continuity and Change* (Albany, 1981), 83–95. For Bihbihani, see *QU*, 143.
28 According to Shi'i sources, the name "Zukurt" derives from the word *suqur* (falcons), referring either to the name the gang members chose for themselves or the hawks they used for hunting. The term "Shumurd" reportedly derives from *masshaf al-shumurdal*, i.e. the youth who is swifter than the camel: Al-Amin, *A'yan*, XV, 426. Alternatively the names may be corruptions of the Suqur branch of the 'Anaza tribal federation and their bitter rivals the Shammar tribes. Both tribes frequented Najaf as a regional market town, and occasionally the word "tribesmen" is applied to members of the gangs. The term "Zukurt" was applied to respected gang members in Tripoli (Lebanon) during the twentieth century: see Salam al-Hajj, "Hikayat fi sirat marajil qabadayat tarablus," *al-Shira'* (Beirut), May 4, 1992. It is unclear whether the term somehow traveled from Iraq, or had local origins.
29 The most detailed account is provided by Mahbuba, *Madi*, I, 324–34. His account as well as those given by other biographical dictionaries is based on an unpublished manuscript by Muhammad Husayn Al Kashif al-Ghita', *al-'Abaqat al-'inbariyya fi al-tabaqat al-ja'fariyya*, which presents the 'ulama"s point of view. See also al-Amin, *A'yan*, XXIX, 255–56. Shaykh Ja'far may have assisted in the formation of the Zukurt as a counterweight to the Shumurt.
30 France, Correspondance Consulaire et Commerciale (CCC) Turquie Baghdad, vol. 7, August 1817; Mahbuba, *Madi*, I, 325–28. Because of their dual capacity, the governors of Najaf during the Mamluk period were often called *al-Mutawalli*: see Muhammad 'Ali al-Husayni al-Farisi Al-Munshi, *Rihlat al-munshi*, trans. from Persian by 'Abbas al-'Azzawi, (Baghdad, 1948), 91.
31 Mahbuba, *Madi*, I, 332–33, III, 383, 398–402.
32 Mahbuba, *Madi*, I, 332, 396–402; Khaqani, *Shu'ara'*, II, 118–19. One example of the Milalis' conduct that aroused widespread indignation was their appearance at the mourning sessions for Ja'far Kashif al-Ghita' with their beards dyed to express their glee. See Mahbuba, *Madi*, III, 141.
33 CCC Baghdad, August 7, 1817, 102–03.
34 Khidr b. Shallal, "Bab al-Khalal," in *al-Tuhfa al-gharawiyya fi sharh al-lum'a al-dimashqiyya*, cited in al-Amin, *A'yan*, XXIX, 255–58.
35 Khidr b. Shallal, *al-Tuhfa*, cited in al-Amin, *A'yan*, V, 87–88.
36 Kirkukli, *Dawhat al-wuzara'*, 289–90; al-'Abaqat al-'inbariyya, cited in Mahbuba, *Madi*, I, 335.

37 Mahbuba, *Madi*, III, 402–03. Hirz al-Din, *Ma'arif*, 3f mentions 1255/ 1839–40 as the date.

38 Abu Talib Khan, *Masir*, 406–07.

39 Nieuwenhuis, *Politics*, 31; Cole, "'Indian Money'," 462–63; Cole and Momen, "Mafia," 113.

40 Kalantar, "Muqaddima," 32–35; Ansari, *Zindigani*, 64.

41 *Waqi'at al-manakhur*, an anonymous Persian manuscript cited in Muhammad Hasan Al Kilidar, *Madinat al-husayn aw mukhtasar ta'rikh karbala'* (Baghdad, 1949), 97–98; Lorimer, *Gazetteer*, I, 1B: 1349; Sulayman Hadi Al Tu'ma, *Turath karbala'* (Karbala', 1964), 268–69; al-'Azzawi, *Ta'rikh*, VI, 287–88.

42 Arjomand, *The Shadow*, 222.

43 Arjomand, *The Shadow*, 228–29, 233–34, 251–52. See also Ann K. S. Lambton, "Some New Trends in Islamic Political Thought in Late Eighteenth and Early Nineteenth Century Persia," *SI* 39 (1974), 95–128; Ali Reza Sheikholeslami, "From Religious Accommodation to Religious Revolution: The Transformation of Shi'ism in Iran," in A. Banuazizi and M. Wiener (eds.), *The State, Religion and Ethnic Politics: Afghanistan, Iran and Pakistan* (Syracuse, 1986), 238–39, who hold similar views. For an opposite approach see Ha'iri, "Legitimacy," 283, which argues that the dominant trend in nineteenth-century Shi'ism was that "on principle, the mujtahids are legitimate rulers who are to enact the rules of the Twelfth Imam during his Greater Occultation."

44 Algar, *Religion*, 42–49, 104. All three shahs, Aqa Muhammad Khan, Fath 'Ali Shah, and Muhammad Shah, gave large amounts for gilding the tombs of the various shrines in the shrine cities. Sayf al-Dawla Sultan Muhammad, *Safarnamah-yi mecca*, 230–32 enumerates the objects that the various shahs had given to the shrines. Nasir al-Din Shah followed a similar policy.

45 Amanat, "Madrasa," 105; Algar, *Religion*, 60–64; Arjomand, *The Shadow*, 238–39.

46 Amanat, "Madrasa," 106–07. For the duality of Shafti's conduct, see Abbas Amanat, "The 'Leader of the Community' and the 'Undeceiving' British Minister Plenipotentiary: A Correspondence between John McNeill and Sayyid Muhammad Baqir Shafti on the First Herat Crisis," *Iranshinasi* 1 (1990), 11–41, and *QU*, 132–67.

47 Bengal Political Consultations February 20, 1818, proceedings nos. 46–47, resident in Lucknow to deputy secretary to government, September 15, 1816; BPC February 20, 1818, proceedings no. 48, the vezier (nawwab) to resident in Lucknow; BPC February 20, 1818, proceedings no. 53, resident in Baghdad to chief secretary of Bombay, September 10, 1817. For the Asafiyya canal, see Nieuwenhuis, *Politics*, 6, 130; Cole, "'Indian Money'," 463–65.

48 Hidayat, *Ta'rikh*, IX, 429–30; Siphir Lisan al-Mulk, *Nasikh al-tawarikh*, I, 92, 169, 134.

49 Siphir Lisan al-Mulk, *Nasikh al-tawarikh*, I, 207–08; Muhammad Husayn Kashif al-Ghita', *al-'Abaqat al-'inbariyya*, cited in Kalantar, "Muqaddima," 36–37n.

50 Mahbuba, *Madi*, III, 201; Khaqani, *Shu'ara'* (1988), XII, 324; Tehrani, *Kiram*, 132.
51 Muhammad Hasan 'Ali Majid, "Wulat al-hilla wa-hukamiha fi al-qarn al-tasi' 'ashar hata nihayat al-hukm al-turki fi al-'iraq (1800–1917) wa-'athrihim fi al-shi'r," *al-Mu'arrikh al-'arabi* 20 (1401/1981), 266–68; Rashti, *Dalil*, 65–66.
52 Nakash, *The Shi'is*, 25ff.
53 Ibrahim Fasih al-Haydari, *'Unwan al-majd fi bayan ahwal baghdad wal-basra wal-najd* (Baghdad, n.d.), 111.
54 Nakash, *The Shi'is*, 30–33; Nieuwenhuis, *Politics*, 130.
55 Nakash, *The Shi'is*, 45; Luizard, *La formation*, 112, 119, 190–91; Batatu, *The Old Social Classes*, 41–42.
56 Nakash, *The Shi'is*, 45.
57 See for instance the Shammar Tuqa who settled near Karbala' and converted to Shi'ism, while the Shammar Jarba whose domain was in the Jazira between the Euphrates and Tigris remained Sunni. This was also the case with the Al Fatlan from the Dulaim, a section of the Jabur, and the majority of the tribes of the Rabi'a confederation, who adopted Shi'ism. In contrast, most of the Jabur, the Kawwam section of the Rabi'a, the Zubu' of the Shammar, the Fadagha, the 'Akaydat, and the Sha'ar to name just a few, who settled near Kazimayn or on the eastern bank of the Tigris, remained Sunnis. Lorimer, *Gazetteer*, II, 2A: 769, 770, 789, 781, 786, 787; Nakash, *The Shi'is*, 43; Batatu, *The Old Social Classes*, 41–42.
58 The 1919 British census put the number of Shi'is in Iraq at 1,500,000 out of a total of 2,850,000, that is, about 53 percent: see Nakash, *The Shi'is*, 13.
59 Cf. Nakash, *The Shi'is*, 29, who mentions the financial motivation, although he himself (at 232) notes that tribal leaders preferred to give money to the tribal sayyids rather than to the 'ulama'.
60 Nakash, *The Shi'is*, 28–29; Haydari, *'Unwan al-majd*, 111; Niebuhr, *Travels*, II, 173; Hamud al-Sa'idi, *Dirasat 'an 'asha'ir al-'iraq: al-khaza'il* (Najaf, 1974), 60–68.
61 See Lawrence Lockhart, *The Fall of the Safavid Dynasty and the Afghan Occupation of Persia* (Cambridge, 1958), 70–71, 73; Amnon Netzer, "The Persecution of Iranian Jewry in the Seventeenth Century," *Pe'amim* 6 (1981; in Hebrew), 32–56.
62 Bahr al-'Ulum, "Muqaddima," 35–36, 50–65; *QU*, 14–15; Shirazi, *Tara'iq al-haqa'iq*, III, 218; Al-Sadr, *Takmilat amal al-'amil*, 237; Shukri al-Alusi, *al-Misk al-adhfar* (Baghdad, 1930), 18; Deringil, "Struggle," 52.
63 Nakash, *The Shi'is*, chaps. 5–6; 'Ali al-Wardi, *Dirasa fi tabi'at al-mujtama' al-'iraqi* (Baghdad, 1965), 238–39.
64 Tehrani, *Kiram*, 766–67, 527–30; Hirz al-Din, *Ma'arif*, I, 65–66; al-Amin, *A'yan*, XXXI, 108–112; Mahbuba, *Madi*, III, 67.
65 Nakash, *The Shi'is*, 46; Batatu, *The Old Social Classes*, 41–42; Tehrani, *Kiram*, 620; Hirz al-Din, *Ma'arif*, I, 43, 203–04, 285ff., 336–81, II, 96–100, 298, III, 64–65, 228–31; Mahbuba, *Madi*, III, 293–94, 356.
66 Pirzadeh Na'ini, *Safarnamah*, 353.

67 See such correspondence in Saʿidi, *Dirasat*, 68–69. See also the case of the nephew of Khidr b. Shallal al-ʿAfakawi who undertook to host leaders from his former tribe whenever they visited Najaf.
68 On the tribal revolts, see Lorimer, *Gazetteer*, I, 1B: 1361–68, 1432–34, 1436–38, 1501, 1505–08; Longrigg, *Four Centuries*, 290–92, 310; al-ʿAzzawi, *Taʾrikh*, VII.
69 Shaykh Muhammad Mahdi al-Fatuni (d. 1183/1769–70) reportedly issued a proclamation in 1146/1734 in support of a tribal revolt led by Sayyid Shubbar al-Musawi al-Huwayzi against the Mamluks, equating it to "enjoining the right" (*al-ʾamr bil-maʿruf*); Hirz al-Din, *Maʿarif*, I, 356n. The ʿulamaʾ did serve as spiritual leaders when the tribes fought the British during World War I and in the 1920 rebellion. The fighting then, however, was against a non-Muslim power.
70 On the Shiʿi attitudes toward Jihad, see Etan Kohlberg, "The Development of the Imami Shiʿi Doctrine of Jihad," *ZDMG* 126:1 (1976), 64–86.
71 For the definition of such communities see Allen Johnson and Timothy Earle, *The Evolution of Human Societies: From Foraging Groups to Agrarian States* (Stanford, 1987), 195–96. For a discussion of the further development of this process toward an aborted state formation following World War I, see Nakash, *The Shiʿis*, 61–66.

7 THE REASSERTION OF DIRECT OTTOMAN CONTROL

1 Issawi, "Iraq," 75.
2 Al-Wardi, *Lamahat*, II, 110–11. See also FO 195/204 Baghdad no. 13, Taylor to Canning, May 15, 1843 on Shiʿi resentment toward Daʾud.
3 Al-Amin, *Aʿyan*, XXXVII, 126.
4 On the abolition of taxes, see FO 195/237 Baghdad no. 4, Rawlinson to Canning, January 24, 1844; FO 195/237 Baghdad no. 10, Rawlinson to Canning, April 8, 1846; al-Wardi, *Lamahat*, II, 110–11.
5 Al-Wardi, *Lamahat*, II, 111; L/PS/9/95, Taylor to chief secretary of the government of Bombay, July 29, 1833. See also L/PS/9/106, Cairo resident to Secret Committee, April 1, 1839 reporting that Muhammad ʿAli stressed to the resident his benevolent treatment of Shiʿi and Iranian pilgrims to the Hijaz and his claim that "the Persian pilgrims always prayed in the Mosques of Mecca and Medina for his life and welfare."
6 Al-ʿAzzawi, *Taʾrikh*, VII, 60. For his weakness as a governor and the general state of anarchy and disorder prevailing in the pashalik see L/PS/9/97A, Taylor to the Secret Committee, December 7, 1834; L/PS/9/105 Baghdad no. 3, Taylor to Secret Committee, March 1, 1838; L/PS/9/120 Baghdad no. 26, Taylor to Secret Committee, September 7, 1841; L/PS/9/120 no. 32, Taylor to Secret Committee, October 22, 1841; James Fraser, *Travels in Koordistan and Mesopotamia*, 2 vols. (London, 1840), I, 318–19. Each purse (*kese*) equaled 500 piasters, which in the latter part of the century amounted to five gold Ottoman pounds.
7 Translation of a circular from the pasha of Baghdad to the political agent in Turkish Arabia, 16 Shawwal 1258 or November 18, 1842 enclosed in FO

195/204 Baghdad no. 2, Taylor to Sheil, February 16, 1843. Lorimer, *Gazetteer*, I, 1B: 1350.

8 FO 78/519, Farrant to Canning, May 15, 1843 (hereafter Farrant Report) and "Translation of a Persian Account of Kerbela, and the Attack and Capture of that Place," enclosure no. 3 in FO 195/204 Baghdad no. 11, Farrant to Canning, May 14, 1843 (hereafter "Persian Account"). Colonel Farrant was sent by Ambassador Canning to conduct a thorough investigation of the events of Karbala'. His report, based on extensive interviews with all parties concerned, is the fullest account of the affair. The following description, unless specified otherwise, is based on this report. For a detailed socio-political analysis of the gangs, see Cole and Momen, "Mafia," 114–20.

9 Tehrani, *Nuqaba'*, 881–82; "Persian Account"; al-Khalili, *Mawsu'at al-'atabat*, VIII, 279–80 also regards Mirza Salih as one of the town's respected sayyids.

10 Translation of a circular from the pasha of Baghdad to the political agent in Turkish Arabia, 16 Shawwal 1258 or November 18, 1842, enclosed in FO 195/204 Baghdad no. 2, Taylor to Sheil, February 16, 1843; *QU*, 7, 12–13.

11 Lorimer, *Gazetteer*, I, 1B: 1348–51; FO 78/518 Baghdad no. 4, Farrant to Canning, April 22, 1843.

12 Translation of a circular from the pasha of Baghdad to the political agent in Turkish Arabia, 16 Shawwal 1258 or November 18, 1842, enclosed in FO 195/204 Baghdad no. 2, Taylor to Sheil, February 16, 1843 and Taylor's letter itself; translation from Turkish to Persian of Najib's letter to Sheil and the French consul (n.d.), enclosed in FO 60/96 Tehran no. 23, Sheil to Aberdeen, March 9, 1843.

13 Farrant Report. See also Muhammad "Nabil" Zarandi, *The Dawn Breakers*, trans. Shoghi Effendi (Wilmette, 1974), 35–36 on the rumor that spread in Karbala' that 'Abbas, Imam Husayn's half-brother, appeared in a dream to an 'alim asking him to declare holy war against the Ottomans and promising him ultimate success.

14 Farrant Report; Muhammad Karim Khan Kirmani, *Hidayat al-talibin* (Kirman, 1980), 153; Zarandi, *Dawn Breakers*, 35–36.

15 Farrant Report; Lorimer, *Gazetteer*, I, 1B: 1352; *QU*, 12–13.

16 Shushtari, *al-Zill*, fos. 52b–53b. At least one 'alim, Shaykh 'Abbas b. Muhammad Al Qurashi, had to flee Karbala' during the siege because he had been on bad terms with Mirza Salih. Tehrani, *Kiram*, 690–91; Hirz al–Din, *Ma'arif*, I, 390–92.

17 "Copy of an authentic report made by Namik Pasha as part of the Inquiry on the Karbala' Event," enclosure no. 5 in FO 78/520 Buyukderi no. 165, Canning to Sheil, July 28, 1843.

18 Farrant Report; Lorimer, *Gazetteer*, I, 1B: 1355. Taylor arrived at a similar estimate to that of Farrant, of between 4,000 and 5,000 people: see FO 195/104 Baghdad no. 2, Taylor to Sheil, February 16, 1843.

19 Farrant Report. On Mirza Salih see I'timad al-Saltana, *Ma'athir*, 148 and al-Amin, *A'yan*, XXXVI, 207.

20 Hirz al-Din, *Ma'arif*, I, 210–17; *QU*, 106.

21 "Persian Account." In 1826 1 shami was worth 10 piasters, but afterwards

its value declined: see Issawi, *Fertile Crescent*, 469. It is unlikely that Najaf paid 1,000,000 piasters: see below on taxation.

22 FO 195/367 Baghdad no. 15, Rawlinson to earl of Malmesbury, August 2, 1852; FO 195/367 Baghdad no. 16, Rawlinson to earl of Malmesbury, August 20, 1852. In early 1854 the gangs, which numbered about 2,000 men, reoccupied Najaf. Although the Ottomans again sought the mediation of the 'ulama', they regained control of the town only after battling the gangs: FO 195/442 Baghdad no. 3, Rawlinson to Redcliffe, January 25, 1854; FO 195/442 Baghdad no. 8, Rawlinson to Redcliffe, April 5, 1854.

23 FO 195/204 Tehran no. 1, Sheil to Taylor, January 7, 1843.

24 Algar, *Religion*, 115–16.

25 FO 78/517 Constantinople no. 55, Canning to Aberdeen, March 18, 1843.

26 For the correspondence see FO 60/96 Tehran no. 23, Sheil to Canning, March 4, 1843; FO 78/517 Constantinople no. 55, Canning to the earl of Aberdeen, March 18, 1843 and its thirteen enclosures; FO 78/519 Constantinople no. 128, Canning to the earl of Aberdeen, June 16, 1843; FO 78/521 Constantinople no. 200, Canning to the earl of Aberdeen, September 17, 1843 and its enclosures.

27 FO 78/521 Buyukderi, Canning to Sheil, September 8, 1843 – enclosure to Canning, no. 200.

28 FO 78/519, Farrant to Canning, May 15, 1843; FO 195/237 Baghdad no. 19, Rawlinson to Canning, April 11, 1846; FO 195/334 Baghdad, Kemball to Sheil, June 10, 1850; Lorimer, *Gazetteer*, I, 1B: 1376.

29 Farrant to Najib Pasha, Baghdad, January 24, 1844 – enclosure to FO 195/204 Baghdad no. 30, Farrant to Canning, January 24, 1844.

30 Al-Wa'ili, *al-Shi'r*, 185–90.

31 Shushtari, *al-Zill*, fo. 49b; Cole, "'Indian Money'," 473.

32 Amanat, *Resurrection*, 60–61; Cole and Momen, "Mafia," 140.

33 The most comprehensive study on the Babi movement is Amanat, *Resurrection*. The following pages are based on that study unless specified otherwise. See also Peter Smith, *The Babi and Baha'i Religions* (Cambridge, 1987).

34 Amanat, *Resurrection*, 153–55.

35 On the situation of the Shaykhi community in Karbala' and the response to Bastami see Amanat, *Resurrection*, 213–15; Momen, "Trial," 115–16; FO 195/237 Baghdad no. 1, Rawlinson to Canning, January 8, 1845.

36 Zarandi, *Dawn Breakers*, 90–91; Amanat, *Resurrection*, 218.

37 Zarandi, *Dawn Breakers*, 91.

38 FO 195/237 Baghdad no. 2, Rawlinson to Canning, January 22, 1845.

39 Hajj Muhammad Mu'in al-Saltana Tabrizi, *Ta'rikh-i amr-i baha'i*, unpublished manuscript cited in Amanat, *Resurrection*, 169.

40 Zarandi, *Dawn Breakers*, 91.

41 FO 195/237 Baghdad no. 1, Rawlinson to Canning, January 8, 1845.

42 *Ibid.*

43 Enclosure no. 1 to *ibid.*

44 *Ibid.*

45 *Ibid.*

46 See Hirz al-Din, *Ma'arif*, I, 216 who attributes such intentions to the Sunnis.

47 Amanat, *Resurrection*, 225–26, 228–29; Momen, "Trial," 130–36.
48 Momen, "Trial," 137–38; Amanat, *Resurrection*, 227–28.
49 Al-Wardi, *Lamahat*, II, 139; Amanat, *Resurrection*, 230.
50 FO 248/114 Baghdad no. 2, Rawlinson to Sheil, January 16, 1845.
51 For the content and an analysis of the *fatwa*, see Momen, "Trial," 130–43. For Shi'i descriptions, see Tehrani, *Kiram*, 318–19; Hirz al-Din, *Ma'arif*, I, 215–16; al-Wardi, *Lamahat*, II, 138–40.
52 *QU*, 186.
53 Momen, "Trial," 140.
54 Amanat, *Resurrection*, 245n.
55 On her life and activity see Amanat, *Resurrection*, chap. 7; Bayat, *Mysticism*, 110–18 and the sources cited there.
56 See Litvak, "The Shi'i 'ulama'," 358 on grants to Shaykhi leaders from the Oudh Bequest.

8 OTTOMAN CENTRALIZATION POLICY

1 "Translation of a Persian Account of Kerbela, and the Attack and Capture of that Place," enclosure no. 3 in FO 195/204 Baghdad no. 11, Farrant to Canning, May 14, 1843; cf. Kirmani, *Hidayat al-talibin*, 154.
2 FO 195/204 Baghdad, Farrant to Sheil, April 15, 1843; al-Wardi, *Lamahat*, II, 259.
3 Baghdad no. 77, Rawlinson to Canning, December 6, 1848 in J. A. Saldanha, *The Precis of the Persian Gulf*, VI, *Precis of Turkish Arabia 1901–1905* (Simla, 1906; repr. 1986), pt. 1, 37.
4 Translation of a letter addressed by Najib Pasha to Sayyid Ibrahim Qazvini – enclosed in FO 195/237 Baghdad no. 12, Rawlinson to Sheil, April 3, 1845.
5 FO 195/237 Baghdad no. 28, Rawlinson to Canning, June 12, 1844.
6 *Ibid.*
7 On the legal status of Shi'ism, see the *fatwa* issued by the Ottoman shaykh al-Islam Ebusuud Effendi in the sixteenth century in M. Ertugrul Düzdag, *Seyhulislam ebussuud effendi fetvalari* (Istanbul, 1972), fatwa no. 481.
8 FO 195/367 Baghdad no. 10, Rawlinson to Canning, February 10, 1852.
9 FO 195/1763, telegram, Mockler to Ford, September 29, 1892.
10 Al-Wardi, *Lamahat*, II, 226.
11 FO 195/237 Baghdad no. 26, Rawlinson to Canning, June 25, 1845; FO 195/272 Baghdad no. 31, Rawlinson to Wellesley, May 12, 1847.
12 FO 195/318 Baghdad no. 47, Rawlinson to Canning, August 14, 1848; FO 195/334 Baghdad no. 12, Kemball to Canning, April 20, 1850.
13 FO 195/318 Baghdad no. 47, Rawlinson to Canning, August 14, 1848.
14 *Ibid.*
15 See FO 195/334 Baghdad no. 12, Kemball to Canning, April 20, 1850 and FO 195/577 Baghdad no. 29, Kemball to Alison, June 23, 1858, reporting that the issue had arisen again.
16 FO 195/367 Baghdad no. 10, Rawlinson to Canning, February 10, 1852.
17 Baghdad no. 77, Rawlinson to Canning, December 6, 1848 in Saldanha, *Precis*, VI, pt. 1, at 37.
18 FO 195/237 Baghdad no. 4, Rawlinson to Canning, January 24, 1844.

19 CCC, vol. 10, Baghdad 325; CCC, vol. 10, Baghdad no. 94, April 2, 1845, at 427; in 1261/1845 revenues from Karbala' declined somewhat to 630,000 piasters (£6,300) while those from Najaf rose to 866,250 piasters; CCC, vol. 10, no. 110, 505.
20 FO 195/237 Baghdad no. 40, Rawlinson to Canning, September 17, 1845.
21 Ibid.
22 Baghdad no. 77, Rawlinson to Canning, December 6, 1848 in Saldanha, Precis, VI, pt. 1, at 37.
23 John R. Barnes, An Introduction to Religious Foundations in the Ottoman Empire (Leiden, 1986), chap. 3.
24 FO 195/237 Baghdad no. 23, Rawlinson to Canning, June 24, 1845.
25 See details on the salaries of the shrine functionaries in IGFD P/3742, proceedings no. 37, Baghdad no. 123, Tweedie to the government of India, March 1890; Mahbuba, Madi, I, 279.
26 See the report on one inspection in Al-Zawra' (the official gazette of the pashalik), no. 1196, 5 Rabi' al-Awwal 1302/December 19, 1884, cited in al-'Azzawi, Ta'rikh, VIII, 74.
27 See for instance FO 195/334 no. 29, Kemball to Canning, November 19, 1849 on the Ottoman refusal to allow the custodians and mujtahids to carry in procession the flags consecrated to Imam Husayn which were deposited at the shrine.
28 Ali Haydar Midhat Bey, The Life of Midhat Pasha (London, 1903), 53; Husayn Khan Malik Sasani, Yadbud-ha-yi sifarat-i istanbul (Tehran, n.d.), 250; Lorimer, Gazetteer, II, 2A: 855.
29 Anne Blunt, Bedouin Tribes of the Euphrates (London, 1879), 205.
30 'Abd al-Razzaq al-Husayn Al Kamuna, Mawarid al-athaf fi nuqaba' al-ashraf, 2 vols. (Najaf, 1968), I, 153–54. See also the statement in Qaysi, "Impact," 9, that the Ottomans shared their authority and prestige with local families in the shrine cities, e.g. Al Kashif al-Ghita' in Najaf and Al Mahdi Qazvini in Hilla, both of them 'ulama' families.
31 Sayyid Ja'far al-Kazimi, Manahil al-darb fi ansab al-'arab, cited in Kilidar, Madinat al-Husayn, 82–83.
32 Kamuna, Mawarid al-athaf, II, 61–62; Bahr al-'Ulum, "Muqaddima," 135–37; Tehrani, Kiram, 102.
33 R. H. Davison, s.v., "Midhat Pasha," EI².
34 Al-Zawra', year 7, no. 557, 1292/1875–76, cited in al-Wa'ili, al-Shi'r, 182; Phebe Marr, The Modern History of Iraq (New York, 1985), 23–24; Luizard, La formation, 23.
35 On his settlement policies, see Albertine Jwaide, "Midhat Pasha and the Land System of Lower Iraq," St. Anthony's Papers: Middle Eastern Affairs 3 (1963), 106–36; Marion Farouk-Sluglett and Peter Sluglett, "The Transformation of Land Tenure and Rural Social Structure in Central and Southern Iraq, c.1870–1958," IJMES 15 (1983), 494; Lorimer, Gazetteer, II, 2A: 895–96; Nakash, The Shi'is, 33.
36 Al-Wardi, Lamahat, II, 239; J. D. Peters, Nippur, or Explorations and Adventures on the Euphrates, 1888–1890 (New York, 1897), 331; Cowper, Asiatic Arabia, 374.
37 Al-'Azzawi, Ta'rikh, VII, 121; FO 195/577 Baghdad no. 28, Kemball to

Alison, June 9, 1858; FO 195/577 Baghdad no. 29, Kemball to Alison, June 23, 1858.
38 IGFD-political proceedings nos. 323–24 – Baghdad no. 10, Herbert to Elliot, September 1, 1869.
39 See, for instance, Shaykh 'Ali b. Khayri Zahid al-Najafi who was included in the conscription lists in order to put a stop to his activities against the Jewish synagogue in Dhu al-Kifl. Hirz al-Din, *Ma'arif*, II, 119–21.
40 Al-Muzaffar, "Tarjamat," 6–7; for the Khalisi family, see Nakash, *The Shi'is*, 82.
41 Among the mujtahids were Radi Najafi and Zayn al-'Abidin Mazandarani of Karbala'. Hirz al-Din, *Ma'arif*, I, 96, 309–10, 332–33.
42 Bahr al-'Ulum, "Muqaddima," 137, 147–48.
43 Lorimer, *Gazetteer*, II, 2A: 869
44 Hirz al-Din, *Ma'arif*, I, 88–89; and Mahbuba, *Madi*, II, 294–95, 286–89, III, 90–91, 184.
45 FO 78/2650 Baghdad no. 33, Nixon to Thornton, secretary to the government of India in the Foreign Department, July 14, 1877; FO 78/2650 Baghdad no. 36, Nixon to secretary to the government of India in the Foreign Department, July 17, 1877; FO 78/2650 Baghdad no. 28, Nixon to Layard, July 19, 1877; Correspondance Politique des Consuls (CPC) Baghdad vol. 6 no. 45, August 4, 1877; George Geary, *Through Asiatic Turkey: Narrative of a Journey from Bombay to the Bosphorus*, 2 vols. (London, 1878), I, 155.
46 FO 195/1142, 'Akif Pasha to Nixon, 1 Rajab 1294/July 13, 1877, enclosed in Baghdad no. 37, dated September 22, 1877; CPC Baghdad vol. 6 no. 45, August 4, 1877.
47 Haidar Ali Khan to Nixon, Karbala', 27 Sha'ban 1294/September 6, 1877, enclosed in FO 78/2650 Baghdad no. 32, Nixon to Layard, September 8, 1877; Haidar Ali Khan to Nixon, Karbala', 21 Ramadan 1294/September 29, 1877, enclosed in FO 78/2650 Baghdad, Nixon to Layard, October 7, 1877; FO 195/1142, Haidar Ali Khan to Nixon, September 16, 1877.
48 Translation of report from Sayyid 'Ali Bahr al-'Ulum, mujtahid of Najaf, dated 28 Rajab 1294/August 9, 1877, enclosed in FO 78/2650 Baghdad no. 52, Nixon to secretary of state for foreign affairs, August 11, 1877; CPC Baghdad vol. 6 no. 54, February 28, 1878.
49 Geary, *Through Asiatic Turkey*, I, 179.
50 Al-Amin, *A'yan*, XLVI, 113, XXIII, 270; Mahbuba, *Madi*, III, 194; Hirz al-din, *Ma'arif*, II, 283–84; FO 195/1142, Haidar Ali Khan to Nixon, September 16, 1877; Khaqani, *Shu'ara'*, II, 4–5, 130ff.
51 See for instance Sayyid 'Ali Bahr al-'Ulum's indignation at the high indemnities the Russians demanded from the Ottomans during the negotiations on the 1877 St. Stefano Treaty: Geary, *Through Asiatic Turkey*, 178.
52 For the Tanzimat in Syria, see Moshe Maoz, *Ottoman Reforms in Syria and Palestine, 1840–1861* (Oxford, 1968); Moshe Maoz, "The 'Ulama' and the Process of Modernization in Syria during the Mid-Nineteenth Century," *Asian and African Studies* 29 (1966), 277–301; Philip Khoury, *Urban Notables and Arab Nationalism: The Politics of Damascus 1860–1920* (Cambridge, 1983), 4–5, 15–17, 29.

53 On the Ottoman identity of local elites in the fertile crescent, see Toledano, "Emergence."

9 THE CHANGING POLITICAL TRIANGLE, 1875–1904

1 Lorimer, *Gazetteer*, I, 1B: 1376; FO 195/237 Baghdad no. 28 Rawlinson to Canning, June 12, 1844; FO 195/237 Baghdad no. 12, Rawlinson to Sheil, April 3, 1845; FO 195/318 Baghdad no. 39, Rawlinson to Canning, July 5, 1848.

2 See, for instance, FO 195/237 Baghdad no. 25, Rawlinson to Canning, March 29, 1844 and FO 195/752 Baghdad no. 24, Kemball to Bulwer, July 15, 1863.

3 Bruce Masters, "The Treaties of Erzerum (1823 and 1848) and the Changing Status of Iranians in the Ottoman Empire," *IS* 27 (1991), 15.

4 Lorimer, *Gazetteer*, I, 1B: 1425.

5 Stephen Duguid, "The Politics of Unity: Hamidian Policy in Eastern Anatolia," *MES* 9 (1973), 139–56; On 'Abd al-Hamid's pan-Islamic policy, see Jacob M. Landau, *The Politics of Pan-Islam: Ideology and Organization* (Oxford, 1990), 9–73.

6 Shirazi, *Tara'iq al-haqa'iq*, III, 498; Ansari, *Zindigani*, 306. On Mazandarani's ability to disregard repeated injunctions by the Ottoman *qadi* and the governor of Baghdad to return a house he had expropriated from an Indian widow, see FO 195/1309 Baghdad no. 53, Miles to Goschen, June 23, 1880 and enclosures.

7 Mahbuba, *Madi*, I, 68–69, 104, 200–03; Sayf al-Dawla, *Safarnamah-yi mecca*, 231; Deringil, "Struggle," 51.

8 FO 195/1935 Baghdad no. 340/57, Mockler to Michael Herbert, July 14, 1896; William Loftus, *Travels and Research in Chaldea and Susiana* (London, 1857), 50–51; Peters, *Nippur*, 333. See similar remarks by George Geary, *Through Asiatic Turkey*, I, 145; Jane Dieulafoy, *La Perse, la Chaldée et la Susiane* (Paris, 1874), 631; and Cowper, *Asiatic Arabia*, 334.

9 For earlier manifestations of such animosities see Shihab al-Din Mahmud al-Alusi, *al-Tibyan fi sharh al-burhan* written in 1249/1833. Alusi also used to engaged in polemical debates with Shi'i 'ulama' in Kazimayn: see Amanat, *Resurrection*, 225; al-Alusi, *al Misk*, 18; al-Sadr, *Takmilat amal al-'amil*, 237.

10 The British consul claimed that Shirazi owned a lot of property in Samarra': see FO 195/1841 Baghdad No. 242/25, Mockler to Currie, May 6, 1894; Yunus al-Samarra'i, *Ta'rikh madinat samarra'* (Baghdad, 1971), 180–81.

11 Deringil, "Struggle," 49–52.

12 Samarra'i, *Ta'rikh*, 180–81; Kamuna, *Mawarid al-athaf*, I, 153–54; Luizard, *La formation*, 95. Batatu, *The Old Social Classes*, 168.

13 CPC Baghdad vol. 7 no. 5, May 12, 1894; Hirz al-Din, *Ma'arif*, II, 235–36n.; FO 195/1841 Baghdad no. 237/24, Mockler to Currie, May 5, 1894; al-Amin, *A'yan*, XXIII, 272–73. On Shirazi's building activities in Samarra', see Tehrani, *Nuqaba'*, 440 and Habibabadi, *Makarim*, 886.

14 For the Sunni view, see Samarra'i, *Ta'rikh*, 178; For the Shi'i view, see "Petition by Indian Students to the British Consul" enclosed in FO 195/1841 Baghdad no. 210/23, Mockler to Currie, April 21, 1894; and "a

memorandum of statements" made by three Indian sayyids enclosed in FO 195/1841 Baghdad no. 237/24, Mockler to Currie, May 5, 1894, and al-Amin, *A'yan*, XXIII, 274. For the Ottoman view, see CPC Baghdad vol. 7 no. 5, May 12, 1894.

15 FO 195/1841 Baghdad no. 237/24, Mockler to Currie, May 5, 1894.

16 CPC Baghdad vol. 7 no. 5, May 12, 1894; no. 7, June 9, 1894.

17 FO 195/1841 Baghdad no. 242/25, Mockler to Currie, May 6, 1894. The French consul believed that had Shirazi left or been forced to leave, a massive Shi'i rebellion might have taken place in Iraq. CPC Baghdad vol. 7 no. 5, May 12, 1894; even if this was an exaggeration, the governor may have shared that fear.

18 Hirz al-Din, *Ma'arif*, II, 235–36n.

19 Tehrani, *Hadiyat al-razi*, 225–26; Hirz al-Din, *Ma'arif*, II, 235–36n; Samarra'i, *Ta'rikh*, 178; CPC Baghdad vol. 7 no. 6, May 16, 1894 and no. 8, June 1894.

20 FO 195/1841 Baghdad no. 242/25, Mockler to Currie, May 6, 1894. For the text in Arabic, see CPC Baghdad vol. 7 no. 8, June 14, 1894.

21 Kashmiri, *Nujum al-sama'*, II, 153; al-Amin, *A'yan*, XXVI, 217.

22 In 1896, for example, 'Abd al-Hamid sent a delegation to Iran to pave the way for a reconciliation between the two countries which was meant to lead to a union at some future date. The assassination of the shah foiled his plan and subsequent Ottoman efforts in the same vein aimed at Muzaffar al-Din Shah failed to produce any tangible results. Landau, *The Politics of Pan-Islam*, 44–45. On Shaykh al-Ra'is, see Juan R. I. Cole, "Iranian Millenarianism and Democratic Thought in the Nineteenth Century," *IJMES* 24 (1992), 19.

23 Al-Amin, *A'yan*, XL, 68.

24 Siphir Lisan al-Mulk, *Nasikh al-tawarikh*, I, 214–15; Algar, *Religion*, 87–91. Cf. Peter Avery, "An Enquiry into the Outbreak of the Russo-Persian War, 1826–28," in C. E. Bosworth (ed.), *Iran and Islam* (Edinburgh, 1971), 17ff., who argues that the mujtahids' pressure was less important than 'Abbas Mirza's own desire to retrieve Iranian losses from the 1813 war.

25 Hidayat, *Ta'rikh*, X, 708–09.

26 I'timad al-Saltana, *Ma'athir*, 136; Shushtari, *al-Zill*, fos. 64b, 82a–84b, 85b–88b, 95a–100a; Tehrani, *Hadiyat al-razi*, 43.

27 See al-Amin, *A'yan*, VI, 5, XV, 401–13; Hirz al-Din, *Ma'arif*, II, 366–69.

28 Siphir Lisan al-Mulk, *Nasikh al-tawarikh*, III, 325.

29 *QU*, 10–11; al-Amin, *A'yan*, XXXI, 105; Arjomand, *The Shadow*, 234–37.

30 FO 78/2124 Therapia no. 135, Elliot to Granville, August 4, 1870.

31 Nasir al-Din Shah Qajar, *Ruznamah-yi safar*, 135.

32 Al-Amin, *A'yan*, VI, 6; al-Wardi, *Lamahat*, II, 258–59.

33 Nasir al-Din Shah, *Ruznamah-yi safar*, 160–62; al-Wardi, *Lamahat*, II, 258–59.

34 Al-Wardi, *Lamahat*, II, 259.

35 See, for instance, Hasan b. Shaykh Isma'il Al Khidr al-Jinaji; the sons of 'Abd al-Husayn Tehrani; Mulla Baqir Shirazi, in Mahbuba, *Madi*, II, 207; Tehrani, *Kiram*, 715 and Tehrani, *Nuqaba'*, 188.

36 Al-Kazimi, *Ahsan al-wadi'a*, 81; IGFD-Internal B Proceedings nos. 167–69,

February 1893; L/PS/10/77 Baghdad no. 432, Newmarch to secretary to the government of India at the Foreign Department, June 15, 1905.

37 Ibrahim Teymuri, *'Asr-i bi-khabari ya ta'rikh-i imtiyazat-i dar iran* (Tehran, 1325s/1954), 131. This is the same Mirza Salih who had played a key role in the 1843 Karbala' rebellion: I'timad al-Saltana, *Ma'athir*, 148.

38 For analysis of the tobacco protest, see Hasan Karbala'i, *Ta'rikh-i dukhaniya ya ta'rikh-i inhisar-i dukhaniyat* ed. I. Dihgan (Arak, 1333/1954); Ibrahim Teymuri, *Tahrim-i tunbaku ya avvalin-i moqavamat-i manfi dar iran* (Tehran, 1949); Keddie, *Religion*; Ann K. S. Lambton, "The Tobacco Regie: Prelude to Revolution," *SI* 22 (1965), 119–57, and 23 (1965), 71–90; Kazemzade, *Russia and Britain*; Adamiyat, *Shurish*; Algar, *Religion*, 210–12.

39 FO 195/1763 Baghdad no. 719/52, Mockler to Ford, October 29, 1892 and enclosures.

40 Correspondence between Malkam Khan and Kirmani in Malkam Khan Supplement Persan, Bibliothèque National, Paris 1996/66 and 1966/73, cited in Bakhash, *Iran*, 329–32.

41 See the text of the shah's letter in Ibrahim Safa'i, *Rahbaran-i Mashrute*, 4 vols. (Tehran, 1344s/1965–66), I, 208.

42 Bakhash, *Iran*, 332.

43 Kirmani to Malkam Khan, S.P. 1996/66, cited in Bakhash, *Iran*, 332.

44 See Arjomand's discussion on "pious withdrawal from politics" in *The Shadow*, 234–37 which deals mainly with Murtada Ansari.

45 Martin, *Islam*, 13.

46 The most prominent examples were Mirza Muhammad al-Akhbari (d. 1233/1818), who was expelled by Fath 'Ali Shah; Mirza Masih Astarabadi (d.1263/1846–47), who led a mob to kill the Russian envoy Griboyedov in 1829; Sayyid Muhammad Baqir b. Sayyid 'Ali Husayni Qazvini, who was banished by the governor of Qazvin, Majd al-Dawla, to Najaf; Shaykh 'Abd al-Husayn Tehrani, who was dispatched to Karbala' to renovate the shrines as an elegant way to remove him from Tehran; and Sayyid 'Ali Akbar Falsiri Shirazi for his activity in the tobacco protest. Nasir al-Din Shah's intention to banish Hasan Ashtiyani from Tehran to the shrine cities was thwarted by public pressure, but it reflected his belief that Ashtiyani would be less harmful there. Hamid Algar, s.v., "Akhbari, Mirza Mohammad," *EIr*; Bamdad, *Sharh-i hal*, IV, 100–01; II, 431–32; *QU*, 69–70; Tehrani, *Kiram*, 713–14; Keddie, *Religion*, 103–05.

47 Among such mujtahids were Radi Najafi, Habiballah Rashti, Hasan Ardakani: see Tehrani, *Kiram*, 529; al-Amin, *A'yan*, XX, 96; al-Kazimi, *Ahsan al-wadi'a*, 81.

48 The period has been extensively discussed in Nikki Keddie, "Iranian Politics 1900–1905: Background to Revolution," *MES* 5:1–3 (1969), 3–31, 151–67, 234–50; Nazim al-Islam Kirmani, *Ta'rikh-i bidari-yi iranian* (Tehran, 1332s/1953; new ed.); Ahmad Kasravi, *Ta'rikh-i mashrute-yi Iran*, 2 vols. (Tehran, 1383), I; Algar, *Religion*; Mangol Bayat, *Iran's First Revolution* (Oxford, 1991).

49 Muhammad Hasan Muhsin to Newmarch, May 27, 1903, enclosed in FO 248/830 no. 425, Newmarch to Hardinge, May 30, 1904; FO 248/830 no. 490, extracts from resident's diary, June 20, 1904. See the letter signed in

1908 by Mirza Husayn Khalili, Akhund Khorasani, and 'Abdallah Mazandarani to Sultan 'Abd al-Hamid in which they referred to him as Amir
al-Mu'minin, a title reserved to Imam 'Ali alone in the Shi'a. See also the
declaration made in 1910 by Khorasani and other 'ulama' that the Ottoman
and Iranian nations should become united, in Ha'iri, *Shi'ism*, 80, 89–90.

50 Hardinge, *A Diplomatist*, 322; memorandum from Hasan Muhsin, the
   consular agent at Karbala', enclosure no. 8 in FO 416/14, India Office to
   Foreign Office no. 286, September 17, 1903.
51 FO60/645 no. 186, Hardinge to Lansdowne, December 1901; Nikki
   Keddie, "British Policy and the Iranian Opposition, 1901–1907," *Journal of
   Modern History* 39:3 (September 1967), 269.
52 FO 60/660 no. 77, Hardinge to Lansdowne, May 5, 1902. For subsequent
   manifestations of ecumenism among Shi'i 'ulama', see Nakash, *The Shi'is*,
   56ff.
53 Enclosures 1 and 2 in L/PS/3/390 Tehran no. 55, Hardinge to Lansdowne,
   April 1, 1902.
54 FO 416/14 no. 53(94) Gulahek, Hardinge to Lansdowne, July 13, 1903.
55 FO 60/650 no. 18, Hardinge to Lansdowne, February 4, 1902; FO 416/14
   no. 53(94), Hardinge to Lansdowne, June 23, 1903. For their other joint
   calls see FO 416/15 at 241, enclosure in no. 243; FO 416/15 at 269;
   enclosure in no. 277; and FO 416/17 at 169, enclosure 1 in no. 143.
56 FO 416/14 no. 46(85), Hardinge to Lansdowne, June 10, 1903. See FO
   416/14 no. 53(94) Gulahek, Hardinge to Lansdowne, June 23, 1903 where
   Hardinge reported that Mu'in al-Mulk, son of the former *Sadr-i A'zam*,
   Amin al-Dawla, gave money to Mulla 'Abd al-'Ali Herati who served as an
   emissary between the 'ulama' from Tehran and shrine cities.
57 Keddie, "Iranian Politics," 163.
58 Muhammad Hasan Muhsin to Newmarch May 27, 1903, enclosed in FO
   248/830 no. 425, Newmarch to Hardinge, May 30, 1904; FO 248/830 no.
   490, extracts from resident's diary, June 20, 1904; Lorimer, *Gazetteer*, I, 1B:
   1521.
59 FO 195/2164 Baghdad no. 464/35, Newmarch to Hardinge, June 13, 1904
   and enclosure; FO 195/2164 Baghdad no. 534/39, Newmarch to Hardinge,
   July 7, 1904 and enclosure.
60 Lorimer, *Gazetteer*, I, 1B: 1522.
61 For this concept see Arjomand, *The Shadow*, 228.

CONCLUSION

1 Anthony D. Smith, *Social Change* (New York, 1976), 40, 42, 70; Robert
  Nisbet, *Social Change and History* (New York, 1968), 209–305.

APPENDIX: TABLES

1 The sample is taken only from those 'ulama' who were residents in the
  shrine cities. It does not include those who returned to Iran or to their tribe.
2 The biographical dictionaries do not provide the exact places of birth for a

large number of 'ulama'. The *nisba* by itself is not a sufficient indicator, as it often describes only the region of origin, e.g. Mazandaran or Gilan. Furthermore, reliance on towns or cities mentioned in the *nisba* would be a mistake, as these references sometimes merely denote the origin of an individual's family in an earlier period. The reference to Shaykh Muhammad Taqi b. Muhammad 'Abd al-Rahim Aywankafi Varamini Tehrani Israhani demonstrates the difficulty of relying on the *nisba*, as it is impossible to determine which of these localities was his birthplace. Consequently, identification of 'ulama' as villagers, town and city dwellers has not been undertaken.

3 The very small number of 'Atabat born Turkish 'ulama' in the sample makes it difficult to draw any significant conclusions about this group. Consequently, both Turkish migrants and natives of the shrine cities have been examined as one group.

4 The distinction between cities and towns is based on Ervand Abrahamian's division which counted eleven cities in nineteenth-century Iran with a population over 25,000 people each. These cities are: Tehran, Tabriz, Isfahan, Shiraz, Mashhad, Yazd, Hamadan, Qazvin, Kirmanshah, Urumiya, and Kirman. Abrahamian, *Iran between Two Revolutions*, 11.

5 The data for this table are taken from the personal entries of the mujtahids in the various biographical dictionaries and from Tehrani's *al-Dhari'a*. The classification of categories is based on Modaressi Tabatabai, *Introduction*, pp. 18–22. Since the classification among the various *fiqh* categories is not always clear cut, this survey should be regarded as *rudimentary* and as pointing to *general trends* rather than to precise numbers. Further studies based on content analysis are necessary before arriving at definite conclusions on the subject.

6 Only four categories have been chosen, as the number of the titles in the other categories is too small for any meaningful conclusions.

7 This group is composed of thirty-four of the seventy mujtahids surveyed for this study.

8 The group is composed of thirty-six mujtahids.

Glossary

akhbar – the Traditions (words and deeds) of the Prophet and the Shi'i Imams as transmitted by chains of narrators

Akhbariyaa – the Shi'i school of jurisprudence, which rejects deductive methodology in the study of law and requires unmitigated adherence to the limited meaning of the *akhbar*

akhund – general title for the Persian clergy; in the nineteenth century often as an honorific designating high-ranking scholars

Al – the people, clan, or house of

aqa – in the Qajar period used to designate people in posts of authority, particularly in the religious class

'atabat-i 'aliyat (lit. the divine thresholds) the Shi'i holy shrine in Iraq and the cities of their location: Karbala', Najaf, Kazimayn, and Samarra'

ayatallah – (lit. sign of God) a twentieth-century title for a senior mujtahid

Bab – (lit. the Gate) in Shi'ism, the human mediator between the Hidden Imam and his followers; in Babi context, the title was assumed by Sayyid 'Ali Muhammad Shirazi in 1844

batin – the inner meaning behind the literal texts of the scripture and hadith

faqih – a jurist specializing in the science of *fiqh*. In the nineteenth century, it implies specialization in applied religious law (*furu'*)

fiqh – the knowledge of religion with emphasis on jurisprudence and the exercise of independent but informed judgment

furu' – subsidiary principles applied to religious law, as opposed to the *usul*

hadith – see akhbar

hashiyya – gloss or marginal notes on a book

hawza 'ilmiyya – (lit. territory of learning) community of learning in a specific city, denoting a communal whole which encompases scholarship, social bonds, organization, and finance

hujja – proof; in Shi'ism the attribute *hujjatullah* (the proof of God) is used for the Imams; *hujjat al-Islam* (proof of Islam) became an honorific of high-ranking mujtahids during the nineteenth century

ijaza – certificate permitting or authorizing the student to transmit hadith on the authority of his teacher and/or exercise *ijtihad*

ijtihad – the process of arriving at independent legal judgment in specific matters of religious law by employing the sources of law and by using the "principles of jurisprudence" (*usul al-fiqh*)

Imam – in Twelver Shi'ism, one of the twelve recognized hereditary successors of Muhammad, beginning with 'Ali and continued in his house; after the

235

tenth century, both titles *Imam-i zaman* and *Imam-i gha'b* (Hidden Imam) referred to the Twelfth Imam

imam jum'a – leader of the Friday congregational prayer, appointed by the government in each Iranian city with broader responsibilities

Ithna 'Ashariyya – Twelvers, the branch of Imami Shi'ism that believes in twelve Imams, beginning with 'Ali and ending with the Hidden Imam, Muhammad b. Hasan

Jihad – the holy war undertaken against infidels to defend or expand Islam

khums – religious tax, originally paid to the Prophet, by Shi'is to the Imam; in the modern period paid to *the marja'-i al-taqlid* in his capacity as *na'ib Imam*

madrasa – the religious seminary where Islamic sciences are taught, often financed by charitable endowments

marja'-i al-taqlid – (lit. reference point for emulation) one who through his learning and probity is qualified to be followed in all points of religious practice and law by the generality of Shi'is

Mirza – in the nineteenth century if placed before the name it indicates religious or bureaucratic training; if placed after it indicates that the bearer is a prince

mujtahid – an 'alim who attained the level of competence in matters of religion necessary to exercise *ijtihad*

mulla – usual Persian term for a person from the 'ulama' class, which does not denote a hierarchical gradation

na'ib – in Shi'ism *na'ib al-Imam* is the representative of the Imam; *na'ib al-'amm* is the general representative of the Imams. Mainstream Shi'ism recognizes this term for the collective body of the 'ulama'

niyaba – deputyship, the status claimed by the *na'ib*

pasha – an honorific in the Ottoman Empire as the title of the governor of a province, synonymous to *vali* in the Arab provinces of the empire

rawda – (lit. garden) from the title of a book of mourning, *rawdat al-Shuhada'* (Garden of the Martyrs); recitation of the suffering of the Imams, particularly of the Imam Husayn at Karbala'. *Rawza-khani* is the gathering for such recital. *Rawza-khan* is the professional reciter of the suffering

rijal – *'ilm al-rijal* is the study of the biographies of the transmitters of the hadith

risala – a treatise

ri'asa – in Shi'ism, the religious leadership of the community, specifically of the 'ulama' - community, by one or several mujtahids

sayyid – master and a descendant of the house of the Prophet

sharh – commentary or interpretation of another work

Shari'a – the canonical law of Islam, as defined by orthodox authorities

shaykh – an elder, but also a designation for 'ulama'

Shaykh al-Islam – in Iran official title of 'ulama' appointed to preside over religious courts

takfir – a formal denunciation, usually by the 'ulama', of a person on the charge of heresy or disbelief

taqiyya – the prudential dissimulation of true religious beliefs in circumstances of danger of death or humiliation, sanctioned by Shi'ism

taqlid – the process of following and emulating the practices and pronouncements of a mujtahid in matters relating to religious law, without practicing *ijtihad*

usul – principles; *usul al-din* – principal elements of religion as distinct from *furu'*; *usul al-fiqh*; *usul al-fiqh* – principles of jurisprudence used for arriving at judgments in *fiqh*

Usuliyya – the school of jurisprudence that emphasizes the use of reason in the study of *usul al-fiqh*

zakat – a religious tax payable by believers intended to assist the poor and needy, travelers, and debtors; it is usually paid to the *marja'al-taqlid*

Bibliography

ARCHIVAL SOURCES

BRITISH FOREIGN OFFICE:

FO 60 vols.: 27; 96; 373; 645; 650; 660
FO 78 vols.: 517; 518; 519; 520; 521; 533; 2124; 2650
FO 195 vols.: 113; 204; 237; 272; 318; 334; 367; 442; 577; 707; 752; 1142;
    1309; 1409; 1763; 1841; 1885; 1935; 2020; 2120; 2138; 2164; 2188
FO 248 vols.: 114; 141; 226; 270; 413; 762; 830
FO 416 vols.: 14; 15; 17

INDIA OFFICE RECORDS

India Government Foreign Department – political vols.: P/124/25; P/199/4;
    P/199/67; P/437/71; P/438/1; P/1026; P/3742; P/3743; P/3996; P/4614;
    P/4184; P/4187; P/4820; P/6652; P/6887; P/7127
Letters Political and Secret 3 (L/PS/3) vols.: 390; 399
L/PS/6 vols.: 93
L/PS/7 vols.: 10
L/PS/9 vols.: G/29/27; 6; 95; 97A; 105; 106; 120
L/PS/10 vols.: 23; 77
L/PS/11 vols. 165

FRANCE

Correspondance Consulaire et Commerciale (CCC) Turquie, Baghdad vols.: 7;
    10
Correspondance Politique des Consuls (CPC): Turquie, Baghdad vols.: 6; 7

UNPUBLISHED SOURCES

Sayyid 'Abbas Shushtari, *al-Zill al-Mamdud* (Arabic MS in the library of the raja
    of Mahmudabad, Lucknow)[1]

---

1 I wish to thank Juan Cole for providing me with a copy of this most valuable source.

OFFICIAL PUBLICATIONS

Admiralty War Staff Intelligence Division, *A Handbook of Mesopotamia* (London, 1916).
Iraq Administrative Reports (1918), II, 86–87.
Lorimer, John G. *Gazetteer of the Persian Gulf, Oman and Central Arabia*, 2 vols. (Calcutta, 1908–15, repr. London, 1970).
Saldanha, J. A. *The Precis of the Persian Gulf*, VI, *Precis of Turkish Arabia 1901–1905* (Simla, 1906; repr. 1986).

PUBLISHED SOURCES IN ARABIC AND PERSIAN

Anonymous. "Safra ila karbala' wal-hilla wa-nawahiha," in *Lughat al-Arab* (Baghdad, 1912–1928).
Abu Talib Khan [Isfahani]. *Masir-i talibi ya safarnamah-yi mirza abu talib khan*, ed. Husayn Hadivim (Tehran, 1352).
Adamiyat, Feridun. *Shurish bar imtiyaznamah-i rizhi* (Tehran, 1360s/1981).
Adib al-Mulk. *Safarnamah-yi adib al-mulk bih 'atabat (dalil al-za'irin) 1273h.q.*, ed. Mas'ud Golzari (Tehran, 1364s/1986).
Al-Alusi, Shukri. *al-Misk al-adhfar* (Baghdad, 1930).
Amin, Muhsin. *A'yan al-shi'a*, 60 vols. (Sidon, 1957).
Amini-Tabrizi, 'Abd al-Husayn. *Shuhada' al-fadila* (Najaf, 1955).
Ansari, Murtada. *Zindigani va-shakhsiyati-i shaykh ansari quddisa sirruhu* (n.p., 1960).
Asifi, Muhammad Mahdi. *Madrasat al-najaf wa-tatawwur al-haraka al-'ilmiyya fi-ha* (Najaf, 1964).
Al-'Azzawi, 'Abbas. *Ta'rikh al-'iraq bayn al-ihtilalayn*, 8 vols. (Baghdad, 1375/1955).
Al-Bahadili, 'Ali. *Al-Hawza al-'ilmiyya fi al-najaf al-ashraf: ma'alimuha wa-harakatuha al-islahiyya, 1339–1401/1920–1980* (Beirut, 1993).
Bahr al-'Ulum, Muhammad Sadiq, "Muqaddima," in Muhammad Mahdi b. Murtada Tabataba'i, *Rijal al-sayyid bahr al-'ulum al-ma'ruf bil-fawa'id al-rijaliyya* (Najaf, 1967).
Al-Bahrani, 'Ali b. Hasan. *Anwar al-badrayn fi tarajim 'ulama' al-qatif al-ahsa' wal-bahrayn* (Najaf, 1960).
Bamdad, Mahdi. *Sharh-i hal-i rijal-i iran dar qarn-i 12, 13 14 Hijri*, 6 vols. (Tehran, 1347s/1971).
Al-Basri, Uthman ibn Sanad. *Matali' al-su'ud bi-tayyib akhbar al-wali da'ud* (Cairo, 1951).
Davani, 'Ali. *Ustad-i kull aqa muhammad baqir b. muhammad akmal ma'ruf bi vahid-i bihbahani* (Qum, 1958).
   Zindigani-yi za'im-i buzurg-i 'alam-i tashayyu' 'allama-yi 'aliqadr hadrat-i ayatallah burujirdi (Qum, 1961).
Dawlatabadi, Yahya. *Hayat-i yahya*, 4 vols. (Tehran, 1341s/1963).
Düzdağ, M. Ertuğrul. *Seyhulislam Ebussund Effendi Fetvalari* (Istanbul, 1972).
Al-Fadli, 'Abd al-Hadi. *Dalil al-najaf al-ashraf* (Najaf, 1966).
Gurji, Abu al-Qasim. "Nigah-i bar tahawwul-i 'ilm-i usul va-maqam-i an dar miyan-i 'ulum-i digar," *Maqalat va-barrasi-ha* 13–16 (1352/1973): 27–80.

Habibabadi, Muhammad 'Ali Mu'allim. *Makarim al-athar dar ahval-i rijal-i dawra-yi qajar*, 2 vols. (Isfahan, 1958).

Al-Hajj, Salam. "Hikayat fi sirat marajil qabadayat tarablus," *al-Shira'* (Beirut), May 4, 1992.

Al-Haydari, Ibrahim Fasih. *'Unwan al-majd fi bayan ahwal baghdad wal-basra wal-najd* (Baghdad, 1962).

Hidayat, Rida Quli Khan. *Ta'rikh-i rawdat al-safa-i nasiri dar dhikr padshahan-i dawra-i safaviya afshariya zandiya qajariya*, 10 vols. (Qum, 1399s).

Hirz al-Din, Muhammad. *Ma'arif al-rijal fi tarajim al-'ulama' wal-udaba'*, 3 vols. (Najaf, 1964–65).

I'timad al-Saltana, Muhammad Hasan Khan. *Kitab al-ma'athir wal-athar* (Tehran, 1306/1888).

'Izz al-Din, Yusuf. *Al-Shi'r al-'iraqi, ahdafuhu wa-khasa'isuhu fi al-qarn al-tasi' 'ashar* (Baghdad, 1958).

Kalantar, Muhammad. "Muqaddima," in Murtada Ansari, *Kitab al-makasib* (Najaf, 1392/1972), I.

Al Kamuna, 'Abd al-Razzaq al-Husayn. *Mawarid al-athaf fi nuqaba' al-ashraf*, 2 vols. (Najaf, 1968).

Kashmiri, Muhammad Mahdi. *Nujum al-Sama': Takmila*, 2 vols. (Qum, 1397/ 1977).

Al-Kazimi, Muhammad Mahdi. *Ahsan al-wadi'a fi tarajim ashhar mashahir mujtahidi al-shi'a* (Baghdad, 1930).

Al-Khalili, Ja'far. *Mawsu'at al-'atabat al-muqaddasa*, 2nd ed., 12 vols. (Beirut, 1987).

Khan Malik Sasani, Husayn. *Yadbud-ha-yi sifarat-i istanbul* (Tehran, n.d.).

Khaqani, 'Ali. *Shu'ara' al-ghari*, 10 vols. (Najaf, 1954).

Shu'ara' al-ghari, 2nd. ed., 12 vols. (Qum, 1988).

Khunsari, Muhammad Baqir. *Rawdat al-jannat fi ahwal al-'ulama' wal-sadat*, 5 vols. (Tehran, 1962).

Al Kilidar, Muhammad Hasan. *Ta'rikh karbala' wa-ha'ir al-husayn 'alayhi al-salam* (Najaf, 1387/1967).

Madinat al-husayn, aw mukhtasar ta'rikh karbala' (Baghdad, 1949).

Kirkukli, Rasul. *Dawhat al-wuzara' fi ta'rikh baghdad al-zawra'*, trans. M. K. Nawras (Beirut, 1963).

Kirmani, Muhammad Karim Khan. *Hidayat al-talibin* (Kirman, 1980).

Al Mahbuba, Ja'far. *Madi al-najaf wa-hadiruha*, 3 vols. (Najaf, 1955–58).

Mahmud, Mahmud. *Ta'rikh-i ravabit-i siyasi-yi iran va inglis dar qarn-i nuz-dahim*, 8 vols. (Tehran, 1949–50).

Majid, Muhammad Hasan 'Ali. "Wulat al-hilla wa-hukamiha fi al-qarn al-tasi' 'ashar hata nihayat al-hukm al-turki fi al-'iraq (1800–1917) wa-'athrihim fi al-shi'r," *al-Mu'arrikh al-'arabi*, 20 (1401/1981).

Mamaqani, 'Abdallah. *Makhzan al-maghani* (Najaf, 1345/1926).

Marjani, Haydar, al-*Najaf al-ashraf qadiman wa-hadithan* (Baghdad, 1986).

Mudarris, Mirza, 'Abd al-Rahman. *Ta'rikh-i 'ulama'-yi khorasan* (Mashhad, 1341s/1963).

Mudarris Khiyabani, Muhammad 'Ali. *Rayhanat al-adab*, 8 vols. (Tabriz, 1967).

Mudarrisi-Chahardahi, Murtada. *Shaykhgari va-babgari* (Tehran, 1345s/1966) .

Ta'rikh-i ravabit-i iran va-iraq (Tehran, 1351s/1972).

Zindigani va-falsafa-yi hajji mulla hadi sabzivari (Tehran, n.d.).

Al-Munshi, Muhammad 'Ali al-Husayni al-Farisi. *Rihlat al-munshi*, trans. from Persian by 'Abbas al-'Azzawi (Baghdad, 1948) .

Al-Muzaffar, Muhammad Husayn. *Ta'rikh al-shi'a*, 3rd ed. (Beirut, 1982).

Al-Muzaffar, Muhammad Rida. "Tarjamat al-mu'allif," in Muhammad Hasan Najafi, *Jawahir al-kalam fi sharh shara'i' al-islam*, ed. 'Abbas Quchani-Najafi (Najaf, 1958), I, 2–24.

Nadir, Mirza. *Ta'rikh va-jughrafi-yi dar al-saltana tabriz* (Tehran, 1323).

Nafisi, Sa'id. *Ta'rikh-i ijtima'i va siyasi-yi iran dar daura-yi mu'asir*, 2 vols. (Tehran, 1340s/1961).

Nasir al-Din Shah Qajar. *Ruznamah-yi safar az tehran ila karbala' va najaf* (Tehran, 1870).

Nawras, A. K. S. *Hukm al-mamalik fi al-'iraq* (Baghdad, 1972).

Nawwar, 'Abd al-'Aziz Suleiman. *Da'ud pasha wali baghdad* (Cairo, 1967).

   Ta'rikh al-'iraq al-hadith min nihayat hukm da'ud pasha ila nihayat hukm midhat pasha (Cairo, 1968).

Nuri, Fadlallah. *Majmu'a-yi az rasa'il-i, i'lamiyaha-yi maktubat-i wa-ruznamah-yi shaykh shahid fadlallah nuri*, 2 vols., comp. Muhammad Turkoman (Tehran, 1362s).

Nuri Tabarsi, Husayn. *Mustadrak wasa'il al-shi'a* (Tehran, 1318–21/1900–03).

Pirzadeh Na'ini, Muhammad 'Ali. *Safarnamah-yi hajji pirzadeh*, ed. Hafiz Farman-Farmayan, 2 vols. (Tehran, 1343s).

[Najafi] Quchani, Hasan. *Siyahat-i sharq ya zindiganinamah-yi aqa najafi quchani* (Mashhad, 1351/1972).

Qudsi, Hasan A'zam. *Khatirat-i man ya rushan shoadan ta'rikh-i sadd-i saleh* (Tehran, 1342).

Qummi, 'Abbas. *Fawa'id al-ridawiya* (Najaf, 1956).

Ra'in, Isma'il. *Huquq-i bigiran-i inglis dar iran* (Tehran, 1347/1968).

Rashti, Kazim. *Dalil al-mutahayyirin* (Kirman, 1980).

Ravandi, Murtada. *Sayr-i farhang va-ta'rikh-i ta'lim va-tarbiyat dar Iran va-urupa* (Tehran, 1364/1985).

Sadid al-Saltana, Muhammad 'Ali b. Ahmad. *Safarnama-yi sadid al-saltana*, ed. Ahmad Iqtidari (Tehran, 1362s).

Al-Sadr, Hasan. *Takmilat amal al-'amil* (Qum, 1985).

Al-Sadr, Muhammad Baqir. *Durus fi 'ilm al-usul* (Beirut, 1978).

Safa'i, Ibrahim. *Rahbaran-i mashrute*, 4 vols. (Tehran, 1344s/1965–66).

Al-Sa'idi, Hamud. *Dirasat 'an 'asha'ir al-'iraq: al-khaza'il* (Najaf, 1974).

Al-Samarra'i, Yunus, *Ta'rikh madinat samarra'* (Baghdad, 1971).

Sayf al-Dawlah, Sultan Muhammad. *Safarnamah-yi mecca*, ed. 'Ali Akbar Khodaparast (Tehran, 1364s/1986).

Sayyah, Hajji. *Khatirat-i hajji sayyah*, ed. Hamid Sayyah and Sayfallah Gulkar (Tehran, 1346/1967–68).

Sha'bani, R. "Siyasat-i madhhabi-yi nadir," *Vahid* 7:9 (1970): 1132–56.

Shahristani, Hibat al-Din. *al-'Ilm* (Najaf, 1911).

Shahrudi, Nur al-Din. *Ta'rikh al-haraka al-'ilmiyya fi karbala'* (Beirut, 1990).

Shirazi, Muhammad Ma'sum Na'ib al-Sadr [Ma'sum 'Ali Shah]. *Tara'iq al-haqa'iq*, ed. M. J. Mahjub, 3 vols. (Tehran, 1345s/1966).

Shirvani, Hajj Zayn al-'Abidin. *Bustan al-siyaha* (Tehran, 1315/1897).

Hada'iq al-siyaha (Tehran, 1348s/1970).

Siphir Lisan al-Mulk, Mirza Muhammad Taqi. *Nasikh al-tawarikh*, 4 vols. (Tehran, 1385/1965).

Al-Suwaydi, 'Abdallah. *al-Hujaj al-qat'iyya li-ittifaq al-firaq al-islamiyya* (Cairo, 1905).

Tehrani, Aqa Buzurg. *al-Dhari'a ila tasanif al-shi'a*, 26 vols. (Tehran, 1355s/1936).

Tabaqat a'lam al-shi'a: al-kiram al-barara fi al-qarn al-thalith ba'd al-'ashara (Najaf, 1954–68) and *Nuqaba' al-bashar fi al-qarn al-rabi' 'ashar* (Najaf, 1954–68).

Hadiyat al-razi ila al-imam al-mujadid al-shirazi (Tehran, 1984).

Teymuri, Ibrahim. *'Asr-i bi-khabari ya ta'rikh-i imtiyazat-i dar iran* (Tehran, 1325s/1954).

Tahrim-i tunbaku ya avvalin-i moqavamat-i manfi dar Iran (Tehran, 1949).

Al Tu'ma, Sulayman Hadi. *Turath karbala'* (Karbala', 1964).

Tunikabuni, Mirza Muhammad. *Qisas al-'ulama'* (Tehran, 1378/1967).

Al-Wa'ili, Ibrahim. a*l-Shi'r al-siyasi al-'iraqi fi al-qarn al-tasi' 'ashar* (Baghdad, 1961).

Wa'iz Isfahani, Jamal al-Din. *Libas-i taqwa* (Shiraz, n.d.).

Al-Wardi, 'Ali. *Dirasa fi tabi'at al-mujtama' al-'iraqi* (Baghdad, 1965).

Lamahat ijtima'iyya min ta'rikh al-'iraq al-hadith, 6 vols. (Baghdad, 1969).

NEWSPAPERS

Al-'Ilm 1911, 1912.
Al-Murshid 1925–29.

SOURCES IN OTHER LANGUAGES

Abbott, Andrew M. *A System of Professions* (Chicago, 1988).

Abrahamian, Ervand. *Iran between Two Revolutions* (Princeton, 1981).

Alexander, Constance. *Baghdad in Bygone Days. From the Journals and Correspondence of Claudius Rich, British Resident in Baghdad 1808–1821* (London, 1928).

Algar, Hamid. s.v., "Akhbari, Mirza Mohammad," *EIr*.

s.v., "'Ali Kani," *EIr*.

Mirza Malkum Khan: A Biographical Study in Iranian Modernism (Berkeley, 1973).

Religion and State in Iran, 1785–1906: The Role of the 'Ulama' in the Qajar Period (Berkeley, 1969).

Algar, Hamid, trans. "Excerpts of the Consitution of the Islamic Republic of Iran," in Arjomand, *Authority and Political Culture*, 371–82.

Amanat, Abbas. "In between the Madrasa and the Marketplace: The Designation of Clerical Leadership in Modern Shi'ism," in Arjomand (ed.), *Authority and Political Culture*, 98–132.

"The 'Leader of the Community' and the 'Undeceiving' British Minister Plenipotentiary: A Correspondence between John McNeill and Sayyid Muhammad Baqir Shafti on the First Herat Crisis," *Iranshinasi* 1 (1990): 11–41.

Resurrection and Renewal: The Making of the Babi Movement in Iran, 1844–1850 (Ithaca, 1989).

Al-Amin, Hasan. *Islamic Shiʿite Encyclopaedia*, 4 vols. (Beirut, 1973).

Anonymous. "Le programme des études chez les Chiites et principalment chez ceux de Nedjef," *Revue du monde musulman* 23 (June 1913): 271–75.

Arjomand, Said Amir. *The Shadow of God and the Hidden Imam: Religion, Political Order and Societal Change in Shiʿite Iran from the Beginning to 1980* (Chicago, 1984).

The Turban for the Crown, The Islamic Revolution in Iran (Oxford, 1988).

"The Mujtahid of the Age and the Mulla-Bashi: An Intermediate State in the Institutionalization of Religious Authority in Shiʿite Iran," in Arjomand (ed.), *Authority and Political Culture*, 80–97.

"The Shiʿite Hierocracy and the State in Pre-Modern Iran: 1785–1890," *Archives européenes de sociologie* 20 (1981): 40–78.

Arjomand, Said Amir (ed.). *Authority and Political Culture in Shiʿism* (Albany, 1988).

Ashraf, Ahmad. "The Bazaar–Mosque Alliance: The Social Basis of Revolts and Revolutions in Iran," *Politics, Culture and Society* 1 (1988): 538–67.

Aubin, Jean. "La politique religieuse des Safavides," in T. Fahd (ed.), *Le Shiʿisme imamite* (Paris, 1970), 236–45.

Avery, Peter. "An Enquiry into the Outbreak of the Russo-Persian War, 1826–28," in Bosworth (ed.), *Iran and Islam*, 17–46.

Bakhash, Shaul. *Iran: Monarchy, Bureaucracy and Reform under the Qajars: 1858–1896* (London, 1978).

Barnes, John Robert. *An Introduction to Religious Foundations in the Ottoman Empire* (Leiden, 1986).

Batatu, Hanna. *The Old Social Classes and the Revolutionary Movements in Iraq* (Princeton, 1978).

Bayat, Mangol. *Mysticism and Dissent: Socio-Religious Thought in Qajar Iran* (Syracuse, 1982).

Berkey, Jonathan. *The Transmission of Knowledge in Medieval Cairo: A Social History of Islamic Education* (Princeton, 1992).

Bill, James A. "Class Analysis and the Dialectics of Modernization in the Middle East," *IJMES* 3 (1972): 417–34.

"The Plasticity of Informal Politics: The Case of Iran," *MEJ* 27:2 (Spring 1973): 131–51.

Blunt, Ann. *Bedouin Tribes of the Euphrates* (London, 1879).

Bosworth C. E. (ed.). *Iran and Islam* (Edinburgh, 1971).

(ed.). *Qajar Iran: Political, Social and Cultural Change, 1800–1925* (Edinburgh, 1983).

Bruer, Mordechai. *The Rabbinate in Eshkenaz during the Middle Ages* (Jerusalem, 1976; in Hebrew).

Calder, Norman. "Doubt and Prerogative: the Emergence of an Imami Shiʿi Theory of Ijtihad," *SI* 70 (1991): 57–78.

"The Structure of Authority in Imami Shiʿi Jurisprudence" (Ph.D. diss. SOAS, 1980).

"Zakat in Imami Shiʿi Jurisprudence, from the Tenth to the Sixteenth Century AD," *BSOAS* 44:3 (1981): 468–80.

Caton, Steven. "Power, Persuasion, and Language: A Critique of the Segmentary Model in the Middle East," *IJMES* 19:1 (1987): 77–102.

Chamberlain, Michael. *Knowledge and Social Practice in Medieval Damascus, 1190–1350* (Cambridge, 1994).

Chambers, Richard L. "The Ottoman 'Ulama' and the Tanzimat," in Keddie (ed.), *Scholars, Saints and Sufis*, 33–46.

Chiha, Habib. *La province de Baghdad* (Cairo, 1908).

Cole, Juan R. I. "Imami Jurisprudence and the Role of the 'Ulama': Mortaza Ansari on Emulating the Supreme Exemplar," in N. Keddie (ed.), *Religion and Politics in Iran: Shi'ism from Quietism to Revolution* (New Haven, 1983), 33–46.

"'Indian Money' and the Shi'i Shrine Cities of Iraq 1786–1850," *MES* 22:4 (October 1986): 461–80.

"Iranian Millenarianism and Democratic Thought in the Nineteenth Century," *IJMES* 24 (1992): 1–26.

"Rival Empires of Trade and Imami Shi'ism in Arabia, 1300–1800," *IJMES* 19:2 (May 1987): 177–204.

Roots of North Indian Shi'ism in Iran and Iraq: Religion and State in Awadh, 1722–1859 (Berkeley, 1988).

"Shi'i Clerics in Iraq and Iran, 1722–1780: The Akhbari–Usuli Conflict Reconsidered," *IS* 18:1 (Winter 1985): 3–33.

Cole, Juan R. I. and Moojan Momen. "Mafia, Mob and Shi'ism in Iraq: The Rebellion of Ottoman Karbala', 1824–1843," *Past and Present* 112 (1986): 112–43.

Cowper, H. S. *Through Asiatic Arabia* (London, 1894).

Dabashi, Hamid. "The Sufi Doctrine of the 'Perfect Man' and the View of the Hierarchical Structure of Islamic Culture," *Islamic Quarterly* 30:2 (1986): 118–30.

Davison, Roderic H. s.v., "Midhat Pasha," *EI²*.

Denoeux, Guilian. *Urban Unrest in the Middle East: A Comparative Study of Informal Networks in Egypt, Iran and Lebanon* (Albany, 1993).

Deringil, Selim. "The Struggle against Shi'ism in Hamidian Iraq: A Study in Ottoman Counter Propaganda," *WI* 30 (1990): 45–62.

Dieulafoy, Jane. *La Perse, la Chaldée et la Susiane* (Paris, 1874).

Donaldson, Dwight M. *The Shi'ite Religion: A History of Islam in Persia and Irak* (London, 1933).

Duguid, Stephen. "The Politics of Unity: Hamidian Policy in Eastern Anatolia," *MES* 9 (1973): 139–56.

Eccel, Christopher. *Egypt, Islam and Social Change: Al-Azhar in Conflict and Accomodation* (Berlin, 1978).

Eickelman, Dale. *The Middle East: An Anthropological Approach* (Englewood Cliffs, 1989).

Eisenstadt, S. N. and L. Roniger. *Patrons, Clients and Friends: Interpersonal Relations and the Structure of Trust in Society* (Cambridge, 1984).

"Patron–Client Relations as a Model of Social Exchange," *Comparative Studies in Society and History* 22:1 (1980): 42–77.

Ende, Werner. "The Flagellation of Muharram and the Shi'ite 'Ulama'," *Der Islam* 55 (1978): 19–36.

Fattah, Hala M. "The Development of the Regional Market of Iraq and the Gulf 1800–1900" (Ph.D. diss., UCLA, 1986).

Fischer, Michael J. *Iran From Religious Dispute to Revolution* (Cambridge, Mass., 1980).

Fontanier, V. *Voyage dans L'Inde et le Golfe Persique* (Paris, 1844).

Fraser, James. *Travels in Koordistan and Mesopotamia*, 2 vols. (London, 1840).

Friedman, Menachem, *The Haredi (Ultra-Orthodox) Society: Sources, Trends, and Processes* (Jerusalem, 1991; in Hebrew).

Geary, George. *Through Asiatic Turkey. Narrative of a Journey from Bombay to the Bosphorus*, 2 vols. (London, 1878).

Gellner, Ernest. "Patrons and Clients," in Gellner and Waterbury (eds.), *Patrons and Clients*, 1–6.

Gellner, Ernest and John Waterbury (eds.). *Patrons and Clients in Mediterranean Societies* (London, 1977).

Gilbert, Joan. "Institutionalization of Muslim Scholarship and Professionalization of the 'Ulama' in Medieval Damascus," *SI* 55 (1980): 105–35.

Gross, Edward and Amitai Etzioni. *Organizations in Society* (Englewood Cliffs, 1985).

Guinet, Vital. *La Turquie d'Asie* (Paris, 1891–95).

Ha'iri, Abdul Hadi. s.v., "Akhund Khorasani," *EIr.*
s.v., "Ansari Murtada," *EI²* supplement
"The Legitimacy of the Early Qajar Rule as Viewed by the Shi'i Religious Leaders," *MES* 24:3 (July 1988): 271–86.
Shi'ism and Constitutionalism in Iran: A Study on the Role Played by the Persian Residents of Iraq in Persian Politics (Leiden, 1977).

Hardinge, Arthur. *A Diplomatist in the East* (London, 1928).

Heyd, Uriel. "The Ottoman 'Ulema and Westernization in the Time of Selim III and Mahmud II," *Scripta Hierosolymitana* 9 (1961): 63–96.

Hjortshoj, Keith. "Shi'i Identity and the Significance of Muharram in Lucknow, India," in Martin Kramer (ed.), *Shi'ism, Resistance, and Revolution* (Boulder, 1987), 289–310.

Hodgson, Marshall G. S. *The Venture of Islam: Conscience and History in a World Civilization*, 3 vols. (Chicago, 1974).

Honigman, E. s.v., "Karbala'," *EI²*.

Hourani, Albert. "Ottoman Reforms and the Politics of Notables," in Albert Hourani, *The Emergence of the Modern Middle East* (London, 1981), 36–66.

Humphreys, Steven. *Islamic History: A Framework for Inquiry* (Minneapolis, 1988).

Imber, C. H. "The Persecution of the Ottoman Shi'ites According to the Muhimme Defterleri, 1565–1585," *Der Islam* 56:2 (1979): 245–73.

Inalcik, Halil. *The Ottoman Empire: The Classical Age 1300–1600*, trans. N. Itzkowitz and C. Imber (London, 1973).

Ingram, Robert. *In Defence of British India, Great Britain in the Middle East, 1775–1842* (London, 1984).

Issawi, Charles. *The Economic History of Iran, 1800–1914* (Chicago, 1971).
The Economic History of the Middle East, 1800–1914 (Chicago, 1966).
The Fertile Crescent, 1800–1914: A Documentary Economic History (Oxford, 1988).

"Iraq, 1800–1991: A Study in Aborted Development," *Princeton Papers in Near Eastern Studies*, No. 1 (1992): 73–84.

Itzkowitz, Norman and Joel Shinder. "The Office of Seyh ul-Islam and the Tanzimat – A Prosopographical Enquiry," *MES* 8:1 (1972): 93–102.

Al-Jamali, Fadil. "The Theological Colleges of Najaf," *Muslim World* 50:1 (1960): 15–22.

Johnson, Allen and Timothy Earle. *The Evolution of Human Societies: From Foraging Groups to Agrarian States* (Stanford, 1987).

Johnson, Benton. "Church and Sect Revisited," *JSSR* 10:2 (Summer 1971): 124–37.

Jomier, J. s.v., "al-Azhar," *EI²*.

Katz, Jacob. *Tradition and Crisis: Jewish Society at the End of the Middle Ages* (Jerusalem, 1958; in Hebrew).

Kazemi Moussavi, Ahmad. "The Establishment of the Position of Marja'iyyat-i Taqlid in the Twelver-Shi'i Community," *IS* 18:1 (Winter 1985): 35–51.

"The Institutionalization of *Marja'-i Taqlid* in the Nineteenth Century Shi'ite Community," *Muslim World* 83:3–4 (July–October 1994): 279–88.

Kazamzade, Firuz. *Russia and Britain in Persia, 1864–1914* (New Haven, 1968).

Keddie, Nikki. "British Policy and the Iranian Opposition, 1901–1907," *Journal of Modern History* 39:3 (September 1967): 266–82.

"Iranian Politics 1900–1905: Background to Revolution," *MES* 5:1–3 (1969): 3–31, 151–67, 234–50.

"Islamic Philosophy and Islamic Modernism: The Case of Sayyid Jamal al-Din al-Afghani," *Journal of Persian Studies* 10 (1980): 53–56.

Religion and Rebellion in Iran: The Tobacco Protest of 1890–91 (London, 1966).

"The Roots of 'Ulama' Power in Modern Iran," in Keddie (ed.), *Scholars Saints and Sufis*, 211–30.

Sayyid Jamal al-Din "al-Afghani": A Political Biography (Berkeley, 1972).

Keddie, Nikkie (ed.). *Scholars, Saints and Sufis: Muslim Religious Institutions since 1500* (Berkeley, 1972).

Kelly, J. B. *Britain and the Persian Gulf, 1795–1880* (Oxford, 1968).

Khomeini, Ruhallah. *Imam Khomeini's Last Will and Testament* (Washington: Iranian Interest section, Algerian Embassy, n.d.).

Khoury, Philip. "Continuity and Change in Syrian Political Life: The Nineteenth and Twentieth Centuries," *American Historical Review* 96:5 (December 1991): 1374–96.

Urban Notables and Arab Nationalism: The Politics of Damascus 1860–1920 (Cambridge, 1983).

Kohlberg, Etan. "Aspects of Akhbari Thought in the Seventeenth and Eighteenth Centuries," in Nehemia Levtzion and John O. Voll (eds.), *Eighteenth Century Renewal and Reform in Islam* (Syracuse, 1987), 133–60.

"The Development of the Imami Shi'i Doctrine of Jihad," *ZDMG* 126:1 (1976): 64–86.

"Imam and Community in the Pre-Ghayba Period," in Arjomand (ed.), *Authority and Political Culture*, 25–53.

Lambton, Ann K. S. *Islamic Society in Persia* (Oxford, 1954).

"A Nineteenth Century View of Jihad," *SI* 32 (1970): 181–92.

"Quis Custodiet Custodes? Some Reflections on the Persian Theory of Government," *SI* 6 (1956): 125–46.

"Some New Trends in Islamic Political Thought in Late Eighteenth and Early Nineteenth Century Persia," *SI* 40 (1974): 95–128.

"The 'Ulama' and the Constitutional Movement in Iran," in T. Fahd (ed.), *Shi'ism imamite* (Strasbourg, 1971), 245–69.

Landau, Jacob M. *The Politics of Pan-Islam: Ideology and Organization* (Oxford, 1990).

Lapidus, Ira M. *Muslim Cities in the Later Middle Ages* (Cambridge, Mass., 1967).

Lewis, Bernard. "Ottoman Observers of Ottoman Decline," in Bernard Lewis, *Islam in History: Ideas, People and Events in the Middle East* (Chicago, 1993), 209–22.

Litvak, Meir. "Continuity and Change in the 'Ulama' Population of Najaf and Karbala', 1791–1904: A Socio-Demographic Study," *IS* 23 (1990): 31–60.

"The Finances of the 'Ulama' Communities in Najaf and Karbala' in the Nineteenth Century," forthcoming in *WI*.

"The Shi'i 'Ulama' of Najaf and Karbala', 1791–1904: A Sociopolitical Analysis" (Ph.D. diss., Harvard University, 1991).

Lockhart, Lawrence. *The Fall of the Safavid Dynasty and the Afghan Occupation of Persia* (Cambridge, 1958).

Nadir Shah (London, 1938).

Loftus, William. *Travels and Research in Chaldea and Susiana* (London, 1857).

Longrigg, Steven H. *Four Centuries of Modern Iraq* (Oxford, 1925).

Luizard, Pierre-Jean, *La formation de l'Irak contemporain: le role politique des ulemas chiites à la fin de la domination ottomane et au moment de la construction de l'état irakien* (Paris, 1991).

MacEoin, Dennis. s.v., "Ahsa'i, Shaykh Ahmad," *EIr*.

"Changes in Charismatic Authority in Qajar Shi'ism," in Bosworth (ed.), *Qajar Iran*, 148–76.

"From Shaykhism to Babism," (Ph.D. diss., Cambridge University, 1979).

Madelung, Wilferd. "Authority in Twelver Shi'ism in the Absence of the Imam," in G. Makdisi et al. (eds). *La notion d'autorite du Moyen Age: Islam, Byzance, Occident* (Paris, 1982), 163–174.

Makdisi, George. "Madrasa and University in the Middle Ages," *SI* 32 (1970): 254–74.

The Rise of Colleges: Institutions of Learning in Islam and the West (Edinburgh, 1981).

Mallat, Chibli. *The Renewal of Islamic Law, Muhammad Baqer as-Sadr, Najaf and the Shi'i International* (Cambridge, 1993).

Malcolm, John. *A History of Persia*, 2 vols. (London, 1815).

Maoz, Moshe. *Ottoman Reforms in Syria and Palestine, 1840–1861* (Oxford, 1968).

"The 'Ulama' and the Process of Modernization in Syria during the Mid-Nineteenth Century," *Asian and African Studies* 29 (1966): 277–301.

Marr, Phebe. *The Modern History of Iraq* (New York, 1985).

Martin, Vanessa. *Islam and Modernism: The Iranian Revolution of 1906* (London, 1987).

Masters, Bruce. "The Treaties of Erzerum (1823 and 1848) and the Changing Status of Iranians in the Ottoman Empire," *IS* 27 (1991): 3–16.

Menashri, David. *Education and the Making of Modern Iran* (Ithaca, 1992).

Michels, Robert. *Political Parties: A Sociological Study of the Oligarchical Tendencies of Modern Democracy* (New York, 1962 repr.).

Midhat, Ali Haydar. *The Life of Midhat Pasha* (London, 1903).

Mitchell, J. C. *Social Networks in Urban Situations* (Manchester, 1969).

Modaressi Tabataba'i, Hossein. *An Introduction to Shi'i Law: A Bibliographical Study* (London, 1984).

"The Just Ruler or the Guardian Jurist: An Attempt to Link two Different Shi'ite Concepts," *JAOS* 111 (1991): 549–62.

Momen, Moojan. *The Babi and Baha'i Religions, 1844–1944. Some Contemporary Western Accounts* (Oxford, 1981).

An Introduction to Shi'i Islam (New Haven, 1985).

"The Trial of Mulla 'Ali Bastami: A Combined Sunni–Shi'i Fatwa against the Bab," *Iran* 20 (1982): 113–43.

Mottahedeh, Roy P. *Loyalty and Leadership in an Early Islamic Society* (Princeton, 1980).

The Mantle of the Prophet (New York, 1985).

Murata, S. s.v., "Akhund Khorasani: His Importance in Usul," *EI*.

s.v., "Ansari, Shaykh Mortaza," *EIr*.

Nakash, Yitzhak. *The Shi'is of Iraq* (Princeton, 1994).

Netzer, Amnon. "The Persecution of Iranian Jewry in the Seventeenth Century," *Pe'amim* 6 (1981; in Hebrew): 32–56.

Nicolas, A. L. M. *Essai sur le Cheikhisme*, 4 vols. (Paris, 1910).

Niebuhr, Carsten. *Travels through Arabia and Other Countries in the East*, trans. Robert Heron, 2 vols. (Edinburgh, 1792).

Nieuwenhuis, Tom. *Politics and Society in Early Modern Iraq: Mamluk Pashas, Tribal Shaykhs and Local Rule between 1802 and 1831* (The Hague, 1981).

Nisbet, Robert. *Social Change and History* (New York, 1968).

Parkin, Frank. *Marxism and Class Theory: A Bourgeois Critique* (New York, 1979).

Pedersen, John. s.v., "Madrasa." *EI²*.

Perry, John R. *Karim Khan Zand: A History of Iran, 1747–1779* (Chicago, 1979).

Peters, J. D. *Nippur, or Explorations and Adventures on the Euphrates, 1888–1890* (New York, 1897).

Qaysi, Abdul-Wahhab 'Abbas. "The Impact of Modernization on Iraqi Society during the Ottoman Era: A Study of Intellectual Development in Iraq, 1869–1917" (Ph.D. diss., University of Michigan, 1958).

Rabbat, Nasser. s.v., "Riwak," *EI²*.

Repp, Richard C. *The Mufti of Istanbul: A Study in the Development of the Ottoman Learned Hierachy* (London, 1986).

Rizvi, Sayyid Athar Abbas. *A Socio-Intellectual History of the Isna 'Ashari Shi'is in India*, 2 vols. (Canberra, 1986).

Rosen, Lawrence. *Bargaining for Reality: The Reconstruction of Social Relations in a Muslim Community* (Chicago, 1984).

Rosenthal, Franz. *Knowledge Triumphant: The Concept of Knowledge in Medieval Islam* (Leiden, 1970).

Royce, William R. "Mir Ma'sum 'Ali Shah and the Ni'mat Allahi Revival 1776–77 to 1796–97: A Study of Sufism in Late Eighteenth Century Iran" (Ph.D. diss., Princeton University, 1979).

Sachedina, 'Abd al-'Aziz 'Abd al-Husssein. *The Just Ruler (al-Sultan al-'Adil) in Shiʿite Islam* (Oxford, 1988).

"Al-Khums: The Fifth in the Imami Shi'i Legal System," *JNES* 39 (1980): 276–89.

Savory, Roger. *Iran under the Safavids* (London, 1980).

Shaked, Haim. "The Biographies of 'Ulama' in Mubarak's *Khitat* as a Source for the History of the 'Ulama' in Nineteenth Century Egypt," *Asian and African Studies* 7 (1971): 41–76.

Sheikholeslami, Ali Reza. "From Religious Accommodation to Religious Revolution: The Transformation of Shi'ism in Iran," in A. Banuazizi and M. Weiner (eds.), *The State, Religion and Ethnic Politics: Afghanistan, Iran and Pakistan* (Syracuse, 1986).

"The Patrimonial Structure of the Iranian Bureaucracy in the Late Nineteenth Century," *Iranian Studies* 11 (1978): 199–258.

Shtampper, Shaul. "Three 'Lithuanian' Yeshivot during the Nineteenth Century" (Ph.D. diss., Hebrew University of Jerusalem, 1981; in Hebrew).

Smith Anthony D. *Social Change* (New York, 1976).

Stark, Rodney and Sims Bainbridge. "Of Churches, Sects, and Cults. Preliminary Concepts for a Theory of Religious Movements," *JSSR* 18 (1979): 117–33.

Stone, Lawrence. "Prosopography," in Lawrence Stone, *The Past and the Present* (Boston, 1981), 107–40.

Al-Tibawi, 'Abd al-Latif. "Origins and Character of the Madrasa," *BSOAS* 25 (1962): 225–38.

Toledano, Ehud R. "The Emergence of Ottoman-Local Elites in the Middle East and North Africa (1700–1900), in I. Pappe and M. Maoz (eds.), *Essays in Honour of Albert Hourani* (Oxford, forthcoming).

Ussher, John. *A Journey from London to Persepolis, including Wandering in Daghestan, Georgia, Armenia, Kurdistan, Mesopotamia and Persia* (London, 1865).

Waterbury, John. "An Attempt to Put Patrons and Clients in their Place," in Gellner and Waterbury (eds.), *Patrons and Clients*, 329–42.

Weber, Max. *From Max Weber: Essays in Sociology*, trans. and ed., and with an introduction by H. H. Gerth and C. Wright Mills (New York, 1946; repr. 1958), 180–95.

de-Yong, Frederick. *Turuq and Turuq-Linked Institutions in Nineteenth Century Egypt* (Leiden, 1978).

Zarandi, Muhammad "Nabil". *The Dawn Breakers*, trans. Shoghi Effendi (Wilmette, 1974).

Zilfi, Madeline. "'Elite Circulation' in the Ottoman Empire in the Eighteenth Century," *JESHO* 26 (1983): 318–64.

The Politics of Piety: The Ottoman Ulema in the Post Classical Age (1600–1800) (Minneapolis, 1988).

Index

Iran *(cont.)*
62, 64–71, 73–80, 85–87, 96, 98–100,
103–04, 110–12, 117–20, 126–29,
137, 142, 161, 163, 164, 169–75, 177,
180, 182–88
1985 constitution, 45, 112
1979 revolution, 3, 33, 111, 184, 186,
Iranians *(see also* Persians), 2, 15, 17, 33,
34, 57, 62, 63, 66, 70–71, 73, 76–79,
81–83, 88, 90, 95, 99, 101–03, 108,
118, 122, 128, 136, 138, 142, 143,
146, 150, 151, 153–56, 158, 160,
165–67, 169, 171, 180, 183, 185,
197n.49, 202n.57.
Iraq, 1–3, 9–10, 12, 14, 22, 27, 31–32, 35,
45, 50, 58, 61, 77, 82–83, 85–86, 89,
93, 96, 143, 146, 148, 153, 154, 156,
163, 166, 167, 171–73
population of, 2, 57, 62, 65, 79, 95, 103,
223n.57
socio-political conditions, 3, 16–17,
118–20, 123–25, 128–34, 135–37,
150, 158, 159, 169, 180–81, 184–87,
203n.73
Iravani, Muhammad, 34, 88–90, 93, 97,
163, 200n.28
Isfahan, 14, 15, 17, 31, 46, 51–53, 65, 66,
77, 79, 82, 85, 86, 98, 112, 127, 173
Isfahani, Muhammad Husayn, 57, 61
Istanbul, 3, 5, 89, 135, 136, 141, 142, 146,
148, 151, 167, 171, 173, 177, 187

jawahir al-kalam, 56, 66, 68, 107
Jawahiri family, 30, 33, 70, 76, 97, 98, 160,
211n.63
Jews, 54, 98, 109, 110, 132, 159, 174, 187,
229n.39
Jihad, 12, 49, 52, 53, 86, 133, 170,
224n.69

Kamuna family, 158
Kani, 'Ali, 86, 172, 173
Karbasi, Ibrahim, 52, 54, 64, 65, 112, 127
Kashan, 52, 112
Kashif al-Ghita' clan, 30, 54–58, 63,
66–70, 73, 76, 82, 98, 102–04, 124,
125, 129, 161, 183, 202n.57
'Ali, 54, 56–58, 60, 67, 72, 125, 209n.29
Hasan, 56, 58, 69, 131, 135, 141, 147,
148, 155, 208n.4
Ja'far Najafi, 26, 27, 32, 46–50, 52, 54,
56, 66, 69, 109, 122, 124, 127, 128,
132, 200n.25, 205n.13, 221n.29
Ja'far (al-saghir), 82
Mahdi, 76, 77, 82, 85, 158
Muhammad, 69, 76, 125, 217n.13

Musa, 54, 55–56, 124–26, 129, 157
Rida, 162
Kashmir(i), 34, 85
Kazimi, Muhammad Husayn al-, 66, 82,
89, 93, 97, 103
Kazimayn, 50, 55, 67, 78, 82, 83, 85, 103,
122, 124, 125, 129, 140, 151, 160,
194n.3
Keddie, Nikki, 117, 176
Khalili, Mirza Husayn, 27, 89, 91–93, 98,
101, 175, 233n.49
Khatunabadi family, 52, 77, 86, 215n.48
Khidr b. Shallal, 69, 124, 125, 131,
224n.67
Khidr al-Jinaji family, 30, 56, 69, 73, 77,
82, 161
Khomeini, Ruhallah, 45, 117, 186
Khorasan, 26, 32
Khorasani, Muhammad Kazim Akhund,
26, 27, 32, 37, 40, 89, 91–92, 94, 99,
101, 102, 107, 175, 181, 210n.47,
233n.49
khums (see also fifth), 15, 35
Khuzistan, 93
Khunsari, Muhammad Baqir, 58, 67
Kifayat al-usul, 92, 181
Kirmani, Mirza Aqa Khan, 87, 172, 173
Kirmanshah, 128, 146, 168
Kufa, 16, 48, 145, 162
Kuhkamara'i, Husayn, 81, 85, 88, 89, 93,
107, 205n.6, 210n.43

Lebanon, Lebanese, 12, 31–34, 57, 82, 93,
96, 131, 211n.70
Libas-i taqva fatwa, 91, 94
Lucknow, 5, 33, 61, 66, 68, 70, 140

Madrasa, 8, 23, 25, 26, 38, 40, 42, 71, 73,
82, 96, 112
Mahdi, *see* the Hidden Imam
Mahmud II, Sultan, 135
al-Makasib, 73, 108, 181
Makdisi, George, 38
Malcolm, John, 5, 110
Mallkum Khan, 87, 172, 173
Mamaqani, Hasan, 33, 34, 37, 88, 89, 91,
93, 97, 100, 107, 174, 175, 205n.6,
209n.33, 217n.27
Mamluks *(see also* Ottomans), 2, 16, 17,
24, 59, 117–18, 120–22, 124–26, 128,
129, 135, 177, 184, 224n.69
Marine report, 91, 93, 94
marja'iyyat-i taqlid, 5–8, 55, 64, 67–70,
74–76, 80–81, 84, 87, 90, 91, 94, 98,
172, 181–83, 186
Mashhad, 17, 32, 68, 78, 79, 112

Printed in the United States
120374LV00005B/229-231/A